Presumed Incompetent II

Presumed Incompetent II

Race, Class, Power, and Resistance of Women in Academia

YOLANDA FLORES NIEMANN,
GABRIELLA GUTIÉRREZ Y MUHS,
AND CARMEN G. GONZÁLEZ

UTAH STATE UNIVERSITY PRESS
Logan

Published by Utah State University Press
An imprint of University Press of Colorado
245 Century Circle, Suite 202
Louisville, Colorado 80027

ASSOCIATION of UNIVERSITY PRESSES The University Press of Colorado is a proud member of the Association of University Presses.

The University Press of Colorado is a cooperative publishing enterprise supported, in part, by Adams State University, Colorado State University, Fort Lewis College, Metropolitan State University of Denver, Regis University, University of Colorado, University of Northern Colorado, University of Wyoming, Utah State University, and Western Colorado University.

∞ This paper meets the requirements of the ANSI/NISO Z39.48-1992 (Permanence of Paper)

IISBN: 978-1-60732-964-0 (hardcover)
ISBN: 978-1-60732-965-7 (paperback)
ISBN: 978-1-60732-966-4 (ebook)
https://doi.org/10.7330/9781607329664

Library of Congress Cataloging-in-Publication

Data Names: Niemann, Yolanda Flores, editor. | Gutiérrez y Muhs, Gabriella, editor. | Gonzalez, Carmen G., 1962– editor.
Title: Presumed incompetent II : race, class, power, and resistance of women in academia / Yolanda Flores Niemann, Gabriella Gutiérrez y Muhs, Carmen G. González.
Description: Louisville : University Press of Colorado, [2020] | Includes bibliographical references and index.
Identifiers: LCCN 2020001586 (print) | LCCN 2020001587 (ebook) | ISBN 9781607329640 (cloth) | ISBN 9781607329657 (paperback) | ISBN 9781607329664 (epub)
Subjects: LCSH: Minority women college teachers—United States. | Minority women college teachers—Social conditions. | Sex discrimination in higher education—United States. | Racism in higher education—United States. | Women in higher education—United States. | Feminism and higher education—United States. | Women college teachers—United States. | Minority college teachers—United States.
Classification: LCC LB2332.32 .P74 2020 (print) | LCC LB2332.32 (ebook) | DDC 378.1/2082—dc23
LC record available at https://lccn.loc.gov/2020001586
LC ebook record available at https://lccn.loc.gov/2020001587

Cover illustration, "Sapiencia, Seshat, Anansi: Encountering Wisdom, Guidance, and Trust," by Veronica Eldredge

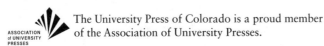

Contents

Foreword

Presumed Incompetent in the Era of "Diversity"

Angela P. Harris

It is a familiar cliché to call the return of a product or service "back by popular demand." In the case of *Presumed Incompetent*, however, the claim is true. After the publication of the first volume, we editors found ourselves met with standing-room-only crowds in university and hotel conference rooms across the country. The book kindled countless reading groups—and action groups. And in private conversations after the talk or workshop, or via email the following week, each of us got the question: "Will there be another book? Because I have a story to tell."

Presumed Incompetent II extends the conversation of the first book, addressing the joys and perils of allyship, the lure of tokenism, and the range of strategies faculty and administrators employ to avoid accidentally making institutional change. And it comes at a crucial historical moment: a time when Women of Color in academic America are facing new threats to their success and their ability to survive and thrive.

In 2012, when *Presumed Incompetent: The Intersections of Race and Class for Women in Academia* first hit the shelves, Barack Obama was still president of the United States, and it was common for liberals to imagine that the nation had become "post-racial." Today, as this volume is released, we all know better. White nationalism is surging around the globe, powering a wave of antidemocratic, pro-authoritarian movements from the bottom and from the top. In many public spaces, the liberal values of pluralism, tolerance, the rule of law, and the objectivity of facts are now being actively attacked. Alongside the discrediting of these values, it is no longer surprising to hear full-throated defenses of White supremacy—sometimes accompanied by open violence, as in Charlottesville, Virginia, in 2017—uttered in "public" and "private" spaces.

At the same time, many hegemonic institutions remain identified with liberalism, where the open espousal of White supremacy remains anathema. The world

DOI: 10.7330/9781607329664.c000a

of higher education in the United States (like the world of the mega-corporations that dominate our daily lives, such as Google, Microsoft, Facebook, Amazon, and Apple), is governed instead by a racial logic known as "diversity." In a recent book, sociologist Ellen Berrey (2015) explains that in the United States, diversity is a form of symbolic politics that has emerged to reconcile a contradiction: it is undesirable for liberal institutions to be portrayed as "racist," but at the same time institutional elites have no desire to change existing racist power structures.

How can Women of Color and working-class women in academia negotiate this difficult moment—caught between outright White supremacy and the "soft bigotry" of liberal institutions driven by diversity logic? Readers of this second volume of *Presumed Incompetent* will find a gold mine of tactics and strategies for disrupting institutional practices that harm academic Women of Color, and a wealth of advice on self-care throughout the process. Above all, readers will find the precious knowledge that they are not alone.

To be a Woman of Color in academia is, too often, to be presumed incompetent. Yet in academia as in other spaces, Women of Color continue to rise, exercising their creativity and expressing their joy. In the face of academia's unspoken norm to be silent about one's vulnerability, the contributors to this volume, like the contributors to the first volume, are committed to telling the truth with wit, bitterness, and insight. This book is a gift.

REFERENCE

Berrey, E. (2015). *The enigma of diversity*. Chicago: University of Chicago Press.

Acknowledgments

I thank the brave women who contributed to this volume. I also thank the many women who are not represented in this volume, but who are pushing back against daily microaggressions, discrimination, and breaches of trust from their peers, students, and upline administrators. I am grateful for our true allies across race/ethnicity. They understand that being an ally does not mean simply declaring that one is not racist. Rather, to be an ally is to take action against racism in its many forms, to be righteously angry when injustice happens to us, to make sure that as we fight back we do not stand alone, and to see, and seek to change, overt and unconscious racism in their own personal and professional contexts. I thank the graduate and undergraduate students on my Critical Race Psychology research team for inspiring me with their seemingly unending energy and tenacity. My special gratitude to my husband of forty-three years, Barry Niemann, and our two children, Russell Flores Niemann and Mychaelanne Flores Niemann. Our family unit continues to be the core and foundation of my own strength, energy, and well-being.

YOLANDA FLORES NIEMANN

First I would like to thank all the women professors who persevered in less than ideal situations, knowing they had much to offer the academy. Thank you for knowing your worth and for insisting on justice. Thank you to the women who hold me up *always*: Marianne Mork, VME, Kathy Cook, Theresa Jones, Mare Blocker, Cynthia Moe-Lobeda, Guadalupe Vega, Graciela Vega, Olga Díaz, Patrice Vecchione, Shirley Flores Muñoz, Lucy Ochoa, and Marú Marquez. Many thanks to my colleagues and friends in academia: Jeanette Rodríguez, Mary-Antoinette Smith, Connie Anthony, Jodi O'Brien, Nalini Iyer, Helena María Viramontes, Norma Cantú, Cristina Herrera, Theresa Delgadillo, Susana Gallardo, Kari

Lerum, Shari Dworkin, Sabina Neem, Jean Anton, Martina Ramírez, and especially Theresa Earenfight. I always acknowledge Yvonne Yarbro-Bejarano for sharing with me her indomitable Chicanx feminism, and thanks to all the holy people who have crossed my path: my mother Socorro Favela, Enrico, Eleuterio, and Eric Muhs, Noemi Natividad, and especially Aldo U. Reséniz, Pierre Loua, and Debbie Radbill, who always bless us. Thanks also to Sheilah Serfaty, John McLean, Armando Miguélez, Alex Flores, Bill Buckley, Jesús Rosales, Steven Bender, John Fraire, Martina Iñiguez, Juan Velasco, Carole Snee, and Ken Weisner. I also want to offer this work to my wonderful cousins, especially those present for my mother: Ofelia Fabela, Maria Elena Reséndiz, Reme Mena, Adela and Lilly Lechuga, Carmen, Eligia, Beatriz, Lourdes, Andrés, and Fidencio Favela, Joel Frías Rivera, Jesen Fayad, and Tania, Conchita, Benjamín, Jesús, and Alfonso Rivera. Thank you so much to Veronica Eldredge for her magnificent cover art and assistance with formatting and improving our manuscript, and of course I would like to especially thank my coeditors Yolanda Flores Niemann and Carmen González, who worked very hard to make sure we included some amazing and innovative work. I thank my dean, David Powers, associate dean, Kan Liang, Natasha Martin, and especially our provost, Shane Martin. For the poets who find poetry everywhere: Demetria Martínez, Xánath Caraza, Claudia Castro Luna, Catalina Cantú, Odilia Rodriguez, Peggy Morrison, Raúl Sánchez, Octavio Quintanilla, Jim Cantú, John Laue, and Carmen Giménez-Smith.

Excerpts from "Silent Bias and Resisting Narratives of Deficit: Social Class and Poverty in the Academy," including the initial poem, first appeared as part of "The Adobe Ceiling over the Yellow-Brick Road" in Menah Pratt-Clarke & Johanna B. Maes (Eds.), *Journeys of Social Justice: Women of Color Presidents in the Academy* (221–224) (New York: Peter Lang, 2017).

GABRIELLA GUTIÉRREZ Y MUHS

I would like to thank the Women of Color whose enthusiastic response to the first volume of *Presumed Incompetent* encouraged us to produce a second. I hope that this book will provide solace and inspiration, and serve as a tool to transform the academic workplace.

CARMEN G. GONZÀLEZ

Presumed Incompetent II

Introduction

Yolanda Flores Niemann, Gabriella Gutiérrez y Muhs, and Carmen G. González

Universities have reputations for being "liberal." We think of collegial environments where people with PhDs engage in intellectually stimulating conversation, sharing ideas and respectfully supporting one another. In large part, that idea is often true. When the reality departs from the myth, however, the context can be ugly enough to derail careers and injure physical and mental health. Such hostile climates are grounded in racism, sexism, homophobia, and classism. The related behaviors include shaming, disregard of cultural values, bullying, harassment, trolling, gaslighting, betrayal, lying, tokenization, coercion, stealing intellectual property, stealing grants, silencing, and blatant disregard for university policies and processes.

In contrast to the myth, when it comes to inclusiveness, universities may be the last bastion of elitism and sanctioned racism in the United States. According to the National Center for Education Statistics (2018), in 2016, 76 percent of all US full-time faculty were White (non-Hispanic), 6 percent African American, 5 percent Latinx, and 10 percent Asian American/Pacific Islander. American Indian/Alaska Natives and persons of two or more races each made up 1 percent or fewer of US full-time faculty. Among those in the tenure-track ranks, the most coveted positions within academia, 82 percent of all full professors were White in 2016 (National Center for Education Statistics, 2018). The fact is Faculty of Color remain underrepresented in comparison to the 2017 US population, which is 76.6 percent White (non-Hispanic), 13.4 percent Black/African American, 5.8 percent Asian, and 18.1 percent Hispanic/Latino (US Census, 2017). University presidents extol the virtues of diversity, and most universities now have diversity or equal opportunity offices, ostensibly to facilitate inclusion of historically underrepresented groups in academia. Yet the numbers of Faculty of Color are disconnected from the various hierarchies of degrees conferred yearly across demographic groups (US Department of Education, 2016). The rhetoric around

DOI: 10.7330/9781607329664.c000b

the importance of diversity seems to be just that—rhetoric without accountability that ends up being meaningless. As Faculty of Color enter tokenized environments, where fewer than 15 percent of their numbers are present, their faculty roles are impacted, even changed, their career opportunities are hindered or halted, and their identities are disrupted by the service they are called upon to engage in by virtue of their uniqueness in the context.

Service in academia comes in many forms. The most common are committee work—at the department, college, university, professional (e.g., advisory boards, journal editorial boards), and community levels (e.g., chambers of commerce, school districts, fund-raising for scholarships, miscellaneous speaking engagements); student mentoring; informal, appointed department roles; and public relations (e.g., speaking on behalf of the university). Formal administrative positions are service that falls in a separate category, as persons in those positions are typically paid a salary for filling those roles. The other service roles, however, are examples of universities asking *some* faculty to engage in a great deal of time-consuming and unpaid service while still actively conducting their scholarship, something that is almost impossible to do at the same time. That is, universities sanction inequitable service from some faculty members, typically women. Then these faculty members are punished for their service through inequitable faculty evaluations.

In other words, faculty who engage in considerable quantity and quality of service, often assigned, and often because they are good citizens, cannot be expected to compete with faculty who engage in comparatively little or virtually no service when it comes to scholarly productivity. Yet the latter faculty receive no retribution or forfeiture of rewards for their lack of service, while the good citizens do, for their comparative lack of productivity. *There is a penalty for service*, which universities claim to value, including student mentoring, *but there is no penalty for lack of service*. Multiple narratives in this volume provide examples of this structural racial tax and emotional labor imposed upon women across race/ethnicity in the science, technology, engineering, and mathematics (STEM) fields and upon Women of Color in all disciplines.

ACADEMIC LEADERSHIP

Women of Color in upper-level leadership positions, such as deans, chancellors, provosts, and presidents, are relatively rare, especially in comparison to White men. Although White women have made some progress entering these roles in the last decades, their numbers are still small, though not as small as the ranks of Women of Color in these high-level positions. Part of the reason for their scarcity is the lack of women across race/ethnicity in full-professor ranks. When there are few or only one in a given context, they enter tokenized situations. The manner and ramification of this token status is elaborated upon in this volume. As noted in narratives here, serving in these roles takes *ganas,* thick skin, and commitment.

Yet we need women in positions of formal power and authority who see and understand what others fail to notice. We need leaders with vision to make changes toward increasing equity. We need such leaders to advocate for the less powerful. Their critical race and feminist lenses will move them to support people, rather than university brands. Such persons can effect institutional, system, and cultural change from within.

DEATH AND DYING IN ACADEMIA

One of the authors of this introduction had two Professors of Color who killed themselves while she was a student—one when she was an undergraduate and the other when she was a graduate student. The author was angry with them—how could they, elite intellectuals at a first-rate university, kill themselves? How could they not choose to fight but instead end their lives? However, they are not the only persons to die while striving to fit into the academic world and achieve success as defined in that elite environment. While we may feel helpless when we hear about scholars who end their lives, we also feel their anguish, desperation, and painful acceptance of their circumstances. And we realize that by not supporting and fully embracing outliers in the academy, especially Women of Color, we are acting irresponsibly. We realize that the best antidote for this disease of death by academia is to be communal and transparent about the hostile contexts experienced by too many of our colleagues.

Yet in the first volume of *Presumed Incompetent* we did not address the fact that people die because of both the dehumanizing tenure process and the sometimes careless and biased judgments and decisions of department chairs, deans, colleagues, and other high-level administrators. We did not address how physical and psychological death and dying might be avoided with appropriate pretenure mentoring by our institutions, departments, colleagues, and the academy at large. This volume directly addresses death and violence. It includes Susie E. Nam's chapter, "Making Visible the Dead Bodies in the Room: Women of Color/QPOC in Academia," about the death of her colleague in a major state university. This volume contains Julia Chang's essay, "Spectacular Bodies: Racism, Pregnancy, and the Code of Silence in Academe," about childbirth and her loss of health due to the inhumanity of her academic workplace. Jamiella Brooks's work also speaks of a certain violence in academia that produces disease and death in "Academia Is Violence: Generatives from a First-Generation, Low-Income PhD Mother of Color." Adrien Wing's chapter, "And Still We Rise," talks about suicide and names African American scholars who died prematurely from a variety of illnesses that may have been caused or exacerbated by their experiences in academia. These narratives provide a somber reminder that sometimes success means surviving, psychologically and physically, and that death comes in multiple forms.

Multiple narratives in this volume also address the issue of damaged mental health. While death is the extreme consequence of severe psychological distress, many Women of Color may be so busy surviving that they lack the time and energy to seek emotional support. Such support can come from a variety of sources: family, friends, mentors and allies, religion and spirituality, meditation, and professional healers and therapists. Meera Deo's chapter, "Securing Support in an Unequal Profession," discusses diverse sources of support as well the policies and practices that universities can adopt to ease the psychological toll on Women of Color.

FIGHTING BACK

The women in this volume of *Presumed Incompetent* provide many examples of how women are increasingly fighting back. They are battling in toxic environments that include bullying, sexual harassment, microaggressions, trolling, gaslighting, shaming, stalking, abuse of power, and misuse of and/or disregard for policies and processes. Women are engaging in battles against hostile climates in different ways, understanding that even small wins can be inspiring and empowering and lead to larger changes. For example, we agree to be the first African American tenure-track faculty member, or the first Asian American department chair or dean. We are preparing students with strong anti-racist, anti-sexist, and anti-homophobic foundations. We are addressing policies and processes that subject students to alienation and trauma. After achieving tenure, we are using our power to fight the system from within, questioning expectations of subservience and kowtowing, and distinguishing accurate from biased evaluative information. We are creating future faculty role models.

We are using university policies and procedures to fight back. We are operating with consciousness about politics—for example, about who may or may not be an ally when we are subject to hostile environments. We are using various survival strategies, such as journaling, to remain sane. We are finding online supportive communities that are lacking in our immediate work contexts. We are embracing our emotions, including anger. We are keeping detailed records that counter the narratives of those who seek to harm us. We are writing about race: calling out hazing, microaggressions, name-calling, stereotyping, passive-aggressive hostility, and White fragility. We are holding diversity offices accountable to effect change, and not just "make paper" and shape empty rhetoric. We are insisting on meaningful inclusiveness, rather than the disingenuousness of "tolerance" and color blindness. We are collecting and publicizing data and using it to effect change. We are calling out patriarchy, "bro-propriating" (a man taking credit for a woman's idea), "mansplaining" (a man patronizingly explaining something, often beginning by interrupting a woman), "manterrupting" (a man interrupting a woman) and "bro-opting" (a man adopting a woman's idea as his own). We are including men in our own identity groups. We are honoring emotions, including anger. We are insisting that the choice to become pregnant must not be punished. We are recognizing and resisting patriarchal females, gossip, whispering cowards, the weaponization of information, expectations of silence, and hegemonic politeness. We are asserting the value of intersectionality—in data, research, hiring, and cultural narratives. We are creating allies and recognizing the collective as social capital for power, strength, success, and healing.

The essays in this volume are organized as follows.

1. TENURE AND PROMOTION

Section 1 sets the stage for the remainder of the book by naming many of the systemic biases that pervade the academic workplace and offering pragmatic, solution-oriented recommendations. These chapters examine the formidable obstacles that Women of Color encounter on the road to tenure and promotion, including inequitable teaching loads, crushing service obligations, race and gender bias in the evaluation of teaching and scholarship, pregnancy discrimination, lack of mentoring, sexual harassment, stalking, bullying, and the painful reminder that skinfolk are not always kinfolk—that those who share our social identities are not necessarily allies. The authors describe in gripping detail the lengths to which colleagues will go to sabotage the careers of Women of Color, and offer a variety of tools that can be deployed to resist, fight back, and prevail.

2. ACADEMIC LEADERSHIP

This section provides a rare window into the working lives of Women of Color who have entered the ranks of senior academic leadership—as well as roadmaps for those who aspire to follow in their footsteps. Creating an equitable and inclusive campus climate requires a diverse leadership team. However, Women of Color who occupy leadership positions quickly discover that there is an inherent conflict between their personal values and the expectations of senior administrators who want to protect the university's brand. Academic leaders who are deemed too ethnic, too queer, too feminist, too angry, too honest, or too radical may find themselves dismissed from their positions. Women of Color who navigate these conflicting imperatives often question whether they are transforming their institutions or facilitating the institution's diversity marketing. They may be viewed with suspicion by faculty colleagues while being excluded from meaningful decision-making by university provosts and presidents.

Women of Color who rise to the highest echelons of the profession also continue to battle the presumption of incompetence along with gender sidelining. They experience challenges to their authority, inconsistent institutional support, ageism, and the perception that they have become "sellouts" or careerists.

The contributors to this section demonstrate that these hurdles are daunting but not insurmountable. These challenges include the hegemonic "politeness" of academic culture that serves to protect White fragility and perpetuate existing power relations. The pioneering leaders whose stories animate this section provide a wealth of strategies to combat the presumption of incompetence and increase the representation of Women of Color in senior leadership positions.

3. SOCIAL CLASS

This section examines class bias in academia and its intersection with race, gender, pregnancy, physical and mental (dis)ability, and other markers of identity. Academia generates voluminous research on poverty but rarely addresses the impact of low academic salaries on faculty, especially adjuncts, who must take on multiple jobs to make ends meet and to support parents and siblings whose sacrifices made their academic careers possible. The professor is expected to be "a poster figure unburdened by anything associated with life, free from poverty and debt, no visible pregnancy or family to support, in full physical and mental health" (see chapter by Jamiella Brooks in this volume). Women of Color who struggle with family financial or care-giving responsibilities, who face debilitating physical or mental illness, or who navigate the tenure and promotion process while pregnant are frequently presumed incapable of diligently and competently fulfilling their professional responsibilities.

Academics from the working class face extraordinary pressure to conform to White middle- and upper-class norms not only in speech, dress, mannerisms, and vocabulary but also in the choices they make about teaching, scholarship, and service. Those who pursue qualitative or community-based research, teach or write from critical class, race, and gender perspectives, attempt to diversify the curriculum, or work with underserved or at-risk communities frequently find their competence questioned and their accomplishments devalued. They may also be shunned and accused of incivility if their working-class candor clashes with middle class passive aggressive communication styles.

The contributors to this volume challenge the deficit model that assigns negative attributes to working-class identity. They identify the unique skills and insights that working-class scholars bring to the academic workplace, including community-building skills honed through years of intersectional class-conscious alliances. The essays in this section demonstrate how working-class coping strategies and values (including solidarity, transparency, sharing, and openly expressing emotion) can create a more welcoming and inclusive environment for all marginalized groups.

4. BULLYING, WHITE FRAGILITY, AND MICROAGGRESSIONS

Women of Color who challenge White, patriarchal norms and defy race and gender stereotypes are often depicted as angry, ungrateful, and threatening. They are frequently ostracized, disciplined, denied tenure and promotion, and silenced, not only by White faculty and administrators but also by fellow Scholars of Color who have internalized racist and sexist beliefs. This section directly and unabashedly discusses the myriad forms of abuse, exploitation, and disrespect endured by Women of Color in academia and their impacts on the bodies and psyches of those who are targeted as well as those who witness the torment of others. The daily microaggressions as well as the premeditated attacks can cause or exacerbate physical and mental illness, and can lead to miscarriages, suicide, or premature death from cancer, heart disease, and other serious ailments. The essays in this section are harrowing, but they provide valuable advice to Women of Color and those who serve as allies on ways to challenge and disrupt oppressive practices and processes.

5. ACTIVISM, RESISTANCE, AND PUBLIC ENGAGEMENT

The final section of this volume is devoted to activism and resistance in a variety of venues and through a variety of means. The contributors to this section share inspiring and courageous narratives about their struggles against marginalization and abuse, including: filing a complaint regarding a hostile work environment while enduring two miscarriages; using social media to create a supportive online community; challenging faculty to incorporate a racial justice lens into the curriculum; healing from racial battle fatigue by talking openly in safe spaces; appealing tenure denial; combating tokenism; confronting racist internet trolls; and filing (and winning) sex discrimination and retaliation lawsuits.

SUMMARY

One of the key lessons of this volume of *Presumed Incompetent* is the importance of building community, mentoring the next generation, and developing intersectional alliances in order to challenge the oppressive practices that have inflicted so much harm on our communities. And of course, we must continue telling our stories. For a glimpse of the impact of the narratives in the first volume of *Presumed Incompetent,* please see the website of the University Press of Colorado & Utah State University. In the space of some of the narratives in this volume, these stories are told, in part, from the vernacular and speech of the authors' cultural context. As such, we are legitimatizing the power of these ways of interpersonal communication.

We received almost 150 narratives for this volume of *Presumed Incompetent*, courageously contributed by women across rank and race/ethnicity. Regrettably, space constraints kept us from bringing to light all of their resolutely presented experiences. Sharing our stories validates the realities of others who face similar experiences, and affords all persons, including academic leaders from a range of power and position standpoints, the opportunity to learn about and intercede in the severe and life-altering forms of violence occurring under their noses.

REFERENCES

National Center for Education Statistics. (2018). Fast facts, race/ethnicity of college faculty. Retrieved from https://nces.ed.gov/fastfacts/display.asp?id=61.

University Press of Colorado & Utah State University Press. https://upcolorado.com/utah-state-university-press/item/2338-presumed-incompetent.

US Census Bureau. (2017). Population estimates, July 1, 2017 (V2017). Retrieved from https://www.census.gov/quickfacts/fact/table/US/PST045217.

US Department of Education. (2016). Digest of education statistics (52nd ed.). Retrieved from https://nces.ed.gov/pubs2017/2017094.pdf.

SECTION ONE

TENURE AND PROMOTION

ONE

"Still I Rise"

Jacquelyn Bridgeman

I am an African American, cisgender, heterosexual woman who has spent over half of my life in Wyoming, first as a child growing up from ages six to eighteen and again when I returned in 2002 at the age of twenty-eight to join the faculty at the University of Wyoming College of Law. I was the first African American tenure-track professor hired at Wyoming's law school. Before hiring me, the college had never hired a minority tenure-track professor. I was the first Associate Dean of Color at the College of Law, I was the second Person of Color to be appointed a dean in the history of my institution, and I am still the only woman to serve as dean of our college in its nearly 100-year history. At the time of my hire there was only one American-born tenured Professor of Color in the entire university, which at that time had 612 full-time instructional faculty.

Mine is a narrative about transformation. Transformation of self, transformation of one's circumstances, transformation of one's institution. It's about how I went from almost not getting tenure to having one of the most secure positions at my university. How I went from being the lowest-paid faculty member in my college to being one of the highest paid in the entire university. How I helped my institution move from a place that had one Tenured Faculty Member of Color to now having so many I don't even know them all. It is about how I learned how to blossom and thrive where I was planted, despite the unconscious racism, overt racism, and rampant sexism I have endured. It is about coming to understand that perhaps the most important work we ever do is not for ourselves, but for others.

THE PRE-TENURE CRUCIBLE AND HOW IT HAS SHAPED MY CAREER

In the nearly sixteen years I have been in academia I have begun to think of a professor position as akin to a polygamous marriage, one that exists between the

DOI: 10.7330/9781607329664.c001

university, oneself, and one's colleagues, with the tenure-track process much like a formal courtship in which all parties are trying to determine if they would like to make a long-term commitment. As with most such relationships, mine with the University of Wyoming College of Law and my colleagues went through a honeymoon period, which lasted almost a year.

I often wonder if the honeymoon period would have lasted longer, perhaps indefinitely, had I done a few things differently. Would it have lasted had I not been an outspoken member of the faculty? Or an unconventional, albeit effective and popular, teacher? Or if I had not written on controversial topics like race, gender, and Black identity? Or if I had continued to straighten my hair? Perhaps it would have lasted longer had I not been the first female professor in many years to have children while on tenure track or if I hadn't also taught in African American studies and insisted on holding those classes in the law school. Even in hindsight it is hard to judge whether doing any of those things differently would have altered the situation I found myself in the year prior to my tenure vote. After all, not doing those things or doing them differently would not have changed the fundamental problem many of my colleagues had with me—the color of my skin. Although it was a problem none of them ever expressed directly, I came to realize over the course of the first six years of my career that the issue affected the evaluation of all aspects of my job.

Teaching: The Unrequited Labor of Love

During the time I have been at Wyoming I have been voted a class hooder, teacher of the year multiple times, and I have received the university's highest award for teaching excellence. In response to the question, "How did you become a good teacher?" the honest answer is "Unmitigated fear." The first day I taught my hands shook during the entire seventy-five-minute class period and I spoke so quickly several students considered dropping the class for fear they would never be able to understand me. I had nightmares—about accidentally oversleeping and missing class, about not being able to answer questions, about missing a big change in the law—that robbed me of sleep nearly the entire first year I taught. I broke out in shingles.

When I took my position at Wyoming I was twenty-eight years old, which meant over half the student body was older than I. I had never taught before. The one African American third-year student and I were the only visible People of Color in the entire school. It became clear almost immediately, when one of my students addressed me by my first name without permission within a few weeks of the start of my first semester, that the imprimatur of respect and deference afforded by virtue of standing in front of the class and being called professor did not apply to me.

I overcame my initial day-to-day fear and survived my first year of teaching by working like a crazy person. In one of my evaluations my dean referred to me as a natural teacher. I nearly laughed when I read that statement because the reality was I was anything but. I just worked hard. I worked hard and I taught for the benefit of my students. Fairly early in my teaching career I had an epiphany that changed everything for me. I realized teaching had very little to do with me and everything to do with my students. Ironically, it was my connection to Wyoming that caused me to focus on my students and fueled my drive to become a good teacher.

We are the only law school in Wyoming. Currently, the governor, all of the state Supreme Court justices, many lower-court judges, state legislators, and practicing attorneys are graduates of our law school. Because of the small practices that most of our graduates will enter, they must hit the ground running. They will not have the luxury of a few years after graduation to learn how to be good attorneys. Consequently, if we do not educate our students well, the entire state suffers. Once I understood this, my teaching became about how I could best prepare my students for the jobs they might do upon graduation and much less about me.

Further, I felt very strongly that I did not want to subject my students to the hostile, alienating, and traumatic experience that law school had been for me. I adopted an approach whereby I wanted each student to feel like they got their money's worth such that they would regret ever missing a class. I called on students in law firms or groups to make answering in class less daunting, and I used group work, simulations, and other activities to encourage active learning, cooperation, and support among the students. I used a variety of techniques to cater to a range of learning styles, and I strove to make class fun.

With respect to the tenure process and my continued longevity, teaching as I have chosen to teach has been a mixed blessing. My teaching approach is extremely time intensive, which makes balancing the scholarship requirements, tremendous service obligations, and now administrative responsibilities that I also have that much more difficult. What's more, being a good teacher, in and of itself, was not enough to save me or to insulate me from attacks on my scholarship or myself when it came time for my tenure decision. This was in part because my teaching received less value during my evaluation for tenure due to race.

The transparent nature of our tenure and promotion process allowed me to compare the work my colleagues did to my own and the kinds of comments they received to the ones I received. Consequently, I was able to witness firsthand how several of my colleagues attributed the poor teaching of my White male counterparts—often characterized in their student evaluations as an inability to convey information in an accessible and understandable way—to the high level of those teachers' intellect. In contrast, those same colleagues postulated that the students liked me because I was too easy on them and too helpful—an assessment made despite the fact that evaluation after evaluation described me as challenging and demanding and my classes as some of the hardest the students had taken in law school. The consequence was that my White male colleagues got the same or even more credit for their teaching as I did, even though they did less work and had poorer evaluations. Consequently, that allowed them more time to engage in other pursuits, such as their scholarship.

While a part of me has resented the fact that I received less credit for my teaching versus some of my colleagues, I don't believe that is the crux of the problem. Rather, I believe my colleagues should have been held to the same standards as I. Since teaching well garnered me little marginal benefit in the tenure and promotion process, there was little incentive for me to be more than a mediocre teacher. This was true despite the fact that quality teaching is something typically valued and rewarded at our institution. Similarly, since my colleagues were rewarded for mediocrity there was little incentive to improve their teaching. None of which served to help students and all of which I worked to change when the opportunity presented itself.

Service: The Structural Racial Tax

While the time I have devoted to teaching has been substantial both before and after tenure, that time has been matched, if not exceeded, by the time I have spent in service work. When I arrived at the University of Wyoming there were four other Black professors. There was an African American studies program in existence, but it was on life support. It became clear almost immediately that if I, and others like me, did not teach in and support the program it wasn't going to survive. At the same time, there were not enough mentors and means of support for Students of Color, African American or otherwise, and there were not enough people from underrepresented groups to add diversity to the many places where it was desperately needed. That meant that the five of us found ourselves very early in our careers being called upon to keep the African American studies program afloat and sitting on, if not running, all of the university committees that wanted or needed an African American presence or just a Person of Color. The five of us mentored graduate and undergraduate Students of Color throughout the university, in addition to our regular advising and mentoring duties within our own departments, and we frequently helped organize, support, and consult with the greater African American community.

In addition to the service burdens that come with being Black, there are those that come from being in a sparsely populated state. In a state of roughly 500,000 inhabitants, people with professional expertise are not plentiful. Thus, all professors, regardless of race or gender, are frequently called upon to serve when expertise of one kind or another is needed.

I think there is no question I could have done much less service without it negatively affecting my tenure evaluation, and now that I am a tenured, full, senior professor, I could also do less. Moreover, less service pre-tenure would have made my life after tenure easier, though not all classes for African American studies would have been covered. It would have meant that there would have been even fewer than five people to help carry the load of mentoring, advocating, and serving in all the many ways our institution needed People of Color to serve.

I have always believed that the opportunities my forebearers fought for mean very little if, once one takes advantage of the opportunity, one does not work to change and better the institution of which one is a part. It means little if one does not speak out regarding things of import and if one does not work to help pave the way for others to follow. Accordingly, I have tried to make all the service work I have done transformative and lasting. Whenever possible I have tried to take on only work that would lead to significant change at my institution or open up opportunities for others. For example, when I served on hiring committees I made sure we advertised and targeted underrepresented populations, often doing extra work to build a diverse applicant pool and to encourage people from underrepresented groups to apply. I then fought for people from these groups to be interviewed and hired. Because I was the token member on so many hiring committees, over time this strategy helped change the makeup of people hired at my institution. Later, when I was in charge of appointing hiring committees, I made sure they were staffed with people committed to diversity and inclusiveness.

Similarly, I found that many in my institution were willing to make changes and were willing to listen and learn if there was someone to lead, or to educate, so I took the lead in a lot of initiatives and worked to educate my colleagues in the process of us doing work together. For example, during my second year, I agreed to co-chair a fledgling university-wide committee that was tasked with creating a weeklong set of events centered around the Martin Luther King Jr. holiday. I used my service on that committee to develop relationships across the university with people who were committed to issues of diversity and inclusion. We developed programming for that event that centered on sparking dialogue and engendering change on a range of issues university wide. Although I no longer chair this committee, it continues and has become institutionalized, carrying on the work we started over fourteen years ago.

Throughout the years, I have pushed for and advocated for change at every turn, employing different strategies depending on the circumstances. In addition to the kinds of service work just described, I have also put myself in administrative positions that have allowed me to make the kinds of decisions that would help bring about change. For example, when I was associate dean and then dean of the law school, I was instrumental in changing the way we targeted and recruited underrepresented students and in changing the kinds of programs we had in place to support them once they arrived. Those improvements significantly increased our minority student population at the law school, at least during the time I was dean.

The university at which I now work in many ways does not resemble the institution I came to sixteen years ago. Whereas I was the first tenure-track Person of Color hired at our law school, four out of our twenty current faculty members are People of Color and all four have tenure and are full professors. I no longer know every American-born Professor of Color at our university. We have created a social justice research center, and in this past year have launched a new school, Culture, Gender and Social Justice. We hold weeklong all-university events twice a year devoted to issues of diversity, equity, and inclusion. We have hired a chief diversity officer and we now require every search committee to undergo diversity training and to actively recruit and try to hire people from underrepresented populations. These are just a few of the significant changes that have transformed my institution and the way we do business. I either spearheaded, led, or was heavily involved in the vast majority of these efforts and I continue to be, as we still have a lot of work to do.

Scholarship: The Tenure-Track Third Rail

> You may write me down in history
> With your bitter twisted lies,
> You may trod me in the very dirt,
> But still, like dust, I'll rise . . .
> You may shoot me with your words,
> You may cut me with your eyes.
> You may kill me with your hatefulness,
> But still, like air, I'll rise . . .
> Bringing the gifts that my ancestors gave,
> I am the dream and the hope of the slave.
> I rise,
> I rise,
> I rise. (Angelou, 1994, pp. 163–164)

There was a day in the spring of 2007, the year before I came up for tenure, when I was bitter, hurt, angry, tired, and very close to throwing in the towel, leaving academia, and finding something else to do with my life. On that particular day, as I sat struggling with an article that I knew I was going to have to once again defend to my colleagues, the refrain from Maya Angelou's poem rang in my head: "I rise, I rise, I rise." It was in that moment that I remembered all the people who came before me who sacrificed and endured so much so that I would have the opportunity about which I was so bitter and angry. An opportunity that still eludes many African Americans: African American professors nationwide are represented in percentages well below the percentage of African Americans in the general population, and 96 percent of tenured African American professors teach in historically Black colleges and universities (Strauss, 2015). It was in that moment that I decided that no matter what, I was going to find a way to hang on and get tenure.

My reviews the first two years I was on the tenure track went smoothly, with no problems, but I began to notice a shift when I received my colleagues' comments in connection with my third-year review. Whereas the comments I had received in my first two years were uniformly positive, now several of my colleagues began to raise subtle questions about my ability to finish enough scholarly projects in time for the final tenure vote. One colleague not so subtly expressed concerns about the quality and quantity of my scholarship. Another called me into her office and, ostensibly making sure I did not run into problems later, proceeded to tell me that she worried my first piece, one centered on issues of Black racial identity, did not demonstrate the kind of rigorous legal analysis my colleagues would require for a favorable tenure decision.

Thankfully, our tenure process is quite transparent, allowing all faculty, regardless of rank, to review the files and sit in on the discussions for all members. Without this transparency, I would not have known that the faculty did not require one of my colleagues to undergo a fifth-year review, as they did me, even though she had fewer publications than I did at the same point in the tenure process. I would not have known that for at least one candidate a legal brief counted as one of the required pieces of scholarship. Or that the faculty never questioned whether another of my colleagues would produce scholarship of sufficient quantity and quality for tenure although he had yet to publish anything, or even submit a work in progress while at Wyoming, having been granted a shortened tenure track due to work completed at a different institution several years prior.

By the time of my fifth-year review, the year before I was to go up for tenure, I had exceeded the college's stated requirements regarding the requisite number of publications. The outside reviews of my previous scholarship were, without exception, positive. I had done more service than several of my colleagues combined and I had earned the university's highest teaching award. One would have thought that determining to reappoint me, and to review me for tenure and promotion the following year, would have been an easy decision. It was not.

In the comments accompanying the fifth-year faculty vote to reappoint me, some of my colleagues did finally reveal their animosity toward the subject matter of my scholarship. One went so far as to refer to critical race theory as alien. Others took a different tack and asserted that the grammar and punctuation in my writing was so poor that perhaps I should no longer be allowed to teach legal writing. There were also those who criticized my writing as too simplistic and conversational to be taken seriously. Yet I sat in another tenure and promotion meeting that year and watched the colleagues I knew were my chief detractors defend and advocate for tenure for a person who clearly fell short of the minimum scholarship requirements. That same person had received a scathing outside review, which the colleagues who were my chief critics blatantly chose to ignore. In that same meeting I listened to my colleagues extol the virtues of another person's scholarship even though his piece had yet to be accepted for publication and even though it took one of my colleagues multiple attempts to be able to read through the entire article. Whereas my clear and straightforward prose was perceived to be simplistic and unanalytical, his turgid prose was construed to be the product of a brilliant mind.

One lesson I have learned is that help can come from the most unlikely places and from people one would never expect. Help for me prior to tenure came in the form of an older White woman who specialized in business and securities law and who could not have cared less about race issues, but who cared a lot about fairness and who actually took the time to read my tenure and promotion packet and to sit in on some of my classes. The year before I was to come up for tenure she came into my office and explained to me that I was having trouble because everyone had supposed I was an affirmative action hire and so even before I took the job they assumed I wasn't qualified.

When I questioned how they could continue to view me in that light given my qualifications compared to recent hires and in the face of all of the work I had done, she explained that most of the faculty never did more than a cursory review of the tenure and promotion packets. Instead they relied on comments made by other faculty members in the tenure and promotion meetings. Because those who chose to attack me made comments consistent with the expectations many of my colleagues had, they never questioned whether the evaluation of me was fair or accurate.

She also helped me understand that despite the way I was being treated, my colleagues did generally like me and did want me to be successful, at least consciously. This realization helped me to recognize that I did not have to do more or better work to get tenure. Rather, I had to change the frame through which my colleagues viewed my work. I was able to accomplish this by doing two simple things. One, I restructured my tenure file. Two, I wrote a narrative explaining how I met all the requirements for tenure and promotion. I placed the narrative at the beginning of my file and arranged my supporting materials as though they were evidentiary exhibits for a brief. I assumed those who were not willing to read the entire file would read my narrative and take it at face value. For those who might delve deeper, the narrative guided them through the materials and helped them read and interpret those materials in the way I wanted them to. In crafting my narrative I did not focus on justifying or explaining any of my work. Instead, I presented as a given that my work was of high quality and great value. Accordingly, my narrative focused on explaining the many ways in which my work far exceeded all of the minimum expectations in all categories, and on all the great things I would continue to contribute if granted tenure. The effect was that my narrative shifted the conversation from one where my colleagues felt free to question the quality of my work to one where my detractors were put in the position of having to prove that my work wasn't good in the face of all the evidence I provided.

The difference between my fifth- and sixth-year reviews was dramatic. The same people who had previously described my scholarship as "alien" and "nontraditional" and who had questioned my discipline, focus, and intelligence now described my scholarship as praiseworthy, carefully crafted, traditional legal scholarship of high quality. Ironically, the content of my tenure packet had changed very little between my fifth- and sixth-year reviews, but the frame through which my colleagues viewed my work caused them to see it in a completely different light.

MY POST-TENURE LIFE

I received tenure and promotion to full professor when I was thirty-four years old. There was a day shortly after I earned tenure that I realized that if I continued to work at my institution until age sixty-five, I would be there for another thirty years. Despite how bitter and angry I was over how my journey to tenure had gone, I still loved Wyoming and I had no intentions of leaving. Yet there was no way I was going to endure thirty more years like the six I had just survived. It was at that point I decided that if I was going to stay, my institution had to change.

That has been the story of my post-tenure life. A year after I earned tenure I became our associate dean for academic affairs. I have spent six of the last ten years in various administrative positions. My approach to administration has mirrored my approaches to teaching and service in that I have become a good administrator because I outwork everyone else, and I have tried to administer according to my values and in a way that is transformative. I have tried to be inclusive and fair, and to recognize and give voice to those who often are overlooked and never heard. I have tried to break down and stop reinforcing institutional instances of oppression, both where they have affected me personally and where they have affected others. For example, I took the associate dean position in part to address the fact that I was the lowest-paid faculty member at our law school because at the time I was hired I did not know that one could negotiate for a higher salary, or the long-term consequences of not doing so. During the time I was associate dean, and then later when I was dean, we changed the way in which we set initial salaries so that we quit systematically disadvantaging women and People of Color. When available, I used raise pools to try to fix existing disparities.

In addition to trying to identify systems of exclusion and working to change them, I have also tried to change the way we think about our institution and the work we do. I have worked to change the culture, such as moving us from a place where no one had children pre-tenure to a place where we embrace and value child care responsibilities and incorporate them as a normal and expected part of doing business. For example, I incorporated my own child care duties into my work as dean. I arranged my schedule around picking up my children, attending their activities, and coaching their teams, and we moved to flexible scheduling that allowed all staff to do the same. We welcomed children into the office regularly, and we created space for them to be there. I kept coloring books, games, and snacks in my office for kids and I brought my own children to meetings, including some I had with the university president. When I had my first child, I was the first woman anyone could remember in the history of our law school who had children pre-tenure, and I was strongly encouraged to stop my tenure clock because our then associate dean did not believe I could have children and still successfully complete the requirements for tenure. Now, nearly every woman currently on our faculty has had children pre-tenure, with some of the nursing newborns even attending our faculty meetings.

Despite the significant progress we have made, there is still much work to do. I have learned over the years that change that is dependent on individuals can be fleeting and illusory. Transformative and lasting change must happen at an institutional level and become embedded in the institution's culture and DNA. The work in which I currently engage seeks to effect that kind of change. I have been able to keep up this work for the last sixteen years because despite how hard it is, it is very rewarding, and it has made the place where I live and work better. Even when the work is hard, it is easy to persevere when one can see tangible and lasting change. Additionally, over the years I have built a wonderful network of family, friends, and colleagues who support and sustain me at every turn. While I may have had a hand in and/or led much of the transformative work at my institution, I certainly have not accomplished anything alone. In a session several years ago at the National People of Color Conference, Michelle Goodwin, who is now the chancellor's professor of law at the University of California, Irvine, talked about the importance of blossoming where one is planted. Over the years, I have taken that to heart and tried to do so, with the hope that over time my narrative would go from one in which "Still I Rise" to one in which "we rise, we rise, we rise."

REFERENCES

Angelou, M. (1994). *The complete collected poems of Maya Angelou.* New York: Random House.

Strauss, V. (2015, November 12). It's 2015. Where are all the black college faculty? *The Washington Post.* Retrieved from https://www.washingtonpost.com/news/answer-sheet/wp/2015/11/12/its-2015-where-are-all-the-black-college-faculty/?utm_term=.e34fbb438b32.

TWO

The Lucky Law Professor and the Eucatastrophic Moment

Lolita Buckner Inniss

Sometimes people are just lucky. They succeed for reasons outside of their control, and even after experiencing hardship, even when they come within inches of failure, things turn out well for them in the end. These sorts of narrative arcs, these tales of luck at the edge of the abyss, are captured by the term *eucatastrophe*, coined by J.R.R. Tolkien in his discussion of fairy tales (Nuttall, 2003).[1] It refers to a "good catastrophe," the joyous, sudden turn of events at the end of a story that results in the protagonist's well-being (Buckner Inniss, 2011). Achieving eucatastrophe involves "recovery" and "restoration," and is a process of defamiliarization with the known world in order to better appreciate its qualities. Eucatastrophe reverses the tragic meaning of catastrophe found in Greek tales and creates, usually within the context of fantasy or supernatural tales, an escape from death (Flieger, 1983). Tolkien, in proposing the word, did not mean to suggest that any and every set of difficult circumstances could or would result in a good outcome. Eucatastrophe is not a restatement of *deus ex machina*, where a good outcome comes from some exterior, sometimes supernatural force even when circumstances make a happy ending highly implausible (Mallinson, 2011). Instead, eucatastrophe is the rejection of cynicism and the embodiment of hope. It is the claim that while all situations of extreme personal difficulty do not end well, many have the capacity to do so. Eucatastrophe does not deny hardships; it embraces the memory of hardships but denies that hardships must, by necessity, cause defeat. Eucatastrophe is the fortuitous satisfaction of long-held desires, and the consolation presented by the possibility of the happy ending (Tolkien, Flieger, & Anderson, 2014).

1. Shakespeare's *All's Well that Ends Well* and *Measure for Measure* have both been described as examples of Tolkien's eucatastrophe, especially in how the disquieting pressure of outside forces is ultimately and happily resolved with a new beginning for the heroines of both plays.

DOI: 10.7330/9781607329664.c002

I adopt the concept of eucatastrophe as a way of understanding the events of my career as a Black woman law professor. I am lucky. My professional story is one of some successes in the face of what at times seemed like insurmountable obstacles—difficulties in obtaining a tenure-track position, professional and social exclusion in the workplace, being passed over for opportunities, workplace stalking and harassment. But ultimately, my circuitous route to becoming a tenured law professor is largely about the eucatastrophic moment: that point when hope and hardship fuse into triumph. In simple terms, my story is about plain old-fashioned luck—both the good kind and the bad kind.

My entry into law teaching was fortuitous. After a half dozen very challenging years of public and private law practice, in 1993 I started work as an adjunct professor teaching a course in legal methods at a nearby law school. I had seen an advertisement for the position in a local legal newspaper, and forwarded my resumé. I later learned that hundreds of people had applied for what were three or four jobs. My resumé caught the adjunct program director's eye because I had obtained my JD from the same California law school the director had attended. This was the first piece of good luck in my journey to becoming a law professor. Upon meeting me, the director expressed surprise that I was Black, an understandable reaction at a time when so very few Black women were in the ranks of either adjunct or full-time law teachers. I was immediately enthralled by the work, and longed to enter full-time law teaching. However, I took no steps to look for such work because, quite simply, I had no idea of how to go about it.

But as luck would have it, the adjunct program director admired my work, and when a job opened for a full-time clinician at the school's Immigration Clinic in fall 1994, she strongly recommended me for the position, which I was ultimately offered, and which I accepted.[2] Much to my delight, I became a full-time law professor at School #1. Readers will note that I choose not to name the institutions that are the subject of this account, or to name most of the persons I encountered along the way. It is better that way, since one person's nurturing mentor is another person's spirit murderer (Williams, 1987).[3]

KNOCKING ON THE BACK DOOR AT SCHOOL #1

I was thrilled to be a full-time law teacher. I could, I thought, finally achieve my dreams of being a scholar and a teacher. It turned out, however, that I could

2. While it may be possible to go from being an adjunct to a full-time professor, it is not the norm. Adjunct law-teaching positions should be viewed as just what they are: temporary, often part-time (and frequently low-paid) employment with little opportunity for a trajectory upward in academia. This is especially true for Women of Color scholars; I have known few to make the transition. Those thinking of adjunct law teaching as a pathway to opportunities for full-time law teaching should forgo adjunct teaching and instead spend that time writing scholarly articles.
3. Law professor Patricia Williams tells the story of being excluded from a Benetton store, ostensibly because of her race. Williams defines "spirit-murder" as the psychological damage caused by racially motivated abuses.

achieve only part of that dream. My job as a clinical law professor was not quite what I had imagined. I worked all day and much of every night: seeing clients as well as teaching and supervising students during the day, caring for my children in the early evenings, and doing research late at night and into the wee hours of the morning. It hit me like a ton of bricks when I learned that the work of my clinic took no hiatus during school breaks that would allow for more writing time—we were lawyers and teachers first, and scholars only if and when time permitted.

Now understanding the lay of the land, I approached members of School #1's faculty appointments committee about applying for a regular tenure-track job. I was told that though my credentials were very good, I had no published writing, and moreover, that other faculty members would be opposed to my effort to "back door" the school. I immediately thought of stories from my grandmother and mother about how, when they worked as maids at various times in the 1950s, White families required them to enter their workplaces only via the back door. Their admission to White homes through these anterior entrances was a reminder of my foremothers' diminished social and professional status, and it was the only way that they would be admitted at all.

I gleaned from my conversation with School #1 faculty members that they meant something pejorative by "back door," but it was not the back door of my ancestors' experience. For these faculty members, back dooring the school meant arriving in one job classification and then moving into another, more favorable classification without the usual formal process required of outside applicants. Where I come from this was called being promoted and usually was encouraged and admired. These faculty members gave me to understand that no such norm existed, either in the context of legal education or in the practices of this institution. Nonetheless, they grudgingly conceded that such things could happen and had happened. Indeed, to my understanding there had been White School #1 faculty members who had entered tenure-track teaching at the school via this route. But this path was clearly barred to me. I would have no such luck.

I watched in dismay and smoldering anger as White faculty candidates with similar and often lesser credentials than mine were paraded through the school during hiring season. After mastering my feelings, I began working on an article in earnest. I also looked for a position where I might be able to write as a part of my job. At the end of the 1994–1995 school year, I accepted an offer to work as a visiting associate professor at School #2, where I would offer lecture courses in immigration law and administrative law, create and conduct an immigration clinic, and design and lead a seminar on law and literature. In retrospect, I marvel that I would have seen such a daunting set of tasks as a piece of good luck, yet lucky I felt. In my happiness at having a new position, I did not notice until much later that I was the only Black woman faculty member at School #2, and the only person assigned such a heavy schedule.

SCHOOL #2 AND THE FAILED LOOK-SEE

I came to School #2 in the fall of 1995 on a two-year "look-see" visit. A look-see is an academic position wherein the professor is under evaluation, usually with a promise of a full consideration for a permanent position after completion of the temporary job. It appeared that all was well during my first year at School #2. I rose at 3:00 every morning and drove ninety miles from my home, spending sometimes over two hours in traffic in order to take advantage of what I believed to be a stellar opportunity. However, early in my second year, I received a faculty-wide memo from which I learned that the immigration clinic would be terminated. "Hmm," I thought, "isn't that my program? Does this mean that I'm out of a job?" It turned out that the answer was yes, as I determined when I called the dean's office and spoke to his secretary.

When I asked for an appointment to see the dean to discuss my indirect discharge, I was told that he could not see me for six weeks. Declining to set such a remote appointment, I hung up the phone in grim shock, not only at being out of a job, but at being treated in such an offhand manner. I got some consolation from the fact that other untenured faculty members had also received notice (albeit theirs was direct personal notice, not the general memo to the faculty that I had received) that budgetary concerns would make it impossible to retain many of us. In their notices, these other untenured faculty members were advised to seek jobs elsewhere. I adopted this advice, though it was clearly not intended for me.

As discouraged as I was after this turn of events, I was determined to remain a law professor. I sought other work immediately. Given the timing of my discharge, I entered the legal academic job market later than is usual for candidates. By early spring 1997, I had received no permanent offers that I wished to accept. After what had just happened at School #2, I proceeded carefully in considering the next position, mindful of the danger of once more moving from frying pan to fire. Strictly speaking, however, I did not consider my failed look-see as a move into the fire. My experience had put me in a position where I had resources equivalent to a regular tenure-track faculty member and I had been able to accomplish some writing. Still, I began to understand that a law school's financial footing and other aspects of its treatment of faculty members were important factors in evaluating a job and so, after making inquiries about the few schools from which I had received offers of a permanent position, I declined those offers.

I turned instead to offers I had received to visit. All of these, however, were far from my home, and I seriously considered giving up my dream of law teaching altogether. I was encouraged to persevere, however, by a Black colleague in the academy who told me about his own odyssey leading to attainment of a permanent tenure-track job. He told me to get over my hurt feelings, to pack my things (though he used a rather more crude, yet apt, term for my things), and to go on to the next job, wherever it was. The other valuable advice this colleague gave me was, come hell or high water, to keep writing. I had written one article during my first year at School #2. I completed another article just before leaving the institution.

Looking back, I see now that writing was and is a substantial key to my survival in this business of academia, and I am forever grateful to that colleague. I pause here to also note that I came to know this colleague, and many others like him, by attending the regional People of Color Legal Scholarship Conferences (Prince, 2000).[4] The People of Color Conferences provided me and other Faculty of Color with much-needed support and advice in navigating the ins and outs of law teaching, and I commend them highly.

I took my colleague's advice and accepted a visiting professorship a few states away from my home, thereby upping the ante on commuting, now traveling by air instead of car. Though my luck had taken a rather substantial beating at School # 2, I collected its tattered remnants and moved on to School #3 as a visiting associate professor.

SCHOOL #3 AND THE HOSTILE FACULTY

At my third law school, I learned to steel myself against some hardcore faculty hostility. My only substantial interactions with faculty members at the school were with two tenure-track Black women professors who were facing their own difficulties. Though they had been there for years before me, and though none of us looked anything alike, sometimes we were confused for one another by our White colleagues. We joked that maybe we were all the same person, and that we should avoid being in the same room together lest we disappear in some odd process of science fiction.

I was cynically pleased to be mistaken for my School #3 Black women colleagues since most members of the faculty who knew who I was ignored me completely, never speaking a word to me even when we met face-to-face. At the first-year student orientation I waited patiently as the dean called the names of the other new faculty members, tenure-track and visiting professors alike. When he finished without naming me, I caught his eye and signaled. He turned away and moved on to the next part of the program. Some members of the faculty made it crystal clear that I was barely tolerated as a visitor and entirely unwelcome to apply for a permanent job. Several weeks into my visit, a White male faculty member expressed interest in my work and asked me to show him drafts of my scholarly writing. I happily complied, grateful for the interest. Not much later, I learned that these early drafts were being shared with some other members of the faculty to bolster the decision not to offer me an interview for a permanent job. I was deeply stung by the betrayal.

Soon, however, I was able to take School #3's shoddy treatment in stride. I worked diligently to research and outline a job talk even while, as at School #1, mostly White job candidates with often lesser credentials were hosted during hiring season. The one Woman of Color among the many interviewing candidates

4. People of Color Legal Scholarship Conferences are comprised of groups of law faculty from six regions: the Midwest, Northeast, Southeast, Southwest, Mid-Atlantic, and West. Regional People of Color Conferences are parallel legal communities for law Faculty of Color wherein writings can be presented without fear and where scholars can find support that may be lacking at their home institutions.

asked me whether I was being considered for a permanent job at School #3. I was ashamed to say that I was not. I now know that the shame involved was not my own. Armed with my job talk, I once again entered the job market, and this time I was successful in receiving several interviews and offers of permanent tenure-track employment. I accepted an offer of permanent, tenure-track employment at School #4 and I began there in the fall of 1998. After an odyssey of five years, I had finally reached a tenure-track, regular teaching position. My luck had come through. But alas, it was not to be easy.

THE VERY ROCKY ROAD AT SCHOOL #4

My beginnings at School #4 included some rocky patches. I started out on a bad footing, stemming mostly from having a truly oppressive schedule. I taught two large first-year classes at the same time, the only junior person to be assigned such a course load. I worked in both the day program and the night program four days of the week, all while commuting to my home in another state. Not surprisingly, it was difficult to keep up with my scholarly writing. I also suffered from social and professional loneliness, as there were very few people at work with whom I had managed to become acquainted. There were a few faculty members who, as at School #3, did not acknowledge me at all. Most others greeted me in the hallways, but never engaged me in any substantive conversation. Many years before, I had heard the saying that to have a friend you have be a friend, so, after several months of isolation, I began to invite senior colleagues to dinners in my home and to lunches between classes, and I stopped in at their offices to chat. There was very little in the way of reciprocity. I found this especially painful as I watched a White male colleague with whom I was hired being feted upon his arrival, and regularly hosted at professional and social events with administrators and faculty members. My role as the invisible faculty member made me feel decidedly less lucky.

One of the unluckiest things that happened to me in my early teaching years occurred when the grades I submitted electronically at the end of my first year were somehow scrambled when posted by the law school. I became aware of the problem only when a few of my best students called me and asked very respectfully where they had gone wrong on their exams. I downloaded and reviewed the spreadsheet I had emailed and saw nowhere that they or I had gone wrong. It was then that I understood that a snafu must have occurred after my grade delivery. Over the next several weeks I dealt with a range of student emotions, from ecstasy to anger, as the grades were corrected. All of this occurred within an eerie administrative silence—no one seemed to know how the grades could have been scrambled after I delivered them, and no one bothered to explain to the students that it was very clearly an administrative error and not my personal mistake.

As the only junior Black faculty member, and as a woman, I was already subject to a presumption of incompetence. School #4's failure to offer me support in the face of its administrative error left me at the mercy of naysayers among the students and faculty. A rumor arose that I had engineered the grade scramble in an effort to give higher grades to the students I liked. I never understood how that made any sense at all, but no matter. After this incident, students avoided my classes for years. I didn't realize the extent to which this was true until I received a student evaluation a few years later: "She's nothing like they say—she's really knowledgeable and she really cares about students."

There was a particularly dark and unfortunate time at my first tenure-track job that I call "the stalker years." One of my senior colleagues began shadowing me, polling my students, discussing my competence with other faculty members, going through my trash, reviewing my already graded and submitted examinations and, worst of all, standing outside my classroom while I taught. At first I assumed that he was looking for students in my class or that he was looking at the photo gallery posted outside my classroom. I simply never imagined that he was spying on me until one day he made it clear to me. I was working in my office on a Saturday, finishing some work after having led a Black Law Students Association study session. He asked me to come into his office. Puzzled, I followed him.

He told me that he had been talking to students, trying to determine why they hated me so much. He then detailed all of the watching, checking, and reviewing that he had been doing. I was dumbfounded. I felt ill. I felt as if I had been physically violated. It took every ounce of my self-control to remain calm. I composed myself to speak clearly, though my hands shook violently.

"Well," I said, "Sometimes new professors, especially those who may seem youthful, have a hard time being accepted by students." He assured me that this was not the problem. Rather, he told me, I was someone who very clearly needed his help. He told me that he planned to sit in on my classes for a while and then, based upon his observations, figure out how to fix my problems. I was stunned into silence. I did not need or want this kind of "help." I stammered that I didn't think I really wanted a regular classroom visitor. He insisted that I needed his help, and he assured me that the matter would not go away, and that he would not go away. He informed me that he would not retire until after I went up for tenure. He told me to think about it and get back to him. He was sure, he said, that I would make the right decision.

I was in a daze as I thanked him and walked out. Even as I write these words now, I feel waves of revulsion at the thought that I thanked my abuser. My mind was racing, and I desperately wanted to go home. Although I had taken the train to work that morning, I asked my husband to drive in and pick me up. I trembled as I related the story to him. It all suddenly seemed clear to me and I felt that I was being set up, big time. I worried about what to do. Should I give in to the stalker? Should I ignore him? Should I tell anyone? This felt very much like organized schoolyard bullying where neither cooperation nor resistance will assuage the assailant. One way I had dealt with bullying in my childhood was by standing my ground and fighting back while screaming loudly so as to be heard by others. It is surprising how sometimes even the most vicious bullies do not want to be observed attacking people so much less powerful than themselves.

I first reported my dilemma to someone outside of School #4, a wonderful mentor, the late great Marilyn Yarbrough. Marilyn was then a professor at the University of North Carolina at Chapel Hill. Before going to Chapel Hill she had been the first Black dean of a majority-White law school, the University of Tennessee. Marilyn knew much about faculty bullying. She knew even more about the difficulties that Black women law professors sometimes experienced. We talked for over an hour, with most of that time spent calming me down. Her advice to me was simple, and jibed with my own thoughts on the matter. "Don't panic." "Don't isolate yourself."

Following my mentor's advice, I shared what had happened with some women colleagues at my institution. Some laughed it off, saying that he was a "great guy" and that he likely meant nothing by it. Others, fortunately, took my concerns seriously, and became my allies. One of this latter group shared with me that the stalker had a reputation for racist behavior. Another ally came up with a brilliant plan. She told me to invite the stalker to come to my class, asking him to schedule the visits at his convenience. After obtaining a schedule of his planned visits, the pièce de résistance was executed: I told him that I had taken to heart his assertion that I needed help with my classes to such an extent that I had asked a few other colleagues to also come to my class on the same days that he would be there. That way, my "panel of mentors" could talk together about what they had observed and figure out how best to help me. As expected, the stalker did not wish to participate in group evaluation of my work. He never appeared in any of my classes, and he never raised the matter again. He did take many of his misdeeds underground and I experienced some other problems as a result, but no matter. My winning of the first round sent a message: I am a fighter, and I am a survivor. I am the lucky law professor. With the exception of a one-semester medical leave in the fall of 2002, I taught for five years at School #4 before seeking tenure and promotion to associate professor.

Throughout my time at School #4, I was buoyed by a carefully cultivated pose of stoicism and defiance. For many years, the signature at the bottom of my faculty email declared, *Les jours s'en vont je demeure* (The days go away, I remain). This wistful quote from Guillaume Apollinaire's poem "Le pont Mirabeau" was entirely apt for I, like Apollinaire, had so many times experienced the sharp edge of hope's violence (Apollinaire, 1995, p. 12).

My years since attaining tenure have been a remarkable journey, during which my luck seemed to go from bad to good to bad to good again. No longer consumed with reaching the Big Rock Candy Mountain of tenure, I began remembering why I had wanted to be a professor in the first place. I gave new attention to my scholarly agenda, firmly establishing myself as writer of interdisciplinary race and gender scholarship. Though I had hedged early on, attempting to make sure that my work was well steeped in mainstream legal doctrine, after attaining tenure I began to think about the ways that disciplines outside of law informed law, especially in the areas of race and gender. I greatly furthered my scholarly agenda by becoming a full-time LLM student during my first and only sabbatical, and thereafter a PhD student. I was understandably hesitant after so many years of not only being away from the role of student but also of being in authority in an educational setting. I wondered whether I still had sufficient humility to "sit at the feet of the master."

I was joyous to be back in school, and yet my joy in this new educational endeavor was tempered with some sadness. My world was so greatly enlarged that I wondered if I had made a mistake in not having gone on leave earlier in my career. I will never know the answer to that. I do know that whether it entails going back to school to take another degree or some other scholarly endeavor, spending time at an academic institution other than one's own can be enriching, motivating, and possibly even career saving. This is not to suggest that any and all time away from your own institution will necessarily be a valuable experience in which you will be well received and appreciated. However, there is no denying the wisdom of the biblical verse: "A prophet is not without honor, save in his own country, and in his own house."[5]

After six years of patchwork scheduling, sporadic unpaid leaves, and predawn scholarly work, I earned an LLM and a PhD. Now, I thought, I can be "the Professor in the Office," that accomplished, respected scholar who had earned a place of honor among her peers and students (Koh, 1995). But no, not quite. My luck turned. The administrator who led my institution when I was hired stepped down, which led to six years of going from bad treatment to even worse. Exacerbating my chagrin was the fact that much of this mistreatment came from the hands of White women and a Person of Color. This was a painful reminder that social group affinity does not necessarily mean personal or ideological affinity.

It turns out that being a tenured full professor and the holder of post-JD degrees is no protection from institutional scorn, neglect, and abuse. A set of shiny achievements is no protection from being passed over for promotion, assigned burdensome teaching schedules, having complaints of sexual harassment ignored, being assailed as a "troublemaker" for speaking out against abuses and inequities, or being underpaid and charged with duties well outside of your job description. Yes, my luck had gone terribly bad at School #4. So I worked harder than ever, hoping for the chance to go where I might find not a better career fit, but a fit—plain and simple. By now it had occurred to me that I had been the proverbial round peg trying to fit herself into a square hole.

SCHOOL #5 AND THE EUCATASTROPHIC MOMENT, AGAIN

As a senior law professor, finding a lateral position requires a certain finesse. Senior law professors may ask their colleagues for leads, and tell them that they are open to a job change. They may attend professional conferences and give incisive scholarly talks and hope to be noticed. But typically, what they may not do is formally and publicly announce their desire for a new position. Instead,

5. Matthew 13:57, King James Version. Some may recognize that essentially the same verse is contained in the New Testament synoptic gospels at Mark 6:4, Luke 4:24, and John 4:44.

lateral job–seeking senior law professors work well and work hard, and then wait by the phone like 1950s high school girls hoping for a date to the big dance. Being a senior Black woman law professor requires even more patience. Although few would admit it, some schools seem to have an unacknowledged racial and gender quota. This means that even more waiting may be required.

So work and wait I did. And once again, as at the very the beginning of my career, good luck smiled upon me. I was invited to interview for a position at what seemed like a wonderful school. In true eucatastrophic fashion, I failed at first—I did not get the job. But then, several months later, I was offered another job at that institution. I accepted it. At School #5, I am finally in a place where, from the very beginning, I have felt a full sense of belonging. Will it last? Will I be ever lucky? It's impossible to know. But as long as hope and hardship can come together to form the eucatastrophic moment, I soldier on as the lucky law professor, and I urge all to do the same.

REFERENCES

Apollinaire, G. (1995). Le pont mirabeau. In Donald Revell (Trans.), *Alcools: Poems* (p. 12). Middletown: Wesleyan University Press.

Buckner Inniss, L. (2011). It's the hard luck life: Women's moral luck and eucatastrophe in child custody allocation. *Rutgers Women's Rights Law Reporter, 32*(1), 56–80.

Flieger, V. (1983). *Splintered light: Logos and language in Tolkien's world.* Grand Rapids, MI: William B. Eerdmans.

Koh, H. H. (1995, July). The professor in the office. Speech presented at the meeting of AALS New Law Professor's Conference, Washington, DC.

Mallinson, J. (2011). Eucatastrophe. In Eric Michael Mazur (Ed.), *Encyclopedia of Religion and Film* (p. 175). Santa Barbara, CA: ABC-CLIO.

Nuttall, A. D. (2003). Measure for measure: The bed-trick. In C. M. Alexander (Ed.), *The Cambridge Shakespeare library* (pp. 52–57). Cambridge: Cambridge University Press.

Prince, H. G. (2000). Foreword: A parallel community—people of color legal scholarship conferences and the advancement of legal education. *Boston College Third World Law Journal, 20*(1), 1–11.

Tolkien, J., Flieger, V., & Anderson, D. (2014). *Tolkien on fairy-stories.* London: Harper Collins.

Williams, P. J. (1987). Spirit-murdering the messenger: The discourse of fingerpointing as the law's response to racism. *University of Miami Law Review, 42*(1), 127–157.

THREE

Tenure with a Termination Letter

Penelope Espinoza

Last fall, I stood on the hardwood floor in the parlor of the university president's home, looking at a room full of faculty who were looking back at me as I was being recognized for receiving tenure and promotion to associate professor. Yet on my dresser at home, I had a form letter, signed "Yours truly" by the university president, notifying me that this was my "terminal year of employment." As I shook the president's hand to polite applause from those gathered at the ceremony, I thought about the termination letter and about my competence—felt, perceived, assumed.

I did not celebrate earning tenure the way I had imagined in my most optimistic moments. The accomplishment did not bring a wave of joy and pride as it should have. But, perhaps because things occurred as they did, I have a greater appreciation for the collective struggles of Women of Color in academia, and a heightened sense that action is long overdue. As a social psychologist and professor in educational leadership, and the first in my family to graduate from a university, I had firsthand awareness of the inequities in higher education, but this situation revealed the convolutions of the tenure process.

The previous spring semester, I had taught a course for our doctoral students, most of whom are education practitioners, and like all the courses I taught, it was offered in the evening. I had invited the chair of my department to speak to the class, and the next morning, I passed by him on the way to my office. He said, "I wanted to tell you this when I visited your class last night, but it somehow slipped my mind: the dean said that she talked with the provost, and he told her that he would be recommending you for tenure." I recall my chair telling me that as if he couldn't get the words out quickly enough, and then he awaited my response, which was a bit delayed because I was still processing its reality. "Oh, wow . . . really? So the provost told her that . . . directly?" My chair replied it was only a matter of time until everything would be made official.

DOI: 10.7330/9781607329664.c003

Some months prior to that, also good news. The dean of my college paused at my open office door and asked if I had a moment. She asked if I had reviewed her letter for my tenure portfolio—did I have any concerns, questions, or feedback? Earlier, she had emailed me a copy of her letter addressed to the provost in which she outlined the overall positive recommendations I had received from my department chair, the department committee, the college committee, and external reviewers; then, she concluded with her own support. Not only had the dean shared this letter with me directly, she was willing to discuss it with me in what I read as a genuine, straightforward, and even supportive manner.

Fast-forward to events proximate to the termination letter. I was heading out to pick up my children from school when my department chair called on my cell phone, signaling something urgent. "I'm sorry to have to tell you this . . . The dean just came into my office to tell me that the president did not recommend you for tenure. I'm sorry . . . I don't know what else to say . . ." This time, it seemed that the words were choking him, and this time, I awaited more. He could only refer me to the dean. I called the dean, and she could only offer a nugget more, that the president had concerns about the trajectory of my productivity. "You should be receiving a letter in the mail; maybe that will have more information," the dean said.

After I hung up, one of my first thoughts was that I had to clean out my office. I had to gather up various work artifacts, pack them in boxes, and take them away, leaving the space ready for someone else, someone who belonged there. My next thought: I need to go pick up my kids. Next thought, a letter in the mail. I'll need to pick up the kids, check the mail, then clean out my office.

IN THE TENURE DOSSIER

In my personal statement for my tenure dossier, I had described my grant-funded research, which supported a number of graduate students; my peer-reviewed publications that reflected my interdisciplinary research in social psychology and education; my mentorship and service on numerous dissertation and thesis committees; and the integration of technology in my statistics and methods courses. I connected my research, teaching, and service to my unique identity as an experimental social psychologist examining issues of equity to inform educational leaders. Well in advance of submitting my tenure dossier, I sought assessments of my body of work, soliciting faultfinding feedback on my materials from a retired colleague and mentor, a formally assigned mentor, an associate dean, an associate provost, and others—almost hoping they would dissuade me from final submission, or warn me of probable failure. I put my competence on the chopping block.

In my tenure dossier, at the suggestion of some wise senior faculty, I inserted a one-page timeline after the table of contents that clearly identified when I had taken maternity leave through the Family and Medical Leave Act (FMLA) and received approvals for extensions to the tenure clock. Neither extension was my idea. Separate college administrators advised me to request each extension, and each was approved according to university guidelines. At the time, almost all of the faculty in my department were men, and most were senior, so there were few conversations about motherhood or parenthood and the tenure clock. When I had interviewed for my faculty position, I was hugely pregnant; I delivered my job talk mostly sitting because standing felt like my belly would be on display. I had been relieved to find my colleagues respectful and supportive.

When I finally sent my dossier forward with a click, thinking, *C'est la vie*, I resigned myself to accepting the outcome, whatever it was. Then I began to receive positive feedback at each phase of the tenure review process—external reviewers, department chair, department committee, college committee, college dean, provost—and it buoyed my hope for an academic career. At faculty meetings and in other interactions with my colleagues, I heard myself speaking up and sharing my hard-earned perspectives, and I thought to myself, This is what it means to find your voice. But then came that phone call and the letter, and I was going to shut up and clean out my office.

ASKING QUESTIONS OF POWER

From initial self-blame and introspection sprang a desire to ask questions. Specifically, I wanted to understand how a decision was made by upper administration to reject the recommendations and overall consensus of senior faculty at multiple levels in the tenure process. I requested and received a meeting with the university provost, who oversees faculty appointment and retention matters. Whether or not it made a difference in my case, I didn't want to leave without asking questions.

Prior to the meeting with the provost, I practically memorized the university's handbook on all things faculty-related and read all references to the regents' system rules. Thus, I was not at all surprised when the provost said he was under no obligation, legal or otherwise, to discuss the decision with me. I thanked him for agreeing to meet with me and asked if he would willingly provide information to help me understand why the final decision negated the consensus. He told me that the president had concerns about my productivity, given the length of time I had been with the university in various capacities. This echoed what the dean had said about the president's conclusion, and I responded by reiterating his phrase: "Length of time . . . did the president discuss with you the timeline in my portfolio where I outlined when I had taken leave with FMLA and was granted extensions?" The provost bristled at my mention of FMLA and said that the president did not know I had taken FMLA, and that he also did not know I had, but even if I did, it had nothing to do with the review. I explained it seemed pertinent because he referenced the length of time I had been at the university. "Length? No, pattern." He repaired his wording and went on to say he had grown uncomfortable with my questions. He mentioned the unpleasantness of this outcome for himself as well as for the faculty members on the receiving end. Nervously, I pressed my fingers on the edge of the glass-topped table between us and said that if I had had any indication of this outcome at the other levels of review, I would not be sitting across from him right now. He said that although he was not required to do so, he could consider any material—including material from me—concerning this decision. He told me that if I felt there was additional material to consider, I should send it to him, and he politely yet certainly ushered me to the door with a final "So, I'll be expecting material to review."

As a professor in educational leadership, I was sincerely interested in how a critical decision was made in opposition to other levels of recommendation, and due to a factor (length of time/pattern of productivity/trajectory of productivity) not evaluated in the context of a vital piece of information, my timeline of appointment and leave. It was a fact that I received extensions to the tenure clock and approvals for FMLA leave (during which time the clock stops), all in accordance with university policies. I illustrated that fact in a timeline at the front of my dossier. Yet the president and provost were not aware of that fact, and the president's decision was based on a factor connected to a fact of which she was unaware. Much of my research deals with attributional processes, but I could not have predicted the extent of their activation in this situation. Why did the president reject the overall consensus of other recommendations? She found the recommendations unreliable? She thought the reviewers were not credible or biased? She did not trust the judgment of the administrators and faculty at other levels? Does the president review each portfolio autonomously, bypassing review of recommendations? What was it about my dossier that prompted skepticism of the recommendations? Which portfolios warrant scrutiny at the ultimate levels of the tenure review process? Who is presumed competent?

Several days after my meeting with the provost, I sent him a letter and an updated CV outlining recent accomplishments that were in progress during the tenure review process. These were submitted based on advice from colleagues about what "additional material for review" means in a situation like this. With my termination letter in hand, I didn't see how there was room for consideration of additional material, except that the regents' meeting was yet to take place, wherein recommendations for faculty tenure are received from the university presidents in the system. Besides, the materials felt redundant, given that I had already submitted a complete dossier, and an insult to the faculty labor applied to the review process. In my letter to the provost, I expressed my confusion and disappointment with the president's decision, which contradicted the sum of reviews and diminished the value of faculty governance. In the letter I also called attention to the timeline in my dossier that identified my FMLA leave and extensions.

Almost three suffocating summer months passed before I received any response to the material invited by the provost for reconsideration of my tenure decision. On the very day I was planning to submit completed job applications, I was informed that the president had reversed her decision and would be recommending me for tenure to the regents. In meetings that followed, I learned that I essentially received tenure with a big *but*, so to speak. The president reversed her decision, yes, but the number of thesis and dissertation committees on which I served was "disturbing" and I should have said no to students, and I would need to immediately catch up on building my academic capital.

Between the time I received the termination letter in May and when I stepped back on campus for the fall term with tenure via the president's reconsideration of her decision, I encountered a range of responses to my tenure situation. Shortly after I had met with the provost, I reached out to two mentors from my undergraduate and graduate programs for advice and to double-check my own questioning of the outcome. They each listened actively and sympathetically, offering suggestions. It was invaluable validation and affirmation. They reassured me that the actions of the president, while within her power, were not typical and would have prompted protest by their respective departments.

My department did not exactly protest the decision, except the chair, who attempted to resign over this and related matters but was persuaded to retain his position amid various transitions taking place in the college, including the departure of the dean (who had supported me) from the university. I had contacted several retired faculty with whom I had worked closely, and they conveyed their shock and dismay over the president's decision. They graciously submitted letters of support on my behalf to the provost while he was reviewing my additional material. Additionally, a couple of my former students who entered the professoriate submitted letters of support.

Outside of my department, a male Colleague of Color, whom I had known since I was a doctoral student and had told me for years that I had his support, turned out to be not so supportive. He called my letter to the provost "awkward," and suggested that I was being emotional and that I probably needed sleep. As we discussed the legitimacy of the president's decision, he pointed out that I had once taken too long to respond to a doctoral student of his who had emailed me. He also happened to be close friends with the provost.

The responses of other faculty were mitigated by their feelings toward the president of the university. Iconic and seemingly immovable, she had been serving as president for nearly thirty years with a leadership style most would likely concede was authoritarian and hierarchical. The president, a linguist who auspiciously spoke Spanish fluently, had been serving as the leader of this Hispanic-serving institution for so long that she signed my offer for a presidential undergraduate scholarship when I was a local high school senior. It was not uncommon for faculty and staff to affectionately tease about not daring to challenge the president.

QUESTION, CONTEXTUALIZE, PERSIST

I suppose I found that I was someone who dared to challenge the president. The challenge did not come to me immediately, as I was picturing myself carrying packed boxes out of my office. The challenge arose from wanting answers to questions—mainly, how and why. The importance of asking questions has become a moral of my story. Questions can be instruments of change. When you confront those in power with informed, reasoned questions, you have the potential to provoke responsive action. When I met with the provost, I had only a plan to ask questions—not a set of points to be made or feelings to express—and I believe those questions turned the key in my case.

This heavy-handed decision by a university president prompted me, as a professor in educational leadership, to examine the decisions of higher education leaders even more closely, especially in regard to equity. If leaders indeed strive to attain diverse and inclusive campuses (as with this leader's rhetoric about serving a "twenty-first-century demographic"), they must consider the extent to which their decision making is equitable. When leaders evaluate the merits and worth of an individual—in a range of decisions from hiring to promotion—they may do so narrowly, by itemizing with an arbitrary ruler. That approach, while pertinent to equality, will not likely result in achieving equity. However, if individuals are evaluated holistically, in context, with regard for circumstance, this elucidates the unique value of a person to the institution. Such evaluations with depth of perspective offer greater potential for achieving equitable and diverse academic communities.

Thus, from this lived narrative about holding in my hands a letter of termination and months later shaking hands in congratulations for tenure, I have come to a few conclusions: ask questions, especially of those in power; for the sake of promoting equity, challenge leaders to evaluate others contextually and holistically; if you are in a leadership position, do the same; if you feel it is right, persist, even in the face of termination.

FOUR

Picked to Pieces

The Cost of Opportunity

Pamela Twyman Hoff

Somebody almost walked off wid alla my stuff/
Not my poems or dance I gave up in the street/
. . . I want my . . . quik language back/
I want my own things/ how I lived them/
. . . give me my memories/ how I wuz when I waz there/
Somebody almost run off wid alla my stuff/
. . . & I waz standin there lookin at myself/ the whole time/

(SHANGE, 1997, P. 64)

A dynamic Latinx sis-star came for a job talk today, and it was all kinda mind-blowing and affirming in so many ways. She was new, dripping freshness filled with the promise of opportunity. I knew this was not going to be the same ole, same ole campus visit. She was too vibrant; the way she wielded that Spanglish like a machete hacking through the dense hegemonic forestry to make her own space was exhilarating. As is customary, we filed into the room tightly wound and tenure smug prepared for the rite of individualism, the job talk. Some glanced at the job announcement, remembering that we desired someone with a social justice orientation, but they had to "fit." She started to speak, but the words would not come. We sat like bumps on a log with fixed-forward gazes extenuating the silence. Some shifted nervously, others offered stoic assurances. I worried, thinking, "Please don't cry." "I'm sorry," she said, "I just had a vision that I've got to acknowledge . . ." With care and reverence, she began to speak of her mother's and grandmother's love and care of her. She acknowledged that at that moment she was standing in their dream for her. Their prayers, commitment, teachings, sacrifice, work, and tears were promises that carried and nourished this opportunity. The sheer force of that energy pushed its way through the deafening silence and baptized us in authentic heart speak. As she stood weeping, I wanted to go to her, stand in solidarity; instead, I turned to a colleague and whispered, "Somebody should go to her."

DOI: 10.7330/9781607329664.c004

I start the chapter with an entry from my journal as an attempt to provide insight into the peculiar turmoil I experienced during and after a dynamic sis-star's job talk. Reflecting on my thoughts and feelings brought to the forefront of my mind an awareness that I have been changed by my experiences as a Black woman on faculty at a historically White university. I came to the realization that this change was a result of my being *picked to pieces. Picked to pieces* is an idiom, identified as a *sayin'* in the African American oral tradition, that conveys and reinforces cultural wisdom and deeper understanding of the lived experience. It is used to make conscious any change in physical, spiritual, or emotional self. I use this *sayin'* as a conceptual frame to ground the discussion in the cultural act of reclamation and moving forward.

As a way moving of forward, it is essential that I develop a deeper understanding of what has *picked me to pieces* and what has been *picked.* I use the concept racial opportunity cost (ROC) as an analytical tool to apprehend the underlying nuances and contradictions that characterize my experiences. Opportunity cost is an economic concept that on the most basic level considers the risk/loss associated with the pursuit of one opportunity as opposed to another. There is some contention about its definition; some assess opportunity cost by its quantifiable measures, while others define it as the *value forgone* (Parkin, 2016). Venzant Chambers and colleagues (Venzant Chambers, 2011; Venzant Chambers & Huggins, 2014; Venzant Chambers, Huggins, Locke, & Fowler, 2015) resolve the ambiguity in the appropriation and expansion of opportunity cost in an educational context. In education, ROC makes transparent the cultural, psychosocial, and emotional costs Students of Color pay to pursue challenging opportunities in White-normed schools (Locke, Tabron, & Chambers, 2017). ROC brings into focus the pervasive ways these norms are coded in the perceptions, behavioral expectations, cultural cues, systems, and processes that disempower People of Color and normalize domination. These costs have dire cultural, identity, relational, and overall well-being consequences. Though this research is situated primarily in secondary school settings, ROC is applicable to higher education. The widespread debasement of Black folk and other People of Color in higher education is indicative of structures that promote and normalizes domination, colonization, and injustice (Peavy, 2000; Richardson, 2018; Sharpe & Swinton, 2012; Wilson, 1998). I utilize both *picked to pieces* and racial opportunity cost to make transparent the ways in which the inherently dominating structure of Academyland (Edwards, 2018) normalizes, sanctions, rewards, and facilitates the complicity and perpetuation of White norms and domination.

This chapter serves multiple purposes. First, putting your business in the streets for the world to judge is unnerving, though necessary in the reclamation of those things *picked.* Second, the chapter seeks to make transparent the pervasive ways domination is ideologically structured in higher education, interlocking, normalizing, and replicating itself on every institutional level. I am also attempting to understand the ways in which domination is an inherent feature and function of the professoriate. Finally, I am hopeful that in some small way this narrative joins with the collective voices of resistance against those individuals, processes, systems, institutions, and ideologies that denigrate us as incompetent, irrelevant, and pugnacious, as well as simultaneously invisible and hypervisible, as if having an *attitude* is not warranted.

DIGGING IN MY OWN CULTURAL KNOWLEDGE WELLS

After the experience of the sis-star's job talk, I was instinctively aware that something inside me had changed. I struggled to understand if the change was spiritual, cultural, social, psychological, or all four. I started with what I knew. I knew that my narrated experiences mirrored the perspicacious research put forth by Women of Color (see, e.g., Carroll, 2017; Collins, 2002; Gutiérrez y Muhs, Niemann, Gonzàlez, & Harris, 2012; Perlow, Wheeler, Bethea, & Scott, 2018; Stanley, 2006; Turner, 2002). I have experienced apparent and veiled acts of dehumanization. These acts include being mishandled (touched without consent), macro- and microaggressions (indirect and direct) (Smith, Yosso, & Solórzano, 2006), alienation (Saunders, 2006), devaluation, and marginalization (Turner, 2002).

Through the conceptual lens of my lived experiences, the language of resistance helped me understand and articulate the change that has occurred slowly over my eight years as a faculty member. Part of my resistance to the ideological domination of higher education has been to rely on my own cultural knowledge to assist my understanding and thinking through complex issues. Acknowledging and starting with my feelings is an essential part of the analysis. In African and African diasporic culture, the rational is not separated from the emotional heart (Ani, 1994; Peavy, 2000). Feelings are ontologically valued as interrelated indicators bridging the known and unknown. I began to understand that what I was identifying as change was more akin to a sense of loss. To apprehend the amorphous aspects of the loss I was feeling, I sought the fluidity and familiar waters of my cultural knowledge wells.

Without fail, reading my journal entries shifted me from joy to shame to anger. I felt immense joy meeting someone real. I define "real" according to my own cultural norms. For me, realness stems from the lessons learned and valuation of working in community, for the sake of bettering the community. It comes in the prioritization of people over institutions. Realness privileges "we" over "me." It demonstrates an appreciation for reciprocity over the accumulation of transactions. Realness attempts to resist the desire for prostrations, affirmation standardized by Whiteness as the metric of achievement or progress. Realness comes from culturally grounded, regular folk, flawed and vulnerable yet purposeful in trying to be better, though not at the expense of another.

Real folk in the academy are few and far between. Holding onto them is essential as we hope and pray that they are who their curriculum vitae says they are. The young sis-star felt as real as they get. She was fire: compassionate, passionate, unapologetically Latinx, community minded, open to possibilities, and unafraid to speak to the contradiction that mars our experiences in the academy.

After much reflection, I found I was wresting with what seemed liked conflicting emotions—shame and anger. I was confused because my understanding of these feelings was more aligned with the praxis of resistance. I had long embraced the tenacity of the angry Black woman. To be Black in America and not be angry seems impossible. However, there was something different about these particular feelings of anger. They were complicated by feelings of shame. In the same vein, I had long since decided that I would not fall victim to the collective shame generated when someone or something is deemed unworthy or inappropriate by the dominating culture. Hearing her real talk, I was hoping she would not cry, "not look weak in front of the White people." In reality, there was nothing weak about her talk or her tears. Earlier in my career, I would not have hesitated to stand in solidarity with her. Part of my shame emanated simply from being a faculty member, a representation of the colonial interest. I cannot deny I wanted her to demonstrate command of the literature by augmenting academic language with her own. I was hoping that she would beat them at their own game, in essence play the smartness game (Hatt, 2012). I rationalized that she just needed to get the job, play the game, after which she could be her whole self. However, there is an inextricable cost in playing the smartness game for People of Color because, according to Hatt (2012), smartness is socially constructed around the norms, values, and behaviors of Whiteness. I questioned, "When did I start co-signing or believing in this mess? When did I step into the colonial performance as a full actor?" In the midst of this emotional storm I had a moment of clarity, so much so that I could hear my momma's voice, "Honey, you been picked to pieces," and I knew it to be true.

PICKED TO PIECES AS A CONCEPTUAL FRAME OF REFERENCE

My grandmother's primary teaching tools were sayin's. In the African American community sayin's function like proverbs. They contextualize and reflect the wit and verve of African American language and the culture of resistance (Hoff, 2014). I value sayin's as my superpower providing me with a layer of protection against the hegemonic indoctrination of higher education. They anchor my thoughts and assist me in making deeper connections that render it possible to extrapolate multiple meanings and context. They give me words when the verbosity of the academy is incapable of allowing me to articulate the complexity of a concept, thought, perception, or experience.

Picked to pieces is used to convey change to one's physical, psychological, spiritual, or emotional self. It is the recognition of a gradual loss of one's uniqueness, joy, or happiness. Using this sayin' is no trifling matter as, more often than not, close friends and family use it. There are unspoken rules that govern its use. First, there is a certain amount of empathy required in its delivery. It is not intended to belittle or shame. Rather, it functions as an alarm triggering a type of introspection for self-determination. Use of *picked to pieces* necessitates some responsibility on the part of the speaker and hearer. The user is expected to provide the necessary support for the process of self-discovery and reclamation. Likewise, the listener is expected to act, to identify the source of the picking, and to work to reclaim what was picked as a way of moving forward.

To locate the source and reclaim what has been picked from me, I draw heavily from the knowledge in my blood memory. I have always been suspicious that the African American collective memory of education and schooling serves two masters. I also rely on the body of work and deeds of radical justice-loving scholars. It is my contention that the normalization, reinforcement, and subsequence internalization of the dominating ideological values that structure higher education have worked in tandem to pick me to pieces.

WOKE AND STILL PICKED

On an intuitive level, I knew I was being picked to pieces. That is par for the course. Higher education was not designed to work in our favor (Carroll, 2017). I had reservations about relocating to this area, a town where sundown sensibilities rest easy against the backdrop of fermented corn. Neoliberalism blends with midwestern respectability politics, bending and warping into a social justice falsetto that masks and normalizes deep racial animosities. The position announcement read like a social justice educator's philosophical mantra. A major selling point was the carefully placed language, anchored by the university's commitment to its Democratic Ideals.

Becoming a tenure-track faculty member was not my first career. I had been a community organizer, high school teacher, and an administrator for several community-based educational organizations. In the latter role, I had the amazing opportunity to learn and grow with some vibrant women who lived and worked in disenfranchised communities. Through my work with them I first learned what it means that the personal is political. Speaking truth to power and building coalitions to resist oppression were part of my identity politics.

I did not walk into the valley and shadow of White supremacy (Hoff & Martin, forthcoming) unarmed. I carried in me a mother's wit, love for my people, and a "Don't start none, won't be none" attitude grounded in a deep commitment to resistance pedagogy. I entered troubled waters when I learned that the university's lab schools where not considered diverse by the university's own standards. In spite of that glaring contradiction, I remained hopeful and optimistic. Upon arrival I found my daughters a school and then immediately sought community. I literally drive around town looking for the Black folk. For the first time in my life, I took up residence in an overwhelmingly White neighborhood. I spent the vast majority of my time protecting and defending my daughters from all forms of racism, from overt to unconscious (King, 1991), at home and school.

At the end of the first semester, while still negotiating my new identity as faculty, I was sucker-punched by the student evaluations. No matter how aware I thought I was, I was unprepared for the vitriol that dissected every part of my being. My pedagogy, capacity, identity, physical appearance, attributes, intelligence, and worth were laid bare for discussion (Evans-Winters & Hoff, 2011). I was admonished for wearing "fancy pants," condemned to hell for "wearing colored loc'd hair," and written off as too Black. I was branded guilty of having a "crazy preoccupation with race," "race baiting," and just being a plain ole "racist." I felt violated and demoralized, forced to defend my embodied experiences in a way that was acceptable to the institution. I began collecting data and found that for the vast majority of my students I was their first Teacher of Color, and specifically, their first African American teacher. I pushed back against the use of student evaluations in the assessment of my teaching. I asked for consideration of implicit bias and racism that underlie students' qualitative comments.

The contentiousness that marked my classroom experiences also marked my campus experiences. One memory in particular stands out. After teaching one evening, colleagues and I had a late dinner. We returned to the parking lot to find a campus police officer waiting at my car. I was informed that "someone"—who, I found out later, was a White woman also employed at the university—alleged that my vehicle had been involved in a hit and run. The complaint was based upon her seeing my van parked in the same lot where her car was supposedly hit two days prior. The light-colored scratches on my twelve-year-old van, according to the unknown woman, matched the color left on her car. For over three hours, I was detained and interrogated, forced to explain every mark on my car. I was asked the same question multiple ways as the officer tried to elicit different responses. When a White colleague tried to interject that she was with me two days ago and that I did not hit anything, she was silenced. When she refused to remain silent, she was threatened. Humiliated and demoralized, I held myself tight, spoke my mind, and lived to fight another day. I filed a complaint, which amounted to nothing. I decided that, tenure or not, I would not sacrifice my dignity and self-worth.

Over the years, I have gained the reputation of someone who will speak truth to power. I am empowered by my community and the counter-spaces we have built to recharge and be (see hooks, 1993; Richardson, 2018; Taylor, 2017). I rely on my community of like-minded folk who represent every aspect of the university community. As a community family, we have created spaces for advocacy and resistance. Yet in spite of all it, I still find myself picked to pieces.

MAKING THE INVISIBLE VISIBLE

Being a sista soldier has not shielded me from the barrage of microaggressions ranging from the subtle to the extreme. Being candid and having the "Don't start none, won't be none" look does not make me immune to the violations that contribute to racial battle fatigue (Smith, Yosso, & Solórzano, 2006). On a regular basis, I field questions about my hair, clothing, and accessory choices. I navigate perceptions that make me simultaneously hypervisible and invisible, creating socio-psychological landmines on campus and in the surrounding community. I challenge beliefs that dehumanize and mark us as undeserving and unworthy of having the benefit of the doubt. White ways of knowing that render us guilty until proven innocent characterize the pervasiveness of anti-Blackness—and also characterize my experiences in the academy. In the academy these perceptions, beliefs, and ways of knowing are hidden in the interpretation of policies, expectations, who gets tenure, what types of narratives are built around whom, and whose work is considered valuable. Apple (2004) uses the concept of hegemony to describe the ways in which these perceptions and beliefs are institutionalized: "Hegemony acts to 'saturate' our very consciousness, so that the educational, economic and social worlds we see and interact with, and the commonsense interpretations we put on it, become the world *tout court*, the only world" (p. 5).

Our collective experiences in higher education as matrix of domination have been articulated in various ways. A considerable body of literature demonstrates how the constellation of White-normed values and beliefs dictate and govern expectations, interactions, and behaviors (Collins, 2002; Kupenda, 2012; Wilson, 2012). Edwards (2018) uses the concept of "Academyland" to highlight the confluence of White norms, behaviors, and ways of knowing that structure and govern the responsibilities of the professoriate. Ani's (1994) work is critical to this discussion. Through her analysis, we see the ways in which the interlocking ideological pillars that gave rise to European global domination shape and structure its institutions. Ani's brilliance lies in unmaking the underlying ideological assumptions of "great" European thinkers who have affected culture (e.g., Aristotle, Plato, and Kant).

Ani's synthesis identifies four ideological pillars that unified, justified, and transmitted European domination—individualism, rationalism, progressivism, and universalism. These ideological concepts constitute the foundation of European dominating culture. Through their structure, institutions transmit these values as norms and standards. Invisible and historically situated in the deep structures of academic culture, these interlocking and related concepts work in tandem to secure complicity gradually over time. That is part of the process of being picked to pieces. Ani writes, "The characteristics [ideological pillars] we have discussed are basically those that determine European interpersonal behavior. The institutions and forms of the culture can be understood as structured sets of rules that are based on these given norms and that act to regulate the behavior of individuals so that a support system for its intercultural behavior is maintained. In other words, what accounts for the survival of the culture as a cohesive whole is its ideological objective of the control and subjugation of all other peoples and the related commitment to technological and material superiority" (1994 p. 381).

Individualism as a principle of domination values and encourages separation from community. It is rooted in the premise that individual potential and autonomy are constrained and limited in community. The goal of the individual is to make oneself better than the community. Individual needs, attributes, and accomplishments are valued and prioritized over community needs. This social arrangement breeds competition. The competition is predicated on the development of specializations used to organize and bind individuals to institutions such that institutions become the epicenter of community (Ani, 1997). Rationality works to validate and normalize individualism. The general assumption is that individual success is oriented around the ability to be rational. Rationality is achieved from the separation of the head (perceived as order) from the heart (perceived as unstable and irrational). This separation creates a callousness in the human psyche associated with the slavocracy and heinous acts of colonization (Ani, 1997). In higher education, this separation is held up as the standard in formal and informal contexts lauded as objective, positivistic, reasonable, thoughtful, and rational.

According to Ani, rationality is the hallmark of standardization. As such, it generates the force and justification on which progressivism is grounded. The ideology of progress presents itself as forward thinking and productive. The final ideological pillar, perceptions and valuation of higher education, is perhaps the most visible because it is taken for granted. The function of universalism is in the creation of hegemonic rhetoric and practices that propagate the universal benefit of internalizing and operating by these dominating assumptions, ostensibly for the benefit of the individual and the larger society.

These ideological constructs act as the barometer determining academic standards and shaping norms and rules of engagement. They are the underlying referents used to evaluate all aspects of the professoriate. The implied and stated expectations that all must adapt to and function within the guidelines of these dominating principles are the powerbrokers' indicators of productivity, collegiality, value, and capacity.

THE RECLAMATION OF WHAT HAS BEEN PICKED

Internalization and compromise are inevitable, but not without tension. "The establishment, whatever rewards it gives us [Black people], will also, if necessary to maintain control, kill us" (Wilson, 1998, p. 21). I have experienced psychological violence, degradation, and betrayal (Carroll, 2017) in the context of institutionalized norms. Education and schooling are sites of Black suffering (Dumas, 2013). Suffering is the expressed sense of dread, frustration, "the loss of hope for oneself individually, and for the group, collectively" (p. 8). Part of the suffering comes from having to endure, negotiate, and navigate the process of being ritualistically and racially dishonored. Yet this pain is inflicted in the context of invisible but standard underlying norms and structures. Reflection compels me to recenter my own value system and remember my purpose. Although the permanence of racism and the internalization of dominating values that normalize oppression have picked me to pieces, I remember another sayin'—*That which does not kill you makes you stronger.*

REFERENCES

Ani, M. (1994). *Yurugu: An Afrikan-centered critique of European cultural thought and behavior*. Washington, DC: Nkominfo.

Ani, M. (1994). *Yurugu: An African-centered critique of European cultural thought and behavior*. Washington, DC: Nkominfo Publishing.

Apple, M. W. (2004). *Ideology and curriculum*. New York: Routledge.

Carroll, D. (2017). A faculty woman of color and micro-invalidations at a white research institution: A case of intersectionality and institutional betrayal. *Administrative Issues Journal: Connecting Education, Practice, and Research,* 7(1), 39–50. doi: 10.5929/2017.7.1.2.

Collins, P. H. (2002). *Black feminist thought: Knowledge, consciousness, and the politics of empowerment.* New York: Routledge.

Dumas, M. J. (2013). "Losing an arm": Schooling as a site for black suffering, *Race and Ethnicity,* 17(1), 1–29.

Edwards, K. T. (2018). Stories of migration: Passing through, crossing over, and decolonial transgressing in Academyland. In O. N Perlow et al. (Eds.), *Black women's liberatory pedagogies* (pp. 85–100). Gewerbestrasse, Switzerland: Palgrave.

Evans-Winters, V. E., & Hoff, P. (2011). The aesthetics of white racism in pre-service teacher education: A critical race theory perspective. *Race Ethnicity and Education,* 14(4), 461–479.

Gutiérrez y Muhs, G., Niemann, Y. F., Gonzàlez, C. G., & Harris, A. (Eds.). (2012). *Presumed incompetent: The intersections of race and class for women in academia.* Logan: Utah State University Press.

Hatt, B. (2012). Smartness as a cultural practice in schools. *American Educational Research Journal,* 49(3), 438–460.

Hoff, P. T. (2014). Just like momma use to say: African American mothers as teachers and keepers of culture. In L. D. Matthews and K. C. Phillips (Eds.), *Liberating minds, liberating society: Black women in the development of American culture and society,* (pp. 88-99). CreateSpace Independent Publishing Platform.

Hoff, P. and Martin, K. (2020). Colonizing communities: smartness and the ideology of domination. From Beth Hatt and Pamela Twyman Hoff (Eds.), *The Social Construction of smartness: Pushing Back.* Boston: Sense.

hooks, b. (1993). *Sisters of the yam: Black women and self-recovery.* Boston: Southend.

King, J. (1991). Black student alienation and Black teachers' emancipatory pedagogy. *Readings on equal education: Qualitative investigations into schools and schooling,* 11, 245–271.

Kupenda, A. M. (2012). Facing down the spooks. In G. Gutiérrez y Muhs, Y. F. Niemann, C. G. Gonzàlez, & Angela Harris (Eds.), *Presumed incompetent* (pp. 20–28).
Logan: Utah State University Press.

Locke, L. A, Tabron, L. A., & Chambers, T. T. (2017). If you show who you are, then they are going to try to fix you: The capitals and costs of high-achieving Latina students. *Educational Studies* 53(1), 13–36.

Parkin, M. (2016). Opportunity cost: A reexamination. *The Journal of Economic Education* 47(1), 12–22.

Peavy, L. (2000). I can see clearly now: The kuona process—a teaching strategy for liberation. *Urban Education,* 35(1), 57–78.

Perlow, O. N., Wheeler, D. I., Bethea, S. L., & Scott, B. M. (2018). *Black women's liberatory pedagogies: Resistance, transformation, and healing within and beyond the academy.* Gewerbestrasse, Switzerland: Palgrave.

Richardson, J. L. (2018). Healing circles as black feminist pedagogical interventions. In O. N Perlow et al. (Eds.), *Black women's liberatory pedagogies* (pp. 281–294). Gewerbestrasse, Switzerland: Palgrave.

Saunders, S. (2006). I'm just a black woman troubling the status quo. In C. A. Stanley (Ed.), *Faculty of color: Teaching in predominantly white colleges and universities* (pp. 283–298). Boston: Anker.

Shange, N. (1997). *For colored girls who have considered suicide when the rainbow is enuf*. New York: Scribner Poetry.

Sharpe, R. V., & Swinton, O. H. (2012). Beyond anecdotes: A quantitative examination of black women in Academe. *Review of Black Political Economics, 39*, 341–352.

Smith, W. A., Yosso, T. J., & Solórzano, D. G. (2006). Challenging racial battle fatigue on historically white campuses: A critical race examination of race related stress. In C. A. Stanley (Ed.), *Faculty of color: Teaching in predominantly white colleges and universities* (pp. 299–327). Boston: Anker.

Stanley, C. A. (2006). Walking between two cultures: The often misunderstood Jamaican woman. In C. A. Stanley (Ed.), *Faculty of color: Teaching in predominantly white colleges and universities* (pp. 328–343). Boston: Anker.

Taylor, K-Y. (2017). *How we got free: Black feminist and the Combahee River collective*. Chicago: Haymarket Books.

Turner, C. S. (2002). Women of color in academe: Living with multiple marginality. *The Journal of Higher Education* 73(1), 74–93.

Venzant Chambers, T. T. (2011). Mergers and Weavers: Using racial opportunity cost to frame high-achieving African American and Latina/o students' school culture navigation styles. *Journal of Educational Administration and Foundations, 22*, 3–26.

Venzant Chambers, T. T., & Huggins, K. S. (2014). School factors and racial opportunity cost for high achieving students of color. *Journal of School Leadership, 24*, 189–225.

Venzant Chambers, T. T., Huggins, K. S., Locke, L. A., & Fowler, R. M. (2014). Between a "ROC" and a school place: The role of racial opportunity cost in the educational experiences of academically successful students of color. *Educational Studies, 50*, 464–497.

Wilson, A. N. (1998). *Blueprint for black power: A moral, political, and economic imperative for the twenty-first century*. Chicago: Afrikan World InfoSystem.

FIVE

Surviving a Difficult Tenure Process

Tips for Junior Faculty of Color

Cynthia Lee

A ROSY BEGINNING

My story begins when I was a third-year law student. I received a call from a man who had been an associate at the law firm where I had clerked the summer between my second and third years.

"Hello, Cynthia," he began. "I don't know if you remember me, but we met when you interviewed last summer with my old law firm." Of course I remembered him. How could I have forgotten an associate who had left the law firm life to go into law teaching, the career path that I eventually hoped to take myself? "Of course I remember you," I replied. "You left the firm to teach law, didn't you?" "Yes," he replied. "That's why I'm calling. Have you ever thought about law teaching?" My heart skipped a beat. Ever since my first year in law school, I had wanted to become a law professor. I did not expect to be invited to do so as a law student. "As a matter of fact, yes," I responded. "Ultimately, that's exactly what I'd like to end up doing. Why do you ask?"

He then proceeded to tell me, "Well, I was in the faculty mailroom the other day and one of my colleagues was xeroxing an article. I looked down and saw your name. I told him, 'I think I know that woman. I interviewed her for a summer associate position at my old law firm.' He told me to contact you and find out whether you were interested in law teaching."

I could not believe my ears. I had recently published a student note in the *California Law Review*. A law professor had read it, thought it was good, and was suggesting that I be considered for a law professor position! This was unbelievable.

I quickly told him, "Yes, as a matter of fact, teaching law is my ultimate career goal, but I have a judicial clerkship lined up right after I graduate from law school so I wouldn't be able to start right away."

DOI: 10.7330/9781607329664.c005

He cut in, "Not a problem. Many academics clerk right after law school. A judicial clerkship is considered a plus." He continued, "I'm coming up to the Bay Area with another colleague to interview prospective candidates. Would you like to be interviewed?"

"Actually," I responded, "I want to practice for a few years before I start teaching, so I don't think I want to be interviewed just yet."

"It's not necessary to practice before teaching," he told me. "A lot of law professors start teaching right after their clerkships."

"I know, but I really want to practice for at least a few years," I insisted. "I'm not ready for an interview right now, but perhaps we could meet for coffee when you come up and you can tell me about how you like being a law professor." I held my breath waiting for his answer, hoping that I was not cutting off my chances of becoming a law professor by insisting on practicing before going into the academy.

"Okay," he responded. "I'll be in touch to schedule a time to meet." I breathed a sigh of relief.

Several weeks later, this professor and one of his female colleagues came to town. The three of us met for coffee and chatted informally.

Three years later, when I was in practice, the female colleague called and asked me if I wanted to come to visit her school. That visit led to an invitation to interview, which led to an offer to join the tenure-track faculty.

LIFE AS THE ONLY ASIAN AMERICAN FACULTY MEMBER ON MY FACULTY

When I joined the faculty at the law school that offered me my first teaching job (Law School #1), I was the only Asian American law professor. There were only four other minority faculty members on the faculty at that time—two of each gender. All of the minority faculty members were very kind to me. The two female Professors of Color reached out and made special efforts to welcome me and mentor me in my early years. I am eternally grateful to them for making these efforts. The one African American male on the faculty later became one of my best friends and mentors. The other minority male faculty member was also very kind to me.

Being the only Asian American on the faculty was a novel experience for me. I had grown up in the San Francisco Bay Area, where there are many successful Asian Americans. In the suburb where I grew up, most of our neighbors were other middle-class Chinese American families. I went to Stanford University, where there seemed to be a lot of other Asian Americans. After graduating from Stanford, I worked in San Francisco, where I was one of many Asian American professionals. I then attended law school at the University of California at Berkeley, where again I had many Asian American law school friends. After law school, I went to Hawaii to clerk for a Chinese American judge. There too, I was surrounded by many powerful Asian American judges, lawyers, politicians, and other professionals.

In the city where I began my law teaching career, there were far fewer Asian American professionals than in my previous environments. The absence of Asian American professional role models may explain why some students were skeptical of my competence when I first started teaching. I remember a student in my very first class questioning me at length about my qualifications in front of the other students. He suggested in no uncertain terms that I was not competent to teach since I had never taught before. Some students called me "Cynthia" even though they called their other professors "Professor."

Fortunately, these initial setbacks were just temporary. Soon I had a great relationship with the students at my first institution. Unfortunately, however, I did not have a good tenure experience. I do not claim that the things described below happened to me because of my race, ethnicity, or gender, but my experience does discredit the notion that the Asian-as-model-minority stereotype works to make life easy for all Asians and Asian Americans.

THE FIRST SIGNS OF TROUBLE

I came up for promotion from assistant professor to associate professor during my third year in law teaching. When I received the internal review of my first article published as a law professor, I couldn't believe how negative it was. My article had been accepted for publication in the *UCLA Law Review*, a well-respected journal, and I'd already received several unsolicited letters from scholars in the field, telling me they thought it was an excellent piece of scholarship. This internal review, however, made it sound like my article was quite substandard, concluding that my thesis was "fairly deeply flawed." Damning with faint praise, my colleague, whom I'll call Cheshire, added that "the piece would likely greatly assist any practitioner." In the legal academy, such a comment is code for saying the article has no theoretical value and is not that good.

I thought perhaps Cheshire had not read my article carefully because his review claimed I did not address several issues that I had in fact addressed. Hoping that this was just a misunderstanding, I approached Cheshire and explained that I was puzzled. To my relief, he seemed very receptive to my concerns. He apologized for any misunderstanding on his part, and told me that if he had misinterpreted anything I said, he would be happy to revise his review. He asked me to give him a list of the places in his review that incorrectly accused me of not addressing particular issues and the places in my article where I had actually done so. I quickly assembled this list and left Cheshire several voice mails with this information.

To my surprise, when the revised review came back, it was even worse. Cheshire had used the information I had provided to strengthen his negative comments. I was so taken aback that I went to a professor who seemed very supportive of me when I first came to the school, thinking that he would help me. I'll call this professor Would-Be-Mentor because that was what I initially thought he would be to me. Would-Be-Mentor, however, did nothing to help me in this situation, saying that Cheshire had the right to his own opinion about my scholarship. Would-Be-Mentor advised me not to write a response to Cheshire's review because doing so would serve no useful purpose. This was the first inkling I had that the road to tenure was not going to be smooth.

THE DANGERS OF WRITING ABOUT RACE

My intention when I started law teaching was to play it safe by not writing about race. I had been warned by colleagues that certain members of the faculty were hostile to race scholarship and I saw evidence of this hostility on more than one occasion. At one lunch, for example, Would-Be-Mentor remarked that he had seen a story in the *New York Times* about affirmative action on the top law reviews. He surmised that this was probably why the *Harvard Law Review* and other top journals published articles on race. Others at the table chimed in, agreeing with Would-Be-Mentor. Would-Be-Mentor opined that this explained why it was so hard to get "good" articles published in the top journals. I was extremely surprised by these comments. Did my colleagues really think that one or two Persons of Color on a law review could influence the entire article selection process? Did they really think that affirmative action on the law reviews was the reason their own articles had not been selected for publication in the top journals?

I also remember Would-Be-Mentor talking negatively about the work of an Asian American female law professor who had interviewed for a position on the faculty many years earlier. Would-Be-Mentor said he had opposed this individual's candidacy because her scholarship was "weak." This professor, who wrote about racial subordination, went on to be hired by a top-ten law school and became a very well-respected and often-cited critical race scholar.

Given this hostility to race scholarship by some members of my faculty, I had decided early on not to write about race because I felt it would be too risky, but despite my intention, I did end up writing about race because I felt there was a need to call attention to some injustices in the application of self-defense doctrine.

One of the customs at my original institution was for junior faculty to share their drafts with certain senior faculty, ostensibly so the junior faculty could benefit from the wisdom of their more senior colleagues. In accordance with this custom, I shared a very early draft of an article on the ways in which racial stereotypes can influence jury determinations in self-defense cases with Would-Be-Mentor. He told me he did not think there was an article to be written on race and self-defense. Believing that I truly did have something worthwhile to say, I continued to work on the article and later shared a revised draft with Would-Be-Mentor. When we met to discuss my article, Would-Be-Mentor was very cordial and told me the paper was well researched and showed a lot of hard work. While Would-Be-Mentor had a few relatively minor critiques, he was generally positive, so I thought he recognized that my article was a solid piece of good scholarship.

Not so. Later I heard that Would-Be-Mentor wrote a scathing line-by-line critique of this article, worse than Cheshire's review of my first article, which surprised me because he had been generally positive when we met to discuss it. I decided I would not publish the article if it were not accepted by a top-thirty law journal. Fortunately, the article ended up being published in the *Minnesota Law Review* and was later excerpted in several casebooks and readers.

After this incident, I was invited to present a paper at a symposium. Several well-respected scholars had been asked to speak so I knew it was an honor for someone as junior as I was at the time to have been invited.

When Cheshire found out that I had been invited to this conference, he contacted the person organizing the symposium and tried to finagle an invitation to speak. The conference organizer, who told me about this, politely declined Cheshire's offer, saying that the panelists had already been chosen and the panels were full. Cheshire flew out to attend the conference anyway.

During my talk, Cheshire sat in the back row next to a professor who would later be selected as one of my outside reviewers for tenure (I'll call this professor BigWig). During the question-and-answer period following my panel, BigWig raised his hand and started asking me questions. After I answered, he would follow up with another question. When others tried to interrupt with questions of their own, BigWig said he was not finished and continued to direct questions to me. He monopolized almost the entire question-and-answer period. It seemed as if BigWig was trying to trip me up in a game of verbal jujitsu, but I responded to all his questions with respectful disagreement. During the break, BigWig gave me his business card and said to call him if I ever needed anything. I thought that quite strange, but figured perhaps he was trying to indirectly apologize for his earlier behavior. Not so.

A short time before my tenure vote, I found out that BigWig was one of my outside reviewers. Even though the names and institutional affiliation of all outside reviewers were blacked out so the tenure candidate would not know their identities, it was pretty easy to figure out that BigWig had written this particular review because he spent about three sentences discussing the article he was assigned to review (my *UCLA* article). The rest of his review was devoted to trashing the presentation I gave at the symposium. BigWig opined that my presentation was barely comprehensible. Even though I do not speak with an accent since I was born in the United States and grew up speaking English at home, I worried that BigWig's negative assessment of my presentation could feed into stereotypes about Asians not being able to speak English fluently and thereby undermine the good teaching evaluations I had received from the students at my institution. I also worried that at my tenure meeting, Cheshire would back up BigWig's allegation and agree that I gave a horrible presentation, which I suspect was the real reason he went to the symposium.

Unfortunately, things got worse before they got better. A few weeks before my tenure vote, I ran into a professor at a conference who greeted me by saying, "I heard you are coming up for tenure, Cynthia, and that everything is going swimmingly." Since things were not going swimmingly, I asked him how he knew I was coming up for tenure. He told me that he had heard about it from one of his female colleagues. She told him that someone from my tenure committee had contacted her to say that since my tenure case was going well, she did not need to write a review letter for me; he would report all the good things she had to say about my scholarship to the committee.

When I heard this, I became quite alarmed. This female law professor had sent me a handwritten note shortly after my first article as a law professor was published in the *UCLA Law Review*, saying that she thought my article was excellent, so I had recommended that she be one of my reviewers. I had been told by the chair of my tenure committee that she was too busy to write a review. It now appeared that someone on my tenure committee (or someone pretending to be on my tenure committee) had tried to keep her from writing a review of my work, knowing that a positive review from such a well-respected scholar in the field would undermine an effort to convince others to deny me tenure. I went to the chair of my tenure committee and told him what I had learned. Fortunately, he was able to get in touch with this professor, and within just a day or two, she wrote a glowing review of my *UCLA* article in time for it to be included in my tenure file. On Monday, December 8, 1997, the faculty voted to grant me tenure.

Even though I got tenure, I felt that the attacks on my scholarship during the tenure process affected the way others on the faculty viewed me. No one said anything overtly to indicate that they presumed my scholarship was incompetent, but I could tell that most of my colleagues at my first institution thought I was a nice person, a good teacher, but not a very strong scholar. After I received an offer to join the faculty at my current institution, at that time a top-twenty law school, I noticed a subtle shift in the way I was treated. Suddenly, some colleagues treated me with a newfound respect.

PSYCHOLOGICAL HAZING

One might say that the things that happened in connection with my tenure process constituted psychological hazing. Psychological hazing, I have learned, is fairly common in the academy and is often deployed as a weapon to cripple another person's scholarly productivity. Several of my friends have been paralyzed from the trauma of unconstructive feedback disguised as constructive criticism. For example, one of my friends on the faculty at Law School #1 shared a draft of an article she wrote with one of our more senior colleagues, an older White male. When she got the draft back from him, she was devastated because it was filled with gratuitous comments that expressed the senior colleague's view that most of her ideas were utterly stupid. She asked me to read those comments and filter out the ones that might be helpful from those that were simply hurtful. Not surprisingly, my friend found writing in this kind of hostile environment difficult.

Another friend, an Asian American female who started her law teaching career at a top-ten law school, told me that every time she discussed her scholarship ideas with her colleagues, they would say they were "insufficiently theoretical," "not scholarly," "pedestrian," "uninteresting" and/or "too practice oriented" to constitute really good legal scholarship. This friend also found it difficult to write in light of such negativity and ended up being encouraged to leave before she came up for tenure.

WHAT HELPED ME SURVIVE MY DIFFICULT TENURE PROCESS

One thing I learned from my difficult tenure battle was the importance of good relationships with colleagues both inside and outside one's institution. I know that one reason I got tenure was that so many people on my faculty were willing to speak up in my favor and fight for me. I am deeply grateful to my colleagues at my first institution who went out of their way to speak in my favor both at my tenure meeting and in the hallways beforehand.

I was particularly touched when I heard that one member of the faculty, a conservative White male, spoke in support of my getting tenure at my tenure meeting. This colleague rarely went to faculty meetings. I had heard that certain members of the faculty would persuade him to attend faculty meetings when there was a contentious issue and they needed his vote. I wonder whether they encouraged him to attend my tenure meeting, thinking that he would be a negative vote. They must have been surprised when he spoke out in support of my tenure. This colleague had come to my housewarming when I was in my second year of teaching. He and my father hit it off. The next time my parents came to visit me, this colleague and his wife invited us to their home for dinner. After that, we took turns inviting each other over to our respective homes whenever my parents were in town. I never spoke about my scholarship with this colleague as I was pretty sure he would not have agreed with anything I had to say. We were on opposite sides of the political spectrum, but that didn't matter. When my tenure at the institution was on the line, this colleague went to bat for me and spoke in my favor. This is why I tell junior faculty, "Get to know your colleagues and let them get to know you."

I was also deeply grateful to one of my female colleagues who wrote a response to Cheshire's internal review, pointing out places in his review that unfairly described my work. I am also deeply appreciative that one of my male colleagues apparently walked the halls before my tenure vote, encouraging colleagues to attend the faculty meeting to vote in favor of my tenure and promotion.

I am also indebted to my Colleagues of Color at other law schools who helped me when I was desperately fighting for survival. These colleagues gave me guidance and concrete support. They helped me to manage the tricky political terrain of the tenure process. Without them, I would not be where I am today. I met many of these colleagues at various People of Color Conferences, the Conference of Asian Pacific American Law Faculty, and LatCrit meetings.

I strongly encourage junior Faculty of Color not only to attend such conferences but also to sign up to present scholarship at their work-in-progress sessions. This was the advice one of my female Colleagues of Color gave me when I was a junior faculty member. I did not realize at the time just how valuable this advice was, but I appreciated it later. By presenting your work at these conferences, you can receive excellent feedback in a safe environment that can help make your scholarly work stronger. Moreover, presenting your work is a way to get yourself known and your ideas out in circulation. Most law professors are too busy to read every single article that is published, but they might attend an hour-long work-in-progress presentation. I have received numerous invitations to speak in large part because someone who heard me speak at a work-in-progress session recommended me to their faculty colloquium committee. Speaking at conferences can also lead to publication opportunities. When I presented my very first work-in-progress (my article on race and self-defense), I did not realize one of the professors in the group was an editor for a university press. Because this person liked my work-in-progress, he helped me obtain my first book contract.

I do not, however, recommend sharing early drafts of your work with colleagues. These colleagues may form negative impressions of your ability to write if they see lots of grammatical errors and typos in the draft. They may think your scholarship is insufficiently theoretical if your draft is in its early stages and you have not yet had a chance to fully develop your thesis. If a colleague or even your dean wants to see a draft, ask why. One friend of mine, a fellow Asian American female law professor, told me that when she was in her fourth or fifth year of teaching but not yet up for tenure, her dean asked to see a draft of an article she was working on. She gave him the draft without asking why he needed to see it. She later learned that the dean shared her unfinished draft with the provost of the university. The two of them decided—based on their review of this one draft—that her scholarship was problematic, and she was told that she should look for a job elsewhere.

I was also able to survive the experience of a difficult tenure process in large part because deep down I believed in myself. Even when my writing was under attack, I believed I had something important to say, so I kept on writing. Yet I would be lying if I left the impression that the attempts to derail my tenure had no effect on my psyche. These attacks wounded me deeply. After the horrible experience of being grilled by BigWig, whose objective seemed to be to make me look bad, I shied away from presenting on panels at conferences and mostly presented at People of Color Conferences and other safe spaces.

I know that I am very fortunate to have survived the attempts by some to convince others on my faculty that I was not worthy of being tenured and promoted. Several of my Friends of Color who experienced similar or worse hostility were either denied tenure or left their institutions before getting it. One of my friends, who was the first Black female law professor at her institution, found a *National Geographic* magazine with a gorilla on the cover in her faculty mailbox when she was untenured. After this incident, my friend decided to give up her tenure-track position and move to a more hospitable environment. Even though she had several publications in good journals, she was unable to secure another tenure-track position and eventually gave up on her dream of becoming a tenured professor. Fortunately, she is now very happy, serving as an administrative law judge.

MOVING ON

Moving to a different institution was an important step in the process of getting beyond a brutal tenure and promotion process. When I received a lateral offer from my current institution, I sat down and wrote a list of the reasons to stay on one side of the page and the reasons to go on the other. For many people, getting an offer from a higher-ranked institution would be reason enough to leave. When I tallied up my list, the reasons to stay outnumbered the reasons to go.

One reason to stay was the excellent relationship I had with students at my first institution. A few years before I came up for tenure, they voted to grant me and another professor the honor of Professor of the Year, an accolade I still cherish. I remember Would-Be-Mentor remarking that the Professor of the Year award was just a popularity contest and that the students did not know anything about good teaching. If the comment was intended to take the wind out of my sails, it worked.

I also cherished the friends I had made at my first institution. Two of my former law school colleagues were and still are my best friends. Outside the law faculty, I had several very good friends who either taught in other departments at my first institution or at other local law schools. Moreover, I loved the year-round sunny weather and the fact that I was a short plane ride from my parents and my siblings.

So why did I leave? The main reason was because continuing to stay in an environment where many of my colleagues did not respect me was emotionally draining. I knew that having to constantly face colleagues who thought I was nice but not smart was going to suck the joy out of living from me. It already had. Many of my more senior colleagues who had endured similar or worse battles dealt with this by withdrawing from the life of the law school, coming onto campus just to teach their classes and meet with their students, but otherwise having as little to do with the institution as possible. I, however, did not want to live out the rest of my professional life in a cocoon. I wanted to be part of an intellectual community that respected me and my scholarship. I did not feel I was respected at my former institution. While my colleagues who had systematically tried to derail my tenure did not succeed in this objective, they had succeeded in creating a caricature of me as a nice person who was popular with the students and a good citizen, but whose scholarship was weak. At my current institution, I feel respected. I also love that the faculty here prides itself on its institutional commitment to collegiality and that teaching is valued almost as much as scholarship.

Eighteen years later, I see even more clearly that my decision to leave was the right choice. At my current institution, my scholarship has flourished. I published my first book, *Murder and the Reasonable Man* (NYU Press, 2003), two years after joining my current institution. Two years later, I published a criminal law casebook, *Criminal Law: Cases and Materials*, coauthored with Angela Harris, with West Academic Publishing. In 2010, the dean at my current law school named me the Charles Kennedy Poe Research Professor of Law. In 2011, I published my third book, *Searches and Seizures: The Fourth Amendment, Its Constitutional History and the Contemporary Debate,* an anthology on the Fourth Amendment, with Prometheus Books. In 2016, I published my fourth book, a criminal procedure casebook, coauthored with L. Song Richardson and Tamara Lawson.

More than two decades have passed since the events described in this chapter. At the time, a few of my supporters on the faculty warned me to stay silent about the things I have written about here. Heeding their advice, I kept my mouth shut and got tenure. I continued to stay silent about the events I have disclosed here for many years. I finally decided to tell my story and the stories of some of my friends who did not get tenure and either chose or were forced to leave their institutions so that those who come after us can learn from our travails. Know that you too can succeed if you foster good relationships with colleagues inside and outside your home institution, if you have confidence in yourself and your work and, above all, if you continue to write even when others are telling you that what you have to say is worthless.

SIX

They See Us, but They Don't Really See Us

Jessica Lavariega Monforti and Melissa R. Michelson

Over the last decade or so, the field of political science has lost a significant number of Women of Color scholars at all points of their academic careers—the graduate school level, entrance to the academy, and at post-tenure points in the pipeline.[1] Despite higher than average interest in political science as undergraduates, Latinas represent less than 2 percent of all PhDs in the field. These women face formidable barriers in their pursuit of higher education and subsequent careers in political science, one of the most male- and Anglo-dominated fields of study in the social sciences. The barriers include lack of sponsorship and mentorship, limited financial resources, and significant familial responsibilities.

To combat the erosion of Women of Color's participation in our discipline, we developed a series of workshops to foster deep mentoring and engage in data collection to investigate the experiences of Women of Color in political science from graduate school through faculty and administration positions. We were inspired by the two-day Workshop on Women of Color Studies in Political Science, held in August 2002 at Northeastern University. Renowned political science scholars and graduate students met to discuss the study of Women of Color through diverse theoretical and pedagogical perspectives, empirical methods, curricula development, and scholar activism. Based on feedback from the

1. Generous support for the workshops came from the National Science Foundation; the American Political Science Association; Latino Decisions; Scholars Strategy Network; Pacific Lutheran University; Menlo College; Pace University; Emory University; University of Chicago; University of Texas–Pan American; University of Washington; University of California, San Diego; Stanford University; University of Illinois, Chicago; Center for Latino Policy Research; University of Maryland; Research Institute for Comparative Studies in Race and Ethnicity; Columbia University School of Arts and Sciences; and Politics, Groups and Identities.

DOI: 10.7330/9781607329664.c006

participants, we knew that the experience and information gained at the workshop had a significant impact on their ability to successfully navigate the profession. In 2013, 2015, and 2017 we held Women of Color in Political Science Workshops (WCPS) in keeping with the legacy of the inaugural workshop.[2]

Attached to each of the workshops were a series of participant pre- and post-workshop surveys and focus groups; further, participants were encouraged to submit narratives about their experiences at the workshop and in academia. In particular, we asked participants to share the attitudes and perceptions they hold about their experiences as graduate students and faculty in the field. Over the last five years, we have collected data from 186 survey participants and nine focus groups. This is the most comprehensive dataset about the contemporary experiences of Women of Color in political science.

In this chapter, we focus on the experiences of Women of Color in political science in our disciplinary and institutional cultures and how they are simultaneously invisible and hypervisible. Nearly every participant remarked that she was either the only Faculty of Color or one of two in her department. A few were among the only Faculty of Color in their college or school. Lack of other Faculty of Color, often combined with very small numbers of admitted graduate Students of Color, reinforced for many a sense of exclusion and isolation. Even women who felt they were situated in a supportive department and who had "strong White allies and mentors" noted that the culture of the department sometimes reproduced biases. Small but frequent slights often undermined a sense of belonging. These microaggressions generated a feeling among these Women of Color scholars that they were unwelcome. Focus group participants provided examples of deeper biases, such as tenure and promotion denial and outright discrimination. As one participant observed, "They see us, but they don't really see us."

Here, we provide space and light for the voices of Women of Color in political science to explain their lived experiences, and to highlight the ways they view progress and/or solutions (or lack thereof). Focus group participants were asked what changes they've seen occurring over time related to race and gender in academia. Many, especially senior Women of Color, were heartened by increasing numbers of women and Women of Color joining the discipline. Others described positive institutional changes, such as the establishment of national association sections related to the study of race, gender, and ethnicity. Some described the intellectual vibrancy that Women of Color had been contributing to the discipline.

There was also significant reflection on countercurrents to progress, including stories of Women of Color leaving their graduate programs and academic jobs, and of Women of Color political scientists choosing to present their research at women's studies or ethnic studies conferences rather than at political science conferences. Of political science as a discipline, one woman concluded a session

2. Jessica and Melissa worked with a committee of women to organize the first workshop in 2013: Drs. Marisa Abrajano, Khalilah L. Brown-Dean, Renee Cramer, Andra Gillespie, Shayla C. Nunnally, Amalia Pallares, and Janelle Wong.

TABLE 6.1. Diversity among political science faculty in the US, 1980 and 2010

	Political science faculty, 1980 (n=7,473)	*Female political science faculty, 1980 (n=769)*	*Political science faculty, 2010 (n=9,302)*	*Female political science faculty, 2010 (n=2,660)*
Anglo	96.4%	93.4%	88.9%	86.6%
African American/Black	2.4%	4.3%	5%	6.1%
Hispanic/Latina/Chicana	1.2%	2.3%	2.7%	3%
Asian/Pacific Islander	—	—	3.4%	4.4%
Female	10.3%	n/a	28.6%	n/a

Note: Data on Asians/Pacific Islanders are not available for 1980.
Source: Fraga et al., 2011.

by claiming, "I don't think we should give this space up." We provide some context to understand this complexity.

CONTRADICTORY EXPERIENCES

In recent years, the number of women who have earned advanced degrees in the United States has increased. Women earned the majority of doctoral degrees in 2016 for the eighth straight year and outnumber men in graduate school 135 to 100 (Hendel, 2011). In the social and behavioral sciences there are 151.3 women per 100 men with doctoral degrees. Looking specifically at data on political science degrees, the profession includes an increasing (but still less than proportional) percentage of women, but most are not Women of Color (see table 6.1).

Although gains have been made in the number of women and members of historically underrepresented groups in full-time faculty positions at colleges and universities, these gains have been small and incremental. Gender diversification in political science has been uneven across racial and ethnic groups, as the overwhelming majority of women political science faculty members are White.

Harris and González (2012) frame colleges and universities as champions of meritocracy, encouraging free expression and the search for truth, and prizing the creation of neutral and objective knowledge for the betterment of society. They argue that these values are supposed to render racial and gender identities irrelevant. Yet Women of Color in the academy frequently find themselves "presumed incompetent" based on their demographic characteristics alone. While colleges and universities have for decades undertaken efforts to diversify their faculties (Shinnar & Williams, 2008), Faculty of Color face persistent challenges in trying to succeed within the academy. A recent national study of campus climate, retention, and satisfaction found that 75 percent of faculty of underrepresented backgrounds identified their campus climates as moderate to highly negative, and that perceptions of high racial hostility on campus were correlated with low job satisfaction and an increased desire to leave the academy. Institutions with the highest levels of perceived hostility were also those with the highest retention rates of White faculty (Jayakumar, Howard, Allen, & Han, 2009).

The lives of Women of Color faculty are "filled with lived contradictions and ambiguous empowerment" (Chase, 1995 p. 74; see also Viernes Turner, 2002). Harris and González (2012) write, "Despite their undeniable privilege, Women of Color faculty members are entrenched in byzantine patterns of race, gender, and class hierarchy that confound popular narratives about meritocracy" (p. 2). Faculty of Color, especially women Faculty of Color, can face unique challenges to their authority in the classroom (Rockquemore & Laszloffy, 2008; Thomas & Hollenshead, 2001; Viernes Turner, 2002). Faculty of underrepresented backgrounds are also more likely to have to be especially careful about their tone of voice, facial expressions, body language, and dress in the classroom because these choices can have direct consequences for perceived levels of competence (Constantine, Smith, Redington, & Owens, 2008). Faculty of underrepresented backgrounds frequently report feelings of isolation, which can have a detrimental effect on morale and lead to these faculty leaving the academy (Constantine et al., 2008; Cooper, 2006; Fries-Britt & Kelly, 2005; Laden & Hagedorn, 2000; Rockquemore & Laszloffy, 2008).

In sum, Women of Color with academic positions, even when tenured, often confront situations that limit and/or question their authority, expertise, and sense of belonging. Addressing the steady flow of a mixture of racism, nativism, sexism, and microaggressions is draining and often leads these women to leave the discipline and/or higher education entirely (Carter, 1988). In this chapter, we focus on the experiences of Women of Color faculty and graduate students in political science. Using original data, we relate the stories of these women in their own words. This research is essential as we see significant increases in the number of women entering and successfully completing their undergraduate and postgraduate programs. Data for this investigation come from surveys and focus groups with Women of Color faculty and graduate students who participated in our Women of Color in Political Science Workshops in 2013, 2015, and 2017.

DATA AND METHODS

Pre- and post-workshop survey data were collected in 2013, 2015, and 2017 from a total of 186 self-identified Women of Color in political science. In addition to demographic information, we asked respondents about confidence in their knowledge and skills across a variety of areas that are key to a successful career in academia, such as navigating the job market, getting tenure, and post-tenure options. We also asked participants about their main concerns related to the profession. Additionally, we conducted nine focus groups in those three years, including a mix of workshop participants and other Women of Color in the discipline.

The survey data give us a sense of larger trends regarding Women of Color in political science.[3] Each workshop participant was given the option of completing

3. Data from the pre- and post-workshop surveys collected in 2013, 2015, and 2017 have been pooled for the purposes of this research.

TABLE 6.2. Demographic characteristics of the sample

Ethnicity/race	*Status in political science*	*Socioeconomic situation*
African American/Black (36%)	Grad student (35%)	Caretaker (32%)
Asian/Pacific Islander (23%)	Post-doc, lecturer, visiting (13%)	Breadwinner (57%)
Hispanic/Latina/Chicana (33%)	Part-time instructor (2%)	
Multiethnic/multiracial (12%)	TT Assistant prof (30%)	
	Tenured prof (21%)	
	Administrator (4%)	

her survey via email or paper and pencil upon arriving at the workshop, as well as at the workshop's conclusion. The focus group data provide us with rich details and narratives that supplement the quantitative data. Focus group participants provided informed consent at the beginning of each session, which was reviewed before initiating the discussion, as well as permission for audio recording. In both instances, each respondent was guaranteed confidentiality and anonymity if she chose to participate.

While obtaining informed consent is often considered obligatory and not particularly notable, several focus group participants had concerns about the consequences of their participation in this study. Many were worried that they would be identified and that, as a result, their careers would be negatively impacted. We reassured them that we would not include identifiable data in the final manuscript. Other respondents thanked the focus group facilitator for taking on such an important—and potentially explosive—topic, and a few even expressed that their participation in the focus group triggered trauma and/or was cathartic. These comments reveal the significance and seriousness of the subject of this research. We now turn to the survey data.

THE RESPONDENTS

Among our survey respondents, about 35 percent were graduate students; 13 percent identified themselves as postdocs, lecturers, visiting professors, or other full-time instructors; 2 percent as part-time instructors; 30 percent as assistant professors on tenure track; 21 percent as tenured professors; and 4 percent as administrators (see table 6.2). These findings mirror earlier work on Women of Color in political science, specifically Latinas (Lavariega Monforti, 2012). About 13 percent said they were employed at Hispanic-serving, historically Black, or tribal colleges and universities.

The low proportion of Women of Color in administrative ranks reflects the relatively young average age of our respondents (thirty-five years old) but also the shallow pool of senior scholars available, given how recently women, and particularly Women of Color, have joined the political science professoriate. The first woman to earn a PhD in political science was Sophonisba Preston Breckinridge, in 1901 from the University of Chicago. The first African American woman to earn a PhD in political science, Jewel L. Prestage, did so in 1954 from the University of Iowa, and in 1971, a full seventy years after Breckinridge, Adaljiza Sosa-Riddell became the first Latina to earn a PhD in political science, from the University of California, Riverside (Telgen & Kamp, 1993). Among our respondents, the earliest PhD earned in political science was in 1991.

Our respondents identified with a variety of ethno-racial groups: 36 percent identified as African American or Black, 23 percent as Asian/Asian American, 33 percent as Latina or Hispanic, and 12 percent as multiethnic or multiracial. The vast majority of respondents identified as cisgender (not transgender) and heterosexual. About one-third of the respondents are the primary or co-primary caretaker for a parent/elder, spouse/partner, children, or another individual, and 57 percent are the primary breadwinner in their households.

In the pre-workshop surveys, we asked respondents to rate their confidence in the following areas: navigating the job market, getting tenure, post-tenure strategies for advancement, becoming an administrator, teaching and identity in the classroom, public intellectualism, receiving and providing mentoring, negotiating a job offer, and careers outside academia. Possible responses were five-point Likert-type scales, with categories ranging from strongly agree to strongly disagree. Across all areas, significant proportions of our respondents indicated a lack of confidence (see table 6.3). The percentage of participants indicating that they strongly agree or agree that they feel confident across these nine areas never surpassed 60 percent. Women of Color graduate students and faculty do not feel confident in their level of knowledge and skills about areas of professional development that are essential for a successful career in academia.

We also examined these data for subgroup differences, as recommended by prior research (García Bedolla, Lavariega Monforti, & Pantoja, 2007). Participants who identified as tenured faculty and administrators reported higher levels of confidence than did their more junior counterparts. Despite the success these women have already accumulated at every level of the profession, and with accomplishments including acceptance and graduation from top PhD programs, publishing books and articles, winning fellowships and grants, and even earning tenure, Women of Color in the discipline lack confidence in their academic knowledge and skills.

Thomas and Hollenshead (2001) argue that, despite their marginalized position in the academy, Women of Color need not consider their place as one solely of deprivation. They find that Women of Color engage in resistance strategies across five areas: organizational barriers, institutional climate, lack of respect from one's colleagues, unwritten rules governing university life, and mentoring. Similarly, we argue that Women of Color have been resilient and persistent in the face of significant discipline-wide failures to mentor, sponsor, and incorporate Women of Color into the field's ranks. We turn to the data from our nine focus groups to help us explain this phenomenon.

TABLE 6.3. Confidence in knowledge and skills

	Navigating the job market	*Getting tenure*	*Post-tenure strategies for advancement*	*Becoming an administrator*	*Teaching and identity*	*Public intel-lectualism*	*Mentoring*	*Negotiating a job offer*	*Careers outside academia*
Strongly agree	12% (21)	14% (23)	18% (30)	19% (32)	7% (12)	12% (20)	5% (6)	19% (23)	20% (24)
Agree	29% (49)	30% (50)	39% (65)	37% (62)	21% (35)	31% (53)	20% (24)	31% (38)	40% (48)
Neither	19% (32)	20% (33)	15% (26)	18% (30)	29% (49)	24% (41)	20% (25)	22% (27)	21% (25)
Disagree	32% (54)	25% (42)	17% (29)	15% (25)	33% (55)	21% (36)	38% (47)	20% (24)	11% (13)
Strongly disagree	8% (14)	12% (20)	11% (18)	12% (20)	11% (18)	12% (20)	17% (21)	9% (11)	9% (11)
Total number of respondents	170	168	168	169	169	170	123	123	121

FOCUS GROUPS: WOMEN OF COLOR EXPERIENCES IN THEIR OWN WORDS

Between 2013 and 2017, seventy-four Women of Color participated in nine focus groups. Participants were asked a series of questions that included: areas of disciplinary focus; institutional climate (in general for Women of Color as well as the climate of the participant's particular department); challenges and opportunities; support they receive from their departments/institutions; and changes they have noticed over time in terms of being a Woman of Color in the profession. From these focus groups several themes emerged: hypervisibility, invisibility, and complexity of change.

Hypervisibility/Invisibility

Women of Color feel hypervisible. Participants talked at length about being heavily recruited into graduate programs and on the job market. Upon accepting offers, they were frequently asked to include a picture on the department/institutional website to help recruit other students and Faculty of Color, and to be involved in service work to represent Communities of Color. These requests were often more about their presence as symbols of diversity than about those departments and institutions genuinely wanting to build a pipeline of Women of Color in the field. For example, one African American woman who recently completed her PhD program said, "They've got me on the website and talk about their diverse students and faculty, but I felt invisible. White faculty kept reintroducing themselves to me like we hadn't met and I was the student they highlighted on the webpage." A senior faculty member who is African American chimed in, "Universities are good at rhetoric, on the surface talking about diversity." An Asian American woman added, "You want to say to them, 'You used me.' After two years I felt used." Another African American tenured faculty member closed this part of the conversation by saying, "This is business. They tell us we are friends. They talk about collegiality, but this is business. At the end of the day, we have to make visible the invisible work we are being uncompensated for because they know we are going to do it."

Hidden labor—especially the labor of working with students—was a theme in another focus group. Women of Color, particularly junior faculty, believed that they were seen as especially accessible to both White and non-White students. Their younger age often made them "relateable." Students of Color, not used to seeing a Woman of Color in a faculty position, wanted to share their own experiences with race and gender. Two described having to set a timer for ten minutes during office hours to accommodate "the line out the door" of students eager to talk with them. Inevitably, these student meetings would extend beyond office hours. And yet, one faculty member observed, "It's service, but it's not counted as service."

Senior Women of Color faculty who participated in one focus group took mentorship very seriously. There are relatively few Women of Color in political science at the full-professor rank. As a result, especially if they are seen as strong mentors, these women not only write many letters, they also spend a great deal of time helping junior colleagues navigate experiences related to race or gender in the academy. In fact, this dynamic was part of the focus group as senior Women of Color turned part of the focus group into a workshop on how to survive feelings of alienation and isolation in the discipline.

Teaching is also an area where Women of Color faculty encounter some unique time-related challenges. The literature on teaching evaluations consistently shows that women receive lower teaching evaluations than men (see Andersen & Miller, 1997; Arbuckle & Williams, 2003; Basow, 1995) and that Scholars of Color receive lower teaching evaluation scores than Whites (see Andersen & Smith, 2005; Hendrix, 1998; Smith & Andersen, 2005). One Woman of Color in our focus group was urged by her department chair to improve her teaching after she received lower than average teaching evaluations during her first semester. When her evaluations improved, she was then told that her high teaching evaluations indicated she was spending too much time teaching. Another faculty member said she believed she had to work twice as hard as her White male colleagues to achieve similar scores on teaching evaluations. Few in her department seemed familiar with the bias that women and Faculty of Color face when students evaluate their teaching. In many cases, spending less time on teaching is not an option for Women of Color faculty who want to mitigate these biases in student evaluations. In another focus group, there was a lengthy discussion of frequently being dismissed or challenged by both undergraduate and graduate students—particularly in courses that dealt with themes of race, gender, and ethnicity.

Participants cited examples of being addressed as Ms. or Mrs. as opposed to Dr. or Professor, having their names continually mispronounced, and frequently being referred to or described as "exotic," "sassy," "overbearing," "uppity," or "greedy." One African American who had become department chair said, "My colleagues were fine as long as I didn't have power . . . but once I became chair people sent emails referring to me as the 'Grand Poobah' and 'queen.'" Others provided similar examples of name-calling and condescension. One Latina postdoc recounted comments from a group of all-White male peers: "They said, 'You're very exotic. We thought you were a foreign student.'"

Focus group participants shared how small but frequent slights often undermined a sense of belonging. A Black faculty member noted that she was one of three Black women faculty in her college, including one senior colleague and another junior colleague. Although there were only two junior Black faculty, her college dean consistently called her by the other junior faculty member's name. White junior faculty in her program did not complain about such instances of misrecognition. Another senior Black faculty member in the focus group said that she taught for more than ten years at her state flagship. At a celebration held when she left for another position, only one of her department colleagues pronounced her name correctly. Over the years, these microaggressions undermined a sense of true inclusion among Women of Color faculty.

Many of the participants also talked about competing at the national or international level for grants and fellowships while having their accomplishments ignored at their home institutions and departments. One Latina on postdoc fellowship explained, "They were not there for me when I needed institutional support. I was awarded a National Science Foundation Fellowship, but the university is fucking with me. They sent me students to mentor and then some of them complained that I wasn't helping them. Then White female peers dumped their mentoring loads on me, and then one of them complained that she wouldn't get a job because she is White." An African American graduate student shared, "I received a fellowship, and asked [my institution] for additional support to be able to pay my expenses. I was told by my department chair that I was greedy. He became a gatekeeper at that point and said I had a target on my back. He wanted me to be ashamed that I won a fellowship."

Several of the focus groups engaged in conversations about the lack of support from male co-ethnics, while some women talked about having active, supportive male co-ethnic mentors and peers. Another theme was co-ethnic "bro clubs"—described as the Black and brown version of the good ol' boys networks. Men of Color in political science have experienced many of the issues laid out here, but have simultaneously benefited from male privilege. There were significant questions about how to navigate this landscape given that the participants felt reliant on their relationships with these men for letters of recommendation, favorable reviews and evaluations, and other forms of support.

Not all conversations in the focus groups were about challenges and negative experiences; some participants shared positive experiences. One African American graduate student said, "Faculty in my department are giving me constant feedback, encouraging me to apply for funding, and networking with me. I feel supported." An African American tenured faculty member said, "I love my department, although it is far from perfect. My comments [in department meetings] are valued and I am not silenced." One woman said, "My institution provides good financial support. I found community early on with the Black Graduate Student Organization, and I can be my true and authentic self there. It has given me the opportunity to work with top administrators too." Many acknowledged that they had good interpersonal relationships with their colleagues and that their colleagues seemed "thrilled" to have a Person of Color in their programs. There were a number of women who felt their department was supportive and that they had "strong White allies and mentors," communities of support within institutions that went beyond their departments, and Scholars of Color to work with and be mentored by.

Complexity of Change

We asked focus group participants about perceived changes in political science over time related to race and gender. Many respondents, especially senior Women of Color, were heartened by increasing numbers of women and Women of Color joining the discipline. Others described positive institutional changes, such as the establishment of an American Political Science Association Section on Race,

Ethnicity and Politics, affinity group caucuses, and more published scholarship on race, ethnicity, and politics. Some described the intellectual vibrancy that Women of Color had been contributing to the discipline over the years. One woman said, "Being a witness to others' promotion and progress, and seeing their paths helps me develop my own." One African American senior faculty member was surprised to hear that junior scholars were experiencing the same challenges she had faced earlier in her career: "These stories are coming from behind me. All the work I did to create pathways for all of you—what happened?" There were expressions of excitement about progress, as well as disappointment in the glacial pace of change in the discipline despite decades of work around diversity and inclusion.

A common topic involved the narrative of being the first Person of Color or Woman of Color to be hired or recruited to a department. One Latina tenure-track faculty member said, "I am the only Person of Color in my department, and maybe first one ever. I have light skin privilege—I'm White enough for them. The department is not hostile, but it's too kind and too nice to deal with these issues. People in the department are inexperienced and naive. I have to spend time educating others. My challenge is that I see the world differently because I am Latina. They want to do better, but they just don't know how." An African American faculty member shared, "You have to develop a persona to deal with growing pains [of departments and institutions]. Being people's first Black friend, you have to educate them. I have to be a human dictionary."

There were reflections on countercurrents to progress, including stories of Women of Color leaving their graduate programs and academic jobs, or presenting their research at women's studies or ethnic studies conferences rather than at political science conferences. One African American woman said, "I am comfortable at my institution because I found my community early on in African American Studies. I found folks to work with across ranks, and was supported in that department. They invested in me. They protect me from service." In contrast, a Latina graduate student said, "Interest [by faculty] in my work started falling off as I engaged more with issues of race and ethnicity in my research. The attitudes of the faculty are being imprinted on graduate students, so the problem is being replicated. I withdrew from the department. Nothing will convince them that this way of thinking [about the discipline] is wrong, and it is crushing to be there."

In sum, Women of Color in political science are persisting and succeeding despite a variety of micro- and macroaggressions, and there are significant disagreements among those women about how best to respond to those aggressions and challenges. Continued diversification of the academy requires recognition of and attention to these challenges. While these women clearly have agency and are taking steps to mitigate the issues they face, the burden of reducing those problems should not fall on those who are disadvantaged by them. That burden more appropriately belongs to departments and institutions, and to the profession as a whole.

CONCLUSION AND DISCUSSION

In this chapter, we focused on the experiences of Women of Color in political science, and in our disciplinary and institutional cultures. Our data highlight Women of Color political scientists as simultaneously invisible and hypervisible, and the complex nature of ethno-racial and gender inclusion in the discipline. We provided some context to understand this complexity. Progress toward their inclusion as full members in the discipline has been uneven and fragmented. While some of our respondents shared positive experiences about their time as graduate students and professionals, they were few and far between. The larger pattern is summed up by one of our focus group participants, "You see me but you don't acknowledge me. I am invisible." Moreover, there is concern that, rather than creating an inclusive path forward, departments are replicating exclusionary behavior by failing to train graduate students with different perspectives toward their Women of Color colleagues, graduate students, and research in the subfield of race and ethnic politics.

The results offer a serious wake-up call for those who laud the increasing diversification of our graduate student and faculty ranks without recognizing the harsh reality Women of Color often face in the profession. There is considerable room for improvement in political science, and the academy in general, in the representation, mentoring, and treatment of Women of Color (Lavariega Monforti, 2012). We offer these suggested survival skills for Women of Color:

- Know that you belong—*we see you.*
- Prepare yourself to handle the issues that are discussed in this chapter.
- Talk to colleagues you can trust, even if they are outside your field of study or at a different institution.
- Get everything in writing (including funding offers, workload issues, information on salary and benefits, and tenure and promotion expectations) and document everything if something does not feel right.
- Get a posse—a group of friends and family that will support you.
- Shape your own narrative; don't let others tell your story.
- Celebrate the positive relationships you have and accomplishments you reach, even the small ones.
- Engage in self-care.
- Delineate healthy boundaries for your work/life continuum.

However, it is also important to realize that these are *not solutions*. Individual Women of Color are not responsible for bringing about the changes that are needed in academia. That responsibility falls directly on the shoulders of institutions, administrators, department chairs, and faculty. White administrators and faculty, who comprise the largest portion of those working in political science, need to make investments of time, energy, and funding in Women of Color.

Perhaps more aggressive suggestions should be implemented. One tenured professor suggested in a focus group that Women of Color should develop a system to rate the best and worst departments for Women of Color graduate students and faculty. She went on to propose that the best departments should be publicly praised and the worst ones should be publicly chided; information from top-performing departments could be the basis for training other departments around inclusion and equity.

Significant literature exists regarding how institutions and department can engage in institutional transformation around issues of inclusion and equity; there is no need to repeat those suggestions here (Ng, 1993). Unfortunately, until there is a shift in thinking among those who have the power to implement those changes—among the White men who dominate the profession and hold most of the power within it—we do not anticipate any sudden embrace of those necessary reforms. Echoing the concerns of many of our workshop and focus group participants, we believe that institutional challenges and institutionalized racism and sexism are likely to persist for some time. We call on all scholars, of all genders and ethno-racial identities, to continue to push for equal opportunities and respect for all political scientists.

REFERENCES

Andersen, K., & Miller, E. D. (1997). Gender and student evaluations of teaching. *PS: Political Science & Politics, 30*(2), 216–219.

Andersen, K. J., & Smith, G. (2005). Students' preconceptions of professors: Benefits and barriers according to ethnicity and gender. *Hispanic Journal of Behavioral Sciences, 27*(2), 184–201.

Arbuckle, J., & Williams, B. D. (2003). Students' perceptions of expressiveness: Age and gender effects on teacher evaluations. *Sex Roles, 49*(9–10), 507–516.

Basow, S. A. (1995). Student evaluations of college professors: When gender matters. *Journal of Educational Psychology, 87*(4), 656.

Carter, D. (1988). Double jeopardy: Women of color in higher education. *Educational Record, 68*(4), 98–103.

Chase, S. E. (1995). *Ambiguous empowerment: The work narratives of women school superintendents.* Amherst: University of Massachusetts Press.

Constantine, M. G., Smith, L., Redington, R. M., & Owens, D. (2008). Racial microaggressions against black counseling and counseling psychology faculty: A central challenge in the multicultural counseling movement. *Journal of Counseling & Development, 86*(3), 348–355.

Cooper, T. L. (2006). *The sista'network: African-American women faculty successfully negotiating the road to tenure.* Boston: Anker.

Fraga, L. R., et al. (2011). *APSA task force on political science in the 21st century.* Retrieved from https://www.apsanet.org/portals/54/Files/Task%20Force%20Reports/TF_21st%20Century_AllPgs_webres90.pdf.

Fries-Britt, S., & Kelly, B. T. (2005). Retaining each other: Narratives of two African American women in the academy. *Urban Review, 37*(3), 221–242.

García Bedolla, L., Lavariega Monforti, J., & Pantoja, A. D. (2007). A second look: Is there a Latina/o gender gap? *Journal of Women, Politics & Policy, 28*(3–4), 147–171.

Harris, A., & González, C. G. (2012). Introduction. In G. Gutiérrez y Muhs, Y. F. Niemann, C. G. González, & A. Harris (Eds.), *Presumed incompetent: The intersections of race and class for women in academia* (pp. 1–14). Logan: Utah State University Press.

Hendel, John. (2011). A U.S. gender milestone: More women have advanced degrees than men. *Atlantic*. https://www.theatlantic.com/national/archive/2011/04/a-us-gender-milestone-more-women-have-advanced-degrees-than-men/237913/.
Hendrix, K. G. (1998). Student perceptions of the influence of race on professor credibility. *Journal of Black Studies*, 2(6), 738–763.
Jayakumar, U. M., Howard, T. C., Allen, W. R., & Han, J. C. (2009). Racial privilege in the professoriate: An exploration of campus climate, retention, and satisfaction. *Journal of Higher Education*, *80*(5), 538–563.
Laden, B. V., & Hagedorn, L. S. (2000). Job satisfaction among faculty of color in academe: Individual survivors or institutional transformers? *New Directions for Institutional Research*, *2000*(105), 57–66.
Lavariega Monforti, J. (2012). La lucha: Latinas surviving political science. In G. Gutiérrez y Muhs, Y. F. Niemann, C. G. González, & A. Harris (Eds.), *Presumed incompetent: The intersections of race and class for women in academia* (pp. 393–407). Logan: Utah State University Press.
Ng, R. (1993). A woman out of control: Deconstructing sexism and racism in the university. *Canadian Journal of Education/Revue canadienne de l'éducation*, *18*(3), 189–205.
Rockquemore, K., & Laszloffy, T. A. (2008). *The black academic's guide to winning tenure—without losing your soul*. Boulder: Lynne Rienner.
Shinnar, R. S., & Williams, H. L. (2008). Promoting faculty diversity: The faculty fellows program at Appalachian State University. *Planning for Higher Education*, *36*(2), 42–53.
Smith, G., & Andersen, K. J. (2005). Students' ratings of professors: The teaching style contingency for Latino/a professors. *Journal of Latinos and Education*, 4(2), 115–136.
Thomas, G. D., & Hollenshead, C. (2001). Resisting from the margins: The coping strategies of black women and other women of color faculty members at a research university. *Journal of Negro Education*, *70*(3), 166–175.
Telgen, D., & Kamp, J. (1993). *Notable Hispanic American women*. Detroit: Gale Research.
Viernes Turner, C. S. (2002). Women of color in academe: Living with multiple marginality. *Journal of Higher Education*, *73*(1), 74–93.

SEVEN

Promotion while Pregnant and Black

Jemimah Li Young and Dorothy E. Hines

Historically, as female tenure-track professors, we have been advised implicitly and explicitly not to grow a family while seeking tenure. Although substantial progress has been made to dismantle this perspective, it remains an unspoken White patriarchal rule within the confines of predominately White institutions (PWIs). What we as academics do not discuss in the literature is that when White women have a baby on the tenure track, their Whiteness may garner sympathy, compassion, and support from their male and female colleagues. However, Women of Color, especially Black women, endure systemic micro- and macroaggressive actions designed to usher them and their unborn children out of the academy. As such, the purpose of this chapter is to examine the unspoken realities of pursuing promotion and tenure while growing a family as young Black female assistant professors. To this end, this chapter has two goals. Our primary goal is to describe our experiences as Black female assistant professors through the lens of presumed incompetence. Our secondary goal is to provide recommendations for other Black female academics navigating the tenure and promotion process while pregnant.

The concept of presumed incompetence is fundamental to our narrative regarding pregnancy and promotion for Women of Color in the academy. We argue that some faculty members presume that Black mother-scholars are incompetent. We base this argument on the spoken and unspoken rules of the promotion and tenure process, as well as the unforeseen consequences that we have incurred while utilizing the policies designed to support academics who choose to grow their families. For instance, while mothers are on leave they are at risk of having their research projects mishandled by graduate students, their courses reassigned to less qualified faculty, or their leadership positions revoked. All of this occurs under the veil of support, but when senior faculty members retell our narrative, we as Black mother-scholars are characterized as unfocused, uncommitted, and

DOI: 10.7330/9781607329664.c007

incapable of simultaneously managing our professional and parenting obligations. These are just selected samples of the challenges we have faced as Black mother-scholars seeking promotion and tenure.

In the first section of this chapter, we clarify how our pregnancy and familial experiences on the tenure track diverged from the trends we observed for White female faculty. This is important because the presumptions of incompetence and consequences of the choice to have a child while on the tenure clock were not the same for us as for our White peers. Then we unpack the hidden burden of accepting a stop to your tenure clock for Women of Color. Finally, we discuss how our success as mother-scholars was met with disbelief and denigration. This discussion is at the heart of our presumed inability as Black women to soar above our peers, despite the additional challenges of pregnancy and parenting, which many assumed would cripple our productivity. Finally, we provide recommendations for future Mother-Scholars of Color and their administrators.

THE INTERSECTION OF THE PROFESSORIATE, PREGNANCY, AND PIGMENT

Some often jokingly say, "You need to be promoted before you can be devoted to your family." We contend that Black mother-scholars face dual marginality, and this burden is multiplied exponentially due to the intersection of racism and sexism in higher education. It is a well-known yet often denied fact that family comes second to the job in heteronormative, hyper-masculine White spaces like the academy. Behind the rhetoric university officials provide to avoid discrimination lawsuits is a systemic and systematic cycle of disdain for women giving birth while seeking tenure. Yet we are among the many women who have begun to do it with more success recently.

Our pigment has a unique effect on our experiences as pregnant scholars seeking promotion and tenure. Faculty of Color routinely encounter racism while on the tenure track, and researchers have confirmed the ways in which racism and stereotyping shape the tenure and promotion process (Allen, Epps, Guillory, Suh, & Bonous-Hammarth, 2000; Turner, Gonzalez, & Wood, 2008). Sexism likewise affects the career trajectories of both White women and Women of Color, and pregnant women face even greater ridicule from male and female scholars. Unfortunately, we as Black, female, pregnant, tenure-track professors represent an anomaly, which means that we bear the burden of paving the way for the Black women of the future. In this first section, we recount our challenges and accomplishments as Black mother-scholars at PWIs navigating the intersections of our pigment, pregnancy, and the professoriate.

Being Black in the academy placed us on full display for our students and colleagues. Because Black women were not commonplace at either of our institutions, our baby bumps were extra noticeable. Nonetheless, as mothers, especially new mothers, we believed that the changes to our bodies should be celebrated, not masked, hidden, or otherwise concealed. Often, however, we were subject to comments and actions that made us feel embarrassed or ashamed, while simultaneously being encouraged to maintain our physical and emotional composure as we came to work each day. We understood that, as Black women, our tenure and promotion was automatically more political and personal than academic—that we would be held to a higher standard and presumed incompetent and unworthy. Thus, we knew that any need to attend to our pregnancy and growing child might be misconstrued as an act of weakness or a lack of focus—including sitting down to teach our class in the third trimester, stepping out periodically during lengthy department meetings to empty our bladder, or being placed on bed rest. All of these natural pregnancy experiences contributed to negative perceptions and presumptions of us as scholars. Lack of support from our departments through policy or a set of established departmental practices only compounded our difficulties.

My story is unique because I was the first woman to have a child in our department in over fifteen years. Not surprisingly, no one knew of any resources or procedures to assist me because, as I was repeatedly informed by my chair, "it has been so long." Fortunately, I was aware of the Family and Medical Leave Act (FMLA) and quickly began to navigate the process on my own. With the support of God, my husband, my mother, and an active online mentoring circle, my pregnancy and birth were relatively smooth processes. However, shortly after my pregnancy, a cohort of White female tenure-track professors became pregnant, and the differences in our experiences could not have been more stark.

The first of three, after announcing her news to the department, quickly began the "Woe is me" campaign. She immediately suggested to all who would listen that she was overwhelmed and worried about promotion and tenure. Her words were heard, and the department sprang into action. All of a sudden, the department was well informed and extremely accommodating. For instance, my White colleague was advised by our shared mentor that she could teach online during her pregnancy instead of taking unpaid leave provided by FMLA, and was excused from having to be physically present during office hours. During my pregnancy, I also taught an online course that I had to redesign to increase student access and enrollment, only to learn later that the department chair was telling students that I moved the course online because I was pregnant. When this was brought to my attention, I swiftly informed my chair about the negative impact of such statements on student perceptions. He replied that I was being sensitive and reading too much into the situation. Moreover, I personally advocated for the same office hours accommodation my White colleague was granted, only to have it denied by my chair. Finally, my White peer was also assigned a teaching assistant, which is typically reserved for the endowed chairs, one of whom just happened to be the mentor we shared. Hence, we had the same White female mentor and experienced the same pregnancy circumstances, yet the level of compassion, support, and sound advice I received was remarkably different.

I would be remiss not to acknowledge that my White female mentor and White female colleague shared the same ethnicity, which understandably made their interactions less arduous and more natural. Ethnic nepotism enhances the support that White women receive, as their senior faculty members find their challenges more relatable. Additionally, other White women in my department were encouraged not to teach classes during the final stages of their pregnancies, whereas we, as Black women professors, were encouraged to "place our students first" and subsequently completed our teaching assignments with minimal or no support.

During my second pregnancy, I made sure to remain the chair of several time-consuming departmental committees, and continued to work on my current research projects, in light of the lessons learned from my first pregnancy. For example, during that earlier pregnancy, several of my departmental colleagues replaced me on their ongoing research projects without consulting me. When I inquired, they said they had assumed I was no longer interested in the project. Furthermore, many senior faculty members used my motherhood as a mechanism to discourage graduate students from working with me, claiming that I had too many family responsibilities to chair new dissertation committees. Furthermore, I was overlooked for graduate teaching opportunities because the program chair assumed I would not want to teach courses in the evening while pregnant. These are just a few of the presumptions that hindered my growth and development as a scholar when I became a mother. Women of Color are presumed incompetent for getting pregnant while pursuing promotion and tenure. The presumption is not usually imposed on our White colleagues, nor does it carry the same career consequences.

TO STOP OR NOT TO STOP THE CLOCK

Our biological clock, unlike the tenure clock, is unpredictable. Six years of success on the tenure track could yield a lifetime of personal regrets. Studies consistently indicate that most women should consider starting their families before the age of thirty (Moos et al., 2008). Advances in fertility science and better overall health care have extended this timetable substantially. Thus, women are entering the professoriate earlier with an unapologetic ambition to have their cake and eat it too. It is not surprising that increasingly more women are opting to start or grow their families while pursuing tenure and promotion (Acker, Webber, & Smyth, 2016). One out of three women on the tenure track will become mothers (Baker, 2014). This represents a marked increase compared to several decades ago (Mirick & Wladkowski, 2018). Women are becoming more empowered and informed, and in some small instances, the academy has followed suit.

The tenure and promotion process was designed in an era when the typical academic was a White man whose wife stayed home to raise children. Despite efforts by universities to accommodate changing faculty demographics, certain cultural assumptions and expectations remain. Many universities have established policies to allow faculty to adjust their tenure clock to help manage family responsibilities. In this section, we discuss our experiences with the tenure clock adjustment process and the benefits and drawbacks we faced as Black mother-scholars.

Most universities will *stop the clock* during the probationary period of tenure-track faculty and grant an additional year on the tenure track to accommodate parental obligations. The stop the clock can be used for the birth/adoption of a child or to care for an elderly family member. Unfortunately, regardless of the written policy, senior faculty are free to hold the extra time against their colleagues and vote accordingly. Thus, these policies could subject faculty who take parental leave to negative tenure recommendations later. Although these policies have existed for decades, there is little research examining the correlation between taking a stop the clock and negative tenure decisions, especially for Black female faculty. According to Manchester, Leslie, and Kramer (2010), receiving a stop the clock does not affect one's probability of earning tenure but it does influence earnings. This, however, was not our experience.

Pregnant women are "encouraged" to stop their tenure clocks, and this is frequently presented as a courtesy and/or means of support. However, in our experiences, this accommodation is often misconstrued as a modification of the expectations for promotion and tenure, which in turn further perpetuates ideas of inferiority. Some senior colleagues regarded stopping the clock as a sign of inadequacy and treated this period as research leave, even though university policies indicate that this time should not count at all toward tenure and promotion. Our White female peers were well aware of these perceptions and presumptions because they received strong, unbiased mentorship from senior faculty. For instance, one of my White female colleagues was offered an opportunity to take a stop the clock, but was advised to obtain written confirmation that she could revert to her original timeline if she later deemed the stop the clock unnecessary. The same mentor failed to mention this to me when she informed me of my options, thus placing me at a disadvantage and in a very vulnerable position.

Although parental leave is presented as gender neutral, the reality is quite different. For women, the act of giving birth and caring for a child is assumed to interfere with our work as teachers and scholars. By contrast, men who father children during the pre-tenure years are celebrated and are less likely to be encouraged to request a stop the clock. Men who do avail themselves of stop the clock programs are often rewarded rather than stigmatized for taking parental obligations seriously, even though they do not face the physical challenges of childbearing.

Additionally, although men are free to take advantage of stop the clock programs, they often do not. Nevertheless, male parents are substantially more successful at earning promotion and tenure than female parents. According to Mason, Wolfinger, and Goulden (2013), 70 percent of men with children earn tenure, compared to only 44 percent of women with children. When their tenure files are reviewed, men benefit from the presumption that they published *and* parented, while the assumption is that female scholars parented *rather than* published. Hence, a gender-neutral policy to support male and female parents actually does more to support male academics. Men who take parental leave are rewarded for being concerned and involved parents, while women who stop the clock are perceived to be taking advantage of the system. This is especially so for women who become more productive during and after pregnancy.

REPRODUCTIVE AND PRODUCTIVE

Black women are often taught that they must work twice as hard to get half as much. This is the sentiment that surrounds everything we do within the academy. Thus, it is not surprising to us when our accomplishments are questioned during the promotion and tenure process. However, it becomes problematic when questioning leads to the presumption that we are incapable of amassing strong, high-quality publication records while pregnant or parenting. As discussed earlier, the promotion and tenure process presents unique challenges for Black women and other Women of Color related to presumptions of incompetence. However, arguably the most egregious challenge is the assumption that we cannot establish work/life balance.

Scholarly publications are the currency of the academy, as reflected in the old adage "Publish or perish." In evaluating a tenure-track professor's research, committee members often focus not only on the quantity published but also on the nature of research and where it was published (Blackwell, 1988; Schuster & Finkelstein, 2006). When Black women "publish and parent" they are often faced with subtle as well as explicit criticism from senior faculty. For instance, several of my senior colleagues reviewed my record with disbelief or disregard. Those who were skeptical of my accomplishments wanted me to provide proof of publication, a condition that is neither departmental policy nor a requirement for other junior faculty members. These senior colleagues insinuated that I had fabricated my publication record or had somehow inflated my productivity. Others acknowledged the quantity of published research, but suggested that my work lacked empirical rigor or was disjointed.

Scholarship, teaching, and service are all given attention in the promotion and tenure process. Yet senior faculty often attempt to amass evidence of negligence or deficiency to justify devaluing a Black woman's work by *cherry-picking* within each category to identify the smallest of weaknesses. For instance, senior colleagues have argued that I do not have as many graduate students as my peers and am therefore not carrying my fair share of service. Likewise, student evaluations of teaching are often scrutinized, as the presumption is that the Black woman must be neglecting some of her commitments if she outperforms her White colleagues. We experienced these patterns of bias before we had children, but they have become more acute now that we are mothers. The only difference is that colleagues now highlight our responsibilities as mother-scholars to explain our presumed academic inadequacy. Based on our experiences, we contend that Black mother-scholars are at an increased risk for negative tenure decisions. Given this reality, we provide the following recommendations for Black mother-scholars seeking promotion and tenure.

RECOMMENDATIONS

The realities for Black mother-scholars are unique. Therefore, it is essential that their experiences and needs be given full consideration during the probationary period and the tenure and promotion process. To counteract the presumption of incompetence, we provide the following recommendations for Black mother-scholars, their academic peers, and administrators.

1. *Every day should be a writing day.* Most scholars suggest that untenured faculty should set aside at least one day each week to scholarship. This may not be enough for scholars who face racism and sexism in the academy. Therefore, we suggest that to achieve a consistent work-family balance and excel professionally, at least some part of each day must be devoted to scholarship-related tasks.
2. *Mentorship is essential to the success of Black mother-scholars.* Black mother-scholars must receive mentorship from tenured Black mother-scholars, even if these mentors are outside of their institution or discipline. These relationships should be honored, respected, and supported by senior faculty and administrators. Social media can facilitate these interactions, but face-to-face meetings are invaluable.
3. *Departmental and college accountability training for reviewing the tenure materials of early career scholars with children must be implemented.* Because all review processes are subjective, training and accountability measures are necessary to help minimize the ill effects of bias on the probability of promotion and tenure. As noted earlier, many of the mechanisms designed to support mother-scholars can place them at risk for negative tenure decisions. Through training and accountability, biased perceptions that often jeopardize the careers of mother-scholars can be identified and mitigated.

CONCLUSION

The presumption of incompetence is a problem for faculty across many unique circumstances and disciplines. Here we examined the structures and mechanisms that reinforce this presumption against Black mother-scholars. We hope that the information provided in this chapter will be useful to Black mother-scholars, their peers, and administrators. Additionally, we hope that this chapter helps to foster further discussion regarding the unique challenges at the intersection of race, gender, and pregnancy during the tenure and promotion process.

REFERENCES

Acker, S., Webber, M., & Smyth, E. (2016). Continuity or change? Gender, family, and academic work for junior faculty in Ontario universities. *NASPA Journal about Women in Higher Education*, 9(1), 1–20.

Allen, W. R., Epps, E. G., Guillory, E. A., Suh, S. A. & Bonous-Hammarth, M. (2000). The black academic: Faculty status among African Americans in US higher education. *Journal of Negro Education*, 69(1–2), 112–127.

Baker, K. (2014). Are children career killers? *Chronicle Vitae*. Retrieved from https://chroniclevitae.com/news/569-are-children-career-killers.

Blackwell, J. E. (1988). Faculty issues: The impact on minorities. *Review of Higher Education*, 11(4), 417–434.

Manchester, C. F., Leslie, L. M., & Kramer, A. (2010). Stop the clock policies and career success in academia. *American Economic Review*, *100*(2), 219–223.
Mason, M. A., Wolfinger, N. H., & Goulden, M. (2013). *Do babies matter? Gender and family in the ivory tower*. New Brunswick, NJ: Rutgers University Press.
Mirick, R. G., & Wladkowski, S. P. (2018). Pregnancy, motherhood, and academic career goals: Doctoral students' perspectives. *Affilia*, *33*(2), 253–269.
Moos, M. K., Dunlop, A. L., Jack, B. W., Nelson, L., Coonrod, D. V., Long, R., et al. (2008). Healthier women, healthier reproductive outcomes: Recommendations for the routine care of all women of reproductive age. *American Journal of Obstetrics & Gynecology*, *199*(6), S280–S289.
Schuster, J. H., & Finkelstein, M. J. (2006). *The American faculty: The restructuring of academic work and careers*. Baltimore, MD: Johns Hopkins University Press.
Turner, C. S. V., González, J. C., & Wood, J. L. (2008). Faculty of color in academe: What 20 years of literature tells us. *Journal of Diversity in Higher Education, 1*(3), 139–168.

SECTION TWO

ACADEMIC LEADERSHIP

EIGHT

Senior Chicana Feminist Scholars

Some Notes on Survival in Hostile Contexts

Donna Castañeda, Yvette G. Flores, and Yolanda Flores Niemann

We, the three authors of this chapter, are psychologists of diverse backgrounds. Collectively we represent more than seventy years as faculty members and administrators in public universities. In this essay we briefly discuss our paths to full professor and administration, focusing on two major themes from our experiences: (1) how we are seen and not seen; and (2) maintaining positive and hopeful perspectives, in spite of often challenging and hurtful situations. The theoretical approach that informs our work is the intersection between Chicana feminist theory and Latina/o critical race (LatCrit) theory. Chicana feminist theory and practice emphasizes overcoming sexist oppressions, including legacies and remnants of historical power, with a focus on intersections of gender, race, and social class (Cuadraz, 2005; Garcia, 1997). Like Chicana feminists, LatCrit theorists believe that structural and institutionalized racism persists as a function of the routines, policies, and practices that keep members of historically underrepresented groups in subordinate positions, and that the social construction of race is central to how People of Color are constrained in society (Delgado & Stefancic, 2012; Trucios-Haynes, 2000). Following are some of our experiences through these lenses.

CHICANAS IN UPPER ADMINISTRATION—YOLANDA FLORES NIEMANN

I am a cisgender, heterosexual Tejana whose family has lived under all six flags that have flown over Texas, who grew up in economic poverty, and who was the first in her immediate family to be formally educated beyond seventh grade. In the sixteen of the twenty-six years since obtaining my PhD that I served in formal administration positions, the road has been perilous, heartbreaking, validating, and fulfilling.

DOI: 10.7330/9781607329664.c008

My first assistant professor position was in a hostile workplace (see Niemann, 1999) in which I was the only Person of Color the year I was hired in this moderately large department, and where the White senior male faculty saw me as an affirmative action hire forced upon them. I left after four years, with a mission to effect change toward social justice in higher education, which meant that I needed to become a full professor and administrator. I entered administration by way of faculty service in my second position at a predominantly White Research I university. I was one of the few Women of Color faculty, so leaders who wanted a "diverse perspective" got a "two-fer"—a woman and a Person of Color—by appointing me to committees at every university level. I soon learned that what they wanted was my ethnic identity, not my Chicana perspective. I consistently completed never-ending service and teaching during the day, while grading, conducting research, writing grants, preparing teaching materials, and producing scholarship in the evenings and weekends, often after my husband and children went to bed. With successes resulting from that schedule, I earned tenure and promotion to associate professor.

About that time the Latinx faculty and staff association, which I had helped develop, persuaded the university president to create administrative internships to help us prepare for leadership positions in academia. Thanks to the group's nomination, the week I got my tenure and promotion letter, the provost offered me my first formal administrative position as special assistant to the provost. He asked me to examine faculty morale and underlying reasons for low numbers of Latinx students. Based on my findings, I recommended that the president develop a position for director of outreach. He approved my plan and asked me to step into that new role. I agreed, even though it required moving to the branch campus situated in a Latinx community. In part to increase the university's low numbers of Latinx students, I constructed and obtained my first major federal outreach grant, for $14 million. The work I accomplished in that position led to future Latinx degree programs and collaborations with the local community. My next position was chair of the Department of Comparative Ethnic Studies when, after two failed national searches, my faculty colleagues nominated me for that role. I was concerned because, according to university guidelines, I was still two years away from going up for full professor. It is almost impossible to produce scholarship while serving in these demanding roles. The dean reviewed my CV and reassured me that I could go up early, during my first year as chair. However, that following year the college promotion committee refused to consider my file, insisting that I adhere to the conventional promotion timeline. I then obtained another $12 million federal outreach grant. In my second year as chair, the large grants and the journal articles I had published before becoming chair earned my promotion to full professor.

At that point I took the initiative to meet with the president, who had complimented what he called my courageous leadership, and asked for his guidance to obtain upper-level administrative positions. He nominated me for the prestigious American Council on Education (ACE) Fellowship. In that role I shadowed the president of Penn State University for one year, gaining access to various divisions, leaders, and reports of the university, as well as to information gleaned from being a fly on the wall in his meetings.

After this role I obtained a dean position, overseeing the largest college at another predominantly White institution (PWI) and Research I university. Not only was I the only Person of Color in the administration, I was an individual who had been raised Catholic working in a predominantly Mormon university and community. I was an outsider whose appointment coincided with the national economic crisis of 2008. Deans were ordered to cut budgets; my share was $1 million, in addition to resolving $1 million college deficit that I inherited. I successfully saw my college through the financial crisis, accomplishing the enormous feat of maintaining all of our academic programs and protecting tenure-track faculty, though I had to let some popular lecturers go. Some faculty rebelled, refusing to believe that I had no choice in making the cuts, even though I was completely transparent with all budgeting documents. They accused me of behavior I did not recognize. The unpopular upline administrator who hired me (and who, coincidently, had previously received a vote of no confidence from the Faculty Senate) did not back me up. He thanked me for my effectiveness during the crisis, asked me to leave the deanship immediately, and offered me a vice provost position. I felt coerced into doing as he asked.

After almost a year as vice provost, I received a stellar performance review in that role. However, carefully selecting my words to say nothing negative about the senior upline administrator, I supported the all-White faculty diversity committee in a meeting when the upline administrator started relentlessly berating them. Immediately after the meeting the upline administrator asked me to step back into the psychology faculty, saying he could no longer trust me to be loyal to him. I was quite devastated at the unjust turn of events. As word got out about how the upline administrator had treated the committee (and me), the president announced there would be a new Women's Center to address university diversity needs. I did not benefit from that decision.

Although the psychology department faculty were welcoming, I still had administrative aspirations, thinking I might achieve the most change if I could become president of a Research I university. A year later, I accepted a position as the first senior vice provost at another PWI. Once again I was the only senior Person of Color from academic affairs in the offices of the president or provost. Again, I had the bad luck of entering a role when the university had a financial crisis, a fact I was not informed about during my interview, though I had asked multiple questions about the university's financial state. That situation meant that I had to help the university cut the budget, which is never popular with faculty or staff. Nevertheless, in my first year, I led the implementation of changes that increased freshman enrollment by 3 percent and hugely improved our budget; addressed revision of academic affairs policies that were out of compliance with accreditors; empowered associate deans to effect needed changes in their units such that they would more efficiently serve students and improve service to faculty and students; encouraged deans to address hiring of Faculty of Color; provided a safe space in my home for the female, Latinx, and Black faculty to meet; and helped the Latinx faculty develop a Latinx studies program. Because women streamed through my office with grievances about a hostile climate, I compiled data that validated their claims, demonstrating gender and race/ethnicity salary, hiring, and retention inequities. These successes were challenging but invigorating, as they were in line with my mission to effect change toward social justice. In general, I felt as if I was filling in for the provost, who traveled to Mexico frequently and spent much time in his research lab. However, I functioned as provost without the formal position, power, and authority of that role, which left me out on a precarious limb.

In my second year as senior vice provost the university hired a new president who, after a year in office, fired the provost. Although most persons who worked with me expected the president to appoint me provost, even congratulating me on my upcoming promotion, instead, a month after firing my boss, the president asked me to step back onto the faculty. He thanked me for my significant accomplishments, but told me that there were some complaints that I only cared about People of Color. He said that reputation made me "scorched, but not burnt earth," but that I would have other administrative opportunities for which he would nominate me. I asked him how he justified my firing to search committees to which he was nominating me. He replied that he told people that he had fired the provost and that I was "collateral damage."

Overarching Lessons

The excess university service helped me hone administrative skills and gave me insight into university functions and decision-making that underlie changes in system practices but are not typically transparent to faculty. For those who aspire to formal administrative roles, please keep in mind the following:

- Accepting formal administrative roles before earning full-professor rank is perilous to your career and your ability to lead change at high levels.
- Be assertive in pursuit of administrative roles.
- A network of colleagues who actively support and promote you is key to obtaining administrative positions.
- Being mobile makes it more likely that you will receive an upper-level administrative position.
- Keeping the administrative role can be at least as challenging as obtaining it, not because we are not effective leaders, but because the changes we lead are threatening to the powerful status quo.
- Without our perspectives at the table, it is likely that the status quo will not be challenged.
- Upper-level administrators are expected to protect the university brand, not the individual. This clash of Chicana values and university role expectations makes it challenging to maintain personal integrity.
- Our Chicana values and voice enable others to unfairly peg us with the notion that we only care about diversity-related matters.

- Administrators work at the will of their supervisors and can be removed without cause (for precepts of Chicana leadership, see Niemann, 2016), so plan on living on a salary considerably closer to faculty than to administration to prevent panic and concern for your family's economic well-being resulting from a lowered salary.
- Upper-level administrative work is 24/7, so plan accordingly.

It was painful to be unjustly removed from administrative positions in which I was totally invested and had achieved excellent outcomes for the university. What kept me going was believing that I was making a difference in matters of equity and justice—for faculty, staff, and students. As of this writing, I do not know if I have another administrative role in me. I am enjoying the opportunity to be a change agent as a full professor through my writing, teaching, scholarship, and mentoring—sharing lessons learned from administrative experience and preparing the next generation of formal leaders.

TENURE AND BEYOND FOR LATINAS IN THE ACADEMY—DONNA CASTAÑEDA

I am originally from Texas, the daughter of a third-generation Mexican American father and Canadian-born mother, and the first in my family to receive a college education. As the second child in a military family of seven children that lived in many places, including two foreign countries (Germany and Panama), crossing boundaries of culture, class, language, ethnicity, and geography was an everyday experience for me. Maybe it was from this experience that, while I do not have a family history of higher education and never had models of anyone, female or male, who was an academic, I developed the idea that obtaining a PhD was possible for me.

Nonetheless, the journey to this point was not an easy one. To be honest, this is the first opportunity I have taken to reflect deeply on this journey. Up to now, I spent many years just working to do what I believed was necessary to reach the designated benchmarks, which were also my personal goals—getting into a graduate program, securing a tenure-track job, attaining tenure, getting promoted, and being appointed as associate dean. At this point, however, I realize that although professional advancement has brought me a measure of legitimacy and status in the academic context, at the same time, old challenges do not disappear and new ones have emerged.

Biased Perceptions Do Not End

The idea that Latinas at the senior academic level have nothing more to say about marginalization, denigration, or unfair sexist and racist expectations applied to them is not true. For example, at my university, job evaluations continue for professors at the senior level and, in order to receive resources, such as lab space and release time, I must continue to publish, make conference presentations, and engage in student research mentoring. I engage in these activities because they are intrinsic components of my work, but promotion to professor has never ended the fact that I continue to face biased perceptions of my scholarly work in my department, institution, and the top journals in the field. This is particularly the case if one's work focuses on People of Color and integrates feminist, intersectional, and critical race perspectives and meanings.

Moreover, hurtful microaggressions (or macroaggressions, I would say!) do not end at promotion, or even after moving into administration. For instance, I was recently told by my psychology department chairperson that the work I do is not important and that my small satellite campus, located within blocks of the US-Mexican border, produces no academic programs or research of value. I do not know what prompted this disturbing revelation, but as I was driving home I had the sensation of having to psychically put myself back together.

Increased Workloads

For tenured Latina professors, workloads may actually increase. With promotion to professor I have been implicitly and explicitly expected to take on greater committee and service demands, course teaching loads, and student mentoring tasks. One small example, out of many, is that I have acted as the faculty advisor for the undergraduate psychology club at my small campus for seventeen or eighteen years. I would like to turn this position over to newer faculty, but they understandably feel compelled to focus on their research and publications to advance in the tenure process.

A common piece of advice I receive when I mention my feelings of being overburdened with service, teaching, and nonresearch work is that I should just say no. This advice implies that if I feel unfairly burdened by such work, I am somehow at fault for not being sufficiently assertive in declining it. Such advice ignores the hierarchical nature of the university. For Latinas, the ability to say no is not necessarily an aspect of one's individual assertiveness; rather, it is a reflection of the institutional power relations in which Latinas are embedded and within which they must operate to survive. For example, I was personally asked a few years ago by the provost at my university to chair a dean search committee for the second year in a row, due to a failed search the first year. While this work is, of course, voluntary, the disparity in my status compared to the provost's meant that declining this burdensome task did not seem an option to me at the time.

Mentoring

After Latinas receive promotion to professor, some may falsely believe that they no longer need mentoring, but this is not the case. On the other hand, traditional mentoring models, where an individual in the early stages of her career is partnered with a more senior colleague, are not particularly useful to Latina senior faculty. Alternative mentoring models that may be most appropriate for senior Latina faculty include more fluid and cross-hierarchical relationships, such as peer mentoring, collaborative relationships with other Latinas at the same or different levels, and linkages between Latina faculty and administrators. Unfortunately, I have seen little institutional emphasis on these or any other types of mentoring strategies that focus on the needs of Latina professors at the senior level.

Although I have encountered many helpful people throughout my career, the most useful continue to be my peers and other Latinas and allies facing the same demands and concerns that I do. I basically create my own mentoring models. For example, when I needed letters of support for the tenure process, for appointment to important professional committees, or to achieve fellow status in a prestigious professional association, I turned to a network of women I developed on my own. Most of these Latinas helped me tremendously. And I, in turn, help them.

Ageism

Although the topic is almost never discussed, a new challenge that has emerged for me at this stage of my career is ageism. I am taken aback at new, subtle, but definite messages I have received from certain colleagues about how my age makes me less knowledgeable about my field and less useful as a mentor to students. I am experienced, knowledgeable, and wise, yet my age, combined with other dimensions of my identity, is used to discount me and make my contributions invisible. Instead of viewing me and women like me as repositories of skill, knowledge, and institutional memory, others often perceive us as having a lesser ability to make continuing contributions to our departments, universities, and the profession.

What Has Helped Me in My Journey

Despite the difficulty of this career journey, I feel free of bitterness. Why? First, love of my discipline and profession has been fundamental to reaching this stage in my career. I remember sitting in my first social psychology class as an undergraduate, listening to the professor, and thinking, "This is what I want to study." I vowed to continue to work in this field. Where I am today is a result of that promise to myself, as well as the joy and satisfaction I continue to find in my work. For example, I love playing a small part in the lives of so many Latinx students I see graduate each year and I hope I will always be able to support their ambition to succeed. There is nothing more fulfilling.

I have also successfully sought information, help, and mini-mentoring at every stage of my career from many people, which has been an essential survival strategy over the years. While I have never had a mentor in the traditional sense, my peers, trusted colleagues, friends, and family have been instrumental in providing the support I needed to advance in my career.

I have also been fortunate to have spent the largest portion of my career as a faculty member at a small branch campus of a larger university with over 80 percent Latinx student population. But in the beginning, I viewed the situation differently, believing I was in the same pattern in academic psychology I saw so often, where Latinas and Women of Color were hired only in nonpsychology departments, such as public health, social work, and ethnic studies. I would fret that I was located on the sidelines of the true center of academic psychology, and many times I planned to leave for what I considered "real" psychology departments. With time, however, I realized that being at the margins provides a space where Women of Color may actually survive and thrive, and it is from within these "inter-faces" (Anzaldúa, 1990, p. xv) that some of the most creative and thought-provoking scholarly work comes. As a person from a mixed and varied background, I found a place in which I fit—and it is from within this space, sidelined as it is, with its mixed blessings, that I could plot my trajectory and achieve my goals.

PEDAGOGY FROM THE MARGINS—YVETTE G. FLORES

I am a first-generation, immigrant, heterosexual female who never imagined becoming a full professor at a University of California (UC) campus. When asked to reflect on what it took to become a full professor, I responded, "*Ganas*, tenacity, thick skin, mentorship, and commitment." As I contemplate retirement after twenty-eight years at a UC campus, I offer a brief reflection on how I got "there" and what helped me thrive despite presumed incompetence by colleagues and administrators.

I chose psychology as a field of study while in high school. When an African American psychologist explained to me what psychologists did, I saw the possibility that a science focused on the well-being of people, even immigrants like my parents and me, was a good career choice.

Mentors

Throughout my academic journey from K-12 through the baccalaureate, I found teachers who believed in my abilities and helped me see that I could succeed. I did not know the term *mentoring* at the time, but their interest, guidance, and encouragement put me on the college path. My working-class parents, who migrated to the United States to afford me greater opportunities, were the first to support my aspirations. My mother, an elementary school teacher in her native Panama, encouraged me because she valued education. My father supported me financially because poverty had thwarted his academic dreams.

While a graduate student, I sought the guidance of faculty in the Chicano studies department, as the mostly White psychology faculty had limited knowledge of, or expertise and interest in, the work I wanted to do. Minimal mentoring helped me stay on track. I quickly learned that there are different types of mentors, and both students and faculty must find a supportive team that will provide them with important sources of information, navigational capital, and networking contacts.

I did not have a plan or even imagine that someone of my class, gender, and national origin could ever teach at a University of California campus, even though I had a PhD from UC–Berkeley. It was during my pre- and postdoctoral years at UC–San Francisco that two Latino psychologists encouraged me to apply for an assistant professor position at a professional school of psychology.

Tenacity and Thick Skin

Academic psychology was too often a hostile environment where I encountered daily doses of microaggressions, from comments about how well I spoke and wrote in English to comments about my exotic looks that were not "typically Mexican." My commitment to mentoring Students of Color and focusing on the mental health needs of diverse groups was seen as unimportant and "not central to the discipline of psychology." I was invisible to the administration, unless struggling Students of Color needed a mentor or dissertation chair. When I was falsely accused of leaking information from a contested faculty meeting, my physical and mental health began to suffer. Despite my apprehensions, rooted in my working-class origins, about the wisdom of quitting a job that provided financial security, I left a professional school of psychology and accepted a position at UC–Davis in Chicana and Chicano studies.

I had lectured in a Chicano studies department previously, where my psychology background was viewed as problematic, given the racist history of the field. Nonetheless, the chair of the search committee convinced me that the university's program had a gender focus and was committed to supporting my research on Latinx mental health. I joined the faculty and developed a health and mental health curriculum that remains very popular with students. My pedagogy and research were rooted in an intersectional understanding of Latinx utilizing Western psychological theories, mestizo psychology (Ramirez, 1998), and Chicana feminist theories (Flores, 2012; Flores-Ortiz, 1997).

Ganas

I was fully cognizant that the road to tenure might be difficult, as I would be judged not as a Chicana/o studies scholar but as a psychologist. In a campus that privileges the hard sciences, the interdisciplinary nature of my work might not be understood and valued. My senior colleagues, all Latinx, advocated for me, and explained, when needed, the nature and importance of my published work, and I was granted tenure. Shortly thereafter I became director of the Chicana and Chicano studies program, which is typically marginalized within academic institutions. My colleagues and I have fought arduously with administrators and review committees for over four decades to change the perception that we are a service rather than an academic unit, and to demonstrate that our scholarship merits advancement. When it comes to seeking spokespersons or representatives of the Latinx community regarding academic matters, administrators routinely ask faculty not in our department for input. However, when

Latinx students protest about any issue that affects them, our chair is told to get our students in check.

Like so many other Women of Color, I assumed excessive service workloads too early in my career, which resulted in a longer time to full professorship. I directed our program through a difficult college reorganization while serving on countless committees, chairing dissertations from professional schools, teaching on our campus and abroad, and eventually taking on the directorship of our quarter abroad program, at a time of financial crisis in our state that adversely impacted the funding of public education. Yet I remained largely invisible to higher administration.

I was promoted to full professor largely due to the excellent extramural letters that served to contextualize my work, and its relevance, to multiple disciplines. As a full professor, I joined and chaired important personnel committees, wherein I finally began to understand how merits and advancements are negotiated. Having gained "insider information," I began to mentor junior colleagues regarding advancement and work/life balance.

I never expected to break the glass ceiling at my institution. However, over the past six years, largely due to engaged support from a more senior Chicana scholar, I have become part of two highly important extramural grants that have increased my visibility within and outside the campus. Through these projects, I have been able to utilize my intellectual and clinical skills, as well as my passion, to promote the needs of Chicanx and Latinx in and outside the academy.[1]

In the fall of 2015, I was eligible to apply for professor step 6 (considered the glass ceiling on my campus) and submitted my packet with the support of my colleagues in the department and the dean of our college, who voted that I should receive an additional half step due to my record of teaching and service.[2] However, the vice provost of academic affairs, a White woman scientist, decided I should receive a two-step acceleration because she judged my scholarly work, rooted in community-based participatory research and intersectional approaches, as critical to the fields of psychology and Chicana/o studies, and as representative of the future of the academy. I felt vindicated at last. After twenty-six years on the campus, higher administration had recognized the importance of the scholarship created by a Latina faculty in a nontraditional department.

The road to full professorship for interdisciplinary scholars can be arduous because review committees often do not understand the nature or relevance of

1. These projects are a USDA-funded project to address overweight issues among Chicana/o children (de la Torre et al., 2013) and an NSF institutional transformation grant to increase the numbers of Latinas in STEM (Katehi, de la Torre, Rodriguez, Stanton, & McDonald, 2012).
2. The UC–Davis campus has nine steps within the full-professor series. Step 10 is a designation of Distinguished Professor. Our campus recently implemented the Step Plus system to recognize faculty who have outstanding records of teaching and service, or whose scholarly record exceeds what is expected of the rank (Higher Education Recruitment Consortium, 2016).

our work and because we often carry heavy service burdens. Lack of advancement often precludes Latinas from reaching and breaking through the glass ceiling and obtaining leadership roles.

After my promotion to full professor, I applied to various administrative positions on our campus, but was not selected. A provost noted that while my work was stellar, the selection committee felt I would be more suited to a student affairs position rather than an academic one. In the next breath, he asked my opinion on who might be a good interim dean for our division. In this instance, as in many others, I had to swallow the indignity of the situation. As female scholars, we tend to be viewed as laborers, not scholars with leadership potential. Ironically, our positionality as marginalized women often gives us a broader and deeper view of what the campus needs to do to promote success and excellence among faculty and students. Yet conscious and unconscious bias often prevents those in leadership roles from seeing our potential and inviting our contributions. Still we go on, fighting against bitterness and disillusionment, by strengthening our resilience with the help of our *familias*, networks of support, and healers, and because of our commitment to mentor the next generation.

CONCLUSION

One of the most critical aspects of thriving in academia is to remember that, in spite of all the challenges, professors and administrators hold privileged roles in our society. They are roles that afford some independence and unlimited opportunities to grow, to effect structural change, and to mentor people from multiple generations and ranks. It is that mentorship and the small individual and structural wins that keep us going.

REFERENCES

Anzaldúa, G. (1990). Haciendo caras, una entrada: An introduction by Gloria Anzaldúa. In G. Anzaldúa (Ed.), *Making face, making soul: Haciendo caras: Creative and critical perspectives of feminists of color* (p. xv). San Francisco: Aunt Lute Books.

Cuadraz, G. H. (2005). Chicanas and higher education: Three decades of literature and thought. *Journal of Hispanic Higher Education*, 4(3), 215–234.

de la Torre, A., Sadeghi, B., Green, D. R., Kaiser, L. L., Flores, G. Y., Jackson, F. C., et al. (2013). Niños Sanos, Familia Sana: Mexican immigrant study protocol for a multifaceted CBPR intervention to combat childhood obesity in two rural California towns. *BMC Public Health*, 13, Article 1033.

Delgado, R., and Stefancic, J. (2012). *Critical race theory* (2nd ed.). New York: New York University Press.

Flores, Y. (2012). How many Latinas does it take? Reflections of 30 years of life in the academy. In H. Curtis-Boles, D. M. Adams, & V. Jenkins-Monroe (Eds.), *Making our voices heard: Women of color in academia* (pp. 145–153). Hauppauge, NY: Nova Science.

Flores-Ortiz, Y. (1997). Voices from the couch: The co-construction of a Chicana psychology. In C. Trujillo (Ed.), *Living Chicana theory* (pp. 102–122). Berkeley: Third Woman.

Garcia, A. M. (1997). *Chicana feminist thought: The basic historical writings*. New York: Routledge.

Higher Education Recruitment Consortium. (2016). Academic Senate: Step Plus System. Davis: University of California. Retrieved from http://academicaffairs.ucdavis.edu/.

Katehi, L., de la Torre, A., Rodriguez, R., Stanton, M., & McDonald, K. (2012). UC Davis ADVANCE Institutional Transformation Grant. NSF Funded 2012–2016.

Niemann, Y. F. (1999). The making of a token: A case study of stereotype threat and racism in Academe. *Frontiers: A Journal of Women Studies, 20*(1), 111–135.

Niemann, Y. F. (2016). The social ecology of tokenism in higher education institutions. *Peace Review: A Journal of Social Justice, 28*(4), 451–458.

Ramirez, M., III. (1998). *Multiracial/multicultural psychology: Mestizo perspectives in personality and mental health*. Lanham, MD: Rowman & Littlefield.

Trucios-Haynes, E. (2000). Why "race matters": Latino critical theory and Latina/o racial identity. *La Raza Law Journal, 12*(1), 1–43.

NINE

Can I Charge My Therapy to the University?

Jodi O'Brien

Being included can be a lesson in "being not" as much as "being in."
(AHMED, 2012, P. 163)

There is difference and there is power; and who holds the power decides the meaning of the difference.
(JORDAN, 1994, P. 197)

Conocimiento es otro mode de conectar across colors and other differences to allies also trying to negotiate contradictions, survive the stresses and traumas of daily life, and develop a spiritual-imaginal-political vision together.
(ANZALDÚA & KEATING, 2002, P. 571)

In a voiced community, we all flourish.
(WILLIAMS, 2012, P. 129)

In May 2010, I became a household name in Milwaukee, Wisconsin. The occasion for this midwestern notoriety was my dismissal as the recently hired dean of arts and sciences at Marquette University, a Jesuit Catholic university, on the grounds that my scholarship was "anti-Catholic." I am a lesbian feminist sociologist and my qualifications at the time included sixteen years as a faculty member at another Jesuit university where I had held several faculty administrative positions and was teaching and conducting research on the social psychology of prejudice and discrimination, with an emphasis on gender, race, sexuality, and religion. I have been openly queer throughout my career in academe. With full knowledge of these facts, a well-established professional search firm working on behalf of Marquette pursued me for two years, courting me for the position.

DOI: 10.7330/9781607329664.c009

When they rushed to shortlist me for the position in the first year, I withdrew on the grounds that I couldn't, in good conscience, continue the process knowing that I would likely decline an offer. But they persisted. Apparently, the university had identified me as a potential "diversity dean"—someone capable of building bridges between the university and the diverse groups and communities in the region. Additionally, my deep familiarity with Jesuit higher education gave me the added edge of being a "mission" candidate.

Despite considerable hesitation on my part, when I finally agreed to visit the campus I was moved by the collective embrace I experienced. Students, staff, faculty, administrators, and community members welcomed me with open arms and assured me that I was the one they were looking for to help them write Marquette's next chapter. I was eventually persuaded to take the position and I signed the contract. While preparing to move from Seattle to Wisconsin, I received an unanticipated and bewildering phone call from the Marquette University president informing me that the dean's position had been "revoked." His explanation was muddled and confusing, but the gist was that a small but influential group consisting of a regional archbishop and some longtime donors didn't want me at Marquette and they had prevailed in their efforts to have my contract cancelled. The university community reacted to the news of my "non-hire" with wide-scale protest. The eruption of dissent was chronicled in the *New York Times* and the *Chronicle of Higher Education* as well as local and regional news outlets (O'Brien, 2012).

Although the event was deeply unsettling for me and upsetting to friends and family, in subsequent public talks I stressed that the Marquette debacle was not so much about injury to me as it was a betrayal of a community that had followed every procedure to the letter in finding and hiring the dean *they* had chosen. Yet, when my candidacy became problematic, the president simply overturned this collective process. My illegal and unceremonious unhiring at Marquette drew such a large reaction, in part, because it was a lightning rod for all the pent-up energy that crackles just below the surface in institutions that make strenuous claims of diversity and inclusion, only to betray these commitments and turn to a politics of containment when these commitments encounter pushback from the established status quo. This story resonated so broadly precisely because so many people have experienced some version of it themselves or among members of their own communities—a welcoming invitation of inclusion followed by a dis-invitation when you turn out not to be the correct subject—too queer, too ethnic, too angry, too feminist, too "not one of us." The upshot is a chilling reminder of the "just us" justice of institutional logic.

After a protracted but ultimately victorious legal battle focused on requiring Marquette University to be accountable to its community through financial and symbolic reparations, I returned to my faculty position at Seattle University. I was battle-weary, but also more clear-headed about the tensions and contradictions inherent in institutional logics of diversity and inclusion. This event was a watershed moment for me, an experience that has shaped much of my subsequent thinking and action as a faculty administrator engaged in social justice work within the constraints of a university. In the ensuing nine years, I've held many additional faculty administrative positions, including several years as the chair of the university tenure and promotion committee, an endowed chair in gender and diversity studies, and as the director of a National Science Foundation–funded program for advancing women and minoritized faculty. What I've come to know is that this work is fraught with tensions, contradictions, and paradoxes, all of which turn on the incompatibilities between communities of liberation and institutionalized diversity programs. The politics of institutional belonging is obstinately exclusionary for all but the "correct" subjects, and while the definition of "correct subject" may shift to incorporate broader social categories (for instance, women and People of Color, once actively prohibited from a place in higher education, are now formally recruited), belonging is still contingent on "fitting in" with institutional practices rooted in discriminatory histories.

This is a far cry from liberatory action in which the aim is to be set free from institutionalized systems of oppression. One of the great tensions of contemporary higher education is that this is a site where so many of us have encountered transformative knowledges, ideas in which we have found voice and a promise of liberation, only to find ourselves reensnared by institutional logics. Despite a public rhetoric of higher education as "too liberal," academe continues to be one of the most colonized, patriarchal, elitist, racist, and homophobic institutions in contemporary society. Can we transform it? In my own work, I vacillate continually between energetic optimism and anguished disillusionment. Are we really making a difference, or just aiding the institution in the neoliberal business of diversity as branding: achieving demographic diversity, generating diversity information, and checking boxes? Am I a savvy trickster helping to destabilize entrenched systems and breaking paths to new paradigms, or a naive fool being played as an institutional pawn? Many days it feels like both. In wrestling with these incongruities and my own complicity, I turn often to Gloria Anzaldúa's instructive method of auto-historia. She counsels us to go deeper into the complexities—the messiness and pain—of this experience to move toward a more informed consciousness from which we are able to shift from the inside out. This always-shifting-self paradigm is what I bring to this work and the perspective from which I attempt to write new scripts, or terms of engagement. I share some of these reflections in this chapter.

WHAT ARE WE DOING WITH DIVERSITY WORK AND WHAT IS IT DOING TO US?

In her timely and inspired book, *On Being Included*, critical race scholar Sarah Ahmed implores us to keep asking what we are doing with diversity work and what it is doing to us (2012, p. 17). For her, "inclusion could be read as a technology of governance," a way of bringing strangers into the nation and making them into subjects whose citizenship is conditional on consenting to the terms of inclusion (p. 163). These terms are defined by those in authority and reflect institutional "narratives of repair" and a "conditional hospitality" whereby the institution is host and we diversity subjects behave as appreciative guests who show our gratitude by putting our injuries behind us and accepting the logic that, through its equality regimes, the institution has repaired systems of oppression (pp. 43, 168). Rather than transforming institutions, the logic of diversity work too often requires individuals to transform themselves to fit the rhetoric of repair and hospitality, to serve as correct subjects whose presence and involvement indicate that the institution is, indeed, doing its part to undo oppression by incorporating us.

This question of what diversity work is doing to us resonates deeply for me. To paraphrase sociologist Dorothy Smith (2005), how do we track our own lives within the inequality regimes that characterize universities, especially as faculty administrators intent on transforming institutional agendas that were not established with us in mind? This work requires us to navigate multiple contradictory spaces, logics, and rhetorics, to be nimble, innovative bridgers. How do I locate myself in this? Patricia Hill Collins calls this work a form of intellectual-administrative activism undertaken by the "outsider-within"—the person within an institutional context whose location on the edge provides necessary alternative perspectives for institutional reorientation. In her words: "Speaking the truth to power in ways that undermine and challenge that power can often best be done as an insider . . . Challenging power structures from the inside working the cracks within the system, however, requires learning to speak multiple languages of power convincingly" (2012, p. xiii). These words serve as my compass in navigating inequality regimes. In particular, I aim to remove hurdles and open gates to welcome a wider range of voices and perspectives to academe *without* requiring those expressing them to eclipse or cleave off huge chunks of themselves in order to "fit." Doing this has required me not only to learn multiple languages—the languages of budgets, administration, fundraising, grant-writing, and general institutional bureaucratese—but to translate these languages across different groups (e.g., explaining to department hiring committees why selecting candidates only from elite universities necessarily limits the likelihood of diversity hiring, or effectively teaching tenure and promotion review committees how to identify systematic racism and sexism in student evaluation comments, or helping a dean to understand how a Woman of Color's fear and anger in her department reflects institutional patterns of injustice, not emotional imbalance on her part). I'm grateful for these skills of institutional multilinguality and have honed them studiously and intentionally. But in the constant navigation through and across these varied domains, I often lose myself.

Recently, I suggested to my therapist that I may be "overidentified" with my professional work. Even as I uttered these words, I felt tremendous anger at taking precious therapy time to talk about work (and I fantasized about sending the bill to the university). But the fact of the matter is, I need help managing an unhealthy amount of time in the shower spent puzzling over and anguishing about my work, specifically, about navigating the isolation and inbetweenness that increasingly plague me in my bridging position. While I like to think that I am robustly critically aware of the tensions of diversity work *on* institutions—we are both complicit with and agents for change in systems of institutional oppression—it's more challenging for me to admit the ways in which I may have become *of* the institution as a consequence of my deep engagement in working to change the institution. Minoritized faculty members drawn into administrative positions through a desire for institutional transformation typically face a choice of being dismissed as "too radical" or finding themselves becoming administrative allies who take on the perspective of authority, which is one of internalized dominance. Those of us trying to navigate these dynamics, to be strategic change-agents rather than co-opted instruments, experience tremendous isolation, self-doubt, and a constant struggle to find an effective voice—one that doesn't betray our deepest commitments. There is a constant sense of inbetweenness—of being viewed with suspicion and envy by supposed collegial friends (I've sold out and am just clamoring for power) combined with an awareness that one's worth in administrative circles is instrumental, never truly relational. The urge to simply walk away is always there, yet, at the same time, I feel "bound"—both committed and obligated to the possibilities of the work.

NEVER AT HOME

Anzaldúa suggests that the consciousness forged in the borderlands of the mestiza's experience is the wellspring of more complex, innovative thinking—a perspective that, again, may be valued in institutional diversity work, but typically in ways that are transactional: the mestiza never really belongs. Ahmed reports on the deep institutional ambivalence that diversity practitioners experience: we value the opportunity to engage in this work and find it satisfying in many ways, but we are also continually reminded through many everyday experiences that the institution does not represent us, is not our home, and requires us to adhere to unspoken but firmly entrenched rules for being *acceptably* different in order to maintain our place.

Expectations of relational engagement alongside unwritten codes for acceptance constitute an insidiously unstable terrain for minoritized faculty administrators doing diversity work, and this includes not only formal "diversity officers" but department chairs, deans, and other mid-level administrators. We may feel as if we're being invited to the table of power, and, to some extent, we have been. The lure of inclusion, especially in significant administrative processes, may temporarily blind us to the fact that, ultimately, we are operating from entirely different paradigms. The challenge is exacerbated by the fact that I work with many well-intentioned administrators who very much want to "get it." But that earnestness invokes even more tension as I seek to maintain my footing with those who often really don't get it, but with whom I must continue to diplomatically engage if I want to advance the work that matters to me. A question I ponder regularly is whether to step away from university administrative work and focus instead on community organizations, where I'm more at home.

This question came to the foreground in a recent dissertation defense conversation. Building on his superb book of oral histories on transgender intersectionalities

(*Trans/Portraits*, 2015), Jackson Shultz recently completed doctoral research on the institutional experiences of transgender and gender-nonconforming university administrators. His advisory committee included me and two other feminist scholars with long histories of university administration, including one as chief diversity officer. Jack was describing the relentless "emotional labor" required of the administrators whose stories he was chronicling (cf. Hochschild, 2012). Jack had synthesized this concept with the ideas of "covering" and "comforting," terms used by sociologist Erving Goffman to explain the interpersonal work required of people with "stigmatized" identities (1986). As Jack explained, trans administrators must constantly assess whether, when, and how to reveal their status in the workplace. In addition to the daunting daily dance of covering, they must also engage in constant "comforting"—everyday practices of putting others at ease in their presence. These practices, which include humor, educational commentaries, and efforts to highlight sameness, are exhausting.

As we talked further, the conversation turned to the fact that Women of Color and LGBTQ folk head the ranks of university administrators engaged in diversity work. But despite our significant presence in numbers, we feel routinely blocked in our work (Ahmed's brick wall), excluded from meaningful decision-making bodies, tokenized, and repeatedly "put in our place."

Add to all this the emotional labor of comforting and covering—well, it's a wonder we show up at all. Quoting Ahmed, Jack noted that the trans administrators he talked with frequently lamented that all we do as diversity practitioners is "make paper," or promote the "diversity as brand" efforts of the institution while simultaneously protecting it from litigation. Through our efforts, we generate extensive knowledge of institutions, but with very little likelihood of actual transformation. We three committee members nodded in solemn recognition as Jack articulated a common thread across the stories he'd gathered: administrative diversity work by minoritized faculty and staff requires exhaustive emotional labor that is draining, demoralizing, and often harmful to actual communities and personal well-being.

For Jackson, these interrogations come down to a sense of home. In the contemporary university, despite our attempts at inclusive curricula, practices, and policies, the prevailing terms of engagement—the everyday practices and languages—remain stubbornly grounded in a paradigm of power and control that is fundamentally at odds with the generative, collaborative engagement that is the wellspring of liberation. The paradox is that, even as we advance critical understandings of university inequality regimes, we become increasingly alienated through our own instrumentalization. Much of our confusion and anguish lies in the tension of recognizing the utility and possibilities of our work, while slamming up against continual reminders that this is not our home.

DIVERSITY EMBRACEMENT AND RELATIONAL ENGAGEMENT

My colleague Holly Ferraro studies diversity in organizational management and has introduced the idea of "diversity embracement" as a counter-practice to the instrumentalization of minoritized employee experience. She suggests, "The paradox of inclusive practices not leading to inclusive experiences led me to study diversity embracement which I define as the transformation of interpersonal situations (i.e., the 'small moments') and relational identities to allow people to interact across difference" (Ferraro, 2018). For Ferraro, a missing question in inclusion work is, inclusion in *what* or belonging to *what*? She asks, "To what does one belong or in what is one included?" Ferraro's framework can be powerfully applied to considerations of engagement. How do institutional dynamics tear us apart, and how can we come together in more sustained solidarity?

Diversity practitioners typically practice ongoing self-interrogation so as to not become reensnared by the institutional paradigms and the internalized dominance we hope to crack. Yet one of the most insidious aspects of mid-level university leadership is how our positions isolate us from—and even turn us against—one another. Dynamics of divide and conquer are common in institutional environments with hierarchical authority structures and cultures of competition. We have to be ever vigilant against these self-defeating divisions. For instance, how do I navigate having my integrity and motivation questioned as a result of a colleague, someone I thought a friend, throwing me under the bus in what feels like a maneuver to advance theirown agenda? During such moments (which are more frequent than I sometimes want to acknowledge), I strive to stay focused on the institutional logics that pit us against one another in the first place, the internalized dominance practiced by persons in positions of received, unexamined authority who resort to a parental script and treat us as if we are misbehaving children—fighting siblings in need of discipline and time out. This individualization of minoritized faculty as troublemakers who can't get along with one another and need to be contained reinforces lines of institutional authority and divides us even further. These are the occasions that most try my capacity to stay in solidarity with my colleagues, and yet this is also when it's most important to seek them out for honest discussion about what's really going on, to remember that staying aligned is our only way through these mechanics of containment and diminishment.

Another question Ferraro prompts is, in the midst of annihilating institutional mechanics, where and how are our voices heard, renewed, and cherished? What are the practices, the "small moments," that cultivate vibrant diversity embracement? For me, this begins in genuine and generous curiosity about one another's stories with the intent to learn and stretch rather than to control and incorporate. This can be especially challenging for administrators concerned with keeping order and discomfited by stories and experiences that disrupt the logic of the institution as inclusive host. Faculty administrators concerned with protecting the institution (feeling accountable to administrative superiors) will attempt to shut down or redirect stories and experiences that implicate institutional leaders and systems in injurious practices. Alternatively, when we are genuinely engaged with one another, we are open to these stories and all the pain, anger, and discord that they hold. We not only make room for them, we are prepared to be moved and changed by them. Another closely related aspect of relational engagement is recognizing, highlighting, and counting the relational/educational work that minoritized faculty contribute. Minoritized students, staff, and faculty are expected to "educate" those whose positions reflect the status quo, but with no recognition of the implications. Much has been written about how wearisome this burden of diversity work can be, but we need to give considerably more attention to reframing this work as a *contribution* in its own right: knowledges and skills that add value and enhance institutional life, rather than educational experiences that institutions are entitled to use as a price of inclusion. This work, which includes countless hours spent advising and mentoring minoritized students and colleagues, participating in ubiquitous diversity committees and panels, and fielding numerous requests to "help us 'get it,'" enhances the university mission in tangible ways (O'Brien, 2016), but the work is often hidden, or deemed a hobby interest of diverse faculty, the fruits of which the university is freely entitled to.

Ferraro notes that one of the tensions of institutional diversity is that minoritized subjects may be ambivalent or even resistant to being absorbed into the culture of the institution. Yet one of the demands of hospitality is showing appreciation for the including institution and, more insidiously, being grateful for the appropriation of one's experiences and stories into the institutional fabric. In exploring this issue from a relational rather than an instrumental/institutional entitlement paradigm, Ferraro flips the question to suggest that relational embracement means that persons who hold traditional institutional dominance are not entitled to anything; rather, they have an opportunity to stretch into and learn from others' experiences, but doing so relationally means being vulnerable, disoriented, and not in control of the experience. This is the sort of "inescapable scratchiness" wherein genuine personal transformation can occur, but only if institutional leaders let go of the safety reins of authority and embrace the freefall of relational engagement.

Full recognition of the value of social justice work undertaken by minoritized faculty means not only counting it in formal appraisal processes but learning to embrace the scratchiness of it when practiced outside the lines of existing organizational hierarchy charts. Done well, which is to say when forms of shared governance enable diverse groups to participate fully without the expectation that they will change themselves to conform to existing institutional practices (i.e., to speak and engage only in ways that reflect languages of dominance), these practices *are* a form of transformation. For this to happen, those in positions of power much stretch through their own discomfort and learn to be with difference without trying to contain it or make it conform. If this sort of transformation is truly under way, it will be unsettling.

There is tremendous potential in this approach, but it also exposes more clearly the inherent tensions between administrative roles and social justice advocacy. Provosts or presidents might be personally moved, even committed to deeper personal transformation and engagement, but they are constrained by additional external institutional dynamics, such as the demands of a board of regents unimpressed by social justice concerns except as branding. Contemplating the way through this labyrinth is beyond the scope of this chapter, but my own brief observation is that these dynamics of the status quo are pliable in response to perceived shifts in wider cultural circles: a savvy administrator can move governing bodies into new, potentially transformative terrain by demonstrating the promise of "value added" through embracing diverse perspectives and directions. But for this to truly crack through entrenched systems, such administrators must be grounded in and operating from a place of paradigm shift in themselves. They must be literate and nimble in the multiple languages of both the status quo and *transformation à la libération* (rather than instrumental). Such administrators are reflexively motivated by and accountable to the diverse groups they serve and strive to bring more recognition and voice to. These are the stealth academic administrators who can say, I am a *faculty* dean, or a *faculty- and student-oriented* provost and who are champions of shared governance and practiced in generative mid-level collaboration (as opposed to top-down authority), who understand that they must stake a commitment of accountability: seeking to raise the voices and contributions of those with whom they feel solidarity while educating and persuading those in positions of power without succumbing to the lure of dominance. Such administrators are bridge-builders par excellence.

SOME CONCLUDING THOUGHTS

Recently, my therapist asked me what distinguishes the strong conviction I felt in responding to the Marquette debacle and the creeping desolation that sometimes overtakes me in my current work. Immediately, I recalled the collective solidarity that characterized those weeks following the unhiring. Rather than seek terms of personal settlement, which has become a routinized formula by which a university washes its hands of its own misdeeds, I sought community retribution. Working with a team of astute attorneys and advisors (all of whom enthusiastically volunteered their time and expertise), we drew up a plan obligating the university to create ongoing funding for education and programming in gender and sexuality studies. The illegalities of the case were so publicly egregious that I was in a strong negotiating position, buttressed by ongoing campus protests on my behalf, and a mostly positive media portrayal. I was also buoyed by the more than 400 letters I received from Marquette students and alumni as well as Milwaukee-area residents, many of them practicing Catholics, expressing outrage at the university's actions and offering support and encouragement. Despite all this, Marquette threw up multiple obstacles, but we never wavered, and eventually we prevailed. The process itself was grueling—I often felt nothing in my life could have prepared me for it—but, as my therapist eight years later pointed out, my conviction was firm throughout. That the case was so clearly a wrongdoing helped me in this conviction, but mostly it was the collective support, the shared truth of the wrongness of the actions, that kept me focused and animated.

In contrast, the everyday bridging work of the outsider-within is not so straightforward. The relentless business of framing "our ideas in a language that is familiar to and comfortable for the dominant group" (Collins, 2002, p. 7), working against the grain of unquestioned "commonsense" practices of hierarchy, and maintaining internal equilibrium in the face of destabilizing disbelief from those in power leaves us tattered and frayed. We barely have energy for ourselves, let alone those with whom we wish to be in solidarity. In Anzaldúan terms, this place of extreme vulnerability is where we are least likely to be able to access the inner resources that mobilize us. For her this is *nepantla*—an in-between place, a threshold from which we are invited to go deeper into the "chaos of living between stories" (Anzaldúa & Keating, 2002, p. 545). This threshold is where we develop *conocimiento*, a way of being and knowing that enables us to "negotiate contradictions, survive the stresses and traumas of daily life, and develop a spiritual-imaginal-political vision together" (p. 571). We zigzag repeatedly between ignorance and awareness, but the hallmark of the journey is going deeper into our own breakdowns so that we can break free from habitual coping strategies and emerge with new ways of knowing/being: to arrive at "the critical turning point of transformation, [and] develop an ethical, compassionate strategy with which to negotiate conflict and difference within self and between others, and find common ground by forming holistic alliances" (p. 545).

What I am learning from this struggle is that real liberation includes cultivating new habits for staying engaged. Despite my strong urge to retreat into myself when wounded, I am at my best, with potential for synergistic renewal and unwavering conviction, when I am in community, in genuine engagement with others, working collaboratively. Alternatively, when I'm too isolated, I become confused and doubt myself and then begin to doubt others, including (and sometimes especially) those with whom I desire to be in solidarity. Thus, I'm learning to recognize the importance of renewal—not just for ourselves but collectively.

I have a cherished colleague who is beautifully practiced in the art of collective renewal. She never misses an occasion to celebrate with festive gatherings the accomplishments of our other colleagues. Making time to sit with one another sharing food, stories, tears, laughter, and music (she always makes us sing and dance) reminds me, if not entirely who I am, at least of where I might regain voice. When I gather with my colleagues in a spirit of camaraderie, these self-defeating voices are magically vanquished (and in a manner much less costly and more sustainable than the many hours of billable therapy). During these moments of coming together in genuine curiosity and generous respect, I am reminded of all the ways my dear colleagues delight me; their intelligence of mind, body, and spirit consoles and renews me and (re)sources me for returning to a politics of possibility. I feel inspired to be more fierce with my detractors, and more sustainably aligned with my allies. In other words, I am, once again, more assured in myself.

I am not so naive as to think that my suggestions here will transform the longstanding oppressions of institutional inequality regimes. But I do think that we have choices in how we engage with these institutional practices, especially those of us with the relative privilege of institutional authority as faculty administrators. Small but persistent, mindful practices of relational engagement that confer dignity, respect, and voice shift us all and allow us to come together in ways other than narratives of instrumental hospitality. These "small moments" push against the edifices of institutional oppression and may, indeed, create some cracks. For me, staying engaged in these practices requires a sort of alchemy, a transformation that can only be achieved through nepantla, in the threshold places where I'm thrown off balance and forced to confront my own (dis)identifications, beliefs, and practices. Genuine, relational, emergent collaborative engagement *is* messy. In growing our capacity to engage with this messiness we expand and become more whole. We are motivated to articulate commonalities from which to build bridges and to invite others to do the same.

The lessons I carry with me these days include fiercely mindful collaboration with those like-minded folk (and they come in many guises) who are literate in the multiple languages of institutional dominance and oppression; an appreciation for "stealth" colleagues working intelligently and subversively behind the scenes to confront discrimination in its many forms; a more cautious, curious response to those "sellouts" I may have been too quick to condemn and dismiss (as others have often done to me); ongoing interrogative reflection on who/what I'm feeling accountable to (who's the audience in my head?); and, perhaps most important, the absolute necessity of sustained collective recognition and renewal in solidarity with others. This practice is, in itself, the spirit of transformation, the everyday graces in which we see, honor, and hold each other up in all our splendid possibility.

REFERENCES

Ahmed, S. (2012). *On being included.* Durham, NC: Duke University Press.

Anzaldúa, G., & Keating, A. (2002). *This bridge we call home: Radical visions for transformation.* New York: Routledge.

Collins, P. H. (2002). *Black feminist thought.* New York: Routledge.

Collins, P. H. (2012). *On intellectual activism.* Philadelphia: Temple University Press.

Ferraro, H. (2018). Inclusive organizational practice vs inclusive experience. Research proposal in progress.

Goffman, E. (1986). *Stigma.* New York: Simon & Schuster.

Hochschild, A. (2012). *The managed heart: Commercialization of human feeling.* Berkeley: University of California Press.

Jordan, J. (1994). *Technical difficulties.* Boston: Beacon.

O'Brien, J. (2012). Stained-glass ceilings: Religion, sexuality, and the cultural politics of belonging. *Social Philosophy Today, 28,* 5–26.

O'Brien, J. (2016). What counts as success? Recognizing and rewarding women faculty's differential contributions in a comprehensive liberal arts university. National Science Foundation Institutional Transformation ADVANCE Grant #1629875.

Shultz, J. (2015). *Trans/portraits: Voices from transgender communities.* Hanover, NH: Dartmouth University Press.

Smith, D. (2005). *Institutional ethnography: A sociology for people.* Landham, ND: AltaMira.

Tempest Williams, T. (2012). *When women were birds.* New York: Picador.

TEN

Racial Harm in a Predominantly White "Liberal" University

An Institutional Autoethnography of White Fragility

Lynn Fujiwara

As an Asian American Woman of Color, an associate professor from a working-class background in a predominantly White university that ostensibly champions a commitment to diversity, it is challenging to expose the injuries of institutional violence and the persistence of racial harm. By institutional violence, I refer to both structural and cultural practices of White privilege that marginalize Faculty of Color, but are legitimized and "normalized" as objective, color-blind operations that deem any detriment to the Faculty of Color to be caused by their own doing or explained by extraneous circumstances for which the institution is not at fault. Racial harm, then, is the outcome experienced by Faculty of Color who have endured some form of institutional violence with no recourse, expected institutional accountability, or hope for amelioration. The struggles of being Faculty of Color in situations that are impossible to name result in what Eng and Han (2000) refer to as racial melancholia, a physical and psychical haunting caused by the distancing and estrangement of Asian Americans from America's mainstream culture of "Whiteness."

In a college administration that is 100 percent White, with no particular training in race or inequality, the inability to respond to racial harm contradicts every verbal commitment the administration makes to diversity. Part of the struggle stems from the unconscious workings of liberal racism, whereby seemingly well-meaning White faculty and administrators are unable to see their biased behaviors as a form of racism because their actions are either not overt or not intended. In campus meetings on diversity White colleagues and administrators have invited me to share my experiences of racial degradation. However, they then often explain away the impact by questioning my perspective. They respond: "These sound like petty interpersonal issues"; "Maybe you misunderstood; did you ask for clarification?" "You need to communicate your needs more clearly"; "You need to get over the past and move forward";

DOI: 10.7330/9781607329664.c010

or "You don't know what violence is—I experienced violence of the worst kind as a child."

Liberal racism is steeped in individualist understandings of personal choice and intentionality such that, if actions do not appear overt, like racial epithets or threats, then they do not constitute a serious problem. White colleagues and administrators do not seem to recognize systematic patterns of bias against or devaluation of Faculty of Color. They do not understand the alienation experienced by Faculty of Color in all White departments. The subtle but consistent racial harassment experienced by Faculty of Color is explained away as misunderstandings that can be addressed with a diversity talk facilitated by a department head.

These patterns in liberal White-dominant universities are a challenge that Robin DiAngelo (2011) calls White fragility—the accumulation of protective pillows of resources and/or benefits of the doubt that protects White people from racial stress. According to DiAngelo, "White people in North America live in a social environment that protects and insulates them from race-based stress . . . This insulated environment of racial privilege builds White expectations for racial comfort while at the same time lowering the ability to tolerate racial stress" (p. 55). In the face of racial stress, White faculty and administrators tend to utilize a myriad of defense mechanisms that Faculty of Color must then negotiate.

Asian American women occupy a precarious place in the academy. Our gendered racialization as quiet, passive, submissive, and obedient plays into our colleagues' expectations. The model minority myth feeds assumptions that we are hard-working, responsible, self-disciplined, organized, and loyal. I fulfill the characteristics of being a diversity hire, an obedient colleague, and a skilled worker who contributes to the university. Consequently, when I started to express my criticisms of systematic patterns of marginalization, or to challenge oppressive behaviors, I encountered defense mechanisms by my White colleagues and White administrators. These usually took the shape of oppositional narratives that questioned my perspectives and experiences as particular to my own individual choice of reaction. Their insistence on my complicity with model minority expectations of conformity resulted in manipulation, overpowering, or public disciplining. In their eyes my resistance demonstrated a "failure to assimilate into the university's regimes of Whiteness" (Eng & Han 2000, p. 677). In this chapter I discuss my experiences of racial harm, and the challenges of White fragility and liberal racism. I weave a narrative of racial harm and institutional violence as a Woman of Color moving through the ranks of assistant professor, associate professor, and department head.

WHITE CHAUVINISM AND THE EMOTIONAL LABOR OF WHITE FRAGILITY

I was the first tenure-track Woman of Color faculty member hired in a women's studies (WST) program. I began straight out of graduate school, six months pregnant, with a teenage daughter, in massive debt, with such a low salary that we could barely afford groceries at the end of each month. Although my senior colleague earned nearly twice as much as I did, I was told that my salary was on par with other assistant professors hired in comparable units. I was hired to teach the only Women of Color required course in the entire curriculum at that time. We were a program of three with a governing board of all-White faculty from across campus.

Early in my position we were granted a search to replace a faculty member who resigned. One senior faculty member expressed her disappointment to me that we had to conduct an open search because she wanted to hire a longtime instructor who was also her very good friend and was friends with several other senior women associated with the program. In their use of arcs of "friendship" and "loyalty," I experienced the systematic devaluation of Women of Color candidates and the elevation of the merits of their friend. I was still unfamiliar with the members of our search committee. The chair had also served on *my* search committee; she was a senior faculty member in my tenure home department, and an unofficial mentor to me. I realized that I was in an impossible situation when, after our conference interviews, I expressed my elation about several amazing Women of Color candidates. The chair's response confused me. She sat me down and said, "I know how hard this is for you" because candidate A, whom I barely knew, was the clear choice of the chair and the other WST representatives on the search committee. Their invocation of friendship and loyalty felt manipulative.

Colleagues across campus who were watching the search closely shared their concern for me. One said, "Lynn, everyone knows you are in an impossible situation: 'the friend candidate' will likely be voted in, and she will be your senior colleague." In the search committee meeting, the chair said we needed to be unanimous in our decision. I advocated for Women of Color candidates who were doing exciting intersectional work in queer, race, and sexuality studies, but my senior colleagues systematically devalued their work. I was deferential to their authority. I was still a new assistant professor and did not feel that I could challenge their presumed knowledge. Being told that "we have to be unanimous, regardless of how we decide" felt oppressive, particularly when, with every argument I made for a Woman of Color candidate, they replied with multiple reasons why their friend was stronger (even though the candidates were at very different stages of their careers). I felt disempowered as they minimized my perspective. They implied that I was playing identity politics, while they held the authority to claim "objective measures." One said, "I know you really like the other candidates, but the records speak for themselves." In the White racial regime, my White senior colleagues were automatically granted universal objective reality, while I was positioned as the other, seen as operating out of racial intent (DiAngelo, 2011, p. 59).

In the WST executive committee meeting, the search chair gave an impassioned speech about how stellar the friend's work was compared to that of the two Women of Color. She argued, "Though one of the Women of Color is doing promising scholarship on race and sexuality, she is a transnational feminist scholar, and we already have one of the best transnational feminist scholars right here with us, Lynn Fujiwara." I looked up, shocked, and said that that my work on immigrant communities in the United States did not make me a transnational scholar. Other women on the committee jumped in to say, "Oh, yes, you are, Lynn." I was silenced, manipulated, and felt vulnerable to the pressures of this strong group of senior women who wanted to hire their friend. Even though I argued that the friend's research was far less developed in the field we were searching in, her scholarship lacked theoretical sophistication, and she showed no demonstrable record of working intersectionally, my senior colleagues systematically cut down the Women of Color candidates and elevated their White friend as unquestionably the top candidate. She was offered the position. Later, my new senior colleague thanked me for staying committed "the whole time," for "focusing on merit, not race." My colleague ostensibly rationalized meritocracy over diversity. In actuality, the friend hire was foisted to the top through White women's affirmative action. She sought my validation to legitimize her entitlement to the position. As a side note, the top Woman of Color candidate ultimately received an offer from a much higher-ranked university.

For the majority of my time in the department, I remained the only Woman of Color. For most of my untenured time, it was just the three of us, the two close friends and me. They validated each other over every decision, often speaking from a "we" identity, regarding teaching assignments, guest speakers, graduate student employees, student awardees, and salary increases. One year I chaired the student awards committee. After we came to a decision, my senior colleague followed me to my office to argue for a different applicant. When I replied that the applicant she wanted had weak materials, my colleague retorted, "Did you read all the files?" About an hour later, already home, I received a voicemail from my other colleague. "Lynn, I hear you did not pick student A for the department award. I really want to argue for her; she is a hard worker, and we"—meaning her and my other colleague——"know her well. Maybe her materials weren't so strong, but she deserves the award." At that point she thought she had hung up the phone, but she had not, and her voice continued recording on my voicemail. Yelling over clicking computer keys to her friend colleague across the hall (this was a frequent practice), she said, "There, I did it. I called her and told her what I thought, and I'm glad, because student A really deserves it; she should get the award." I complained to the director, who listened sympathetically. Our office manager, who overheard the conversation in the hallway, asked if official protocol was in question, but that went nowhere. To satisfy the White women, we gave out two awards that year.

We held a retreat to work on the program curriculum, renting rooms and a suite at an inn on the coast. The others each had their own room, but I got the pullout bed in the living room of the meeting suite. Nobody questioned that the only Woman of Color had to sleep in the pullout bed in the same room we held all of our meetings.

Discussions over curriculum development were exhausting. I was the only person invested in race and Women of Color feminisms, but my ideas for multiple classes were treated as potential duplication. After steamrolling discussions, we ended up with a curriculum in which out of six required core courses, students would be guaranteed to have one course with me (the same course I was hired to teach). Our social time at the retreat was dictated by their desires for fast-paced walks, shopping at expensive boutiques, and talking about their lives in intimate detail. Because they were close friends, conversations were about each other's children and family issues. They dominated conversations, often interrupting, asking questions about my life, then not waiting to hear my full response before jumping back to each other. They continually bantered with a familiar intimacy. When I brought up experiences with racism, they replied with comments like, "That is just like what I experienced in a similar situation because of my . . ." (gender, sexuality, faith). When I attempted to engage in discussions of racism, my colleagues' need to divert to their own experiences of marginalization persisted. It was a form of White fragility that worked to reestablish White racial equilibrium (DiAngelo, 2011, p. 57).

While I was away on a postdoc, we had a conflict over a course my colleagues wanted to eliminate. Since I had not had a chance to teach it, I resisted. In the context of yet another mundane issue that set two colleagues against me, I sent an email sharing my feelings about our dynamics. I said that I experienced them as a duo, as a "we," and that I felt I always needed to negotiate the two of them in unison against me. One responded, "I don't see it that way, but I hear that you do, and when you return we will talk about it." The other colleague expressed that she was so sorry to read that I felt this way. She didn't see it like that at all, and was bothered that I was reading her actions in such a way. Her response was defensive, as if I had hurt her for saying such words. In her White fragility, she became the victim and expected me to make her feel better. Through their White fragility, they denied my perspective, yet took a quick way out by postponing the discussion. We never did talk about it. I asked them to stop saying "we," but that didn't happen either.

We eventually brought in an external director and continued to operate through the WST all-White board of directors. Other White women faculty would talk to me privately about my colleagues, checking in to see how I was doing, because they could see their forceful dynamic. At times these other women would even say, "I don't know how you tolerate their dynamic, they are so authoritative and entitled. If I ever act with that level of entitlement, please tell me." All of these comments were made directly to me, and never to them.

Before a campus visit by a prominent Woman of Color feminist scholar whose work was central to mine (I was the lead organizer), my colleagues shared how much they disliked her book. At dinner, the two friends co-opted the conversation away from this scholar's work to talk about things familiar to them: one's son's prom—what he wore, the corsage, the date, the dress, on and on . . . The other friend joined in to talk about her own children. They asked the scholar about her own personal life; she hesitatingly responded but did not elaborate. It appeared as if they were avoiding any intellectual conversation about the guest speaker's scholarship.

Years later, I invited a different prominent Woman of Color feminist scholar, and organized a dinner with Women of Color from a campus group I had developed. I announced my plans for the scholar's visit in two different department meetings, but neither of my colleagues expressed any interest. On the day of the event, they both asked a newly hired junior colleague (a Queer of Color scholar) what the dinner plans were. The junior faculty member emailed me immediately, letting me know they were upset that they were not invited to dinner. When I explained to them that it was a dinner planned for the Women of Color project, one responded, "Don't exclude me from discussions of race." The other said I was not being collegial, and I should have planned a dinner that included them. This turned into a tense email exchange right up to the event. Days later, during a meeting, they argued that any event planned in WST had to include them centrally. I was put in my place. At the end of the meeting, a colleague said, "You seem mad. Why are you mad?" I said I was tired of constantly dealing with conflict, especially when neither of my colleagues had expressed any interest in the speaker until the day of the event. It was hard to introduce the scholar and welcome everyone after such a harsh email exchange. Their White fragility, their narrative of victimization, was couched in demands for a collegiality that centered them. Once it was established that I was required to include them in my programming, one colleague said, "Can we just be jolly? I just want us all to be jolly, I just hate conflict." I said, "I'm afraid I'm not jolly," and that was the last event I planned in the department.

Once tenured and less vulnerable, I pushed against their steamrolling. In my entire time in the department there was not one conflict in which one of the friends was in agreement with me and in disagreement with the other. I insisted on diversifying our program, which also required me to serve on most substantive and time-consuming committees. I fought against merit review procedures that benefited our highest-salaried faculty. The friends did not respond well to my pushing back. They would often argue that I was creating a competitive environment, or that my actions were politically motivated. They would say they did not like tension, and ask why I seemed so mad when I was just expressing my point of view. I was characterized as overly emotional and political. One colleague actually asked me if I was "PMSing."

Even though our unit grew in size, we could not seem to stop the bulldozing of the close colleagues. We openly discussed the steamrolling conversational pattern in a mediated meeting. The conclusion was not that they should stop their behavior; instead, it was up to the "less assertive" speakers to make ourselves heard. Since we could not productively talk in meetings, issues usually remained unresolved. If my anger and frustration showed up when I pointed out systematic patterns of domination and marginalization, I was immediately accused of "being *at* people," of being stuck in the past, of needing to move forward. To invalidate me, they would ask, "Why are you angry?" I was not allowed to be angry. I often relied on Audre Lorde's "Uses of Anger" (1981) to strategize my validation elsewhere.

Ultimately the department imploded. Several of us left for other units, and another left the university. Months later, after radio silence through all the departure emails, the incoming leadership asked us two Faculty of Color who had left the department to "have her back," to provide our "solidarity" in her efforts to rebuild the department. I gave her an honest response about how painful my departure from the department had been, and that after so many years of dealing with the silencing, invisibility, and being pathologized, I wondered where the solidarity had been then. She responded with a curt email, and a couple months later she refused to greet me after I said hello to her, even as I was waving and standing in front of her. She stared at me, bobbing her head as if to say, "You dare to speak to me," and then she turned and walked away. Three other Women of Color witnessed the exchange and asked, "What was that? That was so violent, are you okay?" Later, this same person became an administrator with power over our unit. Under her leadership, our department's resources were reduced, we were excluded from programmatic developments under our academic purview, and our award-winning faculty received poor personnel evaluations. Her White fragility could not handle that although I offered to work with her collegially as a fellow department head (as I had been), I would not put myself back in the WST mix. She appeared defensive when I called out her own complicity and stated that I would not validate her by taking on the job of rebuilding a department that systematically marginalized Faculty of Color.

INSTITUTIONAL VIOLENCE AGAINST A DEPARTMENT HEAD

I was appointed department head (of my new home department) three years after promotion to associate professor. I can unequivocally say that I enjoyed many aspects of my role as department head. I thrived in program and community building, supporting my department's faculty, and I fostered a rewarding institutional presence with my colleagues. I appreciated working with folks across campus with whom I would not normally interact. Leading a department is a clear step into administrative work. You see the inner workings of university politics, and develop skills for negotiating institutional governance and procedures. From what I witnessed, serving as a department head is a natural pathway into upper administrative positions.

I was one of the only Department Heads of Color (among forty-five), in a college with an all-White administrative body. Not one member of the college's administrative office possessed expertise in race, diversity, or about Faculty of Color, yet they validated one another for their good intentions by wearing safety pins touting inclusion. They did not have a handle on a growing diverse faculty that was negotiating institutional racism. Year after year we witnessed the departure of talented and successful Women of Color faculty, sometimes to lower-paying, less desirable positions. They could no longer tolerate the ineptness of the administration in dealing with the racist and sexist faculty members in their departments. These departures were hushed, framed as "an unfortunate situation" in which all had done their best, but unfortunately, some decided to leave.

The racism was veiled under administrators' continual proclamations about how they were working to make the university a place of welcome and inclusion.

They engaged in a diversity shuffle whereby they created overly complex, meaningless diversity plans with lots of pages, categories, tables, and charts. These suggested ways units could think about making their departments "welcoming and inclusive." Administrators provided competitive soft programming money, created diversity strategy groups that never met, and they even went to implicit bias workshops. Because they knew so little about institutional racism, they thought those efforts were sufficient, that their diversity work was done—at least until the next campus racial explosion, when they scrambled again to look like they were taking the issues seriously.

I did not expect the degradation and marginalization I experienced at the college administrative level, or the cost of not remaining silent and complicit. At first others welcomed me, complimented my achievement in becoming a department head, and valued my input. They recognized my leadership and my adeptness at "soft skills": communication, community building, mentoring junior faculty, and working collaboratively with other department heads. As a third-generation Asian American from a working-class background, I recognized that I was accessible to these college administrators. In their Black/not Black racial binary, they felt I was approachable, and they were comfortable sharing their racial insecurities with me. During lunches, coffee dates, and over drinks we got to know one another. They confided their moments of racial intimidation when they had to interface with our star-studded external review committee of highly esteemed professors who studied race. I heard about their doubts regarding their competency as White people trying to understand the circumstances of Faculty of Color, wanting so badly to make the university a more friendly and welcoming place. We would end these "meetings" with hugs and an expression of gratitude for being able to share openly and see one another on a human level. Departures were preceded by "Thanks, Lynn, I'm so glad we are working together—these are the parts of the job I truly enjoy, getting to know people like you." These relationships ended quickly when I started challenging their perceptions of the good liberal work they were doing. My loyalty to them was no longer evident. When I challenged administrative patterns through a racial lens, I become the culprit for their racial discomfort.

I appreciate Patricia Hill Collins's plantation metaphor of the structure of the university's institutional oppression. In this model, elite White men are joined by a growing number of elite White women helpmates to maintain and perpetuate existing inequalities and a culture of Whiteness that congratulates itself for its liberal propensity to care about people (1993, pp. 595–596).

An administrator forwarded an email stream to me, writing, "We need to talk as soon as possible. I am now counting three different personnel issues that you have never even bothered to inform me or [the administration] about. This is not only disrespectful, in my opinion, but causes lots of miscommunication issues that we then have to clean up." The email stream conveyed a conversation about my "bad behavior" with another department head, who was also the spouse of another college administrator. I wrote back, taking offense at his tone and suggesting that he ask me what was going on before accusing me of disrespect, especially since we were following the written college guidelines. He doubled down and said, "I guess we are both offended now. But drama probably won't allow us to move forward or do what's best for your department, the College, and the University." With this implied threat to my department, I started to cc higher-ranking college administrators, and after a series of back-and-forth increasingly hostile emails, they put a stop to our email conversation and said we needed a restart.

To deal with the situation I met with the administrator and my colleague, who was overseeing a possible hire. My colleague felt bad about the turn events had taken, and wished to explain the steps we followed, which were based on the college's written guidelines. As I tried to explain why his initial email was so troubling to me, the administrator lurched forward, bug eyed, face red, and blurted: "*You really want to go there, Lynn?*" I sat back, took a breath, and said, "Wow, you really are emotional." Continuing in his barrage, the administrator said, "Okay, if I say that I've heard your side, that it was wrong for me to call you disrespectful, will that make you happy, will that allow you to move forward? Is that what you want to hear?" The administrator then turned back to my male colleague and said, "Okay, so let's talk about the resources your initiatives would require." The administrator continued to talk only to my male colleague, who became increasingly uncomfortable as he noticed that I was rendered invisible. It turned out that the hire was a stellar candidate in one of our college administrator's home departments. Suddenly things became much smoother. When the candidate was hired, the administrator sent an email to all interested parties saying the success was due to the college administration's hard work.

I made formal complaints about the problematic interactions between the accusatory administrator and myself through emails to the entire upper administration. I asked for an audit of the college administration. Nothing was addressed. Instead, in a meeting with my department colleagues, our chief college administrator sought their comfort by sharing that I had hurt him by calling him racist. He apparently did not understand the difference between the racial consequences of an all-White administrative body and the label "racist." In an informal setting, I sought support from another college administrator who was often touted as the diversity expert because she was the only one who attended diversity workshops. She said she "heard me," but that unfortunately, "sometimes bad behavior goes unchecked." She also defended the college administration because its members worked hard, truly wanted the college to be diverse, and operated with the best of intentions.

In a completely White space there is no recourse. Your competency relies on your ability to navigate racialized and gendered patterns of degradation, while still representing your department and making sure your faculty members are protected. The White fragility of the college administration perceived my actions as disrespect and being difficult. I was not demonstrating the deference and humility that they expected. The college administration suspected me and the majority of the Faculty of Color of trying to push our agendas without regard to protocol. Actually, we were self-consciously reading and rereading the process they outlined for the college. Instead of asking or inquiring about our actions, they felt completely comfortable chastising me in public and calling me into the office to be disciplined. My second three-year term as department head ended on a sour note. I was emotionally spent. Although I had written requests for transparency, accountability, and communication workshops, none of the issues I raised were addressed.

To my knowledge, no lesson was learned by the all-White administration. Years later, our leading African American studies scholar was publicly degraded due to accusations made against our department. With no understanding of the contentious racial intra-politics within ethnic studies fields, any accusations against us were believed and validated by our administration. They even refused to share the accusations to allow a defense. Already suspect of our intentions, anything negative they heard was further validation of their suspicions. My colleague, one of only a few Black women on campus, was removed from a committee she was co-chairing to develop a new program in her field of study. They replaced her with a White woman faculty member and declared that the new program would be housed anywhere but our department. Instead of fostering a strong, vibrant community of Faculty of Color, the administration pitted new Faculty of Color against our department. This is an example of how the university destroys invested Women of Color from pursuing leadership and administrative positions.

COALITION AND COLLABORATION AS COPING STRATEGIES FOR SURVIVING THE WHITE UNIVERSITY

David Eng and Sunhee Han (2000) argue that racial melancholia is not necessarily a pathology or a state of individual or group destruction. Rather, racial melancholia becomes a form of survival (p. 693). For People of Color generally, and Asian Americans specifically, negotiating the *perpetual foreigner* and *model minority* incongruence and the day-to-day indignities requires survival strategies to cope with ubiquitous normative ideals and practices of Whiteness. In spite of the indignities, I still feel fortunate to be part of a thriving intellectual and political academic community. To survive, I utilized collaborative and coalitional strategies at each stage of my career development. After the problematic search that impacted Faculty of Color across campus, I joined forces with the few other Faculty of Color to form the Faculty and Staff of Color Coalition (FSCC). This process helped build a community of support and camaraderie. It gave us a collective voice. We developed an impactful presence on campus. The FSCC provided a much-needed community in which to talk about issues without being questioned. It allowed us a venue to generate action plans that put our rage into intelligible concrete frameworks and goals. The organization lasted for about nine years. By the end we actually had developed a small but significant critical mass of Faculty of Color.

During my time in WST, I developed and coordinated the Women of Color Project through our university's women's research center. Through a national grant funded by the Ford Foundation, I collaborated with colleagues to create a project designed to support Women of Color junior faculty in reaching academic success. Under the broader theme "Institutional Diversity/Institutional Change," we developed a yearlong set of workshops on tenure and promotion, teaching strategies, and work/life balance. We held a broader university dialogue to work internally on issues of academic survival, while also sharing our most important findings with the university's administration. This project proved incredibly successful; many of the junior women have since become tenured. The formation of a supportive collective proved essential. It provided mentorship, institutional resources, and direct connections with upper administrators. This project still exists, now in its tenth year of providing a space of community, support, and resources for Women of Color faculty.

Professional life in the White-dominated liberal university poses challenges for Women of Color faculty actively working to change existing patterns of racial entitlement and marginalization. Institutional activism in the context of liberal racism requires a constant negotiation with White fragility, which excuses behavior with claims of victimization and innocence, or which claims that, because actions were not overt, appeared color-blind, or were not intended, there was no racism. The idea that White faculty and administrators can be very well-meaning and good people yet still engage in practices, patterns, and behaviors that have harmful racial impact does not seem so outlandish. It is perplexing to me how White fragility still remains a barrier to active, open, and honest efforts to make substantial institutional change from the ground up and the top down.

At each stage of my professional experience, I challenged White normative practices that triggered my colleagues' and White administrators' racial discomfort. Once faced with racial discomfort, my colleagues engaged in denial, victimization, and steamrolling. College administrators resorted to public disciplining, ostracism, and hostility. If my White colleagues and administrators could get over the fear of "being racist," they could see that their behaviors, while maybe not intentional, have serious racial implications. Until White administrators and faculty can recognize this difference, and understand that the university is inculcated with systemic patterns of White domination, Faculty of Color will continue to be harmed by ongoing racial animus.

REFERENCES

Collins, P. H. (1993). Toward a new vision: Race, class, and gender as categories of analysis and connection, *Race, Sex, & Class, 1*, 1.

DiAngelo, R. (2011). White fragility. *International Journal of Critical Pedagogy, 3*, 3.

Eng, D. & Han, S. (2000). A dialogue on racial melancholia, *Psychoanalytic Dialogues, 10*, 4.

Lorde, A. (1981). The uses of anger. *Women Studies Quarterly, 9*, 3.

ELEVEN

Presumptions of Incompetence, Gender Sidelining, and Women Law Deans

Laura M. Padilla

"A Gendered Update on Women Law Deans" (Padilla, 2007) examined the number of women law deans, their paths to deanships, and what the future might hold for law school leadership from a gendered and racialized lens.[1] *Presumed Incompetent* (Gutiérrez y Muhs, Niemann, González, & Harris, 2012), a powerful collection of essays, explored presumptions of incompetence that haunt Women of Color in academia. "Gender Sidelining" (Fink, 2018) addressed harmful gender-generated behaviors that are not significant enough individually to warrant a comprehensive response, but whose cumulative effect can be devastating. "A Gendered Update," *Presumed Incompetent*, and "Gender Sidelining" have different theses, yet each addresses challenges women in leadership face. Drawing upon quantitative data and narrative responses from questionnaires sent to all women Law Deans of Color, this chapter examines common threads and unique fibers in the experiences of female Law Deans of Color, many revolving around presumptions of incompetence and sidelining. It closes with ways to reduce presumptions of incompetence and gender sidelining, and to expand the growing club of women Law Deans of Color.

UPDATE ON WOMEN LAW DEANS

"A Gendered Update" reported that in 2005–2006, 31 of the 166 Association of American Law Schools' (AALS) members had women deans (18.7 percent), including three Women of Color (1.8 percent) (Padilla, 2007, pp. 461–464). As of April 2018, 56 of the 179 AALS schools had women deans (31 percent),

1. Special thanks to Tandis Taghavi and Linda Weathers for their research and library assistance, respectively.

DOI: 10.7330/9781607329664.c011

including twelve Women of Color (6.7 percent), and 59 of the 204 American Bar Association (ABA)–approved law schools had women deans (29 percent), including fourteen Women of Color (6.8 percent). This marks progress since 2005–2006, especially for Women of Color. Since then, five Latinas and the first Native and Asian American women have become law deans.

Women have led many of the top-ten law schools, including Stanford, Harvard, Columbia, Berkeley, and Virginia. Research done in 2005, indicated that only three women had led elite law schools: Barbara Black (Columbia, 1986–1991), Kathleen Sullivan (Stanford, 1994–2004), and Elena Kagan (Harvard, 2003–2009). Now, six of the top-ten schools have had one female dean, and Stanford, Columbia, and Berkeley have had at least two. At present, there is a holding pattern, with women representing about 30 percent of all law deans. While there appears to be a plateau, today's numbers still represent a major improvement from the early days of women deans.

In 1969, the first woman Law Dean of Color, Patricia Roberts Harris, was appointed at Howard Law. From then until 2006, all women Law Deans of Color were African American, as are ten of the fourteen current ABA deans, and nine of the twelve AALS deans. Adding to the ranks, Boston University Law recently named Angela Onwuachi-Willig as its new dean.

Thirty-seven years after Howard Law appointed the first Woman of Color, Drexel Law appointed the first Latina, Jennifer Rosato (acting dean 2006–2007), who is the first Latina to hold serial deanships (Northern Illinois Law, 2009–2015; DePaul Law, 2015–present). Since Dean Rosato's appointment, four other law schools have hired Latina deans: Cuban American Leticia Diaz (Barry University, 2007–present); Rachel Moran (UCLA, 2010–2015); Puerto Rican Vivian Neptune (2011–present); and Maria Pabón Lopez (Loyola, New Orleans, 2011–2015).

In 2011, Arkansas appointed Stacy Leeds, the first and only Native American woman law dean (Dean Leeds stepped down in 2018). Another milestone was recently achieved when UC–Irvine Law named as dean L. Song Richardson, the first woman of Asian descent and "the only woman of color to serve in this role among *U.S. News & World Report*'s top 30 law schools" ("L. Song Richardson Named Dean," 2017). Considering there was only one Woman of Color law dean for decades, we have seen progress—there is a critical mass of African Americans, several Latinas, and the first Native and Asian Americans. It is especially notable that the number of women Deans of Color has quadrupled since "A Gendered Update" was published.

WHY ARE THERE MORE WOMEN LAW DEANS TODAY?

Currently there are more women lawyers than ever, providing a bigger pipeline for potential deans. The ABA reported that women comprised 50.7 percent of first-year law students, 51.3 percent of total JD enrollment, and 52.7 percent of JDs awarded (American Bar Association, 2017). Just as the number of women in law school went from imperceptible to more than a novelty to roughly the same as men, the number of women in legal academia (the source of most law deans) has grown.

While some law deans were previously judges, lawyers, or in business, most were law professors or in administrative appointments. Promisingly, there are now many women in those roles. The ABA's 2013 annual questionnaire reported there were 3,632 tenured (67.3 percent) and 778 tenure-track (51.6 percent) male law professors, totaling 4,410 (American Bar Association, 2013). By comparison, there were 1,766 tenured (32.7 percent) and 731 tenure-track (48.4 percent) female law professors, totaling 2,497. While women's numbers still trail men's, there is improvement. First, the number of tenure-track women and men is nearly equal. Second, the percentage of tenured women has grown significantly since "A Gendered Update" was published: in 2000, women comprised 6.4 percent of tenured law professors; in 2001, 5.9 percent; in 2003, 25.1 percent; and in 2005, 25.3 percent (Padilla, 2007, p. 477).

Some deliberate efforts emerged to increase deanships among underrepresented groups. From the late 1990s through the early 2000s, Dean Judith Areen, and later the AALS, kept a list of women interested in law deanships. One year after the list was created, the number of women law deans increased from fourteen to twenty (Padilla, 2007, pp. 457–458). Starting in 2007, "Seattle Law and the Society of American Law Teachers [SALT] hosted the first Promoting Diversity in Law School Leadership program . . . devoted to preparing women and minorities for the [dean] search process" (Sloan, 2015, p. 3). Forward-thinking leaders have cleared some of the mystery of landing deanships, making it easier for women and minorities to pursue them, resulting in increased numbers of both.

Perhaps there are more women deans because the position is less desirable. Running a law school is particularly challenging now due to application declines, shrinking budgets, more work, and less pay. From 2010 to 2015, law school applicants declined from 87,900 to 54,500, producing smaller entering classes (Padilla, 2017). The dip was accompanied by weaker entering credentials, making it difficult to maintain bar passage rates and respectable employment statistics. Many law schools lack deep endowments and are heavily dependent on tuition. Fewer students coupled with deeper tuition discounts meant a major cut in tuition revenues. Law schools thus slashed budgets and created voluntary and involuntary retirement programs. One dean expressed "concern that women may be getting more opportunities to lead because traditional dean candidates are waiting for legal education's problems to subside. 'It's not a good time to be a dean. It's very difficult. The goal is housekeeping, rather than growth . . . I'm going to be keeping an eye on whether, as things stabilize, opportunities for women decline.'" (Sloan, 2015, p. 4).

NARRATIVES FROM WOMEN AT THE TOP

Women's journeys to deanships and their experiences in deanships have many similarities, from sometimes rocky paths to glass cliffs. Telling stories of these journeys is important because they acknowledge the truth of those who live(d) them; emphasize that Women of Color still face hurdles in the academy even as leaders; provide guidance for future leaders; and allow women deans to share kernels of knowledge and moments of gratification.

I sent questionnaires to the fourteen sitting women Law Deans of Color and some former deans. Seven women completed the written questionnaire and some answered partly in telephone interviews. One question asked about gender sidelining like "manterrupting" (man unnecessarily interrupts woman), "bropropriating" (man takes credit for a woman's idea), and "mansplaining" (man patronizingly explains something, often beginning by interrupting a woman) (DiGeronimo, 2018). Every dean had experiences with gender sidelining. One said that when she was in a leadership role, like running a faculty meeting or hosting an event, she encountered little gender sidelining. However, when she was not in a leadership role, particularly at bigger events, gender sidelining increased, especially manterrupting. In smaller, breakout groups, gender sidelining decreased. Other women shared similar experiences. Another dean, who is in a sparsely populated state where 94.8 percent of the residents are White, said she initially experienced resistance from Foundation Board members. They often mansplained why she did not really understand situations—"You're not from around here." Maybe that was code for "How would an African American woman who is not from here have any idea how to run this law school?" They did not directly challenge her vision with sidelining or presumptions of incompetence, but they did not believe in her—"I just don't understand your vision" or "You have not made your case." However, after a few years in her deanship, she now receives more widespread support.

When asked if they had any "presumed incompetent" experiences, one dean bluntly responded, "All the time. By colleagues, students, when I was on the bench—it's ingrained in many until you have the opportunity to demonstrate your expertise." This is not surprising given that "Latinos and African-Americans of working-class backgrounds are particularly vulnerable to being stereotyped as unqualified, undeserving, and uncollegial" (González, 2014, p. 53). One dean said that from her first deanship to the present, people still tell her what to do, ask her, "Have you thought of . . . ?", question whether she understands an issue, or assume she does not—then proceed to mansplain. Another woman felt dismissed and talked over. When one dean started her deanship, she wasn't necessarily presumed incompetent when she entered a room, but she was treated as almost nonexistent. However, once introduced as the law dean, she was treated differently, practically cloaked with a presumption of competence. Women of Color often face initial presumptions of incompetence, and although these decline once the women are stamped with labels of leadership, they do not truly transition to presumptions of competence until women have proven themselves capable. This contrasts with the default presumption of competence until proven otherwise for White men.

A common response to how gender and/or race impacted their leadership involved adaptation, "a slow, usually unconscious modification of individual and social activity in adjustment to cultural surroundings" ("Adaptation,"

2018). Women of Color are accustomed to adapting to reduce challenges to their authority and make their constituents more comfortable, even if that means losing authenticity. One dean's authenticity was constrained by expectations, which is problematic. "When an academic woman's behavior thwarts expectations, she may be punished for her transgression in subtle and not-so-subtle ways . . . these macro- and micro- aggressions may actually increase as a Woman of Color is promoted from assistant to associate and finally to full professor, assumes administrative responsibilities, and enters environments that are even less diverse than the ranks of junior faculty" (González, 2014, p. 51). Expectations of a law dean are heightened for Women of Color, often requiring them to adapt to a more traditional law dean model for easier acceptance. One dean said some roles are easier because they are more consistent with who she is, but she has to force an occasional "nice response" (even if a different one is called for), think about how she dresses and presents herself, remember to sometimes bring cookies, and not be too assertive for fear of offending. This aligns with observations that "faculty, staff, and students may have particularly adverse reactions—conscious and unconscious—toward Women of Color who are not perceived as adequately nurturing or feminine. The stereotype of the mammy and motherly Latina are particularly strong. Women who do not meet stereotypical expectations that they will nurture students arouse anger, distrust, and feelings of betrayal" (Niemann, 2012, p. 469).

Women law deans spend disproportionate energy considering how they will be perceived, which can be depleting. "Women of color may feel compelled to conceal or mute aspects of their identities to make their students and colleagues feel comfortable—to mask the very diversity that makes their presence in legal academia so valuable. They may sidestep controversial topics . . . and behave in an exaggeratedly lady-like manner to avoid triggering stereotypes, such as 'the angry black woman,' or the 'working-class Chicana militant'" (González, 2014, p. 51). One dean noted a different aspect of adapting to make others more comfortable: "My greatest challenge has been the lack of leadership skills and vision in university leaders and their feeling threatened by ambitious goals and vision—with very rare exception, I always found that I had to 'play small' to make them comfortable . . . very confining and limits progress." Dean challenges are daunting enough when you can bring your best and most complete self to the job. When you have to leave parts behind to enhance others' comfort, everyone loses.

It is draining to remain authentic as a law dean when one is a token, "seen stereotypically. For People of Color, the stereotypes are largely negative, racist, and sexist, and there are damaging consequences of these perceptions" (Niemann, 2012, p. 473). With effort, Women of Color can overcome "token" status by using their intersectionality as a plus. One dean said that while gender and race did not impact her leadership style, they added value to the goal of diversifying the least diverse profession. She recognized that her presence made a difference in the legal profession, where Women of Color are severely underrepresented. One dean noted she is more influential as the Latina voice at the table, bringing legitimacy. Others said they represent frequently missing or underrepresented perspectives. One woman uses her identity as a Black woman to authentically address diversity needs. Despite initial faculty resistance to a program designed to diversify and improve the school's reputation, the initiative achieved great success, bringing in twenty-five Students of Color from rural and poverty-stricken areas. Another dean said, "My experience as a Black woman marks how I treat colleagues, students and faculty members. I do not dismiss personal experiences and I listen to all my constituents." She noted that many former deans dismissed the voices of women and People of Color. As more women take on leadership roles and their "token" label diminishes, there should be a normative shift so they can bring their complete selves and spend less energy adapting. They can thus devote more energy to leading and active inclusion.

Blurring the lines between presumptions of incompetence and gender sidelining, Women of Color are "generally subjected to extra scrutiny (the double standard), and . . . encounter constant pressure to prove themselves and overcome the resentment of their colleagues by making extraordinary efforts to 'fit in' and put others at ease" (González, 2014, p. 51). One dean confirmed that expectations for her were higher and people wanted instant results. She thought there was more patience for White males, who were subject to less scrutiny. Another angle, she explained, is she was judged not just as herself, but as a representative of her entire race. She represented a demographic in a way that privileged deans did not, so if she was unsuccessful there would be behind-closed-doors talk about whether the institution should have taken a risk on a [fill-in-the-race] female. "It is the plight of minorities to know that their whole subgroups may be judged by their individual behavior. If I failed, it might mean that no other Black woman would be hired in the future . . . Yet the administration would never say that the failure of one White male meant that another should never be hired again" (Wing, 2012, p. 356). One woman said someone always wanted to push her out because she was not good enough, and people frequently second-guessed her. A more traditional dean would likely have had more leeway early in his deanship, given more time to learn the ropes than was accorded to her. "Women's mistakes tend to be noticed with greater frequency and are remembered for longer; they tend to be judged more rigorously than men by their superiors; and they tend to receive more polarized evaluations" (Fink, 2018, pp. 81–82). This dean also said there was an assumption she would solve pervasive law school problems like declining applications, yield, and entering credentials. If she could not, the sense was that she was not the right person for the job. Another dean said her leadership was subject to early and frequent scrutiny, as was her commitment to Constituents of Color. There was constant attention to whether she struck the right balance between doing too much and too little for People of Color.

Women described oblique doubts about their skills early in their deanships, which changed as they proved themselves, with presumptions of incompetence gradually waning. One dean said negative presumptions and gender sidelining "happen—if I let [them] happen—sometimes you have to know when to pick your battles." While these deans ultimately were accepted, it took extra work to obtain the vote of confidence a privileged dean likely received on arrival. Their successful leadership highlights the need for more Women of Color to model professionalism and demonstrate that they can effectively run law schools, which minimizes presumptions of incompetence and neutralizes gender sidelining.

Several deans expressed disappointment at inconsistent institutional support. While their hiring was greeted with much fanfare and warm welcomes, many were soon left on their own. In addition to being destabilized by lukewarm institutional support, they are undermined when staff take their lead from the institution and retreat into their silos rather than provide teamwork and assistance. A recent study revealed disturbing effects when women and People of Color are appointed as leaders—White men tend to identify less with their employer *and* became less collegial and supportive of their Colleagues of Color—"White male managers on average experienced a 'lower sense of identity with their company' after the appointment of a female and/or racial minority CEO." The study also reported, "Researchers found that White male executives working under a female and/or racial minority were . . . less likely to provide help to fellow colleagues, with an especially negative effect on help provided to minority status colleagues" (DaSilva, 2018, para. 3). This troubling outcome can create serious morale and productivity problems as well as hinder team-building and collaboration.

Some deans lamented the debilitating loneliness of a deanship. With more Women of Color law deans, mentors, allies, and robust support networks, there are now more resources to counter the isolation of being a Woman of Color in a deanship. In spite of the challenges, Women of Color who serve as law deans uniquely touch lives, shape policy, and make a difference through their deanships. Many deans said they valued the opportunity to serve underserved constituents, and provide sustained and meaningful hope, leadership, and guidance.

PRESUMPTIONS OF INCOMPETENCE, SIDELINING, AND OTHER HURDLES: GETTING AROUND AND OVER THEM, AND MAKING THEM GO AWAY

> From the manner in which men and women conduct themselves in meetings . . . receive mentoring and guidance . . . [and] receive credit (or not) for their workplace contributions, men and women tend to experience the workplace in profoundly different ways.
>
> (FINK, 2018, P. 79)

Women of Color often experience law deanships in radically different ways than their more privileged counterparts. Difference by itself is not bad. However, when it is a proxy for additional scrutiny and disrespect, it is problematic. While increasing Women of Color's presence is part of the solution, improving retention and women's experiences are also important.

Acknowledging Women of Color's underrepresentation in leadership is a starting point. "Critical mass may not be a panacea for the ills of the academic workplace, but it can relieve the soul-crushing isolation, the painful stigma, and the exhausting service requirements" (González, 2014, p. 53). Underrepresentation is aggravated by endless microaggressions, unconscious bias, and presumptions of incompetence. Some deny the problem—"psychological evidence suggests that . . . men and women—will be inclined to dismiss the events described as exaggerations or illustrations of 'oversensitivity'" (Dovidio, 2012, p. 113). However, many women's harrowing experiences belie naive assertions that the problems are fabricated or already solved. While proportionality is not a cure-all, increasing women's numbers will reduce tokenism and demonstrate competence while deterring sidelining behaviors. Change will not occur spontaneously, especially when many are convinced there is no problem, and others fear change or embrace the status quo. "Regrettably . . . academia . . . remains not only remarkably blind to its own flaws, but deeply invested in a thoroughgoing denial . . . The culture of academia . . . is impervious to change because its power structure is designed to reproduce itself . . . When . . . people in power receive a mandate to search out excellence, the first place they look is to people like themselves, and too often that is also where the search ends" (Harris & González, 2012, p. 7). Raw data can highlight the problem, showing roughly equal numbers of men and women initially, even through college and law school, but in tenure-track positions and leadership roles, women's representation declines. Disseminating accurate data may not be enough, as research suggests it is more effective when coupled with statements that disparities persist even when people want to overcome biases that lead to discriminatory behavior (Grant & Sandberg, 2014). Quantitative data should be supplemented with qualitative chronicles of women's experiences to emphasize that change starts with numbers, but does not end there. The numbers resonate more when attached to stories of sidelining and presumptions of incompetence.

Search committees should make diversity a priority and actively seek out Women of Color. Women of Color, in turn, can better position themselves as viable law dean candidates with leadership training and education on budgets, management, and development. Additionally, law schools can move from institutional preferences for male leadership styles toward a broader range of styles. Diverse leadership is likelier to reach more people, resonate with a bigger cross-section, and create more variety in how issues are framed and resolved. A shift from predominantly male leadership to inclusive leadership can reduce sidelining, allow more voices in the conversation, and permit success by different paths, but it will take intentional efforts to support diverse leadership. "We need to be explicit about our disapproval of the leadership imbalance as well as our support for female leaders. When more women lead, performance improves. Start-ups led by women are more likely to succeed; innovative firms with more women in top management are more profitable; and companies with more gender diversity have more revenue, customers, market share and profits. A comprehensive analysis of 95 studies on gender differences showed that when it comes to leadership skills, although men are more confident, women are more competent" (Grant & Sandberg, 2014, para. 17). Law schools tend to be risk-averse and precedent-bound. Disrupting that model with fresh leadership can enhance problem-solving and team-building. Making room for women's leadership helps undo the damage of decades of silencing, normalizes women as leaders, and boosts morale. That leads to greater workplace satisfaction and productivity, which is especially important for women's success. Law schools shortchange themselves and their constituents when there are few or no Women of Color in leadership. As institutions welcome more leadership styles, Women of Color can more readily lead authentically, bringing their unique strengths to deanships while improving their retention and success.

Although institutions celebrate hiring Women of Color and have good diversity intentions, without sufficient support, they can contribute to sidelining and derail deans' prospects for success. Support can range from selecting a point person at the university, on the board, and in other key bodies who can provide information, introductions, and overviews to providing a thorough orientation. Legitimate support has a ripple effect, thus amplifying its benefits. "Women who repeatedly are praised and recognized in the workplace will be motivated to try even harder, while women who feel overlooked and ignored may see their drive and ambition diminish" (Fink, 2018, p. 92). When women leaders validate all voices, including those likelier to have been silenced, sidelined, and presumed incompetent, they practice inclusiveness and allow contributions that may otherwise have been missed. On a smaller scale, many of us have had students say they rarely spoke up before taking a given class, but having a professor who looked like them or shared their life story made them feel competent and more welcome to participate. That is in a law school classroom—imagine the potential that could be unleashed if the "other" was the law school dean? When Women of Color lead and support their communities, especially members of underrepresented groups, they provide affirmation and inspiration, thus improving optimism and outcomes.

Mentoring helps offset presumptions of incompetence and gender sidelining by growing the pool of Women of Color candidates and retaining existing deans. When there were only three women Law Deans of Color, few women had been in their shoes to whom they could turn for mentoring. Now there are fourteen Women of Color, many of whom will serve as mentors for future deans. As more women become deans, they will make an even bigger difference, but it requires deliberate steps given the historical dearth of women Law Deans of Color. The power of an effective mentor cannot be understated. "The academic landscape is littered with landmines and unwritten rules that may torpedo the careers of those who do not receive proper guidance and support. In addition to mentors, Women of Color also need sponsors . . . who will advocate for them in . . . meetings and behind closed doors" (González, 2014, p. 52).

Women Law Deans of Color should seek sponsors like provosts, deans, and board members. Trustworthy sponsors can provide meaningful introductions and invitations, acknowledge your presence, highlight your ideas and initiatives, and otherwise present you as impressive, accomplished, and worthy of respect. Women Law Deans of Color should also sponsor others who aspire to deanships. They can promote them to decision-makers, recommend them as speakers, and make introductions. With leadership comes access to influential people—women law deans should use those relationships to pay it forward.

Sidelining includes the "silencing that women experience in the workplace," which "often becomes part of a vicious circle: The more women feel silenced or 'man-terrupted' or as if their ideas have been 'bro-opted' by male peers, the more they may doubt their real value in the workplace" (Fink, 2018, p. 89). Although women deans are less likely to have silencing issues given their positions, problems remain. "When a woman speaks in a professional setting, she walks a tightrope. Either she's barely heard or she's judged as too aggressive. When a man says virtually the same thing, heads nod in appreciation for his fine idea. As a result, women often decide that saying less is more" (Sandberg & Grant, 2015, para. 5). Even when leading law schools, Women of Color struggle to find the right balance between being heard and acting too assertive. With more women leaders, we should see a new normal where we no longer discount their voices or assess them negatively when they don't align with preexisting expectations.

Sidelining also includes manterrupting, which can be mitigated by being part of a network of allies. When manterrupted, women can play "verbal chicken" (keep talking until the interrupter stops), "lean in" ("If you put your elbows on the table . . . you're less likely to be interrupted)," or "womanterrupt" ("Find a wingman or wingwoman who will interrupt the interrupter when you get interrupted"). ("Seven Practical Ways," 2016, para. 3–8). Women leaders can use these tools to finish their thoughts, reclaim control when men take over conversations, pause for new voices, and give women credit for their ideas. These tools should be effective enough over time to reduce the problem.

Professional women are all too familiar with bro-propriation—where ideas are initially ignored or bro-opted. When bro-propriated, women can "thank & yank" (thank the bro-propriator for supporting your idea but stressing it is *your* idea), or use a "wingman/woman" (someone who publicly supports your idea when proposed or runs interference, giving you credit when a bro-propriator tries to hijack it) ("Seven Practical Ways," 2016, para. 12–13). One dean said sidelining, including bro-propriation, happens, but she developed prevention strategies. "It has not been easy but my faculty meetings and even Academic Senate meetings run smoothly when I run them, providing each participant an opportunity to express [himself or herself]. Especially Women of Color. Humor also works to demonstrate that 'the female professors just said that,' or was the author of the idea and the men are trying to take credit." When leaders look out for others and use humor to point out sidelining and diffuse tension, it is a more hospitable environment for everyone.

Law deanships are mentally, physically, and emotionally exhausting, especially for women who may also be juggling family demands. When asked what sustains them, the deans shared many strategies. One woman is sustained by an "optimistic attitude, family, running, [and] knowing I am doing the right things for the right reasons." Establishing a set point of optimism can help maneuver sidelining challenges and overcome self-doubt. Healthy habits are also vital, given the inherent job stress and a dean's long hours. Family was a common source of support (one dean said her son sustains her, and another credited her faith, family, and friends). Another dean is sustained by meditation and prayer, a happy home life, and diversity of opportunity. These are healthy counterpoints to the demands of leading a law school. One dean was sustained by trust in the excellent education her school provided and the new generation of lawyers, while another said her commitment to equal justice sustains her. These responses stem from the idea of believing strongly enough in what you do that it sustains you when facing sidelining and negative presumptions.

CLOSING

Many Women of Color serve as law deans, but even with increased numbers, they are underrepresented. Gender sidelining and presumptions of incompetence obstruct access to deanships and hinder retention, as the stories in this chapter demonstrate. The battles are real and the impacts can be devastating, but they can also lead to greater resilience and satisfaction. Women's responses to my questionnaire were by turns disheartening and encouraging, and revealed the depth of strength their experiences have honed. Their presence, persistence, and leadership ameliorate gender sidelining and presumptions of incompetence while broadening entry opportunities and improving retention for Women of Color.

REFERENCES

Adaptation. (2018). In *Random House Unabridged Dictionary*. Retrieved from http://www.dictionary.com/browse/adaptation.

American Bar Association (ABA). (2013). *Law school faculty & staff by ethnicity and gender* [data file]. Retrieved from https://www.americanbar.org/groups/legal_education/resources/statistics.html.

American Bar Association (ABA). (2017, January). *A current glance at women in the law* [data file]. Retrieved from https://www.americanbar.org/content/dam/aba/marketing/women/current_ glance_ statistics_january2017.authcheckdam.pdf.

DaSilva, C. D. (2018, March 11). White male workers respond poorly to women and racial minorities in power and take it out on colleagues: Report. *Newsweek*. Retrieved from http://www.newsweek.com/white-men-react-poorly-women-and-minorities-power-positions-study-finds-839862.

DiGeronimo, J. (2018). Manterrupting—bropropriating—mansplaining: Ways men undermine women [blog post]. Retrieved from https://www.jjdigeronimo.com/manterrupting-bropropriating-mansplaining-ways-men-undermine-women/.

Dovidio, J. F. (2012). Part II: Faculty/student relationships—introduction. In Gutiérrez y Muhs, G., Niemann, Y. F., González, C. G., & Harris, A. P. (Eds.), *Presumed incompetent: The intersections of race and class for women in academia* (pp. 113–115). Logan: Utah State University Press.

Fink, J. (2018). Gender sidelining and the problem of unactionable discrimination. *Stanford Law & Policy Review*, 29(1), 57–106. doi:10.2139/ssrn.3010235.

González, C. G. (2014, July). Women of color in legal education: Challenging the presumption of incompetence, *Federal Lawyer*, 48–61.

Grant, A., & Sandberg, S. (2014, December 6). When talking about bias backfires. *New York Times*. Retrieved from https://www.nytimes.com/2014/12/07/opinion/sunday/adam-grant-and-sheryl-sandberg-on-discrimination-at-work.html.

Gutiérrez y Muhs, G., Niemann, Y. F., González, C. G., & Harris, A. P. (Eds.). (2012). *Presumed incompetent: The intersections of race and class for women in academia*. Logan: Utah State University Press.

Harris, A. P., & González, C. G. (2012). Introduction. In Gutiérrez y Muhs, G., Niemann, Y. F., González, C. G., & Harris A. P. (Eds.), *Presumed incompetent: The intersections of race and class for women in academia* (pp. 1–14). Logan: Utah State University Press.

L. Song Richardson named dean of UCI School of Law. (2017, December 21). *University of California Irvine News*. Retrieved from https://news.uci.edu/2017/12/21/l-song-richardson-named-dean-of-uci-school-of-law/.

Niemann, Y. F. (2012). Lessons from the experiences of women of color working in academia. In Gutiérrez y Muhs, G., Niemann, Y. F., González, C. G., & Harris A. P. (Eds.), *Presumed incompetent: The intersections of race and class for women in academia* (pp. 446–499). Logan: Utah State University Press.

Padilla, L. M. (2007). A gendered update on women law deans: Who, where, why, and why not? *American University Journal of Gender, Social Policy & the Law, 15*(3), 443–546.

Padilla, L. M. (2017, April). Whoosh—declining law school applications and entering credentials: Responding with pivot pedagogy. *International Journal of Arts and Humanities*, *3*(2), 43–64.

Sandberg, S., & Grant, A. (2015, January 12). Speaking while female. *New York Times*. Retrieved from https://www.nytimes.com/2015/01/11/opinion/sunday/speaking-while-female.html.

Seven practical ways to combat workplace sexism. (2016, September 15). *Newsweek*. Retrieved from http://www.newsweek.com/seven-practical-ways-combat-workplace-sexism-feminist-fight-club-498751.

Sloan, K. (2015, June 22). Rise in number of women deans at U.S. law schools: They make up 40 percent of incoming leadership. *National Law Journal*, 1–4.

Wing, A. K. (2012). Lessons from a portrait: Keep calm and carry on. In Gutiérrez y Muhs, G., Niemann, Y. F., González, C. G., & Harris A. P. (Eds.), *Presumed incompetent: The intersections of race and class for women in academia* (pp. 356–371). Logan: Utah State University Press.

SECTION THREE

SOCIAL CLASS

TWELVE

Unlikely Alliances from Appalachia to East L.A.

Insider Without and Outsider Within

Desdamona Rios and Kim A. Case

We are seemingly unlikely allies, but our working-class backgrounds inform intersectional analyses of our connections between the cultures of East Los Angeles and Appalachian East Tennessee. Patricia Hill Collins (1986) labeled herself an "outsider within" due to her intersectional standpoint as a Black woman sociology professor in the ivory tower. Using counter-storytelling, we explore Desi's *outsider within* status as a working-class Chicana academic from East Los Angeles and Kim's *insider without* location as a White working-class academic from Appalachian East Tennessee. Expanding on Kim's theorized three-phase "working-class academic arc" (Case, 2017a), we apply intersectional theory (Anzaldúa, 1987; Collins, 1990; Cortera, 1977; Crenshaw, 1989; Gutiérrez y Muhs, Niemann, González, & Harris, 2012) to our personal experiences in the academy.

Working-class studies scholars (e.g., Jensen, 2012) argue class extends beyond income as "a way of being, relating, and thinking that culminates in a shared cultural experience often invisible to the privileged and the marginalized" (Case, 2017a, p. 17). In a professional context, fitting in is often measured by shared speech and expression, food, hobbies, clothing, work ethic, and values (Attfield, 2016; Jensen, 2012; Warnock, 2016). Violation of hegemonic standards based on social class, as well as race and gender, often results in tangible consequences. From a counter-storytelling strengths perspective, we aim to harness our working-class and racialized subjectivities to reject respectability and openly critique White patriarchal middle-class culture performance in the academy.[1]

Phase 1 of the *working-class academic arc* (Case, 2017a) analyzes the promise of education as an escape from home. We received the consistent message that education was the only path to financial stability and expanding our options.

---

1. We use the term "middle class" as inclusive of upper middle class.

DOI: 10.7330/9781607329664.c012

For me (Kim), education required purposely losing my biscuits and gravy accent and keeping my single-wide trailer origins quiet. Phase 2 focuses on working-class faculty's lack of awareness of middle-class invisible rules used to judge us as uncouth. Working-class women faculty experience frequent "moments of cross-class communication slippage" (Case, 2017a, p. 25) as our cultural style clashes with gendered middle-class schemas. Phase 3 culminates in development of critical intersectional class consciousness: (re)claiming identity, endorsing a strengths perspective of working-class culture, and resisting classism in higher education. By further elaborating this three-phase arc, we hope to raise awareness of invisible and intersecting academic cultures that invalidate Women of Color and working-class ways of being and knowing, as well as encouraging coalition building among unlikely allies.

PHASE 1: TRYING TO FIT THE MOLD

Desi's Journey

I embody the predictors of presumed failure in American culture: Chicana, female, from a working-class, single-parent household, a "latch key" kid who struggled in high school. When I was a child, my White female teachers recognized my talent. However, by high school the stereotyping of adolescent Chicanx students manifested in how counselors and teachers treated me. Graduating high school was a major accomplishment in my neighborhood, and the idea of becoming a professor was nonexistent. Like many Faculty of Color, as a child I initially loved school, where I was mentored by benevolent teachers who encouraged me to excel academically. As I progressed, I learned that academia held no place for me both according to what I learned in the curriculum (no Mexican Americans) and how I was treated by (most) teachers and administrators. For example, my mother was once called into a high school counselor's office to be scolded by a White woman who assured her that I would never amount to anything.

My experience in higher education is reflective of "post-traditional" college students (Soares, 2013). Like many working-class parents, my mother hoped my sister and I would go to college but did not have the experience or information to guide us. For ten years, I managed a full-time job and part-time community college enrollment. From my experiences among educated people in corporate America and my community college curriculum, I internalized that to be successful, acceptable, and professional would require learning to speak, dress, and act a certain way, none of which reflected my neighborhood or my family. At the age of twenty-eight, I finally enrolled in a four-year university where I met a statistics professor who was a Woman of Color and took an interest in me. I was introduced to a community of professors who intentionally mentored Students of Color planning to attend graduate school. This was my first academic anchor, one of a cohort of ten working-class Latinx with aspirations to change the world. Eventually, 100 percent of this cohort earned graduate degrees in top programs in the nation, often commiserating about the incongruence between our authentic selves and expectations for our professional selves. We grew to understand that in public academic spaces we had to work against what others perceived us to be: working-class, loud, angry, and entitled to spaces only because they were reserved for us through affirmative action.

Kim's Journey

My greatest efforts to try to fit the model of middle-class academia centered on completely obliterating my Dixie accent (Case, 2017a). Although I managed to convert my voice to mimic a midwestern news anchor dialect, my brain continued to soak in a cast-iron skillet of southern accent lard like fried chicken on Sunday. Once I moved to Texas, the Appalachian came rushing back without my awareness and resulted in my own embarrassment when academics would ask me about my Kraft mac 'n' cheese speak (yes, food was/is a central part of my working-class culture). Both of my parents were first-generation high school graduates, so navigating college and the prospect of graduate school felt foreign, particularly when I encountered others judgmental of my clothes, mannerisms, and vocabulary. On a campus interview for a doctoral program in New York City, the graduate students hosting me made fun of my T.J.Maxx clothing. These students were representing one of the most social justice–oriented doctoral programs in psychology, yet they shamed me for my lack of middle-class performance.

My first year in graduate school included regular arguments with an extremely conservative White man classmate who made it clear my presence in *his* program was a matter of my unearned affirmative action handouts. When I informed him that my admission into the program was the direct result of a White man taking a better offer at another university, he failed to understand the implications—that I had barely made it into a doctoral program due to a White guy's greater opportunities. These encounters with classist and sexist microaggressions and my conscious efforts to murder my own voice (accent) resulted in rebellious behavior such as getting a tongue piercing in my first year as a doctoral student. My faculty advisor/mentor, a White Jewish man in his sixties, was baffled, insisting that I explain why on earth I would do such a thing. At the time, I could not explain. On reflection, I think this served as a way for me to resist being subsumed by the elitist (upper)-middle-class culture that ruled my educational environment by connecting to the counterculture of the late 1990s.

PHASE 2—VIOLATING (INVISIBLE) ACADEMIC NORMS

Desi as Outsider Within

Arriving at graduate school, I suffered from the typical impostor syndrome described by the status of outsider within. There were few Chicanx, and none of the graduate students spoke publicly about being from working-class, single-parent households. Everyone seemed so polished, educated, and knowledgeable about how to behave in an academic context. I was thirty-two years old when

I started graduate school, ten years older than (most) everyone else, and I also lacked the tacit knowledge of how to succeed in this new culture. Nonetheless, I had stumbled into a university whose mission included creating equitable spaces for students. I was generously counseled by my mentors on the importance of rigorous training as preparation for the world of academia, where most people would assume my incompetence from the outset. After I graduated, I felt adequately prepared to challenge presumptions of my inadequacy or lack of fit in the academy. After all, I had learned the jargon, the research methods, the dress code, and how to carry myself (e.g., minimal hand gesticulation) in academic spaces.

It was never explicitly stated that I should tone down my ethnic identity, but norms of academia are firmly grounded in middle-class Whiteness. I regarded my mentors and graduate school friends as my allies, some of whom I connected with on the basis of our shared working-class backgrounds, not necessarily race or gender. Although I still felt out of place, I also felt adequately supported. I was surprised and disheartened to learn that the culture of my graduate program was not representative of the academy more generally. Early in my career, a prominent Afro-Latino scholar advised me that many White people in the academy would offer a warm welcome to me as long as they felt they were fulfilling a diversity checklist by "helping" a Woman of Color. Once the paternalistic fantasy was dispelled by my academic success in achieving equal status—or worse, surpassing their status in the field—I would find myself in a very chilly climate. Violating class-based norms and expectations also has repercussions. For example, when Kim surpassed, in both promotions and salary, faculty who had been at the university for several years longer than she had, she was met with strategic bullying and targeted attacks on her career. This bullying and mobbing involved refusing to provide basic information needed to perform her administrative duties, coordinated gaslighting, passive-aggressive silent treatment, and promoting negative views of her teaching, scholarship, and service, despite her national awards and recognition.

Across academic settings, I am often the only Person of Color in the room. I mostly remain silent on all matters unless asked directly to contribute. If I do comment, responses from colleagues range from polite dismissal to open hostility. Aside from my race and gender, I challenge academic norms in my scholarship (qualitative methods, marginalized groups), teaching (diversifying the curriculum), and service work (working with at-risk Latinx adolescents). Challenging normalized practices and ideologies informed by White male middle-class sensibilities means colleagues dismiss my work as less rigorous and overly scrutinize it to identify any detail that would confirm the illegitimacy of my arguments. For example, my community-based educational research requires years of developing trust and establishing shared research goals before producing a publication. Unfortunately, some colleagues/administrators regard the time spent building relationships with community partners as a lack of productivity rather than legitimate work with underserved communities. I witnessed another example of class-based racism in my experience with a White woman who, discussing the faculty in her own department, declared, "We want one of our own!" after learning of another department hiring a talented Latina. The blatant tokenism and exotification of the future Latina colleague felt analogous to the White woman shopping for a new pet. Then, once People of Color are hired, the implicit expectation is that we will "behave" by demonstrating our mastery of White middle-class sensibilities.

Kim as Insider Without

An unsettling White middle-class norm is the façade of polite respectability. From a working-class perspective, efforts to delegitimize work that challenges oppressive systems take place outside of our awareness. For example, middle-class standards endorse talking behind other people's backs versus the "unseemly" working-class practice of confronting others when there are disagreements. Much to my surprise, I had a rare glimpse behind the veil of politeness when a White upper-middle-class academic called me "bossy" and admitted to gossiping about me with others. When she asked for professional advice, I had responded with phrases such as "Well, you know who you *should* talk to? Kathy. You *should* let her know your course schedule preference." She had held onto this misreading of me for several years without my knowledge. To be crystal clear, my "should" phrasing was in response to being explicitly asked for advice. As an insider without a middle-class culture decoder ring, I was baffled by being called bossy because my deliberate approach to mentoring is take it or leave it, and I regularly state this position out loud. I tell my peers and junior faculty to seek other views to best inform their decisions. After much reflection, I considered how social class influenced this cross-class communication slippage. Unaware that my working-class discourse patterns violated norms, I began to recognize how small phrasing differences can hurt working-class women academics.

Gender undoubtedly plays a major intersecting role in this scenario because we have yet to hear any faculty member label a man "bossy." White men yelling in meetings or demanding obedience from colleagues somehow remain free of this negative label. For me and my family, and arguably for working-class culture more broadly, women regularly give each other solicited advice by using the word *should*. Unlike middle-class connotations of "should" as an attempt to control another person, working-class use of the word simply communicates, "If I were in your shoes, this is what I think I would do." Even though I intended all of these "shoulds" as supportive suggestions, the difference in classed language framed me as professionally problematic and damaged my cultural capital. Indeed, classed miscommunications result in detrimental effects only for the marginalized, with no damage to the privileged upper-middle-class academic's reputation.

As I found when I joined a social media group for working-class academics, these experiences of being misread across class lines occur quite often. In response to a post about microaggressions experienced in academia, working-class scholars related common tales of being labeled by middle-class colleagues as blunt, salty, rough around the edges, brutally honest troublemakers. In our personal experiences, middle-class academics label working-class White women as difficult, unprofessional, harsh, opinionated, overly emotional, irrational, demanding, and reactionary. For Women of Color, the "angry" label is an added descriptor to the list. Working-class scholar Anna Rita Napoleone recounted her surprise at being viewed as aggressive, confrontational, in-your-face, manly, and unfeminine (LeCourt & Napoleone, 2010). Napoleone and many working-class academics pointed out that we already tone down working-class performance and make conscious efforts to conform to middle-class expectations for communication style and politeness, yet it never seems sufficient.

LACK OF CLASS ANALYSIS: MISREADING POTENTIAL ALLIES IN PHASE 2

One way to quickly identify an ally is to assume shared values based on superficial markers of identity such as race or gender. Due to this reliance on identity politics, we often miss the invisible threads that unite us because it is more difficult to determine people's social class background, social justice orientation, commitment to recognizing their own privilege, or political leanings merely by looking at them. Through a (too) slow progression of trusting each other as colleagues and allies, we (Desi and Kim) came to understand the value of making connections across marginalized identities. Informed by our own research on intersectional theory and pedagogy (e.g., Case, 2017b; Rios & Eaton, 2016), we strive to build plans of action that consider intersectional lived experiences. With this in mind, we found common ground at the intersections of social class (both from working-class, single-mother households), gender (cisgender women), and our social justice values.

The University of Michigan served as common ground for us. Kim began collaborating with UM faculty while Desi was a doctoral student in psychology and women's studies. Dr. Elizabeth Cole invited both of us to join her study of the effectiveness of race and ethnicity courses, and Kim visited Ann Arbor to work on data analysis and writing the manuscript in 2009.

Desi's First Encounter with Kim

My recollection of Kim is that she was eager to fit in. She gave us each greeting cards wherein she expressed being excited to work with us. Although her enthusiasm was endearing, I was uncomfortable because it was so out of place. I was very mindful to emulate the cool exterior of a scholar, and certainly no one in my graduate program publicly exuded this type of overt joy about working with colleagues. I painfully hid my own tendency to publicly show emotion that violated middle-class norms. I read Kim's enthusiasm as suspect due to previous experiences with well-intentioned White women who were "excited" to work with a Woman of Color. However, this often resulted in their subtle behavioral rejection of me as their equal. My lack of intersectional consciousness and focus on succeeding in the academy meant that I failed to analyze social class and ask critical questions about why certain expressions were appropriate in this particular space while others were read as unnecessary, egregious, or even uncouth.

Kim's First Encounter with Desi

My first encounter with Desi in the basement lab of Lane Hall at UM made me nervous. My imposter syndrome was at full throttle, so all of my thoughts revolved around my fear she would figure out that I lacked the intellectual fortitude to work on research with UM doctoral students such as herself. Here I was at an elite research institution working with top scholars, and I believed I had no business being in that space. In my eagerness to gain acceptance, I tried to get a read on Desi, but found her a difficult nut to crack. She rarely changed facial expressions or offered any of the nonverbal cues I look for to determine "friend" or "foe." Desi always dressed in the utmost professional attire, while I came to the lab in jeans and a hoodie. That interaction led me to perceive her as middle class (maybe even upper middle class), distant, and quiet. Once we became faculty colleagues, it still took years before I finally had the fortune to overcome her protective wall.

Barriers to Social Justice Ally Coalitions

In essence, we were suspicious of each other. Intersectional ally work cannot move forward when we allow these structural barriers to psychologically block our ability to fashion solid coalitions across perceived boundaries. Identity-based perceptions and middle-class cultural habitus expectations influence perceptions and create barriers that prevent recognition of common ground. Cognitive energy spent (mis)reading others distracts from development of intersectional ally partnerships, thus maintaining oppression in multiple forms (e.g., ableism, transphobia, anti-immigrant). When Kim invited me (Desi) to attend the Liberal Redneck comedy tour of Trae Crowder and friends, which highlights White working-class culture from an intersectional perspective (critiquing racism, homophobia, Islamophobia) while breaking down stereotypes, I found the comedy relatable to my own Chicanx working-class culture. Knowing Trae is from Kim's hometown in East Tennessee, I laughed throughout the show because of the undeniable commonalities between "white trash" and "hood" experiences. Replace a few details in Trae Crowder's show, and it could be George Lopez's standup (e.g., mismatched dishes and free plastic cups as appropriate dinnerware). In this setting outside of academia, we identified common experiences and began our intersectional analysis of systemic class-based discrimination and unearned privilege.

PHASE 3: CRITICAL INTERSECTIONAL CLASS CONSCIOUSNESS

For the small group of working-class academics that make it to phase 3, this stage is characterized by development of critical intersectional class consciousness

(Case, 2017a), (re)claiming devalued working-class identities, recognizing strengths of one's culture of origin, and resisting oppression and rejecting respectability. Our nonprototypical presentations as professors (e.g., anti-racist, LGBT allies, not White middle-class men) define us as radical departures from the Whitestream norm. Phase 3 provides healing through eye-opening realizations and pathways for embracing the previously tenuous position of feeling alienated from both home and profession. As noted by Collins and Bilge (2016), intersectionality requires both critical inquiry and critical praxis. Radical academics insist on inclusion while interrupting and making visible the intersecting academic performances that create and perpetuate injustice. For example, within the faculty search process, if a powerful White woman calls a Woman of Color candidate's credibility into question, stating, "I think someone else conducted her data analyses and created her presentation for her," allies must be willing to publicly question the basis of such (racist and/or sexist) accusations. In this scenario, resistance demands rejecting polite respectability to bluntly point out that the candidate expertly explained each slide and was able to answer complex questions with ease. In fact, we both bring up the topic of race and implicit bias when we experience similar scenarios. This resistance comes with consequences, especially if the perpetrator occupies a position of power and chooses to retaliate (e.g., within annual review ratings and P&T letters).

Critical Intersectional Class Consciousness for Personal Change

Building alliances can be challenging, especially when a social identity like social class can be invisible when intentionally hidden (like Desi) or unavoidable (e.g., Kim's insistent accent). As noted by Stewart (1998), understanding a person's motivation includes consideration of obstacles faced, resources needed, and strategies used to pursue goals, all of which may differ for working-class and middle-class faculty. Like all self-reflexive work, identifying our own biases and finding common ground requires cognitive energy.

As a White woman and ever-aspiring anti-racist ally, I (Kim) continually reflect on my role as senior faculty member and mentor to Women and Men of Color (faculty and students) in these contexts. My personal journey across the working-class academic arc culminated in development of my critical intersectional *class* consciousness (Case, 2017a). Considering the historic groundwork laid by my predecessors, I (Desi) continually reflect on my privilege as a member of the academy, reclaiming my voice so that I can mentor future generations of academics and work toward diversifying the academy. To break down these barriers to allies across race lines, I began to analyze my tendency to avoid certain expressions deemed too "ethnic." I questioned why the "best" way to be a professional must mimic White middle-class people and their ways of being. Over time, I learned to appreciate Kim's speaking up as courageous rather than distasteful and analyzed why I had a negative reaction in the first place. Kim violated middle-class White women's norms by directly challenging social injustices in our professional settings, something I eventually recognized as stemming from her/our working-class culture, which honors transparency and honesty as sacred values.

Strategies for identifying allies include mindfulness about who is speaking up on your behalf. Kim consistently calls for institutional support and inclusion of working-class students and faculty in "diversity" initiatives. For example, Women of Color, who are often working class, frequently receive biased student evaluations. These evaluations create a daunting obstacle to career advancement. On her own initiative, Kim chaired a committee to rewrite the annual review criteria for evaluation of teaching. This new policy included six themed areas related to teaching effectiveness and reduced student evaluations to one item within one of the six areas. In essence, this evaluation policy decentered student evaluations, which disproportionately harm Women of Color during annual review and, perhaps more important, during promotion and tenure review.

Additionally, increasing the visibility of working-class faculty who express an interest in serving as role models and mentors in curriculum and faculty development, and in ally training to help middle-class colleagues understand microaggressions and appreciate the strengths of working-class culture (Case, 2017a) can unite people who are interested in addressing social class issues.

Critical Intersectional Class Consciousness for Institutional Change

Intersectional theory demands going beyond the individual level to critical analysis of power operating at systemic, structural, institutional, and societal levels to maintain inequality (Dill & Zambrana, 2009). Below, we provide suggestions for harnessing critical intersectional class consciousness to transform institutional policies, training, and advocacy to promote Women of Color and working-class women faculty (recognizing these groups overlap, but not entirely) in higher education. Our call to action includes institutional changes to support working-class faculty:

- promoting and rewarding intersectional diversity, equity, and inclusion work (teaching, research, service, leadership) in all evaluations of faculty (e.g., annual review, tenure, promotion to full professor, promotion to department chair);
- training all search committees and individuals involved in faculty review on their own privilege, implicit bias, student evaluation bias, faculty experiences of stereotype threat, the impact of microaggressions, and so on; and
- designing mentorship programs inclusive of Women of Color and working-class White women, from a critical intersectional class consciousness perspective, that illuminate the three phases of the working-class academic arc.

In particular, we call attention to the problem of invisible work done by Women of Color and working-class women. We suggest the following for making invisible work visible, formalized, and documented:

- formalize any roles with titles such that they are included on CVs and tenure and promotion review documents;

- convert informal advising/mentoring of students into an official group with a name and title, such as "director of the Combahee Student Leaders Team";
- document time spent on student emotional support and other crises, especially when it is related to diversity or social justice, to show the disproportionate burden on certain faculty;
- document mentoring of colleagues, including formal (e.g., research collaboration) and informal (e.g., inviting new faculty to lunch or reaching out to colleagues who are struggling);
- develop service checklists that explicitly ask if a faculty member contributed food, took notes for a committee, organized the committee (even if not the actual chair), or arranged social events that contribute to team-building;
- update policies to place the same value on formal committee work and invisible work;
- keep track of the number of new course preparations and who is assigned more/less work (paying particular attention to race, gender, and class).

McIntosh (1988) argued that those without privilege must develop sophisticated coping and survival skills that the privileged class does not possess. We are not romanticizing class struggle, but rather highlighting the importance of diversifying the academy not only in race and gender but in class (as well as other marginalized social groups). Skills, coping strategies, and values held by working-class people help many of us navigate a world that privileges the middle and upper classes. Contrary to the deficit model that assigns negative attributes to working-class character, we reframe these deficits as strengths drawn from working-class origins. Working-class culture validates questioning rules, not trusting authority, expressing emotion, using our hands while storytelling, valuing honesty and transparency, speaking truth to power, laughing out loud, debating with passion and energy, cheering for the underdog, authenticity, using sarcasm/exaggeration as discourse tools, cursing as acceptable vocabulary, giving generously to others, sharing what little you have, celebrating the accomplishments of others, focusing on the welfare of others, saying what you mean, meaning what you say, contributing to your community, pulling your weight, and following through on commitments. By recognizing these strengths and raising awareness of the value of honoring working-class ways of being and knowing, we can express our authentic selves and contribute to social justice transformation in higher education.

Resisting the deficit model that paints working-class ways as inferior, we embrace the call to honor "prickly" women, as proposed by Caballero and Knupskly (2018). They praised prickly mid-career women who ask the tough questions, stand up for justice, question inequality, and lead with courage. As these women resist oppression and reject respectability, they endure a laundry list of negative labels such as "bossy," as in Kim's experience described above, while being systemically silenced, stereotyped as angry, and dismissed as emotional. In our experience, the women who get shunned and isolated due to their prickly ways are most often working-class women who violate middle-class gender expectations of the quiet, deferential, passive woman. As bell hooks (1993) noted, we must reclaim our roots as our most powerful resource. In support of this work, we need middle-class allies to recognize their privilege and become vocal agents of change in higher education.

REFERENCES

Anzaldúa, G. (1987). *Borderlands/La frontera.* San Francisco: Aunt Lute Books.

Attfield, S. (2016). Rejecting respectability: On being unapologetically working class. *Journal of Working-Class Studies, 1*(1), 45–57.

Caballero, S., & Knupskly, A. (2018, May 23). In praise of prickly women. *Inside Higher Ed.* Retrieved from https://www.insidehighered.com/views/2018/05/23/why-academe-should-honor-prickly-women-opinion.

Case, K. (2017a). Insider without: Journey across the working-class academic arc. *Journal of Working-Class Studies, 2*(2), 16–35.

Case, K. (2017b). *Intersectional pedagogy: Complicating identity and social justice.* New York: Routledge.

Collins, P. H. (1986). Learning from the outsider within: The sociological significance of black feminist thought. *Social Problems, 33*(6), 14–32.

Collins, P. H. (1990). *Black feminist thought: Knowledge, consciousness, and the politics of power.* New York: Routledge.

Collins, P. H., & Bilge, S. (2016). *Intersectionality.* Malden, MA: Polity.

Cortera, M. (1977). *The Chicana feminist.* Austin: Info Systems Development.

Crenshaw, K. (1989). Demarginalizing the intersection of race and sex: A black feminist critique of antidiscrimination doctrine, feminist theory, and antiracist politics. *University of Chicago Legal Forum, 1989*(1), 139–167.

Dill, B. T., & Zambrana, R. E. (Eds.). (2009). *Emerging intersections: Race, class, and gender in theory, policy, and practice.* New Brunswick, NJ: Rutgers University Press.

Gutiérrez y Muhs, G., Niemann, Y. F., González, C. G., & Harris, A. P. (Eds.). (2012). *Presumed incompetent: The intersections of race and class for women in academia.* Logan: Utah State University Press.

hooks, b. (1993). Keeping close to home: Class and education. In M. Tokarczyk & E. Fay (Eds.), *Working-class women in the academy: Laborers in the knowledge factory* (pp. 99–111). Amherst: University of Massachusetts Press.

Jensen, B. (2012). *Reading classes: On culture and classism in America.* Ithaca, NY: Cornell University Press.

LeCourt, D., & Napoleone, A. R. (2010). Teachers with(out) class: Transgressing academic social space through working-class performances. *Pedagogy, 11*(1), 81–107.

McIntosh, P. (1988). *White privilege and male privilege: A personal account of coming to see correspondences through work in women's studies* (Working Paper No. 189). Wellesley, MA: Wellesley Centers for Women.

Rios, D., & Eaton, A. (2016). Perceived social support in the lives of gay, bisexual and queer Hispanic college men. *Culture, Health and Sexuality, 18*(10), 1093–1106.

Soares, L. (2013). Post-traditional learners and the transformation of postsecondary education: A manifesto for college leaders. *American Council on Education.* Retrieved from http://www.acenet.edu/news-room/Documents/Post-Traditional-Learners.pdf.

Stewart, A. J. (1998). Doing personality research: How can feminist theory help? In B. M. Clinchy & J. K. Norem (Eds.), *The gender and psychology reader* (pp. 54–68). New York: New York University Press.

Warnock, D. (2016). Paradise lost? Patterns and precarity in working-class academic narratives. *Journal of Working-Class Studies, 1*(1), 28–44.

THIRTEEN

Academia Is Violence

Generatives from a First-Generation, Low-Income PhD Mother of Color

Jamiella Brooks

> Word-work is sublime, she thinks, because it is generative; it makes meaning that secures our difference, our human difference—the way in which we are like no other life.
>
> (MORRISON, 1993)

This essay contains narratives about how academia constructs violence, even from within and by those opposed to it. I will describe three areas of violence and suggest ways to generate discourse against it. In addition to generating anti-violence, some instances will require deep epistemic violence to uproot what the ivory (and sometimes ebony) tower wrought.[1] These three areas include: the subject/ontology, community, and knowledge/episteme. These begin at the level of the self, expand to the self-with-others, and end with the knowledge that the value systems for knowledge constructed by academia are not the only means of knowing. Ultimately, it is important to understand that, as we function *within* academia, we must resist participation in the violent logic of its claims. My aim is to turn these interconnected forms that academia has wrenched from us back in on themselves: philosophy need not be limited to the blanched dead. May thought be wrestled from those who believe that only self-proclaimed "thinkers" are doing all the thinking.

---

1. The use of the term *ebony tower* to designate the involvement of People of Color in academia does not go far enough to erase hierarchical relationships that insist on forms of power to maintain legitimacy. Arguably, an ebony tower is a subset of academia just as is its ivory iteration, yet it must be made clear that "ivory" wields a different form of power, one that is predicated on a historical prominence and saliency. The two are not interchangeable, although they are under the same umbrella.

DOI: 10.7330/9781607329664.c013

SUBJECTIVITY/ONTOLOGY

I did not want to admit that I was situated in violence, but even if I wasn't its core, I was complicit as its hand.

When I first stood in front of a room of academics presenting my research on a Moroccan novel, it did not occur to me that I was inscribed in violence. Despite a sound thesis, the intense research needed to present the subject, and a sense of connection to the African continent via my own Blackness, I had forgotten that while the stories were fictional, the people and the culture were real. Because conference presentations demand a voice of authority, I spoke as though I had knowledge despite my lack of experience. In an effort to connect to the Black diaspora, I falsely believed that the "me" as a Woman of Color could usurp my status as a Western American, whose Blackness was crafted by a different history.

I came to African literature written in the French language because I believed it could offer something my English major did not. I could not relate to Whitman's struggles or Dante's grammar. While characters who traveled the world and never went hungry complained of their affluence while marveling at Othered peoples, I wondered what happened to the *real* people, those who struggled in ways that I struggled as the daughter of a single mom who could barely afford fresh fruit; whose forebears protested in streets under threat of water cannons and guns; whose ancestors contemplated the meaning of their very being. While the field of literary criticism insisted the author was dead and claimed that meaning must transcend history and context, I wondered about my mother's name alongside those of Black authors whose agency was tied to radical visibility, whose histories were inscribed in and through their names.

I resonated with the Cameroonian child in Ferdinand Oyono's *Une vie de Boy* and the pain he endured as he experienced his Blackness colliding with unfamiliar customs and cultures. I shared with Assia Djebar's *L'amour, la fantasia* a love of finding one's voice in a foreign tongue. Her work showed me it was possible to snatch lost history back from the hands of the self-proclaimed victors through storytelling and prose. These experiences eventually materialized, years later, as a dissertation on the representation of women's voices in North African French-language novels.

Yet as my predecessors wrote of *epistemic violence*, I came to discover that my work was a participant in it; the humanities suffer from a center rooted in and governed by anti-Blackness just as other disciplines do. French and Francophone studies still rely on the canonical works from what was called "the hexagon," or France proper. Despite the inclusion of African literatures written in French, only the "sanctioned" literatures of the canon are given attention. Even among these, space is not made to ask the right questions, understand the histories from the perspective of those that lived them, or challenge the disciplinary limitations that still uphold non-African scholars as authorities over African ones. These things were never explicitly taught to me but what I came to learn through the mentorship and wisdom of those who called out "the complicities between state power and corporate academia" (Benyoussef, 2015, p. 120).

The sense of there being something deeply wrong within my own discipline was a move toward Lorde's theory of the *erotic*: I was *doing* what was required, but the feeling in the doing disconcerted me (1984, p. 54).[2] When I began to pay attention to scholars away from the center, particularly Scholars of Color, I found others who articulated why I sensed my own scholarship was failing. I learned that good scholarship was not simply the anthropological excavation of people, places, and things; it went beyond mere resonance. I needed to untrain from my discipline, whose mechanisms were exposed; scholars are disciplined, and in our being disciplined, we do not question the methodological obfuscations that our discipline wields. What potential harm does this create, and whom does this exclude? What violence is required of me by the university, what compliance required by the very structures I claim to dismantle in my thesis? These questions are not deemed relevant by disciplines that draw their lines through exclusion without bringing attention to the logic of their exclusion. As I presented my research, I wondered: what investment did I have in the peoples I interpreted through literary criticism?

In this sense, I *generated* epistemic violence—violence against subjects—with no recognition of such, because I was too concerned with advancing my own scholarship in line with a system whose logic rests on this form of violence. Spivak expresses this in reference to colonialism; we need only shift two words to make the parallel: "Colonialism [Academia] insists upon a certain narrative of a subjugated people, which includes their knowledge of themselves (in particular, *one* narrative of reality is established as the norm) . . . Subjugated knowledge is the subtext of the palimpsestic narrative of [epistemic] imperialism" (1994, p. 76).

The modus operandi of such discipline is this: I, the composer, have knowledge that you, the reader, need to possess. I, the scholar, will inspire a new line of inquiry that you, the learner, will follow. I, the well-meaning text-weaver, will compose the meaning that you, the text-swallower, will decode. One can speak about *poverty* all day long and generate new lines of inquiry, yet never set foot in the house to break bread with the impoverished, except for "research purposes." And if the academic is also impoverished? The positionality is torn: one who exists both inside and outside this research risks turning oneself, friends, and family into objects of research within the system.

Western academia draws its strength by imagining that it creates knowledge where it somehow did not before exist. It assumes that it *generates* knowledge, and that the only way to accomplish this is via an I-Authority that never fully asserts a real *self*—one who says, "Who am I, and what am I doing here?" No, the authority of Western academia must be two-dimensional; she must be a poster figure unburdened by anything associated with life, free from poverty and debt, no visible pregnancy or family to support, in full physical and mental health, without dynamism. Without spirit.

---

2. I am grateful to Cecilia Caballero of Chicana M(other)work for this insight (and for our friendship as mother-scholars), which helped me articulate many aspects of this chapter.

Who am I? I am a first-generation PhD, first-generation bilingual, first to leave the country for educational purposes, mother of two, wife, daughter, believer, descendant of enslaved ancestors. I gave birth to and raised two kids while pursuing my PhD which, through the support of my husband, family, and community, I earned in March 2018.

For my family, I am the outlier, the one who had made it as our first PhD in a root system broken by a history of slavery and anti-Blackness. Not knowing the unspoken rules of the game, they supported me as best they could; for Families of Color, merely possessing a PhD speaks volumes of the difficult work that must be done. In the beginning, I diligently did the work, played by the rules, questioned little, because *I-as-a-subject* was already in question. I was too deep, too three-dimensional, *too much*.

My husband has a picture of me that he titled "Scholar Mom in Red." I had just finished a panel session that I organized; my son, still breastfeeding at the time, is at my hip, with bright, large eyes and tiny, socked feet. His expression reads: skeptical.

He was unimpressed by the whole pomp and circumstance demanded of the conference form, in which we spend excessive amounts of money to visit a gentrified city we'll never get to explore, run around in fancy clothes we never regularly wear, give papers very few will remember. What I do remember is that I did not believe myself to be a scholar: I was an impostor. Graduate student, mother, and new to both of these roles, I stumbled through the conference trying to make connections but ultimately I felt ignored. I was adorned by the twenty-first-century double-consciousness for Scholar-Mothers of Color: ashamed in my scholarly dimension for needing to bring my son to the conference, and ashamed, also, of being a scholar who dragged her son to the corners of the earth for her own selfish professional reasons.

Ashamed to be attending this conference, where I felt like an outsider, for the sake of a line on my CV. One of my scholar heroes was in attendance, and I breathlessly hoped that she would offer some words of encouragement. At the end of the session, when I tried to talk with her, it was clear that she had attended the event only to see a former student, and that my work was of little interest to her. I realized that academia, just like Hollywood, has an idol problem.

While academia tries to claim that the true human is truly alone, pregnancy taught me otherwise. I was a co-inhabited being, sustaining life that would become the thread of my dissertation, the purpose of my labor, a child of Black futurity.

Barbara Christian warned us in "The Race for Theory" that "the critic yearning for attention has displaced the writer and has conceived of herself and himself as the center." (1988, p. 67) The academic-centric position is not simply actively pursued; it is central to the construction of the profile of any academic. At conferences, the talks given by high-profile names are more heavily attended—in plenitude—than the low-profile ones, regardless of title or subject. Very few of us who are on "the other side" reach out to those graduate students whose presentations could have needed more work to offer critical, but beneficial, feedback.

The academic machine gives little time for this, and helping others this way does not contribute to the records of those on the tenure track. I will not mince words: this, too, is violence. Graduate students and other burgeoning scholars need a sharpened scholar who could act as a mentor, if even briefly. Though the conference is a unique space where we can come together across the nation to do so, the power dynamic makes it very difficult for graduate students experiencing impostor syndrome to breach the barriers required to effectively network. I remember meeting another scholar at a different conference and gathering the courage to thank her for her book. She looked at my nametag, perhaps saw the words "graduate student" or did not recognize my name, and walked away.

Sometimes impostor syndrome is real because we make impostors of one another.

A break from the system entails separating subjectivity from the subject: my being isn't "about me," and my history does not speak to selfishness. The sacrifices my mother made as a solo parent raising two children, the sacrifices of her parents before her combating a deeply segregated America, the sacrifices of our ancestors even before them: all these speak to an ontology of multiple beings working toward a shared, equitable existence. Accordingly, in my scholarship, I must privilege voices beyond the canon and take care to include those scholars who also directly critique the discipline; and when it is time to mentor others, I must base my mentorship on a model of sacrifice: *the first shall be last*; the last shall be first.

COMMUNITY

> *I taped this Post-it Note to my computer so that I would read it every time I sat down to work: "The year my papa turned eighty-three—I received my PhD."*

This note, written in the past tense, was intended for the future. By imagining my future, I could keep in perspective that the difficult times would be over some day. By invoking my grandfather, I reimagined time as both continuous and recursive. The year before, he had survived triple bypass heart surgery. By keeping in mind what was really important, I was able to survive the academic wounds.

Our liberation from the violence of academia lies not only in drawing strength from allies within the academy, but also in sustaining and strengthening communities that lie *outside* of academia. Nothing from within the center can move the center (Ngũgĩ 1993). The ebony tower is still a tower, and it towers over those who do not uphold its power.

Sherronda Brown argues in "Decolonizing Black Intellectualism" that although references and homages are important, when Scholars of Color constantly have to fight for visibility, we need not name-drop or devalue those of different socioeconomic classes and education levels in order to do our work. Brown says, brilliantly, "Academia and its language can be useful, but it will never get us free" (para. 20). Indeed, we must return to those things that have sustained us—our faith, our families, our communities for which we fight—in order to fulfill the dream of our ancestors: that of liberation.

Communities from within are also necessary, especially when the academy tells us in whispers to check our identities at the door: those of us caring for aging or ill family members; battling our own illnesses; sending home what little money we make to sustain those we love because the world does not sustain them. Yet how often is space made to discuss these problems outside of those impacted by it? One year I received an annual review of my performance from my graduate program expressing concern that my workload was untenable and that if I were to graduate I should cut back if it was "financially feasible." No—it wasn't. Every quarter I would take on two, sometimes three separate TA and researcher positions in order to make ends meet; I often worked at 75 percent (thirty hours per week), though the recommended was 50 percent (twenty hours per week). From my point of view, I was making a strategic decision; how else could I make ends meet when nearly three-fifths of my salary went to housing alone while I also supported family? Yet in my marginal performance review, it was assumed that my workload—which included mentoring other students—took me away from research. There was no consideration of how departments and those in positions of power might combat the systemic problems that made it necessary for students like me to work more (such as the lack of affordable housing, rising education fees, previous student loan debt, and limited scholarship and fellowship funding.) Even though my husband also worked to support us, we are today haunted by six-figure debt.

It is unsurprising, then, that when I became pregnant, so sick and exhausted that I missed two consecutive classes, I feared repercussions for having needs outside of the academic context. In a ten-week quarter system of one course per week, missing more than one class is the death knell of a graduate course grade. I knew I had to drag myself to my courses despite my extreme nausea, or risk dropping out for the quarter. Fearful of the repercussions, I approached Dr. Timm—a professor of sociolinguistics who also happened to be the associate dean of graduate studies—to explain. Her response was unexpected. She asked me: "Do you know what your rights are as a pregnant graduate student?" I was so used to the idea that there were "no excuses" in graduate school—I was told to get the work done or don't, that I alone was responsible or irresponsible—I no longer thought in terms of "rights." She directed me to the human resources website and to different programs the university offered to pregnant graduate students that I had no idea existed, including breastfeeding rooms and maternity leave.[3] My story ended well, but there were others who did not benefit from these policies because of the stigmas associated with them (Mason, 2013). A graduate student friend of mine knew of the policies, but was forced to pay the student who served as her substitute while she was on leave. She was aware that this was

3. I am in debt to Dr. Lenora Timm, may she rest in peace, for the ways she reached out to her students, both challenging and loving them. I pray that others can see in her work a good model for student advocacy.

a violation, but fearful that her advisor would not graduate her if she refused. The existence of policies does not always result in the affirmation of rights.

Allies such as Dr. Timm are difficult to find in the academy, but they are necessary to speak the volumes of unspoken. Two compelling works exploring oppression in academia both make similar claims: "There are codes and habits that Faculty of Color often don't know about because those unwritten practices are so subtle as to seem unimportant until something goes wrong, and then the assumption is that the Person of Color is incompetent, lazy, or lying" (Matthew, 2016, p. xv). Note this alongside, "A set of unstated rules also shapes your experiences . . . Rooted in white supremacy, [they] afford unfair opportunities to white colleagues while imposing unfair constraints" on Academics of Color (Rockquemore & Laszloffy, 2008, p. 152). Without Dr. Timm's advice, I likely would have attempted to return to my teaching duties immediately after giving birth, unaware of the options I had, in order to avoid being painted as incompetent. One colleague told me that because it was "my choice" to have children, it was also "my burden" to deal with the consequences of the increasingly difficult ways of navigating a system that was not built to support first-generation Academic Mothers of Color.

Yet in community, I found allies with similar struggles. While some of my colleagues complained about trying to sell their house, we built a sense of home in the Solano Park Apartments, a multiethnic, multicultural community on UC Davis's campus, a ten-minute walk or bike ride from most buildings. It was a haven for all of us who lived there, a key reason academics could thrive while parenting. Student parents were given priority for housing; some of our neighbors were indigenous, others from Uganda, Pakistan, Egypt, Italy, Spain, Korea, Mexico, China—the list goes on. Many mornings I worked on my dissertation while my children played with those of other residents. Community programs like La Leche League meetings and gardening ran regularly throughout the year, and one summer our RAs helped obtain free lunch for our children through a social assistance program. While it is clear how such a community promotes academic thriving for those of us balancing multiple roles, it is not valued by the academy: at present, the university is committed to demolishing the housing, replacing it with more expensive apartments in an already predominately affluent, largely White community, while administrators and housing management actively encourage internal dissent, asking that neighbors betray neighbors by calling Child Protective Services on any parents who do not hover over their children like a hawk, and dictating that RAs step out of their community-building role to police residents. The record is as intentionally broken as the system: the people existing within it are used as tools to perpetuate the violence upon which the system depends.

I would not have been able to complete my PhD without my community of mothers and fathers, bound by our collective struggle against academia's discriminations (Mason & Younger, 2014).

In time, my children and the parents who sustained this community will hold a wake for this housing, slated to be torn down and not rebuilt. We know as scholars that we must do the rebuilding ourselves, and ensure that our children carry forth those tools to dismantle structures that try to displace and compromise underrepresented scholars.

KNOWLEDGE/EPISTEME

Things I know:

I brought two children into this world with my body, a miracle given the stress and pressures of obtaining my PhD.

After each child, I successfully (with support) returned to teach when my children were only six weeks old.

I can survive trauma and maintain my teaching and research duties as best I can.

I can hardly fear the academic process when my son is whisked to the hospital for breathing problems.

I can hardly fear the academic process when I get up at 3:00 a.m. to rush my husband to the ER and teach at 9:00 a.m. the next day.

I fear far greater things than the dissertation.

This is what we must tell ourselves to survive the violence of academia.

There is no manual that can encapsulate the graduate student experience. Advice is contingent, both time- and discipline-sensitive. As with parenting, marriage, and death, there are many published opinions but nothing universally acknowledged or applied.

My children know more than the world claims they know, and through my relationship with them, they have helped more knowledge thrive within me. For example, I no longer fear the opinions of others who have no interest in my well-being. I can brush off the scoffing when I announce that I was late because my son decided that his diaper was no longer useful; *they* have no bright-eyed brilliance to behold when they return from work.

I no longer doubt my ability to create meaningful scholarship in seemingly impossible conditions. I fought through exhaustion, interrupted sleep, illnesses, children's hospitalizations, family law battles, financial struggles, and cramped housing: in 600 square feet with four people, there is no "room of one's own." But I produced a dissertation nonetheless.

This is not about pulling myself up by my bootstraps. It is about leveraging the strengths of those who came before me and alongside of me. Invoking my ancestors, my family, and my community is a part of my scholarship. *Everything I write is a testimony to this.*

WE MUST DISMANTLE THE VIOLENCE OF ACADEMIA

We must develop a discourse of who we are as subjects, who we are in community with one another, and the knowledge we collectively hold to maintain our being in our very breaths.

We must care for ourselves and one another. We cannot dismantle anything if, by PhD completion, we end up dismantled ourselves.

For those of us still in the process of earning the PhD, we need to recognize and reject the sites in which we sustain any tower, be it ivory, ebony, or any other shade of hierarchical difference.

For those of us on the other side of the PhD, we must stop reusing systems of oppression and reinforcing inequitable systems of power that have been used against us. We must resist replicating the systems of power against our own students and, in some cases, our colleagues. We need to empathize with our students even as we challenge them to do better. We need to stop dragging and shaming our students. And we should lament when we fail a student after we have measured, fully, honestly, whether it was the student who earned failure or whether the system—or we—failed the student. And if we have done so, we need to use that failure as a signal to change or transform something about our pedagogy, which should *always* be a work in progress.

As I try to mold my classroom into one in which all of my students thrive, I am constantly haunted by the problem of grading as a system that devalues our students as complex human beings and turns their efforts, thought processes, and complexities into a single number, a byte within which all depth is collapsed. Baldwin's "A Talk to Teachers" (1963) reminds me to tell my students that, while I have to grade them because I am held accountable by an unjust and uncreative system, I consider them whole human beings, not numbers, not letters, not standard, and I appreciate their overwhelmingly beautiful minds.

When our students and colleagues mess up—and they will—then we must teach them to think rightly without tearing them down. This work is never not exhausting, even if it is among People of Color whom we might call our own, and it might take distance. I invite my own colleagues who might be reading this to consider deeply what it has taken me nine years to say.

And it is here that this experience comes full circle. My knowledge of myself, of who I am as a scholar, is precisely the knowledge that academia wants to deny me. I must admit both my strength and my vulnerability, because this is what we all must do to reject the tower's power. These lines appear in the introduction of my dissertation:

> As an American academic who holds U.S. citizenship on the one hand, a Black mother first-generation PhD marginalized within this "center," a first-generation French language learner, and a scholar invested in the African Diaspora, I want to make my position as clear as possible as a way of expressing my feminist/womanist praxis. Scholars cannot extricate themselves from their own positionality; this affects the way a text is read, the content is privileged in close readings, and the scholars chosen to frame the reading of the text. As such, if this dissertation makes . . . mistakes . . . , it is because of my own "ideological scotoma" and part of the life-long learning of shifting from the gravitation of the Center.

REFERENCES

Baldwin, J. (1963). A talk to teachers. *Saturday Review*. https://www.spps.org/cms/lib010/MN01910242/Centricity/Domain/125/baldwin_atalktoteachers_1_2.pdf.

Benyoussef, L. (2015). Le freak, c'est critical and chic. In F. Ekotto and K. W. Harrow (Eds.), *Rethinking African cultural production* (pp. 109–126). Bloomington: Indiana University Press.

Brown, S. (2017, November 28). Decolonizing black intellectualism: How society's ideas around knowledge leave some black people behind. *Black Youth Project*. Retrieved from http://blackyouthproject.com/decolonizing-black-intellectualism-how-societys-ideas-around-knowledge-leave-some-black-people-behind.

Christian, B. (1988). The race for theory. *Feminist Studies, 14*(1), 67–79.

Lorde, A. (1984). *Sister outsider: Essays and speeches*. Berkeley: Crossing.

Mason, M. A. (2013, June 19). Family-friendly policies pay off. *San Francisco Chronicle*. Retrieved from https://www.sfchronicle.com/opinion/openforum/article/Family-friendly-policies-pay-off-4611243.php?t=9d211a157acefdcb88.

Mason, M. A., & Younger, J. (2014). Title IX and pregnancy discrimination in higher education: The new frontier. *N.Y.U. Review of Law & Social Change, 38*, 269–304.

Matthew, P. A. (Ed.). (2016). *Written/unwritten: Diversity and the hidden truths of tenure*. Chapel Hill: University of North Carolina Press.

Morrison, T. (1993). Nobel lecture. https://www.nobelprize.org/prizes/literature/1993/morrison/lecture/.

Ngũgĩ wa Thiong'o. (1993). *Moving the centre: The struggle for cultural freedoms*. Melton, UK: James Currey.

Rockquemore, K., & Laszloffy, T. A. (2008). *The black academic's guide to winning tenure—without losing your soul*. Boulder: Lynne Rienner.

Spivak, G. C. (1994). Can the subaltern speak? In L. Chrisman & P. Williams (Eds.), *Colonial discourse and post-colonial theory: A reader* (pp. 66–111). New York: Columbia University Press.

FOURTEEN

Silent Bias and Resisting Narratives of Deficit

Social Class and Poverty in the Academy

Gabriella Gutiérrez y Muhs

All I want to say is yes, I am grateful to be here, but that doesn't mean I'm not hungry.

(PROUT, 2019)

Social Class Captives

(FOR WOMEN ACADEMICS FROM THE WORKING CLASS)

Unable to run from our lives
we construct rubrics
to measure the assets
of our possessions
since the debits are greater than the credits
we think . . .
but how do you count a hug at a university, in pounds or letters?
the hope a student has inside
the tear they reversed into a smile,
because you were the mathematician of their assets . . .
How many universities become accordions, because someone read you?
Because your music played in barns, reservations, hoods, and buses?
Because while you carried your daughter on your back
and held a book with one hand and your breast with the other, you cultivated
the future
in someone
What do we call the thoughts that couldn't happen?
lapsed truth,
or inclusive matter?
Perhaps only they,
the future intellectuals,
can escape

DOI: 10.7330/9781607329664.c014

these captive lives
that social class thought
imposes on us

PERSONAL NARRATIVE

Early on in my career as a tenure-track junior faculty member, one of my mentors told me, "You do not have to say that you come from a migrant farmworker background, or that you worked in the fields as a child." She, who had come from emaciated relatives in the South, who as a White, slender, blond woman had been able to present herself as coming from wealth, was simply trying to give me her best and most sincere advice. She was trying to help me because, from her perspective, I had to pretend I jumped into the academy from a different social class. She thought she should caution me not to look like I popped out of the barrio, or even be read as possibly "undocumented." I understood her genuine perception and interest in my career, because she knew, having served as an administrator in academia, that I needed to find her wisdom useful in order to follow the traditional yellow brick road to success. She was somewhat embarrassed about her background, as well as mine, because she had never claimed this subjectivity as an asset. Lower social class is something from which we are meant to escape via academia.

An elderly dean of another college, who had never claimed that he was Jewish, and in fact pretended to be Catholic at the Catholic institution where we worked, was dumbfounded when I asked him what he did to support the Jewish students on our campus. He was also the professor who had commented in his classes that the other Latinas on our campus and I should not be wearing indigenous clothes because we could not claim that we were fully indigenous. This, he had blurted out in his classes, was something that deeply preoccupied him. The academy is ostensibly claiming that it wants diversity, when in fact it discourages people from representing their diverse facets and fullest potentials to our students or colleagues.

I appreciated the advice of my well-meaning colleagues who came from the working class as well as the advice from the People of Color who came from the upper class but who did not address social class. However, I felt strongly that I *did* have to mention my migrant background and the dire poverty of my childhood. I appreciate the trajectory of my mother's labor, from working in El Paso for $1 a day, paying for six buses or trolleys to clean and cook for ailing and cancerous well-to-do people. I am grateful that she managed to arrive in Juárez and found a way for her children to be born in the United States of America. I carry the experiences of my mother's work, from pulling the long, slender bags for picked cotton with her children on top to working in the sweatshops of Los Angeles to toiling in the factories of Chicago. I carry deep respect for her courage as she attempted to run away from an alcoholic husband with two children in tow. I want young women of that family background to know that if I can I can complete master's degree work in two universities, become a credentialed teacher, teach and work as a social worker, acquire a PhD from Stanford University, and publish my writing, that they too can accomplish those milestones.

As is evident and openly discussed in the introduction to our first volume of *Presumed Incompetent,* the academy was not built to educate the poor or the working class. The structures established for cisgender men, in particular European men, were not made for women, nor for the daughters of the working masses, anywhere in the world, and especially not in the United States. Today, as we see Alexandria Ocasio-Cortez gain respect in Congress as a newly elected US representative, we also witness how unbelievable her presence is to racist, patriarchal America, which continually questions her skills and knowledge, challenging her self-awareness and empowerment. Throughout history, people have pretended to come from a certain socioeconomic and cultural rank to pass as intellectuals and writers. As a professor in the academic land of milk and honey, you almost have to become a trickster to survive, at least—or especially—until you acquire tenure. Academia largely ignores the increasing numbers of working-class students and downwardly mobile middle-class students entering universities. We do not want to acknowledge that students do not have money for food when we could be theorizing space and place, gender and nationalism.

It is not pleasant or philosophical enough to find out that our students are living in their cars, since we are here solely to educate them *intellectually*. Yet when it comes to currencies—students always come to those of us whom they recognize as having grown up in poverty, or at least who are seen by the academy as coming from narratives of deficit. This recognition takes a different form institutionally, in which case your behavior is suspect evidence of difference, shaped by social class, race, fluid sexualities, and of course a Person of Color's perspective.

As a Chicanx scholar who welcomes a variety of students into her events and classes, from diverse experiences, backgrounds, and languages, solidarity has always happened to me across race, class, genders, and sexualities. Poor White students come to me if they need a dollar for the bus. Students have shared news of unexpected pregnancies, and many have sought my office for guidance when they are ready to come out. Working-class students in the military, despite my transparent antiwar politics, know that I can be trusted with their personal tragedies, because we all come from similar circumstances.

Financial and social class standing are a no-man's-land——never inscribed into our discussions, yet existing in a stratified arena. There is a certain shame about the poverty of past, and current, generations, as if somehow the people in our backgrounds had every opportunity to succeed. In fact, for descendants of immigrants, most of their forebearers believe that they did succeed by bringing their children to the United States. We have ascribed failure to economic assets, making this one of our silenced biases that overflows into prescribing the status of recently minted PhDs. "When I got into the University of Iowa's nonfiction-writing M.F.A. program, I cried out of joy and then again out of fear—I had no savings, I'd lived paycheck to paycheck in Chicago . . . I tried to make it work, but during my final August in graduate school, I started going to the food bank" (Prout, 2019).

Academia is for the competitive, and yes, for the morally and mentally strong—but how do we measure strength? Although it is truly immeasurable, it is often assessed in terms of compiled resources. We do not measure whether strength is possessed by the people who are able to compartmentalize and continue to work—no matter how ill their mother is, how disabled their children are, how sick they are, how little money they make relative to what they need to lead a decent life, or how many microaggressions they may suffer daily.

Enduring these institutional inspections refines working-class skills needed to cross social class lines. These skills are the unrecognized and accumulated assets of Academics of Color from working-class backgrounds, and include adaptability, compartmentalization, and creativity. We must resist narratives of deficit, which are central to the academy, and embrace those of collaboration and creativity.

- Adaptability means the ability to:
    - address the needs of colleagues, institutions, and students
    - learn fast
    - multitask
    - transition into new positions
    - shift perspectives and communication style
- Compartmentalization means the ability to:
    - transcribe reality
    - camouflage, fit in suitably with diverse groups
    - navigate obscure and unexpected actions and reactions from institutional apparatuses and colleagues
    - navigate power structures
    - deal with crises efficiently
    - learn your needs and limitations
- Creativity means the ability to:
    - collaborate
    - translate needs of the underprivileged, as well as linguistically translate culture and reality
    - find creative solutions to basic cultural, social, intergenerational, and practical "problems"

Sometimes these survival skills allow professors who emerge from dire poverty to provide positive mentorship to others, although they may not have received it themselves. They are, in turn, able to work with others in solidarity toward the common good, including having the ability to uplift junior faculty from diverse backgrounds, in an attempt to evolve and reshape academia. *Presumed Incompetent* is an ongoing project that has emerged from those familiar with the repercussions of emerging from the lower classes, determined oftentimes by social class behavioral expectations and silent biases (by administrators and institutions as well as colleagues and students).

Professors from low-income backgrounds are also often better acquainted with organizing and collective struggle than their more affluent peers. These faculty are responsive to improving the livability of academia for others, and are more likely aware of different forms of class struggle, perhaps witnessed first-hand in their communities. For example, people who work in factories are able to do more than simply perform monotonous work: they can in fact theorize their lives, organize themselves into unions, and even produce future professors capable of shifting paradigms in academia. Compared with factories and assembly lines, which have long been contested sites of power with vibrant struggles raising questions of race, gender, and class power in the workplace, labor struggles in the university remain relatively unadvanced.

Another conundrum that is newly arrived at the American academy involves middle-class Professors of Color, who grew up with privilege and were not exposed to everyday struggle. They are assumed by appearance to have the experiences and skills necessary to cross social class boundaries with their students and colleagues. However, as middle-class voyeurs in poor Communities of Color, they would not understand the nuanced experiences and cultures of the working class—unless they have lived in relationship with those communities, not merely encountering them as tourists traveling abroad. These cultural nuances include different expressions of gratitude, variations in the language of appreciation, specificity, and overall cultural assets.

Although they may succeed in admission to the academy, the first generations of new Professors of Color often face difficulty without having the support of people like them. They often come from families of educated parents who are themselves new to the middle and upper classes. In this case, these professors may demonstrate the skills that are the unrecognized and accumulated assets of working-class backgrounds.

The current political state of hatred and minimizing of Mexicans and other immigrants is particularly important because at the same time we are seeing greater numbers of upper- and middle-class People of Color hired for important positions in our American universities than their peers who emerge from poverty. This bias adds to the invisibilizing of the trajectory of Professors of Color who initially emerged from poverty.

As a Latina in my early career, I was not given a microphone by administrators or asked to participate in symposiums that influenced or ameliorated the gaze toward People of Color. Yet I know that other Professors of Color, particularly men, were immediately handed a microphone upon their entry to the academy and entrusted with representing their Communities of Color as PhDs. From my lens and experience, it seems that voices of Chicanas/Latinas come last.

As a Latina woman I knew early on that I needed to be able to produce three times the amount of work that White men or women did to be respected in my field. That was a given, but I also actively worked to construct my professional identity before not-so-well-meaning colleagues would do so.

I will never forget the disparaging reaction a Latina student had observing the amount of work I prepared for every day. (She did not work for me but filed papers outside my office.) She saw me working intensely: directing programs, rushing in and out, meeting with students (who often dropped by my office because they had nowhere else to go), printing, copying, and going out loaded with books and materials for teaching, for meetings, for presentations I was to give abroad and across the United States. She witnessed the papers placed in my box for correcting, and how I didn't leave the office until 6:00 p.m. most days. She once looked me straight in the eyes and said to me, in a sorrow-filled tone: "Professor, I don't want your life." Perhaps because she was so sincere, her words impacted me greatly. She said, clarifying: "I don't want to work like you do." She was a middle-class student, and I understood clearly that she did not want a job in which one has to be on top of one's work continually.

Pre-tenure: I learned as I proceeded on the tenure track that I had a lesson to teach the academy about valuing my assets, because I did value them myself. However, I wish I had already known that the power I acquired post-tenure would not be an immediate "click and save," but rather an "erecting" of a reputation—one that I had a large part in building for myself. As Women of Color we also oftentimes face the pressure of being seen as representing our ethnic group, particularly where we are the only Chicana, Latina, African American, Asian American, or Native woman in sight.

> When women of color enter such spaces, they are unable to create any positive interaction because they are already perceived in ways that have altered their reality as human beings (for example, they are seen as nuisances, considered incapable, or assumed inferior). They remain only objects to reaffirm assumptions about who they are. For example, if they fail at a work task, it confirms that they are less able than their white/Anglo counterparts. Or if they become emotional, it is because they are inherently illogical. (Rojas, 2009, p. 142)

Post-tenure: Mid-career in academia, once you achieve tenure, although you are no longer likely to be fired, you must prove to your institution and the academy, especially as a woman, a Chicana, and a multilingual person who may have come from a previous teaching or service career, that you are worthy of being called a professor. This is where you show *them*—they who did not want you to be their equal and acquire tenure, because they did not see that you could contribute as much as they to the academy—that you are in fact invaluable. You are not minimized as an "affirmative action hire," an "opportunity hire," a "gender hire," an "international hire," or a "diversity hire." Instead, you undoubtedly are part of the intellectual class, whatever that may be, at your university.

Mid-career is truly a difficult terrain—your family and friends think you must be grateful for your job, having acquired tenure, the stability of employment and benefits, and so on. But if you are a Woman of Color and have been undermined—never truly given credit for your accomplishments, academic or otherwise—you feel the need to prove to all that you are at least as deserving as others in the academy and that you will become renowned outside of your university, and even your discipline. Because of the aforementioned issues and many more not addressed in this essay, after acquiring tenure you could become completely isolated from the academy, your institution, and your family. The first thing one of my PhD mentors and ex-professors told me when I notified him that I had received tenure was: "Well, I do hope depression doesn't get you now." There are also other emotional issues you must confront post-tenure, for which you can prepare pre-tenure. It is important to understand that (as I have underlined in my previous work) in mid-career and after tenure, you are considered "a played card," your political positions already known by your colleagues. You must prepare for this emotionally, but understand that you cannot attempt to please your colleagues, and underline to yourself that your colleagues are not your friends. You must find friends outside the academy, especially if you do not have a family. Your position in the institution has shifted and now you are seen as a competitor for administrative positions, although you may not be interested in these positions.

WHICH COMES FIRST: THE EQUALITY EGG OR THE EQUITY CHICKEN?

Capital, Assets, and Liabilities in Academia

Being a professor is truly a privilege, and while we have heard this many times, some of us must remember to unpack why that is the case. These privileges include a permanent job, possibilities to have our work published, summers off, the ability to influence the mainstream paradigm, as well as constructively critique it, or improve the world with our research and understanding of various narratives.

Our privileges are often misunderstood by our family members, as they are not familiar with the academic world. For instance, the culturally correct etiquette for my social class and culture, my barrio, my mother, and where I come from is that I give each of my relatives a copy of my books when they are published; nonetheless, mainstream academia would never understand this. "Your books are expensive," says my cousin Lola. "Do you get half of that money?" To her, a working-class factory worker who began this job at age sixteen after marrying and coming to the United States to work and raise three children, there is no meaning or value to my book writing if I am not getting any or much of the money that the press charges for my book. And I'm not even getting free copies for my relatives? In her eyes, I am a PhD and a sap. Thus, publishing a book is a liability for me on a personal level. "I want to be myself in Iowa, but I'm in between selves, betraying one even as I fail to fully inhabit the other" (Prout, 2019).

Has my social class changed now that I am a tenured professor? To acquire notoriety, I would have to incur debt, or be married to a similar intellectual who agrees to give up camping and family vacations for conferences and symposiums. My partner would have to be willing to borrow and invest in order for me to become a top intellectual in my discipline, in the American academy, and in the world—since all of us are globally colonized by the established academic norms of Western universities. Or I need to obtain a position in a rich private institution that subsidizes my travels and other intellectual endeavors as part of my work package.

As a tenured professor, you have honor within your community, but unless you come from the middle or upper class you do not have the financial assets that people anticipate you should have based on your intellectual and social standing. Your life becomes somewhat of a disappointment to others. You will not inherit any money, and your job is not a hobby, but in fact the liquidity you utilize to pay your mortgage. Thus, your working-class relatives could think you are the richest and most influential person in the family, and although intellectually you might be (working-class and immigrant communities respect degrees and education), there are other pressures that accumulate on your financial agenda. If you do not have the capital, you will disappoint both academia and your working-class family. One of the objects of this chapter is to demystify the narrative that once you "make it" your social class changes—or that socioeconomic class is fluid. Once you make it as an accomplished intellectual, there are a series of problems that join your "tenured" status and permanent position.

CONCLUSION

Which comes first: the equality egg or the equity chicken? Can one happen without the other? Social class plays a very important part in the lives of Professors of Color, especially if they are women. Lives become problematized simply by the fact that there is a specific set of expectations for you as a woman Professor of Color, whether you come from the working class, the middle class, or the upper class. Suffice it to say that there are no grids that explain these distinctions, except for testimonials and narratives by these populations. It is, however, clear that the presuppositions and expectations of each of these social classes are different for a Woman of Color and somewhat structurally unsatisfactory, since these silent biases have not yet been thoroughly explored.

REFERENCES

Prout, K. (2019, January 13). Being poor in America's most prestigious M.F.A. program. *Chronicle of Higher Education*. Retrieved from https://www.chronicle.com/article/Being-Poor-in-America-s-Most/245459?cid=cr&utm_source=cr&utm_medium=en&elqTrackId=bbe92886262f45dbb6b1a6b1b08d7877&elq=238d6345db3f4042ad89dfc04fc11652&elqaid=22075&elqat=1&elqCampaignId=10816.

Rojas, M. (2009). *Women of color and feminism*. Berkeley: Seal, 2009.

FIFTEEN

They Don't Call It Work for Nothing

Navigating Classism in Academic Relationships

Amelia Ortega

"They don't call it work for nothing" was a saying often repeated in my family when I was growing up. It is no wonder, then, that the work of being a professor of social work practice is a labor that I take seriously. Through my academic position as an adjunct faculty member who teaches courses on human development, systemic racism, and mental health, my pride in my teaching style and classroom pedagogies has grown. I claim these practices as working class.

I am a mixed-race Chicana queer cis woman who was raised in the working class. These identities have informed my pedagogy, my approach to academic collaboration, and my engagement with students, including how I dress and speak in my classroom spaces. The way I design my courses is a direct result of personal realizations regarding my own internalized classism and the impact of classism on my professional relationships. I understand how to utilize community cultural wealth in my work as a professor, although this understanding can sometimes be perceived as a threat to the structural hierarchies within the university.

I know that there is a high possibility that you, the reader, are also an adjunct faculty member, since we comprise nearly 700,000 faculty nationally (Coalition on the Academic Workforce, 2012, para. 3). The Coalition on the Academic Workforce noted in its 2012 report that part-time faculty represent more than 70 percent of the contingent academic workforce and almost half the entire higher education faculty in the United States. My story is one of many that make up the dense expansion of the adjunctification of higher education. As adjuncts we hold simultaneous institutional insider and outsider status. My personal and professional experiences have led me to intimately know this status. I understand the impact that class-based hierarchies within the university have on relationships among faculty who find themselves sharing course instruction and academic spaces.

I was raised in New England in a small university town close to the Atlantic Ocean. Early in life, my understanding of college came mostly from hearing

DOI: 10.7330/9781607329664.c015

my parents talk about their relationship to the university. My father, an immigrant from Merida, Mexico, attended the university in our town in 1965, thanks to the expectation of parents whose aspirations were deeply embedded in the American Dream. My mother, a White woman raised in a rural mountain town in central New York State, is a product of a long line of paper mill workers, and a family that did not support women attending college. She finished high school in the technical trades program, starting work as a secretary while she was still a high school senior at age seventeen. My family history gives me a sense of self and place when connecting to my students and the social justice content that I instruct. There is a dominant narrative within many working-class communities that reinforces the division between book smart and commonsense smarts. In "Useful Knowledge," Mary Cappello writes: "Higher education in the United States has done much to reinforce lack across the bodies and minds of women, working-class people and People of Color, in part by insisting that they sever themselves from an identity designated as 'prior' to their entry into academe, as though it were as simple as leaving one's baggage at the door" (1995, p. 131).

Every step of the way I ask myself how I can lay claim to both the "prior" and the current in an effort to reduce the divided self. I find my answer not only in my personal experience but also in the voices of other women academics. My contributions to the discussion regarding how I/we are presumed incompetent purposefully includes giving voice to personal narrative as a means of recognizing knowledge produced through and by experience. Because I am a working-class, queer Woman of Color, it is important to include my own personal narrative wherever possible.

My mother's feelings about "college talk" are often expressed through the lens of her own insecurities and her deep belief that she is not on the same level as those who attend college. When I was growing up she often told me, "You might go to college to get book smart, but you can't learn common sense. You either have it or you don't." I was raised to value my common sense, wisdom learned from hard work, and the belief that you cannot survive on "book smarts" alone.

These beliefs affect and inform my presence in the classroom and the voice, values, and approach that I take to teaching and collegial relationships. I inform my students that we will challenge the idea that we can only know something because we have read it. Voices of the working class, raised poor, historically marginalized, and systemically oppressed may not yet be central in many course readings. What does this say to students about whose knowledge is valued? Morley (2018) tells us that academics from working-class backgrounds can be problematically located when they are disconnected from their own communities, and when they are not fully accepted or acknowledged in middle-class academic cultures.

My decision to continue academic work is intentional. Teaching requires that I take on the complex isolation and multiple forms of invisibility present in my family's history, both as immigrants and as poor White people. While the primary university where I teach houses many colleagues who would say vehemently that there are multiple ways of knowing, the experience of speaking from those places of knowing illuminates the hierarchy of knowing as well. Lived experience and personal narrative are often at the ground level of this hierarchy, with formal research at the top. I intentionally choose this labor to reach students who are seeking mirrors of some part of their lives in the classroom and the voices in their texts. Similarly, I write this narrative as I to continue to find my place in academic settings.

COMMUNITY AS CAPITAL

As working-class educators and professors who were raised poor, we carry cultural and social wealth. This can include the capacity and ability to code-switch and to share resources during hardships. It includes relational support that extends into chosen and found family. It includes cultural belonging and sense of home outside of the academy. We lend cultural capital to our work in creative and distinct ways that deserve recognition outside of the income-driven, capital-based models that often frame us. Tara Yosso (2005) describes the importance of shifting our lens from wealth as only income-based capital and posits six forms of community cultural capital. When I first read Yosso's work, I immediately recognized the ways in which my community and I have used the collective as capital. In academic institutions, community cultural wealth is often not recognized as wealth. Rather, wealth is defined as legacy students, family nepotism, family last name, and social class status. Many students and faculty do not carry this status.

I ask my students to use Yosso's framework to analyze the various forms of community cultural capital, such as navigational, familial, and aspirational capital, to identify what they are carrying into the course. As Sherry Linkon (2018) writes, experience is almost always more complicated than income or education. She also reminds us that class is a matter of culture and relationships, and of emotion. Yet professionalism in higher education is often equated with comportment that demonstrates little emotion. For many years, I tried to fit in as a professor by shifting the clothing and shoes I wore, feminizing my body/aesthetic, and monitoring the tone of my voice. This effort to fit in left me to experience my own form of complex isolation. As Dorothy Allison remarks, the essential assumption of the working class is that one is always inappropriate, embattled, and in an argument with the overclass about who and what you are (Wright, 2018). Academia also values individualism, mythologized as the brilliant genius who works alone and possesses learning inaccessible to the masses. These expectations are contrary to the culture and survival strategies of working-class people, but they serve to maintain academic workplace hierarchies, fiefdoms, and silos between departments that might otherwise collaborate (Harris & González, 2012). The experience of developing coursework and co-instructing college courses has led me to *feel* the deep knowledge I hold about the significance and power of collective thinking. It has led me to observe the structural barriers, including classism, that can play out between colleagues who are working closely together.

RECOGNIZING CLASSISM THROUGH CO-TEACHING

Collegial relationships are a place of allyship. They are also a replication of systemic and structural oppression. To address classism in higher education, we have to start with our relationships with one another. To claim working-class identity means to claim the conflicts that can arise when social class is placed front and center in a relationship beside race, ethnicity, gender, sex, and their intersections. Standing in this reality has also meant feeling as though I am neither from here nor from there, caught between two classed spaces. There is no separating my working-class background from my Chicanisma, from my queer femme identity, or from my language choice in the classroom. My relationships with colleagues in co-teaching arrangements have become sites through which I have learned about the replication of class-based hierarchy in the academy.

I aim to turn my teaching experience into language, to turn this language into meaning, and ultimately, to turn this meaning into concrete learning that can be shared. My primary solution to the isolation of performing Professor has been to work in co-teaching partnerships and participate in collective thinking whenever possible. Co-teaching has illuminated the embodied truths of how we each carry institutional norms within us. It has provided me a space to reflect on the ways that co-teaching relationships are complicated by class hierarchies. I have co-developed two courses at two different institutions with faculty who were raised wealthy. Each of these faculty had a PhD, was an adjunct, and identified as queer, like myself.

My first experience with co-teaching initially felt like relief from the position of speaking alone to a group of students. It felt like an opportunity to learn from another faculty's teaching style and approach. My co-instructor and I acknowledged the vast difference in our families' class backgrounds. We shared the same perspective about the lack of representation of Faculty of Color and queer-identified professors. Our brief intensive summer course focused on structural racism and intersecting oppressions. We taught sixty students in a lecture-style classroom, and our final course assignment required students to use the school's databases to conduct a brief literature review. The students were overwhelmed and largely unfamiliar with the library system, reporting in large numbers that they needed extra help. When we called upon the library to offer database search support, we learned that the library and writing center would be closed for the majority of the week our course was running. Because I had worked for years in the school, as a weekend consultant at the writing center, a field advisor, and a teaching assistant, I had developed relationships with the staff in multiple departments, including financial aid, security, the writing center, the library, the advising offices, and the offices of support for the dean. I told my co-teacher that I would go upstairs to speak with the staff. I leveraged the advising office and writing center staff's support to document the institutional issue, to write emails to those in leadership, and to arrange an impromptu lecture from the director of the writing center for all students. The lecture would include how to use the library. I was pleased that we had collectively determined a way to obtain support for the assignment and to introduce incoming students to the writing center.

When I shared this solution with my co-instructor, she expressed anger and frustration with my approach to problem solving. Specifically, she asserted that I had used my privilege to solve the problem, and she resented that she and I had not come up with the solution together. I apologized for not including her in the quick response. However, I was proud of the fact that I could rely on the support of staff within the building, and that ultimately our students were benefiting from these relationships and our collective problem solving.

What I experienced as a triumph and a collective action, my co-instructor experienced as essentially "airing our dirty laundry" and as a power move. We never came to a place of shared understanding about this situation. I listened as she explained that she did not have relationships with staff in the building because she had come from the PhD program and never interacted with those offices. As a working-class academic, I instinctively used community to devise solutions and reap the benefits of collective thinking. My co-instructor perceived my actions as a power grab. As part of our processing, she said that she felt disconnected from the school because of her research-oriented degree and that it was painful for her to observe the networks that existed for some and not others. This felt oddly like a validation of the histories I carry with me, the reliance on collective pooling of concrete resources. My co-instructor did not have the privilege of participating in community resource pooling because *she had never needed it.*

My engagement with structures of informal power was experienced by a person raised wealthy as a privilege. While I do not disagree that cultural capital produces and engages multiple intersecting privileges, my experience at that moment was about leveraging resources not otherwise provided by the school. As Tara Yosso states, "Navigational capital thus acknowledges individual agency within institutional constraints, but it also connects to social networks that facilitate community navigation through places and spaces including schools" (2005, p. 80). While my co-instructor and I were operating nonhierarchically, we were operating as co-instructors within a very powerful university hierarchy. Years later, I am still disappointed that what I proudly considered a helpful contribution and a triumph became a story of in-group and out-group conflict. In this case, I became a representative of in-group power and someone who is used to having access not typically experienced with an out-group identity. I stand behind the decision I made to "out" our problem and to seek the assistance of these other school departments.

As someone who was not raised wealthy, I resent the fact that the cultural capital I offered to the relationship was interpreted as an abuse of power. This experience disrupted the relationship we had built and left me feeling unseen and misunderstood. I walked away with the message that I had not played the game correctly, and that I had missed the rule that stated, "We keep things private and do not show others that we are struggling." To me, that is a very middle-class value. In working-class families and communities, I often hear "Well, they don't call it work for nothin'," a direct acknowledgment that work is exactly that—effort, energy, and problem-solving. In working-class culture, there is often open dialogue about struggle, about conditions of work, and about tensions that play out in the workplace.

THE PERFORMANCE OF PROFESSING

My Chicana identity is often named and welcomed in the university because it serves to diversify teaching teams. Despite the university's rhetoric about valuing intersectional identities, I became aware that my performance of class was not welcomed in the same way as my mixed-race identity. For example, when I disclosed that I shared instructions with all of my students about how to receive food stamps, I was told that was unnecessary. Knowing well that some students would directly benefit from this knowledge, and that clients of some of my students would directly benefit, made sharing this information essential to me. This was one of many instances of class-based treatment that I brought to the dean of my school, a queer-identified Woman of Color. My relationship with the dean became a cornerstone connection regarding my efforts to own *all* my voices, including those that speak from a place of class struggle. The dean mentored me for my first course. Despite occasional debilitating fear and insecurity, I was coached to teach the course that I had TA'd for three years. I was coached to have friends leave me voicemails addressed to Professor Ortega—so that I could hear the words and become familiar with the sound. I was coached to use my own voice in my instruction. The dean pointed out that performing anything else was falling flat.

The coaching I received is consistent with the idea that working-class identity is a site from which to escape (Morley, 2018). Further, society views universities as places that can rescue working-class students from poverty, social exclusion, and unemployment, thereby enhancing their life chances as long as they conform to current academic cultures (Morley, 2018). As such, this perspective reflects a deficit construction of working-class people (Morley, 2018). I have observed my own movement from feeling like an eternal class straddler with internal debates about passing, authenticity, and imposter syndrome, to fully embodying my intersecting identities of mixed race, queerness, and class, such that I emerge now as a confident professor with ownership of all my parts. The way that I present myself in the classroom, the way that I include my own narrative in my teaching, means that all of me can be present, not left outside of the room, not left hidden.

As a professor, I feel great pressure to fit into academia's upper-class legacy, whereby our origins are treated as a problem to solve. Under capitalist White heteropatriarchy, we are asked to work within, around, and through conditions that are designed to uphold a status quo. This status quo is reinforced by statements I've heard, such as "Don't rock the boat," "Better to wait until you aren't angry to speak," and "The dean won't want to hear about your financial problems." These statements represent the pressures to "be okay" and to leave the adjunct pay concerns, class straddling, and affordability issues outside the relationships we build.

I sometimes question my own drive to show up to this labor, to make the university more comfortable, to keep carving a space for myself. I observe the spaces where I am drawn to be quieter, to act more "professional," or to deny the rage and sadness that accompany the cost of education. But then I remember what it was like to be a graduate student who did not see myself reflected in my faculty. I remember the pride I felt in telling my family that I had been encouraged to enter the classroom as a faculty member, despite not having a PhD. Though I may not choose to teach full-time, I choose to remain an adjunct professor as a way of staying in this labor, and also staying grounded in my labors outside the university setting. I have used my personal agency to make decisions contrary to the pressures to conform.

Racism, sexism, classism, homophobia, ableism—all structural oppression informs where and how we move socially. I continue to choose to face the structural impediments to developing a more just workforce in academe. I am choosing to continue to speak this publicly. I stand in line with many very hard-working academics who have given their lives to teaching, but who remain outside the center of the work.

My current approach to teaching is one that centers transparency with students and colleagues. I own my voice through which I instruct. I am mindful of the blind spots that I, too, carry into the classroom. I have developed strategic questions for relationship development—questions that serve to illuminate and open discussions about intersectionality and class.

I inquire about co-instructors' relationship to time. What does "being on time" mean to them? How do our class backgrounds and other identities inform the ways in which we think about time in the classroom, including late students and late assignments? Why might this matter? I also inquire about our relationship to the school's hierarchy. Whom do we find to be allies in the school? Do we have relationships with the staff in the building? How have we worked to build relationships in the space, and if we haven't, what has been a barrier? Have we always wanted to teach? What has been a barrier to seeing ourselves as Professor? What makes teaching difficult? Do we have communities in our lives that do not know about our teaching? And if so, does this inform the ways in which our imposter syndrome may appear? Have our class backgrounds informed any of the responses to these questions?

I have also started to include community cultural wealth mapping in my courses to encourage all students to consider the multiple forms of capital that they carry into the room. Specifically, Tara Yosso's work on community cultural wealth helps to open discussion about multiple ways of knowing, multiple ways of problem-solving, and multiple forms of nonincome-based wealth.

THE WORK THAT REMAINS

I learned quickly in graduate school and through my labor as a professor that working-class pride in academic settings can signify a failing of the systems set up to keep hierarchy in place. The deficit model that encourages us all to think of the working class as a less competent labor force within the academy is a perception that I work daily to reverse. Like many of my colleagues, I start my semester with the internalized voices of outsider and imposter lingering in my mind. My personal work has been to speak back with reminders about the value of work experience, community problem-solving, and connection. I speak openly about family stories and encourage others to do the same, regardless of class background. Thinking and doing through a framework that values problem-solving and acknowledges navigational capital and economic survival are processes that build community. We develop together as an academic community when we can observe classism and its multiple manifestations in our relationships. We develop as thinkers, as activists, and as decolonized bodies when we speak from our places of otherness and reshape these spaces for liberated connection. What it means to be working class is what it means to find a way, to solve a problem together. I call upon you to join me, to enter relationships with colleagues, and to develop new theories about how the structures of academic labor can be unassembled and remade.

REFERENCES

Cappello, M. (1995). Useful knowledge. In C. Dews & C. Law (Eds.), *This fine place so far from home: Voices of academics from the working class* (pp. 127–136). Philadelphia: Temple University Press.

Coalition on the Academic Workforce. (2012). *A portrait of part-time faculty members*. Retrieved from Coaltion on the Academic Workforce website: http://www.academicworkforce.org/CAW_portrait_2012.pdf.

Harris, A. P., & González, C. G. (2012). Introduction. In *Presumed incompetent: The intersections of race and class for women in academia* (pp. 1–16). Logan: Utah State University Press.

Linkon, S. (2018, April 9). Going public with working-class studies [blog post]. Retrieved from https://workingclassstudies.wordpress.com/page/1/.

Morley, L. (2018, February 4). Working-class academics still face discrimination [blog post]. Retrieved from https://www.timeshighereducation.com/blog/working-class-academics-still-face-discrimination.

Wright, A. (2018, May 16). Dorothy Allison: Tender to the bone. *Guernica: A magazine of global arts and politics*. Retrieved from https://www.guernicamag.com/tender-to-the-bone/.

Yosso, T. J. (2005). Whose culture has capital? *Race, Ethnicity and Education, 8*(1), 69–91.

SECTION FOUR

BULLYING, WHITE FRAGILITY, AND MICROAGGRESSIONS

SIXTEEN

Making Visible the Dead Bodies in the Room

Women of Color/QPOC in Academia

Susie E. Nam

The following is a cautionary tale, and much more, for all of us women and queer People of Color who are embarking on careers in academia or are veterans and survivors. It is at once my story and those of many who have sometimes suffered in silence, sometimes raged against the ivory tower, and sometimes not survived. This is especially a tale about the tragic death of my friend and colleague, via what I will always call "death by academia," and the secondary trauma that I and his friends, colleagues, and students who loved him experienced in witnessing his pain and the violence he suffered at the hands of colleagues and the institution where we all worked. I regret that I cannot share more details of his life and journey, of his many contributions and irreplaceable brilliance, so that I might pay proper tribute to the person, scholar, teacher, mentor, and bright star that he was to us all. I cannot do so because I still work in academia, at the workplace we shared, and because I know that the retaliation I would face for telling the truth would be vicious and swift. It is my hope that in the future his many students who loved him and learned so much from him will be able to pay proper tribute to him in ways that even I could not.

Several times this year I have thought of running screaming out of the room, out of academia, out of my tenured position at the University of My Certain Death, out of the only work that I know I am very good at and that I have ever really loved. In years prior, I have had such thoughts many times, and each time I have stayed because of my love for and commitment to my students. I know that I make a real contribution to the world and make "a difference" in my students' lives every day. My decision to stay hasn't been made out of martyrdom, but out of defiance and even arrogance, each time believing that I am one of only a very few people on my campus who do what I do—that is, teach what and how I do. I teach about social justice movements, about intersections of oppression, about violence and resistance, and I give students

DOI: 10.7330/9781607329664.c016

the opportunity to make meaning of their lives and the responsibility to make sense of their worlds.

I teach students who are People of Color, who are immigrants, low-income and first in their families to attend college or graduate school, who are undocumented and unafraid, queer and proud, disabled or differently abled or temporarily able-bodied. I teach students who look for me because they have heard that I "tell it like it is" as a queer Woman of Color, that I will speak to them and the realities of their lives, and that I don't shy away from making White and/or privileged students feel "uncomfortable." They seek me out because they need me and I need them back. And occasionally I teach students who are not looking for me at all, but who need a certain requirement fulfilled and believe that my class will be an easy route to those credits. Often they reportedly hate me at first but come to appreciate something in my teaching beyond what they were originally expecting, and begrudgingly tell me I offered them entrée to new perspectives.

I once had a queer Filipino student approach me after I spoke on a panel at Boalt (now Berkeley Law School) who simply said, "I wish you had been my mother." He did not do the usual, complimenting the talk I just gave or asking me for my contact information (though I wish he had). Instead, he told me he had been having a difficult time in school and after a brief conversation, he walked away smiling. I wonder what and how he is doing now. I have met countless students like him, who connect with me after a class or an event, and often we do keep in touch over time, sometimes over a lifetime. Sometimes they tell me that I made it possible for them to stay in school in some way. It's more than ass-kissing for them or an ego boost for me. It's evidence that there are students who are "at risk" every day of not making it through school, of not "realizing their potential," but not for lack of trying—in fact, not through any fault of their own.

I am ever more worried about my graduate students, who are newly minted PhDs or soon to be. And I am fearful for myself, and the few colleagues whom I can actually call "esteemed," especially the longtime veterans in academia who, like me, sacrificed greatly in order to get these damned degrees, precious tenure-track jobs, and then tenure. We have struggled to stay in jobs where we are not rewarded commensurate to our labors or our worth, and certainly not with parity of salary or other "goodies" in relation to our White colleagues, whether men or women. This might not be so bad if we did not have a myriad of abuses and insults heaped onto these injuries of salary and workload inequities.

One especially common story is that we, as Women of Color and queer People of Color, are recruited to fulfill certain "diversity" categories that look good for the university's public relations, in case any legal questions were to arise. We are told that we are such assets to the faculty, that our arrival on campus was so anxiously awaited, that they are so happy that we are here. Then all of the abuses begin, and we see that we are about as welcome as the plague. But we are indeed welcome to take on extra heavy workloads of everything that was in the job listing—and everything that wasn't, but that we have the unfortunate ability to see is desperately needed. And when we actually try to teach what we were ostensibly hired to teach, we are met with roadblocks, outrage, and outright attacks at every turn.

We are (t)asked to take on huge workloads. We are slated to teach the most contentious subjects, with conservative students seeking easy credits in general education and multicultural requirement courses, addressing social justice issues with students who are neither prepared nor willing to grapple with them, and instead often lash out at us in defensiveness and overt racism. We are expected to accommodate, appease, and entertain these student consumers. Often administrative details are maneuvered so that our "difficult," "controversial," or simply innovative and radical classes mysteriously fail to fill and are canceled, or else are grossly overenrolled, making it impossible to teach such sensitive topics with the attention that they deserve.

Sometimes our courses are stolen from us, after we have spent enormous energy and time developing them, and given to faculty who will cater to students and offer them in more "palatable" (that is, depoliticized and white-washed) ways. Indeed, these are the tactics that our "colleagues" use to try to punish and drive us away, or at least to deter us from our genuine efforts to teach courses about real social justice issues. We also advise and mentor countless marginalized students to earn their PhDs, which causes us to suffer in our own production and promotions when this leaves little time or energy to pursue our own scholarship. This is, of course, an all too familiar story for many of us. We choose to serve our students before serving ourselves the piece of the pie that would merely be a second or third helping for our colleagues.

Let me be clear that we, as Women of Color and queer People of Color faculty, do this not because "we've been there" but because we *are still here*, subject to the very same kinds of exploitation and oppression that our students face. The experiences of our students who are marginalized, neglected, or "underserved" are closely linked to how our colleagues and administration manage to keep us all down and out. They keep us down by forcing us (whether out of their own incompetence or indifference toward certain students) to do countless hours of unpaid labor in meeting the needs of disenfranchised students. They keep us out of positions of power by "letting" us, indeed railroading us, into committees wherein it is made to appear that we were part of fair and democratic processes to keep choosing White men and White women over equally if not more qualified Candidates of Color for positions on the faculty and administration. This is beyond tokenism on search and selection committees. It is outright deception and coercion made to look like complicity or "collegial" cooperation. This is all in the service of what I tell my students was and is the point of so-called public education: to maintain the status quo, and to produce a docile workforce and tractable "citizenry," over and over again.

And why can't we just leave these jobs—take our degrees and go elsewhere? Well, first of all, presumably most of us would like to stay where we have made great and heroic efforts to make a life, a good life. Second, the academic job market is ridiculously narrow and haphazard (with an emphasis on the hazard part). In any given year, there may be one or two positions that are open in our discipline, in our particular area of specialization, at our rank, and in our desired geographic area—if we can be so bold as to ask for an area where we (and possibly our families) could expect to live reasonably well as People of Color.

As Women of Color, each time we take a job, we are taking a chance that we will be able to be "happy" there, sometimes hoping to have and raise families there in relative peace and safety. If things do not work out this way, we face the probability that we will have to stay anyway. I believe that many people who encounter these kinds of discrimination often complain only after they have left an institution—moved to another institution (likely swapping one set of injuries for another), resigned, or retired. I have become one of them.

During the last few years of feeling great emotional anguish and physical pain over the things I've both witnessed and experienced at the hands of my institution and so-called colleagues, I have also read about the effects of chronic stress and lifelong trauma. It turns out that medical research shows that when we experience, swallow, and suppress all of these affronts over a lifetime, we often end up sick, or dead (Nakazawa, 2016). This is, unfortunately, not hyperbole. In the recent past, I lost a dear friend and colleague to what many believe was or would identify as suicide, but what I would call death by academia. This tragedy was not an isolated case, as Linda Trinh Vo has written (2012, p. 100): "I have known faculty who have committed suicide or been homicidal, battled alcohol and drug addiction, struggled with mental illness, or faced debilitating health problems. Some of these afflictions were inherited or triggered by personal problems, but many were aggravated or brought on by their academic careers." This was certainly true for my friend and colleague, whose health struggles and death were exacerbated if not directly precipitated by mistreatment at the hands of his colleagues, which drove him to despair, poverty, disability, and death.

My students and I have been heartbroken and sickened, literally, by the conditions of his death but even more so by the conditions of his life, which we as women and queer People of Color share and relate to as survivors of violence, and victims of the ongoing assaults of this academy. His research focus was immeasurably important to the queer Communities of Color he was both part of and strove to serve through his scholarship. His research methods and teaching were equally radical and invaluable, particularly to graduate students hungrily searching for good models in ethnographic and genuinely community-based research methods. He was truly loved and admired by his students, and especially desperately needed and cherished by queer Students of Color on this campus as a role model. Instead, students witnessed his mistreatment by this institution as an ugly spectacle of the abuse of their urgently needed radical scholar, teacher, and mentor. Those who saw what happened to him suffered as witnesses and secondary victims to this abuse in multiple ways.

I have struggled to decide which parts of my friend's story I should share, out of respect for him, his family, and his beloved communities. I know that even if I were to share certain details, variations of his story are so common in the academy that it might not be so readily easy to identify him or distinguish him from the countless others who have fallen to similar fates. What I can say about my dear colleague and beloved friend is that he was a gay Latino immigrant, a brilliant scholar and teacher who was trying to finish his critically important book and to continue his radical teaching before he died. He was struggling with alcoholism, as his family and trusted friends publicly recognized after his death. His not so trustworthy colleagues also knew this and used it against him, instead of treating him with dignity and his disability with privacy.

His struggles with alcoholism, depression, and anxiety, were not helped but only compounded by his mistreatment and by the mishandling of his situation by his department and the administration. The decision on his promotion and tenure was stalled or delayed beyond the normal time period when faculty are notified, and I believe this was done intentionally to remind him just how tenuous his position was, and how "grateful" or beholden he should be to his fellow and senior faculty. When he was told that he was awarded tenure, it was too late to share this news with those he deserved to celebrate with, and the damage to his mental health was already well under way. This was a triggering event in his breakdown and ultimate demise. When he was deemed to be unable to perform his teaching duties, the courses he taught were taken from him in a manner that shamed and pressured him further.

His classes should have been canceled outright or a replacement faculty should have been found to teach his courses in full immediately. Instead, faculty filled in for him piecemeal, which served only to shame and humiliate him, making him feel compelled to return to campus to finish teaching his classes instead of attending to his health, which only further deteriorated. He should have been given extended paid leave and disability so that he could pursue a path to healing and recovery. Instead, he was given an extra heavy course load upon his return from medical leave, and a drastically reduced salary. His students who loved him are quick to say that his colleagues judged him rather than helping him, and if they had offered true compassion and help, he would be alive today. The gravest shame is that the university and his department should have shown their gratitude for his dedicated teaching, and extended respect and compassion for his struggles with alcoholism, which should have been recognized as illness. Instead, they dishonored him publicly, "made an example of him," criticized him in front of graduate students who admired him, encouraged people to gossip about him by leaving questions unanswered in the campus community about his departure, and made it impossible for him to heal and recover in peace and dignity. Ultimately, I do not feel that I can say that he died of suicide, in the usual ways that people conceive of this or apply this label. I feel I can only say with certainty that this institution killed him—that the cruel pressures applied to him and the compassion and respect withheld from him caused or exacerbated his health issues, forced him to suffer unnecessarily, and brought about his untimely death.

My friend's experience is not an anomaly in the academy, unfortunately. Many have and will meet the same tragic demise, and many more than we would like to believe have missed it narrowly. A Woman of Color scholar in my field whom I admire tremendously once shared with me that she was trapped in a terrible cycle: she had severe chronic back pain, requiring surgery, which was exacerbated by the stress that she experienced from hostile interactions with her colleagues. She told me that most meetings with these colleagues aggravated her so much that she went home and ate for solace and drank as self-medication, which in turn made her gain weight and compounded her back pain. She told me that she had also been suffering anxiety disorders that made public presentations excruciating. At the time, I was shocked to hear this, as I saw her as such a dynamic speaker and world-renowned scholar. In hindsight now, after years of my own ordeals, I understand that her hostile colleagues' aggressions toward her compromised both her confidence and her health to such a degree that she experienced her professional life as I and so many of us have: a veritable minefield of health hazards.

A faculty member at UC Berkeley once remarked to me that to walk down the hallway of the building that houses the Afro-American studies department, past the office doors of its former occupants, is like walking through a graveyard of the brilliant Black women scholars who once taught there. These include June Jordan, whose papers show that while she was battling breast cancer, UC Berkeley denied her medical leave and the teaching releases that she requested several times in 2001, the year she died. Jordan's death followed that of her colleague at UC Berkeley Barbara Christian, not even two years before, and that of Audre Lorde, who was denied medical leave and other teaching accommodations at Hunter College during her struggle against cancer as well (Gumbs, 2016; Hanna, 2016). Too many have died too young, and from illnesses that were undoubtedly tied to the work hazards of stress and exhaustion they experienced trying to serve Students of Color and teach the masses, while simultaneously creating the literature needed to fill critical gaps in scholarship that students need and deserve to be offered in the standard curriculum—the canon we are essentially charged with writing as we go.

In the past year, I have been stunned and sobered by seeing how cold, calculating, heartless, and shameless faculty and the administration have been—both in the cases of these deaths as well as in the daily premeditated maneuvers they enact to keep Women of Color and queer People of Color faculty and students down, out, and silenced here at every turn. I ended up taking a medical leave, in what I am hoping I will look back on one day as a great stroke of luck, because it has forced me to look at the specter of the dead body in the room—my own, and many others'—metaphorically or otherwise.

I know that many of the graduate students of my dear friend and colleague were dismayed and horrified to have witnessed his treatment by the department and administration, and certainly perceived this as much more than a cautionary tale. I am also aware that my graduate students have observed my experiences here as well, and watched closely how I have navigated trying to do my work and secure my power and ability to mentor and advocate for them while retaining my own health and dignity. They have repaid me for my work, for what I would call my "labors of love" and perhaps "labors of sorrow" (Jones, 1985), in manifold ways by showing me the utmost respect and the kind of consideration and concern that they wished had been extended to my dear friend and colleague, and their dear teacher and mentor, by others at this institution.[1]

They have also rewarded my labors by doing brilliant work themselves, by persisting in scholarship that is undervalued or often outright dismissed and challenged by those who wield power over them in various guises. I believe that my graduate students are often targeted secondarily by my colleagues, both because of their association with me and because this is the way that my adversaries know that they can harm me and, at the very least, steal my time and energy. My graduate student advisees in my department have been violated in myriad ways by my colleagues, including having their confidential information about disabilities shared without their consent, and being undermined by passive-aggressive or explicit denigrating, devaluing comments. Despite this, they have been able to do pathbreaking work, earn awards, and secure tenure-track jobs well beyond their peers who have enjoyed relatively "peaceful" and privileged existences here. Graduate students from other departments who have worked with me have also frequently suffered aggressions ranging from not being paid by my department on time or properly for their work, or being blocked from transferring to or working as TAs in the department. These acts are, I believe, at least in part retaliations that are directed toward me, intended to punish me and anyone associated with me, and to block me from building a base of support or community among students who ultimately are seeking a radical restructuring of the academy.

I have been cautioned by my family, friends, and loved ones against speaking out about all of these terrible things I have witnessed and endured. One dear friend begged me to protect myself against "justice"—the kind that this institution would undoubtedly unleash on me for trying to tell the simple truth and have it be heard. She warned me that I would more likely see "justice" done to me in the most violent of ways, in ways that I have seen before. While these loved ones have warned me not to dig my own grave, I already have, and that is not something that can be undone. Nor should it be. The words of James Baldwin, in his allegory of the dead body in the room, call out to me here: "If I know that any one of you has murdered your brother, your mother, and the corpse is in this room and under the table, and I know it, and you know it, and you know I know it, and we cannot talk about it, it takes no time at all before we cannot talk about anything. Before absolute silence descends. And that kind of silence has descended on this country" (quoted in Rich, 2016, n.p.).

There are some who believe that getting tenure releases us from this kind of silence, from fear of reprisal, and enables us to speak out and speak truth to power, freely. A colleague and friend once said that I had never held my tongue before getting tenure and she didn't expect that I would now, post-tenure, either. Truly, I have always spoken and written my mind, "letting my principles get in

1. This reference to Jacqueline Jones's book, *Labor of Love, Labor of Sorrow* (2009), reflects my admiration for her work, and is not intended to equate my labors to those of black women under slavery.

my way," as another colleague has playfully scolded me. So often, I caution my graduate students who are embarking on the job market or simply confronting the question of whether the tenure track is "for them" not to be seduced or deceived that tenure will bring some ultimate state of bliss. I tell them that tenure does not hold out the promise of security unless you are already privileged enough to enjoy that elusive entitlement in the first place, before you have even taken the first step to enter the academy.

This was certainly true for my dear friend and colleague, who did receive tenure (which he more than deserved) years before he died, but it made little difference for him in the continued torment and disregard he endured from his colleagues at our institution. Upon "sending off" some of his cherished graduate student advisees to their first tenure-track jobs, he offered words of guidance to remind them to protect themselves and their health, just as his own ability to protect himself and his health was slowly eroding, and being taken from him on every level. As a former student who shared one of his personal communications with me said, he was "very much conscious of the ways academia consumed and injured him." I know that he feared for his beloved students embarking on academic careers, just as I have and continue to do.

The final injury to him was that they used him, tried to make an "example" of him, to silence other faculty and graduate students who both witnessed his mistreatment and had their own legitimate grievances against a department beleaguered by racism, sexism, ageism, classism, homophobia, and ableism. They rewrote or "hushed" his story to instill fear in those who witnessed his deliberate torment and abuse. Those of us who have witnessed and survived him and his life and death in academia know that our best means of survival will be to continue to speak the truth "to power," to one another, to ourselves and, most important, to tell his story, which is also our story, always.

I often invoke the words of Audre Lorde from her poem "A Litany for Survival," which could well serve as a battle cry or mantra for all of us:

> and when we speak we are afraid
> our words will not be heard
> nor welcomed
> but when we are silent
> we are still afraid
>
> So it is better to speak
> remembering
> we were never meant to survive. (1995, p. 32)

For those of us who will not hold our tongues, especially, tenure will offer no safety and, as many have come to know, no solace in the violent academy. It will only protect those who are already and always the holders or the servants of White racial and class privilege. The rest of us will never enjoy the elusive promises of security—even when we earn and "have" tenure—because we neither look the part nor are willing to play the parts of happy slaves or entertainers in the academy. And when we refuse these roles, we are reminded swiftly and surely that we do not belong in these hallowed halls. And indeed, we should not allow ourselves to be locked in these ivory towers.

As I once said to a theater full of some five hundred Latinx students from across the public university system where I teach: to me, my having tenure only means that I will leave when I want to. Yet I find that I cannot leave this job or academia so easily, for all the reasons I mentioned, even though I can see it could be, will be my certain demise. In a recent conversation with a comrade who is an attorney and disability rights organizer working happily outside of the academy, I found myself calling academia a death trap. Another comrade, also working in the social justice world, astutely called academia a "gilded cage." As someone with both a newfound awareness of my mortality and an acute appreciation for the opportunity to recover my self and my health, I am committed to making sure that I can and will leave this job and academia when I want to, neither prematurely because of abuses heaped on me at this institution, nor after the damage has been irrevocably done.

Whenever I leave, whether imminently or when I'm "good and ready," I will not run screaming from the room. I am committed to mentoring my graduate students in this one final way, by modeling for them how to leave academia before it's too late, but not in a desperate panic. I intend to model, on my way out, leaving and leading with my heart and mind sound, with dignity and compassion, still grounded in my power and passion, in my political commitments and personal convictions, and with my capacity for love and health as strong as ever.

REFERENCES

Gumbs, A. P. (2016). Sounds to me like a promise: On survival [blog post]. Retrieved from http://www.alexispauline.com/brillianceremastered/blog/.

Hanna, K. B. (2016, October 11). Living beyond survival: 11 tips for women of color in academia [blog post]. Retrieved from https://thisbridgecalledourhealth.wordpress.com/2016/10/11/living-beyond-survival-11-tips-for-women-of-color-in-academia/.

Jones, J. (1985). *Labor of love, labor of sorrow: Black women, work, and the family, from slavery to the present*. New York: Basic Books.

Lorde, A. (1995). A litany for survival. In *The black unicorn: Poems*. (pp. 31–32). New York: Norton.

Nakazawa, D. J. (2016). *Childhood disrupted: How your biography becomes your biology, and how you can heal*. New York: Atria Books.

Rich, N. (2016, May 12). James Baldwin and the fear of a nation. *New York Review of Books*. Retrieved from http://kalamu.com/neogriot/2016/05/17/review-essay-james-baldwin-the-fear-of-a-nation/.

Vo, L. T. (2012). Navigating the academic terrain: The racial and gender politics of elusive belonging. In G. G. Muhs, Y. F. Niemann, C. G. González, & Harris, A. P. (Eds.), *Presumed incompetent: The intersections of race and class for women in academia*. (pp. 93–109). Logan: Utah State University Press.

SEVENTEEN

The Alpha Female and the Sinister Seven

Sahar F. Aziz

When I decided to contribute to *Presumed Incompetent II*, a litany of bad experiences came to mind—ranging from outright assaults on my job security to the microaggressions that remind you every day that no matter how hard you work, how many awards you receive, and how frequently your work is cited, you are and will remain at the bottom of the gender and racial hierarchy undergirding American society in general, and the legal academy in particular (Carbon & Cahn, 2013; Monroe & Chiu, 2010).

Being an academic, I could not resist developing a typology of the various characters and forms of racism, sexism, and Islamophobia I have experienced in the academy. Based on my conversations with other Women of Color at various law schools, coupled with the literature on systemic gender and racial biases in the legal academy, I suspect my proposed typology applies to law schools across the country (Deo, 2015). My aim is to theorize why I, and other women like me, have such negative experiences in a profession that purports to be training the next generation of lawyers and leaders to be civil, ethical, and collaborative. In direct contradiction to these values, harms we experience arise from duplicitous, conniving, and dishonest behavior that produces disrespectful and condescending mistreatment.

In attempting to understand this contradiction between law schools' stated commitments to civility, ethics, and integrity on the one hand and the depraved behavior of some faculty toward (some) female Professors of Color on the other hand, I realize my situation is unique insofar as I am a particular type of woman—the Alpha Female. Thus, I am marked as a triple outsider (female, racial/ethnic/religious minority, and alpha) in a profession that expects leadership, intelligence, and confidence from its members and yet penalizes women and minorities for possessing such traits (Aziz, 2014; Moncrief, 2015; Price Waterhouse v. Hopkins, 1989). Despite the common usage of the Alpha Male

DOI: 10.7330/9781607329664.c017

to denote masculinity, leadership, charisma, and social aggressiveness—all traits admired in men—there is no recognition, much less desire, for the female counterpart (Hawley, Little, & Card, 2008; Ludeman & Erlandson, 2004, 2006). The dearth of literature about Alpha Females produces a blind spot in socio-legal analysis on gender equality (Moncrief, 2015; Ward, Popson, & Dipaolo, 2010).

As such, this chapter seeks to incorporate the concept of the Alpha Female into my experiences as a Woman of Color in the legal academy who not only is presumed incompetent because of my immutable racial and ethnic characteristics, but also presumed aggressive (rather than driven and focused) and insolent (rather than confident and competent) because of my alpha personality traits—for which my White male counterparts receive promotions to leadership positions and accolades. I hope this chapter triggers further research on the interplay of alpha personality traits, race, and gender.

THE ALPHA FEMALE OF COLOR

It was not until I began studying identity performance that I had an epiphany about why some men and women with whom I interacted found me to be an anomaly at best or threatening at worst (Aziz, 2014; Carbado & Gulati, 2004). Although I dress like a traditionally feminine woman and am heterosexual, I am confident, ambitious, outspoken, and I exude a sense of entitlement to be treated like my similarly situated White male peers. That is, I commit the ultimate sin for a Woman of Color living in a White male dominant society—I behave and expect to be treated like an Alpha (White) Male (Kindlon, 2006).

In many higher education institutions, alpha characteristics in male professors are (unofficially) treated as a prerequisite for the job. The literature defines the Alpha Male as a dominant, driven, and confident extrovert (Ludeman & Erlandson, 2006, 2007). He is a charismatic, high achiever with a sense of mission. The Alpha Male does not shy away from expressing his opinion in faculty meetings, the classroom, or public debates. His degrees, work experience, and publications earn him full membership in the nation's intellectual elite and in turn deference from students, staff, and colleagues. When the Alpha Male works hard, he expects to be rewarded with higher pay, endowed chairs, and awards. He knows the capitalist system exploits those who allow themselves to be exploited. And as a result, self-advocacy and self-promotion is smart, not selfish. He asks for what he wants because he is convinced that he deserves it. Because he is a man in a patriarchal society, the Alpha Male's actions are respected as rational and smart.

So where does this leave the Alpha Female in the legal academy? And what if this Alpha Female is also a racial or ethnic minority? The few sociological studies on the Alpha Female define her as "a woman who reports being a leader, feeling a sense of superiority or dominance over other females, having others seek her guidance, feeling extroverted in social situations, believing that males and females are equal, and feeling driven" (Ward, Popson, & Dipaolo, 2010), and as "a self-assured, goal-driven, competitive, high achiever who maintained egalitarian beliefs and did not perceive any distinction between herself and her male counterparts" (Ward, Popson, & Dipaolo, 2009). These traits earn the Alpha Male the reputation of leadership and respect and the Alpha Female a reputation for being arrogant, inconsiderate, and aggressive.

My story is that of the Alpha Female of Color—a person simultaneously attracted to the legal profession and rebuked by some of its members. In a society where being an outspoken, smart, driven, and confident Woman of Color gets you a ticket into the gendered "bitch" club and the raced "angry woman troublemaker" club, practicing law can be a reprieve. Because the legal profession trains its members to be zealous advocates who speak and write persuasively in a system designed to be adversarial, it offers respite for women whose alpha temperament refutes gender stereotypes of the "good woman" as docile, deferential, accommodating, perpetually pleasant, and self-sacrificing.

When I entered the legal academy, however, I was surprised by the lack of transparency and gendered cronyism. The unfettered discretion possessed by law school deans and faculty administrators alarmed me as a lawyer whose previous job entailed suing individuals and entities for unlawful actions arising from abuses of discretion. The unspoken rules in law schools are also rife with double standards. White male pre-tenured colleagues who speak up at faculty meetings are perceived as thoughtful, rising stars invested in the institution. In contrast, women (and minority women in particular) who speak up or offer alternatives to the status quo are troublemakers breaching protocol at best or insolent at worst. Such rules are repressive for a self-identifying feminist—and an Alpha Female.

My audacity in acting like I was a full member of the club triggered collective angst (Kindlon, 2006). For my White liberal colleagues, who in the abstract supported strong feminist Arab Muslim women, my presence seemed to produce cognitive dissonance because in practice they did not want a feminist minority colleague. For my minority colleagues, whose identity performances are more accommodating of White supremacy and patriarchy, my alpha personality contrasted with their silence on issues they proclaimed to support in their research, writings, and public engagements. And for my conservative, patriarchal male and female colleagues who believed (either consciously or subconsciously) that minority women are allowed in the building on condition that they be tokens, their antagonism was palpable.

My refusal to abide by these sexist and racist rules came at a high price through daily microagressions and attacks on my job security. Some of my well-meaning senior colleagues privately advised me to pick my battles, talk less at faculty meetings, and keep a low profile like my other pre-tenured colleagues until I received tenure. I was warned that some people on the faculty found me intimidating, without pointing to anything tangible. Why couldn't I just play along for a few years until I received tenure, as others have admitted to doing?

I couldn't follow such repressive rules because they were antithetical to my type A alpha personality and the way I was raised by my Arab Muslim immigrant parents. Like many other women living in the United States, my home and school environment enabled my personality traits (Price, 1982). I had been trained at home and school to be a leader who sought to be the change I wanted to see in the world, even if it made me unpopular among colleagues and students. My parents, and my father in particular, raised me to be a self-confident, hard-working, and competitive person who strived for excellence. That I was female played no bearing on my parents' high expectations for me in school and life. My father frequently bragged about my accomplishments to friends and family, signaling to me that one should not be ashamed of or hide success. At home, I was encouraged to express my opinion, debate with adults, talk politics, ask questions, and never compromise my moral values to please others. That my parents were immigrants with thick accents, obviously Arab names, identifiably Muslim identities, and no social network in America made us lean in more to compensate for the disadvantages rather than be overcome by a sense of defeatism.

In my world, it was normal to be assertive, driven, and ambitious. In legal academia, however, I discovered these traits stigmatize female professors, and more so if they are racial and ethnic minorities, who belong to the sinister seven.

THE SINISTER SEVEN

I entered the legal academy with numerous ideas for student-focused events, research, and ways to make law schools not only more diverse but welcoming to underrepresented minorities. Naively thinking a law school was similar to a law firm, with an institutional mission implemented by faculty and staff, I immediately began sharing my ideas with colleagues and looking for collaborators with similar interests. I assumed there were incentives to share information and work together in support of one another's work because individual accomplishment collectively contributes toward institutional success. I also assumed there were disincentives to hoard information or obstruct your colleagues' work. My assumptions were woefully incorrect.

The legal academy is structurally rife with passive-aggressive behavior, dishonesty, duplicity, and backstabbing—all of which I find to be unprofessional and uncivil, no matter how much those same colleagues smile in your face or include feigned niceties in their emails. The jealousy and insecurities that drive some faculty to sabotage their colleagues' initiatives, quash creative new ideas, engage in ad hominem attacks, impede collaborative work, and oppose transparency constitute a form of professional malpractice that I believe harms institutions and their students. And yet, these forms of unprofessionalism and incivility occur so frequently that they are accepted as "normal" in faculty engagement, while those who are honest, forthright, and transparent in their disagreements or critiques with colleagues become the targets of "incivility campaigns" by the very people whose modus operandi is stealth sabotage, information hoarding, duplicity, and bad faith. Ultimately, the terms *civility* and *professionalism* became arbitrary concepts weaponized to discipline alpha minority professors.

By the time I was up for tenure, I realized I was not like many other female law professors—not simply because of my minority racial and religious background but also because of my willingness to act consistently with my alpha personality. I was outspoken, blunt, confident, not deferential to male authority, emulated White men who self-promoted their work, and had no aversion to confrontation to resolve disagreements. Like others before me, I soon discovered the tenure and promotion process is more of a popularity contest than a meaningful evaluation of merit based on clearly communicated, equally applied objective criteria. Fortunately, I obtained tenure notwithstanding my inability and unwillingness to play by all the unspoken rules, though I know others like me who were not so lucky.

What follows is my attempt to organize my experiences into a typology of characters who likely exist at most law schools to equip other Alpha Females of Color in dealing with prototypes of colleagues prevalent in the legal academy. Although there is certainly a separate typology of colleagues who presume the Alpha Female of Color is competent, treat her with civility, and courageously defend her against the sinister seven's harmful behavior, I am purposely limiting my typology to those who perpetuate subordination in light of the theme of *Presumed Incompetent II*.

The sinister seven are the following faculty prototypes: (1) the Troll, (2) the Patriarchal Female, (3) the Whispering Coward, (4) the Head Minority Man in Charge, (5) the Liberal Hypocrite, (6) the Stealth Pervert, and (7) the Misogynist Racist. Individuals can be multiple prototypes at the same time, and some individuals exemplify a prototype much more intensely than others. Like any theoretical frame, it is not flawless. Nor does it explain every experience of incivility, abuse, or discrimination. Indeed, I hope critiques of the theory motivate sociolegal empiricists to explore the ways in which civility and professionalism are weaponized against male and female Professors of Color who refuse or are incapable of performing their identities to accommodate patriarchy and White racial dominance in the legal academy. Most notably, the typology purposely does not identify specific people at institutions but rather aims to bring order to the myriad forms of subordination experienced by self-identified Alpha Females at law schools across the country.

The Troll

Alpha Females of Color attract attention, both welcome and unwelcome. Supporters of their leadership abilities seek them out for collaboration and new ideas, while detractors seek ways to sabotage their upward trajectory. One of those detractors is the Troll.

The Troll's modus operandi is to create the impression that he is not interested in the Alpha Female of Color's work but in fact surveils her. He seeks out her students and research assistants to gather information about what the Alpha Female of Color is working on, her teaching methodology, student complaints, and her upcoming activities. He secretly follows her social media postings, reads her publications, and tracks her speaking engagements. The Troll passes by her office during office hours to check if she is in fact there; attends her events at conferences even if they are irrelevant to his work; and watches her interact with people. Despite his intense interest in the Alpha Female of Color, oddly, he gives the impression of indifference when she speaks with him. Because his actions are driven by jealousy, personal animus, or opposition to her ideological views, rather than good faith interest in her work, he searches for any breaches of protocol that can be used against the Alpha Female of Color when she comes up for tenure or promotion.

Beware of the Troll on your faculty. If you find that a particular tenured faculty member is always showing up to your events, making comments that evince an unusually high familiarity with your work and speaking engagements, and regularly passing by your office during office hours just to peek in—you may be the Troll's latest target. Because he may be a racist, sexist, or Islamophobe who does not want an Arab or Muslim on his faculty, he will share whatever adverse information he can find with other faculty members as a means of chipping away at your credibility and sabotaging your initiatives. The Troll is well aware of the other faculty members who resent you for your alpha traits or feminist identity, causing him to seek out opportunities at faculty or committee meetings to subtly discredit you through backhanded compliments and insulting "jokes." When others in the sinister seven excessively rely on student evaluations in performance reviews (notwithstanding empirical studies showing systemic student bias against women and minority professors) (Lazos, 2012), the Troll will point out any negative student evaluations. He will portray your op-eds, media interviews, and frequent public presentations as distractions from your teaching duties rather than commend you for raising the profile of the law school.

Do not seek the Troll's guidance on how to improve your teaching, deal with difficult students, or improve your scholarship—this just makes his campaign against you easier. While pretending to be collegial, he'll use the information you share with him in confidence against you when you are most vulnerable—at the promotion and tenure meeting.

The Patriarchal Female

Committee service is tricky for female professors. On the one hand, being at the table means you have an opportunity to weigh in on decisions that shape curriculum, admissions, student mentoring, experiential learning, and other important facets of law school operations. On the other hand, committee service is the least valued work in promotion and tenure evaluations, and as a result is frequently assigned to female professors whose scholarship suffers due to the time demands. But not just any woman will do when it comes to assigning committee chair positions. Deans (particularly male) often prefer the female technocrat over the independent leader. That is, females who implement patriarchy by seeing their roles as merely administrative and facilitative are often the ideal candidates to chair or serve on powerful committees.

The Patriarchal Female is the glue holding patriarchy intact. She is frequently the dean's proxy for keeping the committee on track with a predetermined outcome, whether it be amending policies, adopting new programs, or cutting programs. The patriarchal female foregoes meaningful leadership for nominal leadership because she is culturally indoctrinated to accept male dominance as the norm. Not only does the Patriarchal Female defer to male authority—whether the dean or male committee members, some of whom are more junior—but she silences and marginalizes the Alpha Female of Color who refuses to be a rubber stamp. The Patriarchal Female signals to the Alpha Female of Color, verbally and nonverbally, that her questions and engagement on an issue are a nuisance. Adopting myriad subversive strategies ranging from "accidentally" leaving the Alpha Female of Color off group emails or "forgetting" to send relevant information to sending drafts just before a deadline as a way of preventing group discussion, the Patriarchal Female seeks to sideline the Alpha Female of Color without exposing her biases to colleagues.

To the Patriarchal Female, the Alpha Female of Color is her nemesis—blunt, overtly defiant of patriarchy, and comfortable with open disagreement. In contrast, the Patriarchal Female is the "good girl" who does not challenge male authority, especially in public, reserves her disagreements to private discussions or withholds them altogether, and guardedly performs her gender identity to exude a perpetually pleasant, amicable, and calm demeanor, even if she is fuming inside. Whether the Patriarchal Female is authentic in her gender identity performance is irrelevant insofar as her contribution to stigmatizing the Alpha Female of Color as a "bad girl" whose alpha personality traits would be admired—were she a White male. By joining male faculty who portray the Alpha Female of Color as aggressive, abrasive, and not collegial, the Patriarchal Female is deployed to rebuke the Alpha Female of Color's claims of sexism.

The Whispering Coward

The Whispering Coward will start out wanting to support you, perhaps for ideological reasons or because she does not see you as a threat. But as your strong personality and drive generate high productivity, the Whispering Coward's own insecurities are aggravated, transforming her into an obstructionist. And if she is a woman who has played by the performative rules of patriarchy or White racial dominance, she will resent you for your alpha qualities such that she also takes on the role of the Patriarchal Female.

In contrast to the Troll, who pretends to be uninterested, the Whispering Coward goes out of her way to be collegial to make you believe she is an ally. But, like the Troll, she is duplicitous in her weaponization of information against you. Your creativity, entrepreneurship, and public intellectualism only remind her of her own shortcomings. She exploits the common knowledge on the faculty that you are friends to lend credibility to her critiques and attempts to secretly obstruct your ideas and initiatives. She does not have the courage to speak to you directly about such critiques—likely because they are merely pretexts in furtherance of her agenda to impede your professional growth. Instead, she starts whisper campaigns to poison the well.

If you have colleagues who act like allies, but you observe cowardice in their actions, beware—they may turn against you. A real ally is courageous enough to confront you about any genuine concerns so that she can help you be a better law professor and scholar.

The Head Minority Man in Charge

Minority men in legal academia are scarce. Initiatives to increase diversity have disproportionately benefited White women while the number of minority men law professors remains grimly low (Barnes & Mertz, 2012). When it comes to law school deans, the number is in the single digits (Wolff, 2011). As a result, minority men have to work harder than their White peers while simultaneously being subjected to stringent identity performance rules. Pressures not to fit negative stereotypes of minority men as less intelligent, more aggressive, lazy, and unqualified create significant stress on minority male professors to prove they deserve to be there (Carbado, 2015).

Though minority male professors should be natural allies with Alpha Females of Color due to their shared outsider status and attendant adverse experiences (albeit on different grounds), the opposite is sometimes true. The Head Minority Man in Charge (also an Alpha Male) experiences his own humiliations, microaggressions, or direct affronts arising from a White male–dominant system. Despite his own alpha personality traits, American society's racial hierarchy places him below the White Alpha Male. Thus, a minority male law dean may receive less respect, deference, and credibility by faculty, staff, and students than a White male law dean. Similarly, a senior minority male professor may not have an endowed chair or receive the same salary as his similarly situated (and junior) White male peer. His gender privilege is circumscribed by his racial subordination.

So when an Alpha Female of Color enters the scene, seeking to be treated equally through her willingness to speak out when she does not agree with him or refusal to be blindly deferential, she is perceived as a threat to his status above minority women on the racial-gender hierarchy. He interprets her alpha personality traits as maliciously driven to further discredit and subordinate him as a minority male rather than as her own defiance of the racial-gender hierarchy that oppresses her too. Consequently, the Head Minority Man in Charge openly confronts the Alpha Female of Color to figuratively "put her in her place." He will send group emails openly challenging her authority or criticizing her when she rebukes his attempt to take control or disagrees with him. Because he is a racial minority, the Head Minority Man in Charge may not appreciate how his behavior perpetuates sexism against the Alpha Female of Color. In his mind, he is a victim of racism but never a perpetrator of sexism.

The Head Minority Man in Charge should be an ally with a mutual interest in making legal academia less racist and less sexist. But if he is stubborn and too narcissistic to recognize his own biases, then you should treat him like the sexist he is and accept that he is not an ally.

The Liberal Hypocrite

Legal academia is largely comprised of professors who self-identify as liberal in their ideological leanings (Chilton & Posner, 2014). Pluralism, inclusivity, gender and racial equality, immigrant rights, and multiculturalism are among the values promoted by liberal professors. In theory, a predominantly liberal work environment is more conducive to professional growth for an Alpha Female of Color. In practice, however, the Liberal Hypocrite contributes to the illiberal ways in which law faculty operate.

The Liberal Hypocrite is a male or female faculty member whose writings and public speaking promote liberal values. They bemoan the lack of racial and ethnic diversity in law schools, the shortage of women as law partners, the increasing income inequality in American society, xenophobia, discrimination against immigrants, and other miscarriages of social justice. But when it comes to expending political capital in their law schools to defend these values, the Liberal Hypocrite is either absent or silent. He may join the Alpha Female of Color over coffee to bemoan the few African American and Latino students at the law school but decline to join the committee working on the issue. She will lament the unequal pay between male and female professors but decline to join a collective effort to change it. And when there is a proposal to increase diversity in the student body, staff, or faculty, the Liberal Hypocrite does not come to the aid of the Alpha Female of Color (and other faculty) when she expends political capital to change policies and practices.

If the Alpha Female of Color raises concerns that underrepresented students may be passing the bar at lower rates such that faculty early intervention is necessary, the Liberal Hypocrite just gives a blank stare or distracts herself with her laptop during the faculty meeting. In some cases, the Liberal Hypocrite agrees with the opposition as a means of making himself appear reasonable and objective as compared to the impassioned Alpha Female of Color. Or, more egregious, he doesn't even show up to the meeting when the issue is on the agenda. Although the Liberal Hypocrite may understand intersectionality and oppose discrimination against Women of Color in theory, he takes actions on your faculty in direct contradiction of those values in ways that harm the Alpha Female of Color.

And yet to the outside world of her peers, the Liberal Hypocrite is celebrated as a liberal scholar and advocate. Liberal ideas to her are just that—ideas. Implementing them in her law school is outside the scope of the Liberal Hypocrite's scholarly endeavors or ideological commitments. Yet, she creates the impressions to third parties that she in fact cares about these issues at her institution.

Identify the Liberal Hypocrites on your faculty (there are likely many) so that you are not disappointed or surprised when they openly oppose you, or secretly sabotage you, in faculty debates about diversity, admissions, budget transparency, pay equality, bar passage, and other policies.

The Stealth Pervert

The Stealth Pervert is at every workplace, and law schools are no exception. However, because the law school Stealth Pervert has been trained as a lawyer and knows sexual harassment can ruin careers, he is savvy and subtle. Whether through casual compliments on how you are dressed or asking you to coffee to talk about your work when he clearly has little interest in it, the Stealth Pervert walks a fine line in seeking your attention. As an Alpha Female of Color you are exotic to him, particularly if you are young and he is a senior White male. He may find your strong personality endearing rather than threatening because he is secure at the top of the racial-gender hierarchy. Your minority status makes him less concerned that you would have the audacity to complain about his excessive "friendliness." And even if you did, he knows he has more credibility in the White male–dominant environment when he responds that he was merely being collegial.

The Stealth Pervert's danger to your career lies primarily in his retaliatory response when you eventually rebuke him—either directly or indirectly—once you discover his interest in you is driven by improper intentions. The Stealth Pervert's scarred ego drives him to read every outside review, call colleagues in the academy to ask about you, talk to students, and look for any weaknesses in the Alpha Female of Color's application for promotion or tenure—all under the guise of taking his job as a voting faculty member seriously in the service of the school. As a means of further punishing the Alpha Female of Color, he joins the gang of faculty who find her personality abrasive, although prior to her rebuke he was a vocal supporter. If the Alpha Female of Color never filed a formal complaint, his colleagues are unaware of the Stealth Pervert's ulterior motives, though some of them may notice his intense interest in the Alpha Female of Color's work.

Avoid the Stealth Perverts on your faculty. Make sure there is always a third party present when he attempts to talk to you; or better yet, limit all communications to email. If the Stealth Pervert is persistent in his attempts to interact with you, create a record to protect yourself from his vindictiveness. If his behavior reaches a point where you believe he is seeking to sabotage your job security, request to have him recused from your tenure and promotion evaluation based on the record you have created. Of course, a formal complaint is always an option, but as many of us in the legal profession know, even a meritorious complaint of sexual harassment can be the kiss of death in the secretive, highly discretionary lateral market and tenure process (Feldblum & Lipnic, 2016).

The Misogynist Racist

The Misogynist Racist is usually easy to spot. He is shameless in his belief that the Alpha Female of Color should not have been hired on to the faculty. His White male privilege produces one of two alternative responses: hostility or dismissiveness.

The hostile Misogynist Racist aims not only to humiliate the Alpha Female of Color, but also communicate to his colleagues that he is not afraid of being deemed a sexist or a racist for pouncing on a minority female on the faculty. To the contrary, he claims verbal and public confrontations are integral to his academic freedom to debate ideas—notwithstanding that he does not behave with the same condescension toward other male and White colleagues with whom he disagrees. Usually falling into a conservative ideological camp, the hostile Misogynist Racist resents a strong minority woman who openly challenges White male dominance.

Because she is an Alpha Female, she does not shy away in fear from his attacks. Instead, she confronts him as a peer, including calling out his hostility in faculty meetings and via email. Not being accustomed to being publicly challenged by a Woman of Color, his animosity toward her becomes obsessive. He "replies all" to the faculty in response to the Alpha Female of Color's emails—with a condescending or sarcastic tone. He writes her emails demanding she inform the dean and president of the university of her signing a letter protesting policies promulgated by the (conservative) president of the United States. He feels compelled to police and rebuke every comment she makes in meetings to establish his racial and male dominance, even if his professional record is comparatively weaker and his bad faith is glaringly obvious. That she exudes a sense of entitlement based on her professional record further aggravates his hostility toward her. Put simply, he wants to put her in her place. The more hostile the misogynist sexist becomes, the more he discredits himself among the faculty as a bigot who eventually becomes marginalized.

The dismissive Misogynist Racist is more prevalent in liberal legal academia. His biases, which may be conscious or unconscious, toward the Alpha Female of Color are manifested by ignoring her. He will not respond to emails, attend meetings she organizes, or acknowledge her authority in administrative duties. As far as he is concerned, she is not important enough to warrant his attention. His time is better spent with "real intellectuals" (usually White males) who engage in "serious research" (e.g., corporate, intellectual property, empirical, law, and economics). Whatever accomplishments or accolades the Alpha Female of Color achieves he dismisses as part of identity and diversity politics in the academy, not based on real merit. The only time the dismissive Misogynist Racist pays attention to the Alpha Female of Color is when she is up for promotion equal to him, such as an endowed chair or distinguished professor. At that point, he will weigh in to express his opposition to her candidacy. For although he is willing to tolerate her presence on the faculty, he cannot allow her (and others he deems inferior) to reach his status.

CONCLUSION

Legal academia is treacherous terrain for many faculty. Structural flaws include lack of transparency, unfettered discretion by deans, few incentives for faculty to work as a team in furtherance of an institutional mission as opposed to acting as self-interested independent agents, and arbitrary application of policies based on patronage and personal biases. The more subordinated identities a faculty member possesses, the more these flaws impede her ability to attain tenure, promotion, and respect. The literature is still nascent on the extent to which alpha personality traits adversely impact a minority female professor's student evaluations, performance evaluations, and the workplace environment. While this chapter is not meant to replace the much-needed empirical research, I hope it brings to the forefront how alpha personality traits exacerbate the myriad challenges faced by Women of Color professors as their competence is continually questioned (Johnson, Murphy, Zewdie, & Reichard, 2008).

Being a strong, driven, confident, and ambitious woman should not be stigmatizing. Nor should it be interpreted as evidence of incivility, unprofessionalism, or insubordination. To the contrary, in a profession that trains its members to zealously represent their clients in an adversarial system, alpha traits are treated as ordinary—for men. The same should be true for women, whether as lawyers or law professors.

REFERENCES

Aziz, S. F. (2014). Coercive assimilationism: The perils of Muslim women's identity performance in the workplace. *Michigan Journal of Race & Law, 20*(1), 1–64.

Barnes, K., & Mertz, E. (2012). Is it fair? Law professors' perceptions of tenure. *Journal of Legal Education, 61*(4), 511–539. Retrieved from http://www.jstor.org/stable/42894249.

Carbado, D. (2015) *Acting white? Rethinking race in "post-racial" America.* New York: Oxford University Press.

Carbado, D. W., & Gulati M. (2004). Race to the top of the corporate ladder: What minorities do when they get there. *Washington & Lee Law Review, 61,* 1645–1693.

Carbon, J., & Cahn N. (2013). The end of men or the rebirth of class? *Boston Law Review, 93*(871), 873–895.

Chilton, A. S., & Posner, E. (2014). *An empirical study of political bias in legal scholarship* (Working Paper No. 696). Chicago: Coase-Sandor Institute for Law & Economics.

Deo, M. E. (2015) The ugly truth about legal academia. *Brooklyn Law Review, 80*(3), 943–1014.

Feldblum, C. R, & Lipnic, V. A. (2016). *Report of the co-chairs of the EEOC select task force on the study of harassment in the workplace.* Retrieved from https://www.eeoc.gov/eeoc/task_force/harassment/upload/report.pdf.

Hawley, P. H., Little, T. D., & Card, N. A. (2008). The myth of the alpha male: A new look at dominance-related beliefs and behaviors among adolescent males and females. *International Journal of Behavioral Development, 32*(1), 32–68.

Johnson, S. K., Murphy, S. E., Zewdie, S., & Reichard, R. J. (2008). The strong sensitive type: Effects of gender stereotypes and leadership prototypes on the evaluation of male and female leaders. *Organizational Behavior and Human Decision Processes, 106,* 39–60.

Kindlon, D. (2006). *Alpha girls: Understanding the new American girl and how she is changing the world.* New York: Rodale.

Lazos, S. (2012). Are student teaching evaluations holding back women and minorities? The perils of "doing" gender and race in the classroom. In G. G. Muhs, Y. F. Niemann, C. G. González, & Harris, A. P. (Eds.), *Presumed incompetent: The intersections of race and class for women in academia.* (pp. 164-185). Logan: Utah State University Press.

Ludeman, K., & Erlandson, E. (2004, May). Coaching the alpha male. *Harvard Business Review, 82*(5), 58–67, 150.

Ludeman, K., & Erlandson, E. (2006). *Alpha male syndrome.* Boston: Harvard Business School Press.

Ludeman, K., & Erlandson, E. (2007). Channeling alpha male leaders. *Leader to Leader,* 44, 38–44.

Moncrief, D. J. (2015). *Leadership influences of the veteran alpha female leader.* Unpublished doctoral dissertation, Walden University.

Monroe, K., & Chiu, W. (2010). Gender equality in the academy: The pipeline problem. *PS: Political Science and Politics,* 43(2), 303–308. Retrieved from http://www.jstor.org/stable/40646731.

Price, V. (1982). What is type A? A cognitive social learning model. *Journal of Occupational Behaviour,* 3(1), 109–129. Retrieved from http://www.jstor.org/stable/3000301.

Price Waterhouse v. Hopkins. (1989). 490 US 228.

Ward, R. M., Popson, H. C., & Dipaolo, D. G. (2009). College student leaders: Meet the alpha female. *Journal of Leadership Education,* 7(3) 100–117.

Ward, R. M., Popson, H. C., & Dipaolo, D. G. (2010). Defining the alpha female: A female leadership measure. *Journal of Leadership & Organizational Studies,* 17(3), 309–320.

Wolff, K. (2011). From pipeline to pipe dream: The HBCU effect on law school deans of color. *Journal of Gender, Race Justice,* 14(3), 765–796.

EIGHTEEN

Mindful Heresy as Praxis for Change

Responding to Microaggressions as Building Blocks of Hegemony

Sarah Amira de la Garza

"DON'T CRY; IT WILL MAKE THE PAIN WORSE"

I was a brand-new PhD in December 1987 when I was struck by a car in a crosswalk on the Rutgers University campus, where I was an assistant professor. Although I survived the accident with only minor bodily injuries, the most significant injury resulted when my head hit the front of the car, knocking me unconscious; my body was thrown onto the road. My first thought upon regaining consciousness: "I'm still alive!" My life had changed permanently, however.

I don't remember the arrival of the ambulance, but I can recall having my jeans cut open so the EMTs could treat my leg, a brace being placed on my neck, my mouth hurting from where my lip had been bruised, my tooth chipped from impact with the hood of the car. The EMTs asked me basic questions, at the same time telling me not to move. One of them had found my purse and asked if they could look through it. I noticed that there was a delay when I tried to speak. They opted to read my driver's license instead of getting answers from me. My words came out explosively, even though I didn't intend to yell them. Once in the ambulance, the driver asked me, "Is there a hospital that you prefer?" I recall wanting to tell him to take me to St. Peter's, just down the road from my home. My words didn't come, and I heard the EMT in the passenger seat say to him, "Take her to county; she's Hispanic." The pain in my head was now compounded by the anguish and frustration of my awareness of what was happening coupled with my frightening inability to communicate. I began to cry, and the EMT riding with me told me, "Don't cry; it will make the pain worse." In retrospect, it was like everything happening during those moments was a foretaste of what my experience living with the disability would be like—a disability I still didn't realize I had. A disability that from the earliest moments combined with my presence as a Woman of Color, a "Hispanic" body.

DOI: 10.7330/9781607329664.c018

"YOU'RE GOING TO WANT TO QUIT YOUR JOB"

"You're going to want to quit your job, but if you can avoid it, please don't," were the words of Dr. Ian Livingstone, the neuro-psychiatrist in Princeton suggested by my attorney. He pinpointed the exact area of the brain impacted by my head trauma. Since Spanish was my first language as a child, he tested me in both English and Spanish, discovering that my linguistic ability was not as severely affected in Spanish. This was amazing to me, knowing that my Spanish was not as fluent as my English. When he asked me to list words in Spanish, I had no problem; when I tried in English, I quickly went blank, or repeated words I'd already provided. He told me that my head injury (which at the time was causing aphasia, various memory problems, altered affect, and speech delays) was minor in comparison to most brain injuries he dealt with, but because of the nature of my work, it was considered major. He said context had everything to do with the real, lived impact of a brain injury, and for this reason, he wanted me to know I might be tempted to leave my profession. "Don't do it, if you can hang in there," he said, adding, "These injuries can take years to stabilize, and we won't know for a long time how your brain will compensate, what you might actually be able to do." He then went on to describe the work he wanted me to do with him, so I could begin to rely on my right brain to support the functions my left brain was not able to do. With the help of my partner at the time, I returned to see him over the following months, and the guidance he gave me saved my career, as well as giving me a roadmap for accommodations I could make to assist my cognitive function.

"RIA RODRIGUEZ HAS BEEN IN AN ACCIDENT"

The car hit me in early December, just before finals, sparing me the struggles of teaching for over a month. The chair of our department gave me a pink message slip from the date of my accident. Apparently I had managed to utter to the EMTs that I worked at Rutgers, and they'd found my business card in my purse and used it to call and let someone know I'd been in an accident. However, the message was "Ria Rodriguez has been in an accident." My chair explained he'd thought it was a student and had displayed the note in case someone recognized the name. My first name at the time was Maria—somehow that became Ria, and I was renamed a generic Spanish last name. I recalled the EMT redirecting the driver to the county hospital because of my ethnicity. I laughed along with my colleagues at the "joke," but it stung.

When I returned in January, I had to cancel co-teaching my first graduate class, and my undergraduate classes were frequently disrupted by my random misarticulations, momentary amnesia, and changes in affect, the markers of my brain injury. I could not write more than a few lines without forgetting what I had started to write. In time, I would come to realize that interruptions of any sort could cause me to lose the sense of what I was doing until contextual cues reminded me again. It took me years to learn that I shouldn't write during office hours because of the risk of disruption. During those instants of what I call "no mind," I would feel panic, and any further disruption in the conversation (such as someone asking, "Are you okay?" or "Should I come back later?") would compound the interruption and cause a vicious cycle of hyper-reaction. My fear and panic would translate to the expression on my face and my vocal tone. My nonverbal communication was frantically expressing, "Wait! Let me get my mind back—don't talk—let me finish what I'm thinking!" In trying to explain "I'm not mad at you," or that without time to focus I could forget what I was working on, I began to experience incredulity, suspicion, and dismissive attitudes from others. These were often accompanied by expressions of concern and sympathy that were not as credible as the doubt or judgment on their faces. Dr. Livingstone had accurately predicted the impact on my work, as well as my desire to escape it.

SIGNAL MANTRAS FOR PREJUDICE

I could continue with my account of the ways that the accident influenced my work and career, but that's another story. I choose to share the story of my accident because it caused the brain injury that led to my permanent struggles with PTSD and sequential memory loss. Until 2015, when I had conversations with our associate dean about microaggressions in the workplace, I hadn't formally discussed my disability with any colleague or supervisor without others' reactions becoming microaggressive or dismissive. Statements like "I wish I had an excuse" had become the informal signal mantras for me when I attempted to explain my situation, letting me know that my disability was being framed with an implicit prejudice. I recalled other things that Dr. Livingstone had said to me. He told me people wouldn't believe I had a disability. "Yours is an invisible disability." Because they can't see it, they don't believe it. And, as I grew to learn over the years, the idea of having a cognitive disability is threatening to the very perceptions of how academics think and *exist*. The stereotypes and implicit assumptions about a brain injury project ignorance and fears of "losing our minds," of dementia, of insanity, of lowered intelligence onto the person willing to publicly identify that she or he has one.

I learned to live with the felt sense that I must continually remind people that just because I "sounded smart" and "was organized," it didn't mean I wasn't dealing with a disability. And because I succeeded and managed to achieve international recognition in my field for my work in indigenous/decolonial methodologies and epistemology, it didn't mean that the disability had disappeared. Instead, I grew to see how my presence as a Chicana who was "erudite" (as a university president once told me when I'd defended a graduate student's critique of his strategic plan) threatened assumptions. The symptoms of my PTSD, triggered by the social experiences brought on by my cognitive disability, required that I repeatedly point out my need for accommodation. But the disability was invisible, as Dr. Livingstone had warned me, so what was *visible* was the body of a woman, a Mexican woman, a Latina, a Chicana.

ALWAYS THE ANGRY CHICANA . . . NO NEED TO LOOK FURTHER

So, imagine this scenario. I am working in my office on a manuscript, writing with full attention. My office door is open, and a grad student or colleague comes by and says, "Have a minute?" That's normal and ordinary. But when such a disruption happens to me, my severely low-functioning sequential memory cannot tie together the strings between what I was doing, the person at the door, and what they begin to tell me about—"this student," "this project," or "this gossip." As I struggle to hold the ends of the strings to each piece, my anxiety is aroused, its discomfort subjectively intensified because of the multiple things going on in my mind to attempt to compensate for what I cannot do, and the memory of previous encounters like this that erupted into conflict. My face is reflecting what is happening within me, the product of my disability. But it is the face of a Chicana woman. The affect is quickly and easily read as anger and aggression. It fits the popular stereotype. On top of the familiar agony of an interruption, I must negotiate the frequent narration of my experience by those who witness the affect that is the only visible aspect of my disability. I must defend myself against their perceptions.

My logical response to those interruptions would be to ask that I be allowed to finish what I am saying, to tell people to wait. My words reflect the urgency I feel to stop the interruption. If I offer the explanation "I have a traumatic brain injury that makes it difficult for me to be interrupted," the insistence that what they are witnessing is my *anger*, my *rudeness*, my *aggression* is what lingers. So, I've been asked by Latino men why I can't be "sweet" like White faculty women, White women cry because I'm mean, and when I try to explain, I'm "making excuses." I am a mean Chicana professor, and as my colleagues have said, they wish *they* "had an excuse." These microaggressions have become so agonizing they actually trigger my PTSD. Only a handful of male students, veterans or athletes familiar with traumatic brain injuries (TBIs) or PTSD, have ever responded with understanding and compassion or accommodation. I have lived with the sense that by being a Chicana woman, I was already at risk of being perceived as an angry Woman of Color simply by disagreeing or holding my ground (recalling my professors in graduate school who referred to me as a "saucy señorita" when I expressed disagreement or a critique). The brain injury interacts with this to create a personal context within which the receipt of microaggressions is guaranteed almost daily in my work environment.

TELLING THE STORIES CAN BE TRIGGERING, BUT I MUST

But let me catch my breath. I have written something here that I've never written before. My heart rate has accelerated, my breathing quickened, become shallower. I take a deep breath. "You can do this." Yes, I *must* do this. Because in addition to highlighting the significance of how the stigma and stereotypes of a disability combine with the expectations of incompetence implicit in a racist environment, my task here is to do more than reap the benefits of catharsis from an empathetic or sympathetic audience. I wish to share the insights of my careful consideration and observation of microaggressions as a member of an academic discipline that rewards us for mastering the capacity to speak with a standard sound, where our history includes training to speak Standard American English in our speech classes. Almost no one could do so, but in a world where an accent should be "learned away," guess for whom it mattered most? As stridently explicit as those markers of prejudice and racism are, it is the experience of microaggressions in everyday conversations, the silences, apologies, and politeness that feather the air when they occur, that has led me to believe this is where hegemony is created, maintained, and learned. I must step up and speak. If we do not learn how to exist in these settings so that they do not further oppress and reinforce implicit racism, sexism, ableism, ad infinitum . . . if we do not do that, we're digging our own graves. That's how hegemony works.

"THE BRUISES ON MY THROAT"

"The bruises on my throat look remarkably like the imprints of my own hands" (Gonzalez, 1998, p. 227). I will simply define *hegemony* here as how domination is maintained, specifically emphasizing the learned social rituals, scripts, and routines that keep the hierarchical structures of power in place. We can be said to be agents of hegemony if we behave in ways that keep the powerful who dominate in power, and those who are oppressed remain so. Hegemony is present in any well-functioning organization where people do what they must without having to be told—including families, cultural institutions, schools, and corporations. Critiquing hegemony requires that we critically self-examine how we ourselves have been complicit in our oppression. It requires an awareness of how even though oppressed, we have come to be complacent in the comforts of rewards when we play by the rules. This is fundamental to understanding why, in practice, it is so difficult to change things. Because in a successfully dominated system structured with hierarchical privileging, it is inevitable that undoing even one small piece of how we interact with others will have implications for a multitude of our other interactions, including our self-talk. The rules, or the orthodox ways of behavior, require that we not disrupt these structures. After centuries of religious and colonialist domination around the globe, even our decolonial theories and theories of resistance often describe disruptions that unwittingly uphold and socially construct the norms of what is considered successful. It is difficult to detach ourselves from the habitual enticements of the hierarchies and class structures birthed through colonization.

"BUT YOU DON'T SEEM BRAIN DAMAGED . . . AND YOUR ENGLISH IS SO GOOD"

Counseling psychologist Derald Wing Sue (2010) has come to be known for his work to raise awareness of the reality and ubiquity of microaggressions. His definition is familiar to anyone who has studied them: "Racial microaggressions are brief and commonplace daily verbal, behavioral, or environmental indignities, whether intentional or unintentional, that communicate hostile, derogatory, or negative racial slights and insults toward people of color" (Sue et al., 2007, p. 271). What I'd like to address here is not what they are, whether they exist, or how they can hurt us, but why it is so difficult to address them, and what I believe is required to disrupt them. To do this, it requires that we come to terms with how easily we are manipulated and kept in place by avoidance of discomfort. And when dealing with hegemony, I am talking about discomfort that has been defined as inappropriate. Because in a hierarchically privileged system, appropriate discomfort works to keep it in place. Case in point: cognitive dissonance theory. When I began to consider this possibility, I suddenly understood why White women cry so readily and predictably when faced with evidence of complicity or wrongdoing. I understood why the mistreatment of groups of people is easy for society to overlook, while for others, it is an "outrage." We are not in a modernist vacuum where all things are equal and viewed objectively; we exist in historically and culturally formed patterns of social interaction.

AN ORTHODOXY OF COMFORT; OR, THE ONTOLOGICAL ASSUMPTION IT IS POWER

If our society is racist and rooted in a history that dominated, isolated, and eliminated those with disabilities, then those underlying assumptions are present in what have come to be our implicit assumptions, learned since childhood through observation and participation. Hegemony of racism and ableism is kept in place when we behave in ways that allow people to remain comfortable in the presence of the expression and enactment of racist and ableist ontological assumptions, flawed though they might be. Insisting on our comfort in such a system could be the kiss of death. We need to have a nonorthodox view of discomfort. We need to learn to live with it, with new, disruptive norms. Consider that ontologically, if the powerful and "superior" are privileged and entitled to comfort always, then it would stand to reason that the avoidance of discomfort would come to be a sign of one's place within the society. Those with less power or status become the icons of discomfort. In time, rituals and routines would be established to show that one understands how to operate in the society in exchange for . . . comfort. Being comfortable with conscious, chosen, discomfort disrupts the norms, and is critical to the response I've come to practice in my life, which I'll explain later.

MAYBE WE SHOULDN'T "LET IT PASS"

In my graduate studies, I devoted a large amount of my effort to study with the late Robert Hopper, learning how to analyze everyday spoken conversation as a systematic structuring social ritual almost all humans engage in. It is here I first learned of Grice's cooperative principle (1975) for social interaction. This principle explains that we basically operate on a system of politeness when speaking with others, attempting not to say too much, too little, or to say things in the wrong way. And when someone violates these rules, which Grice calls "maxims," more often than not, the polite thing is to "let it pass." That's what is meant by cooperation. People should not make statements that are ambiguous, erroneous, lacking information, and so on, but when and if they do, we also shouldn't call people out on them. In my (2018a) essay exploring an Anzaldúan approach to microaggressions, I go into more detail about this. The main point is that if you call out someone on a microaggression (which is by definition ambiguous and dependent on unspoken assumptions), the norms for conversation would call that an interruption to a smoothly occurring conversation. And an interruption calls for a speedy resolution, usually with a quick "repair sequence," often experienced as a side sequence in conversation, where you temporarily stop the existing conversation to clarify, then resume (Zahn, 1984, p. 56). We don't want to spend too much time doing this because, well, that would be rude. In organizational literature, we learn that interruptions require "sensemaking" (Weick, 1995), but sensemaking is based on what we know from our previous experience. When considering microaggressions, I quickly saw that based on what we know to be the ways that people in our society respond to problems in conversation, the person who wishes to call out someone for a microaggression is between a rock and a hard place, and even conversations about microaggressions are technically violations of the rules.

A CRY FOR MINDFUL HERESY

Despite my disability, I continued with my career and today find myself with less than five years before I'm eligible for retirement. I was granted tenure at a Research I university, have participated in sponsored research teams, held numerous administrative positions, and received recognition for the impact of groundbreaking work. I made choices during my early career not to confront the microaggressions by supervisors, colleagues, and even other Women of Color—not because I had any strategy for it, but because my greatest challenge was privately dealing with the obstacles my disability often put in my path. But I never lost my zeal for understanding, and my training as an ethnographer, combined with my training as a conversation analyst, assured that I was always watching and reflecting, analyzing, and conceptualizing. In 1992, I wrote an entry in my personal journal that I entitled "A Cry for Heresy." In every area of my life, my PTSD and TBI were turning my capacity to respond within normal parameters upside down. I'd come to realize that what was often called working "outside the box" was considered a plus for decision-making, but once the solutions were found, it was back to the box. I was involved in activism with the Arizona Chicano/a community, and my experiences everywhere seemed to illustrate how patterns of politeness and the familiar (i.e., invoking "familia" as a form of social control) were used to dominate. Not one but two leading Chicano/a professors in higher education advised me to leave the academy. "If you don't want to play by the rules, maybe this isn't the place for you," they said in response to my intention of delaying my tenure plans to do the work I was doing without interruption. "The academy isn't meant for people like you, who write about our dirty laundry," they said in response to my outspoken defense of a colleague who had been silenced through the invocation of a code of "familia" and a criterion of "entre nos" for departmental discussions. I felt that only someone willing to break the rules could live within the society held up by them.

That was the start of my liberation. I began to study heresy historically, and decided to earn a second doctorate in spirituality, inspired by the writings of a formally proclaimed heretic, theologian Matthew Fox, who started a nontraditional doctoral program in collaboration with politician Jerry Brown. I was even hired to work as Fox's academic dean for a year, and it was there I learned most of how hegemony works. The heretical priest ran the school with more domination than the nuns did in my Catholic elementary school in the 1960s. In watching how his fury about his expulsion for heresy prevented any sharing of power in the school, I realized that the only way to be a heretic who had what Fox called "the voice of the prophet" in its capacity to say "*No!*" to the orthodoxy was to be a *mindful* heretic (de la Garza, 2014). A mindful heretic, one who sees that the only way to continue being a part of a group vital to one is to violate its rules. And, beyond that, to mindfully be aware that there will be a backlash. To insist on identical rewards from, and privilege in, a corrupt system is to still be driven by its assumptions.

Because I am rightfully a scholar in the academy, as a mindful heretic, my response to the microaggressive norms, rather than to defect or attack, is to mindfully (with full consciousness) violate the orthodoxy, thereby maintaining a sense of integrity and dignity while *staying*. The "mindful" aspect of mindful heresy implies conscious awareness and acceptance that there will be many repercussions for violating the orthodoxy as yet unchanged. As a mindful heretic, I am aware that simply by standing in disruption of the orthodoxy, I can be framed as attacking. Here, I seize upon the reality that simply existing in a role that defies the hierarchical structuring of a racist and ableist society has already been enough to be experienced as an attack by those threatened by my body and mind. In the academy, the unspoken orthodoxy includes racist, gendered, and prejudicial assumptions that would implicitly require that a Woman of Color be *presumed incompetent*. Similarly, such orthodoxy includes the assumption that a person with a cognitive disability requiring accommodations cannot be equally (or more) intelligent or scholarly.

NEPANTLA FACING TLAHTLACOLLI: A PRAXIS OF COURAGE

Around 2010, I began to share my ideas on mindful heresy that I'd been developing as a private work of scholarly reflection. My life experience and observations were my laboratory. I shared my ideas and even began occasional blogging on my site, Mindful Heretic: Living Narrative Unplugged (de la Garza, 2018b). I taught a doctoral seminar to discuss the fundamental aspects and key distinctions of the concept, drawing on scholars, activists, poets, and legal experts as guest speakers to help me better grasp what I was (and was not) trying to express. This was my "baby," and much like its older sister, "Four Seasons of

Ethnography" (González, 2000), I wanted to bring it to birth with the support of a "village." With this piece, I wanted to be clear that I was not making a call for simple rebellion or anarchy. And I wanted to make clear the difficulty of the path, as well as its potential for power, and its modeling of another way.

Living this way requires what I call a praxis of courage (de la Garza, 2016). Thomas Cahill, in his book *Heretics and Heroes,* tells us that heresy is a "dress rehearsal for permanent change" (2014, p. 9). By risking the attacks and ostracizing social responses to a willingness to call out the inherent racist and/or prejudicial assumptions in microaggressive statements, standing in our dignity as our embodied reality, we are drawing on the strength of nepantla (becoming what we already are but have not embodied) as we face tlahtlacolli (damaging speech/microaggressions) (de la Garza, 2018a). Gloria Anzaldúa, over the corpus of her work, has been a *comadre* in spirit in a lengthy dress rehearsal.

IT'S NOT NICE TO BE NICE ALL THE TIME

Mindfully heretical responses offer an alternative to the ready-made orthodox option of accommodation to the familiar hegemonic "politeness" of "nice White women," which is exceedingly normalized. Microaggressions that are handled through orthodoxy become the "building blocks of hegemony," transforming us into hegemonic police (Gonzalez, 1998) who buy into the system of politeness and unconscious enforcement of conversational norms when confronting difficult and ambiguous, injurious interactions that systematically escape accountability. Think about this—how much hegemony is held in place because we won't challenge or release ourselves from socio-emotional bonds, from the desire to be "liked," from the pain in loss or redefinition? It takes courage, as in *coraje*, the *rabia* of love that dwells in our hearts but starts in our whole being, extending to our ancestors and those who will come after us. Without this conscious (mindful) connection, we run the risk of snapping back to the hegemonic competitive individualism inherent in the hierarchies where we've co-created persistent patterns of politeness serving only the status quo.

"I'M NOT GOING ANYWHERE" IS HERETICAL

When the orthodoxy is to be presumed incompetent, where we're expected to accept microaggressions doubting our reality, and to be proclaimed rude for daring to express difficult truths, I have chosen to be a heretic. Mindful heresy, as I have stated, exists in situations where we highly value membership or association with a group, but that group's orthodoxy is untenable due to its practices or norms. To be a mindful heretic, you claim heresy; you are not accused of it. Traditional accusations of heresy are made to uphold the orthodoxy; claiming the path of the mindful heretic is to align ourselves with the possible. We live in a way that might encourage others to see the reality of expressing our own agency, our authentic existence, even in a colonized and disciplined institution or culture. Orthodoxy often requires support and complicity with unethical, dishonest, prejudicial, or otherwise injurious patterns of behavior. Because of the importance the association holds, a mindful heretic is the person who, rather than defect or attack, chooses mindfully to stay and keep doing good work.

A heretic, by tradition, is an outcast who leaves, hides, and/or camouflages to avoid the negative repercussions of her heresy. What makes the mindful heretic stand apart is the refusal to depart, the continued public affiliation while demonstrating a failure to comply with the orthodoxy, and the refusal to internalize or accept orthodox framings of one's status in (here) the academy. This includes raising one's consciousness to the subtle hegemonic nature of predictable tropes of leadership and the social mores of administration that may unwittingly draw one into the service of the flawed premises of the institution.

I took on the challenge of transcending my experience to guarantee that I would not be prevented from leaving an intellectual legacy. I was able to construct a praxis of courage by finding dignity and not stigma in embodying the heretical and claiming my authority as a scholar from that habitus. On this path, I have had to exert enormous effort, calling on the memories of my grandparents, the elders and exemplars who inspire me, to give me the strength to stand through the autos de fé and social *hogueras* that I could not allow myself to legitimate, no matter how normative. Sometimes it was my fellow Women of Color who insisted I was angry and aggressive, who dismissed my brain injury, insisting that I discipline my affect when daring to question. Mindful heresy does not make me their opponent or public inquisitor, but neither does it make me their ally in supporting the hegemony of "niceness" as politic. I continue to stand, to participate, in violation of the norms that would have me disappear, including the embrace of real allies who stand by me, and don't simply fulfill essentialist and politically correct norms.

THE PROTECTIVE SHAWL OF THE MINDFUL HERETIC

The conscious identification with mindful heresy creates a resistant framework, like a protective shawl, for continued dignified expression of my intelligence and contributions. It helps me frame the backlash for daring to be heretical by the very fact that I continue to show up as an intelligent, competent, and successful Woman of Color in the academy, that I remain whole and engaged.

In my work, this praxis is not just a way to resist, it is a way for future scholars, through creative pedagogy and mentoring, to find a better way. Creating spaces where voices can disrupt oppressive orthodoxy provides subjective experience for them, modeling the promise of possibilities. Despite the evidence of persisting injustice and unfair treatment in my own career, I have turned my senior years as a scholar into "golden years." It is the very attributes of competence, skill, an educated mind, and ability to express myself powerfully that already make me, and every other such Woman of Color scholar, inherently heretical to the orthodoxy of inequality. By seizing the power, rather than the stigma, of heresy, I demonstrate the power of Coyolxauqui, and close with an invocation of she who persists, though broken into many pieces.

Coyolxauqui, patron of the dismembered
let me remember that what I have known as me
is never as powerful as that which *is* me
let me remember that when I am torn into pieces
there is more of me to open to the world
let me remember that what I know I am here to do
will give me the strength to do it
even when the world I will create may not look
like the one I thought I wanted.
Let me dare to be beautiful, powerful, playful.
Give me the courage to break and be whole.

REFERENCES

Cahill, T. (2014). *Heretics and heroes: How renaissance artists and reformation priests created our world.* New York: Anchor.

de la Garza, S. A. (2014). Mindful heresy, holo-expression, and poesis: An autoethnographic response to the orthodoxies of interpersonal & cultural life. In R. Boylorn and M. Orbe (Eds.), *Critical autoethnography: Intersecting cultural identities in everyday life* (pp. 209–221). Walnut Creek, CA: Left Coast.

de la Garza, S. A. (2016, April 20). *A praxis of courage.* Opening lecture. Communication week, California State University, Northridge.

de la Garza, S. A. (2018a). Facing Tlahtlacolli with Nepantla and Conocimiento: A Xicana epistemological approach to understanding microaggressions. In L. H. Hernández & R. Gutiérrez Pérez, (Eds.) *This bridge we call communication: Anzaldúan approaches to theory, method, and praxis.* Lanham, MD: Lexington Books.

de la Garza, S. A. (2018b). *Mindful heretic: Living narrative unplugged.* The official website of Sarah Amira de la Garza, https://www.mindfulheretic.com.

Gonzalez, M. C. (1998). Abandoning the sacred hierarchy: Disempowering hegemony through surrender to spirit. In M. L. Hecht (Ed.), *Communicating prejudice* (pp. 223–234). Thousand Oaks, CA: Sage.

Gonzalez, M. C. (2000). Four seasons of ethnography: A creation-centered ontology for ethnography. *Journal of International and Intercultural Relations, 24*, 623–650.

Grice, H. P. (1975). Logic and conversation. In P. Cole and J. L. Morgan (Eds.), *Syntax and semantics, Vol. 3, Speech acts* (pp. 41–58). New York: Academic.

Sue, D. W. (2010). *Microaggressions in everyday life.* Hoboken, NJ: John Wiley & Sons.

Sue, D. W., Capodilupo, C. M, Torino, G. C., Bucceri, J. M., Holder, A.M.B., Nadal, K. L., & Esquilin, M. (2007). Racial microagressions in everyday life: Implications for clinical practice. *American Psychologist, 6*(4), 271–286. doi: 10.1037/0003-066X.62.4.271.

Weick, K. (1995). *Sensemaking in organizations.* Thousand Oaks, CA: Sage.

Zahn, C. (1984). A reexamination of conversational repair. *Communication Monographs, 51*(1), 56–66.

NINETEEN

Exposure to Discrimination, Cultural Betrayal, and Intoxication as a Black Female Graduate Student Applying for Tenure-Track Faculty Positions

Jennifer M. Gómez

> If you are silent about your pain, they will kill you and say you enjoyed it.
> (HURSTON, 2017, N.P.)

When I was on the job market for tenure-track positions at Research I universities, I was filled with nerves, trepidation, and excitement. Though still a graduate student in clinical psychology, I was keenly aware that I had been in school for ten years, preparing for the opportunity to become faculty. I had successfully made the jump from being surrounded by other Black people in my former career as a ballet dancer with Dance Theatre of Harlem to the predominantly White world of academia. At the time of the applications, I already had been developing my theory on cultural betrayal trauma (Gómez, 2012, 2016a, 2017a, 2017b, 2019; Gómez & Freyd, 2017) for five years and had defended my dissertation the previous spring (Gómez, 2016b). My student status was all but a technicality as I was completing the required, yearlong clinical internship. I felt ready to begin my life as a faculty member. Bright-eyed, bushy-tailed, and naive, I was completely unprepared for what was to come.

In this chapter, I expand on reflections offered in my op-ed in the Conditionally Accepted Blog in *Inside Higher Ed*, "A Time for Arrogance: A Minority Scholar Describes the Challenges She Experienced on the Academic Job Market" (Gómez, 2018c). I flesh out my experiences of discrimination, cultural betrayal, and exposure to faculty's alcohol intoxication as a Black female clinical psychology graduate student on the job market for tenure-track faculty positions at Research I universities (2016–2017). I also provide advice for Women of Color who are currently on the job market, as well as identify avenues for systemic change. Though these stories may seem scary to some, all too familiar to others, and painfully aversive to many, the solution I am proposing is not "Save Yourself! Don't Apply! Get out While You Still Can!" On the contrary, I discuss what I

DOI: 10.7330/9781607329664.c019

went through because I believe in the importance of publicly sharing our pain in academia (Jones, 2018) as a way to foster community, solidarity, and healing (Gómez, 2014).

Eventually, my job market terror had a happy ending: I landed a dream job (postdoctoral fellow in the Wayne State University Postdoctoral to Faculty Transition Program, which focuses on my own research program with room for tenured advancement) in a city I love (Detroit), within an imperfect-but-not-toxic working environment. Though I know that not everyone is lucky enough to have this *ending-beginning*, I feel hopeful that amid the oppression in academia, there is enough freedom to experience happiness and joy, do the work we value, mentor the next generation of scholars, and make positive change in our respective fields and the academy at large. Our goal: to live our professional lives in a way that costs us neither our health nor our souls. I must believe this is possible. Bearing our pain may be the first step.

RACISM, WHITE SUPREMACY, AND "SCIENCE"

I was unprepared for the instances of White supremacy that were heaped upon me during campus visits. As is typical in the field of psychology, these visits were each two days, and consisted of individual meetings with faculty, lunch with graduate students, giving one (sometimes two) job talks, and breakfast and dinner with multiple faculty. The bigotry I experienced came in several domains, including disrespect to me as a scholar and disregard for Black and other minority communities.

Scholarly Disrespect

My job talk centered on cultural betrayal trauma theory, which I developed to study the impact of violence victimization in minority populations through directly implicating societal trauma in outcomes (e.g., Gómez, 2017b). Following my job talk at one institution, a White male faculty member told me that I had explained my theory incorrectly. He condescendingly described how cultural betrayal trauma theory was unrelated to inequality and instead was about something else entirely. During his White mansplaining, I froze in disbelief. The problems with this communication were not lost on me: the absurdity of one scholar telling another that her understanding of her own theory is incorrect is intermixed with the additional layers of a White man telling a Black woman that the way she understands anti-Black racism is wrong.

At another department, I met with a senior White woman faculty. She told me how she was "worried that you won't be able to expand 'your ideas' into sound science." The "ideas" she referenced, using air quotes, were the same theory and supporting research that had granted me the interview in the first place. She further impressed upon me the scientific nature of this department in a way that implied that my work on inequality and trauma in minority populations was not scientific enough.

In another meeting, a junior White woman faculty told me what my next research steps should be. With each idea she thought she had created, I initially responded with variations of "Yes. That is what I mentioned in my job talk," which she had attended. After the third or fourth time of being subjected to her Christopher Columbus complex of discovering things that are not new, I shut down. I started taking notes. "Wow. That's such a great idea!" I told her. I watched myself having an out-of-body experience of playing dumb. My behavior in this meeting is probably what I am most ashamed of throughout my journey on the job market. Simultaneously, it is the reaction that I most viscerally understand. While I have not forgiven myself for placating her, I know I was striving for emotional survival in a situation in which I was drowning under the weight of White supremacy.

Minority Disregard

I additionally was exposed to the unbridled thoughts that some White faculty have toward the minority communities I represent and those I feel allegiance to as a cultural outsider but minority insider. For instance, I repeatedly encountered faculty characterizing minorities in the community as the valueless backs you can stand on in order to get tenure. One junior White woman faculty explained to me that in order to show that my work is scientific, I need to do comparative research in which I compare diverse minority groups with Whites. A senior White woman faculty told me that I could create a measure for cultural betrayal trauma theory (Gómez, 2017a) that I then—with no knowledge, investment, or cultural sensitivity—could shop to various Communities of Color to achieve multiple publications. My attempts to explain the problems with these and other scenarios (e.g., exploitation of Communities of Color) were futile. Using minority communities as currency for self-promotion was normative among several faculty.

Moreover, hearing what some White academics think about Black people in particular shook me to the core. One example occurred during my very first job talk. As I was describing how there is harmful cultural betrayal when a Black woman is raped by a Black man (Gómez, 2019), a senior White male faculty member interrupted me to ask: "I know I'm going to sound racist saying this, but isn't it possible that being raped by a Black man is just worse—for any woman, White or Black?" The in vivo retrieval of the superhuman, hypersexual, violent Black man stereotype (Ray, 2017) that pervasively impacts Black males' lives through policing (Gilbert & Ray, 2016), the criminal justice system (van Cleve, 2016), policy (Dumas, 2016), K-12 education (Brown & Donnor, 2013; Ferguson, 2010), and media (hooks, 1992; Jackson, 2006) was jolting in this academic context. Forgiveness has come to me in no small part due to this same White man being moved to tears by the end of my job talk. However, healing has not accompanied this forgiveness. Whenever the memory emerges, which it does during every talk I have given since, my heart aches. Perhaps it always will.

CULTURAL BETRAYAL

Though I was hurt by the discrimination I experienced from White faculty, I was gobsmacked by mistreatment from fellow Scholars of Color. Right or wrong, I had expected that Faculty of Color across genders would be safe havens for me during the interview process. While I have continued to foster relationships with some Faculty of Color post–job market, I also was harmed by others. My experience mirrors what Bonilla-Silva (2017) describes as "false positives": Faculty of Color who behave in ways that undermine other People of Color (e.g., Faculty and Students of Color). These experiences also hit close to home as forms of cultural betrayal (Gómez, 2018b). According to cultural betrayal trauma theory (Gómez, 2019), because of systemic discrimination, like that found in historically White universities, some Scholars of Color develop (intra)cultural trust—"connection (e.g., dependency, attachment, loyalty, love, and/or responsibility) with other members of one's minority group(s), potentially as a buffer against societal trauma" (Gómez, 2018b). From fellow minorities, violations of (intra) cultural trust such as in-group rejection (Cano, 2018) and cultural invalidations (Durkee & Gómez, in preparation) are cultural betrayals (Gómez, 2018b).

One experience was simple enough—an isolated comment—that, as one of the thousand cuts of such comments, pricked me deeply because of the cultural betrayal within it. In one meeting, the department head, a Woman of Color, was explaining tenure criteria to me. After stating that being invited as a peer reviewer was one criterion, she looked up at me and said, "Don't worry, you'll get there." That simple statement relies on the premise that I do not have any experience as a peer reviewer and am daunted by the prospect. It rings of the microaggression assumption of inferiority (Sue, 2010). Her statement is at odds with my prior experience, which includes coediting a special issue of *Journal of Trauma & Dissociation* (Ford & Gómez, 2015) and serving as an ad hoc peer reviewer for multiple journals. The presumption of incompetence jolted me in such a way that I did not correct her. I just willed the meeting to be over so I could escape the disease of condescension that was beginning to infuse my spirit.

A final example of cultural betrayal came from a senior Faculty of Color. During our meeting, he communicated with me that I might not be a true academic because I strive for my work to have impact beyond the ivory tower (e.g., through publications for the general public; Gómez, 2016a). In addition to questioning my academic credibility, he also implied that I should stay in my lane, as it were. Specifically, he told me that the work I was doing, in addition to the way I presented my work in my job talk, was that of an associate professor. This was not a compliment. Instead, this statement was advising me to do work at a lower level. The kind of work I was doing now—pushing the boundaries of trauma psychology with cultural betrayal trauma theory; publishing for the general public; preparing to write a book—should wait until I am tenured. While I cannot know for sure, I do not believe that he would have advised a man to dull his shine because he was outperforming his rank.

Whereas the former cultural betrayal experience I detailed presumed incompetence, the latter interaction punished my acumen as a Woman of Color and advised behavioral ineptitude. Both serve as reminders of the double bind that academia can put on Women of Color: *You're not good enough* and *You're too good*. The fact that this came from fellow Scholars of Color in the academia is both additionally painful for me due to cultural betrayal, and worrisome for them: likely, they themselves have been victims of similar situations throughout their academic journeys and have survived through assimilation.

INTOXICATION

The final challenge on the job market came out of left field: faculty intoxication at campus dinners. Prior to the job market, I was advised to order an alcoholic drink during dinners in order to make faculty comfortable in ordering alcohol for themselves. I was further told to nurse the drink throughout the night if I did not want to have alcohol. Though I do drink socially, I felt very uncomfortable with this advice, given that: (1) many people do not drink for personal or religious reasons, past alcohol misuse/abuse, or pregnancy (Cohen, 2017); and (2) no one should be pressured to drink alcohol. The problems regarding faculty use of alcohol happened irrespective of my decision to drink. Each problematic dinner brings up issues of power and the potential for harm amid the vulnerability of being a junior Woman of Color scholar on the job market.

White Woman: Power-Pressure

This dinner was reminiscent of stereotypical high school peer pressure to drink alcohol. Out to dinner with two senior White women faculty on one campus visit, I ordered a nonalcoholic drink, which prompted one faculty to complain that my decision inhibited her ability to drink. I ordered a glass of wine to pacify her. This faculty left midway through dinner. What had transpired was clear and absurd: as a woman in my thirties, I had succumbed to power-pressure to order alcohol, whereas the instigator succumbed to sloppy intoxication that prevented her from staying for the whole dinner.

White Man: Belligerence, Drunk Driving, and Sexual Harassment Potential

Race-gender dynamics made another faculty's intoxication at a different dinner problematic in other ways. I was picked up for dinner by a senior White male faculty member. He drank several alcoholic drinks throughout our multi-hour dinner with two other White male faculty members. Throughout the night, his behavior degenerated into making off-color jokes, including one about students with disabilities. I emotionally retreated, knowing that at the end of this sixteen-hour day I was not equipped to deal with such bigotry. Even after he slurred several times, "I want to ask you something about your theory . . .", I continued to avoid engaging with him. I knew this might mean that I would be appraised unfavorably; however, I chose to protect my own well-being as best as I could, knowing that I was not in a position to communicate what I actually thought.

Toward the end of dinner, I began to fear for my safety. I judged this faculty member as too intoxicated to safely drive me to my hotel. When he went to the bathroom, I considered asking the other men for help; yet, since the others had not acknowledged his intoxication, I felt alone in fearing the dangers of getting into a car in which the driver was drunk. Moreover, as a Black woman, I was scared of the potential of sexual assault if I was left alone with this White man. Though this intoxicated White male faculty member drove me back to my hotel without incident, the implications of my own helplessness continue to haunt me. My thoughts at the time remain true now: *If he drunkenly chooses to sexually harass or assault me, I feel I have no recourse as a Black woman or as a graduate student who needs a job.*

ADVICE

Whenever examining how to address injustices that are both mundane and systemic (McClelland, Rubin, & Bauermeister, 2016), I conceptualize a two-pronged approach: (1) triage: address the needs of the individual; and (2) systemic: change the systems so that the triaging becomes obsolete. In the context of being exposed to discrimination, cultural betrayal, and faculty intoxication on the job market, this includes detailing what Women of Color scholars can do for themselves and one another.

Triage: Individual Level

I'm not crazy. My first piece of advice is simple: employ an *I'm not crazy* mantra throughout the job market journey. So much of my pain on the job market came from me thinking I was crazy. My supportive White colleagues were unfamiliar experientially and empirically with the prevalence of gendered anti-Black discrimination (Gómez, 2015) and discrimination against Women of Color in academia (Bhasin, 2018; Gutiérrez y Muhs, Niemann, González, & Harris, 2012; Matthew, 2016; Sensoy & DiAngelo, 2017). Thus, I questioned my own reality each time they told me they were sure everything was going well because I was such a qualified candidate. Trusting your own perception and seeking validation from those who are other-ized in the academy can likely mitigate some of the harms. Additionally, fostering validation within yourself through writing can help. I began my journal, *Against the Banality of Evil*, my third year in graduate school. It is now over 200 pages long and recounts some of the most vile experiences I have had in academia, as well as my own acts of resistance and advocacy. Rereading the passages not only provides me with validation but gives me strength to continue in the academy.

Identifying benefits of campus visits. Even though I experienced discrimination on most of my campus visits, it would be a mistake to conceptualize these visits—or the job market as a whole—as uniformly discriminatory. My professional network in the community of Scholars of Color has increased from these job interviews. Fostering these relationships can help with future career necessities, such as external letters of support for tenure. Attuning to the heterogeneity of experiences (e.g., respect from some faculty; discrimination from others) and multiple goals (e.g., job attainment; development of professional relationships) can ease the hardship of the job market.

Find your people. Another way to help prevent the devaluation of yourself (as a scholar and a sentient being) is to actively seek out and foster community with *your people.* Finding out who your people *are* requires first identifying who they *are not.* For instance, my people are not the faculty who tell me to poach Communities of Color to further my research career. They are not those who scold me for being "too sensitive" when I detail discriminatory experiences. Painfully but importantly, not all People of Color, including Women of Color, in academia are my people. Instead, my people are those who share my worldview of inequality, while further stretching my thinking about how it affects my communities. My people are the professors at the historically Black college or university (HBCU) who shared reflections of us, as Black people, in accepting cultural betrayal trauma theory (Gómez, 2018a). My people are Ford Fellows (National Academy of Sciences, 2018), who support and challenge me. I have found that reorienting my conception of who I see as my people has pushed my intellectual work forward. More important for my soul, finding my people has given me a safe haven—not by providing comfort without challenge, but through imbuing hope, strength, knowledge, and solidarity within the intellectual heights where I live.

Fostering self-worth. Finding your people can aid in fostering professional and personal self-worth. When we work in predominantly White fields, we can start to adopt oppressive mindsets, even when we consciously strive for equality. For instance, in my field of psychology, peer-reviewed publications in high-impact journals "count" for hiring, tenure, and promotion. However, the impact factor is not a good measure of an individual scholar's merit (Freyd, 2009), and mainstream researchers and journals may underappreciate (e.g., undercite or underpublish) work done by and for minorities. Moreover, other kinds of publications, including those that translate research for the general public, are ethically important but not systematically "counted" in hiring, tenure, and promotion decisions. Nevertheless, I consciously adhere to my own frame: the publications I "count" are peer-reviewed articles, book chapters, other scholarly publications, and pieces for the general public. In this and other ways (e.g., mentoring, teaching, promoting equality in the department), I foster my own self-worth within an academic environment that will likely systematically devalue much of what I hold dear.

Allyship. Beyond focusing on what Women of Color on the job market can do to deal with their oppression, I want to highlight the role of Women of Color and other allies in addressing discrimination on the job market. Examples of allyship are (1) countering *scholarly disrespect*: to combat bias that Women of Color are likely to be unqualified for the position (Bhasin, 2018), allies can review an applicant's CV prior to meeting with her and/or simply assume she is qualified; (2) resisting *minority disregard*: if allies ever think "asking this question may make me sound like a bigot," refrain from speaking; instead, become informed through reading empirical and experiential information, attending workshops or trainings, and eliciting feedback of your work (e.g., research, teaching); (3) opposing *cultural betrayal*: take steps to understand the toll that working in predominantly White, oppressive academic spaces has had on you, including how some of the bigotry has become internalized, as evidenced by the advice you give to junior Women of Color scholars, the research methodologies you employ, and the citation patterns you utilize; and (4) avoiding *intoxication*: refrain from drinking alcohol at dinner in order to provide applicants a freer choice regarding their own alcohol intake on job interviews.

Allyship can be as simple and as profound as this example: an academic administrator at my university emailed me after my op-ed piece about discrimination on the job market was published (Gómez, 2018c). In addition to commending my bravery for speaking out honestly as a junior scholar, he detailed the importance of proactively working for inclusivity. As a White man, he expressed bearing witness to the discriminatory behavior Students of Color detailed through PhinisheD.org, an online platform for scholars finishing their theses and dissertations. I was moved by the humility of his statement: "If you ever think we're coming up short . . . I hope you will feel free to speak with me or [the director] about it." His response is an important reminder to me that change does happen one person at a time.

Systemic Change

Creating systemic change is likely the best way to ensure that applicants in the decades to come do not have similar negative experiences on the job market. A strategic plan can proactively correct problems with discrimination in the department, including but not limited to campus visits. A model is the United Nations Office on Drugs and Crime's (UNODC) "Strategy for Gender Equality and the Empowerment of Women (2018–2021)" (2018). This strategy includes two broad goals: (1) "strengthen delivery of global results on gender equality and the empowerment of women through our activities: . . . systematic efforts to understand and respond to gender inequalities"; and (2) "strengthen institutional capacity and effectiveness to enhance delivery of results on gender equality and the empowerment of women: . . . to build and sustain a modern organization and workforce capable of attracting, retaining, and motivating top talent." Each of these goals has strategic performance areas (the first is "report on gender-related results"; the second is "build and communicate knowledge of mandates and expertise with regard to gender equality and the empowerment of women," with target years for meeting and exceeding requirements). Departments could create such plans for broader equality—proactive inclusivity practices regarding race, gender, class, sexual orientation, gender identity, religion, dis/ability, and their intersections—to increase the likelihood that efforts result in verifiable change that mitigates, reverses, and ultimately eliminates oppression across departmental and university-wide facets (e.g., job searches, campus visits, coursework, faculty meetings). Beyond individual diversity, such models can institutionally invest in Faculty of Color (Mercado-López, 2018) through doing real diversity work (Ahmed, 2012).

CONCLUDING THOUGHTS

Discussing discrimination and harm of this magnitude on the job market can be demoralizing. I believe we need to take the time and the space, perhaps particularly for junior Women of Color scholars, to mourn the lack of the academia we have been working toward. An academia that does not now, and never has, existed. Nevertheless, even with the experiences I have described in this chapter, along with all the others I did not share, I remain eternally hopeful. Part of my hope comes from necessity: I find solace in envisioning myself as a rose emerging from White supremacy concrete (García, 2018). I am also heartened by the positive work I witness around me. While I understand the necessity for change, I am cognizant that we already have so many resources, connection, community, and solidarity—within and outside of academia—close to us, provided we know about them and consider ourselves worthy enough to connect and contribute to them.

REFERENCES

Ahmed, S. (2012). *On being included: Racism and diversity in institutional life.* Durham: Duke University Press.

Bhasin, R. (2018, May 8). 4 ways I am underestimated as a woman of color [Ritu blog]. Retrieved from https://ritubhasin.com/blog/4-ways-im-underestimated-as-a-woman-of-color.

Bonilla-Silva, E. (2017). What we were, what we are, and what we should be: The racial problem of American sociology. *Social problems, 64*(2), 179–187.

Brown, A. L., & Donnor, J. K. (Eds.). (2013). *The education of black males in a "post-racial" world.* New York: Routledge.

Cano, A. (2018, March 23). The power of academic role models "like me." National Center for Institutional Diversity. Retrieved from https://medium.com/national-center-for-institutional-diversity/the-power-of-academic-role-models-like-me-7f4f2c59279d.

Cohen, J. J. (2017, June 4). Drinking and conference. *Chronicle of Higher Education.* Retrieved from https://www.chronicle.com/article/DrinkingConferencing/240258.

Dumas, M. J. (2016). My brother as "problem": Neoliberal governmentality and interventions for black young men and boys. *Educational Policy, 30*(1), 94–113.

Durkee, M., & Gómez, J. M. (in preparation). Does it matter who the perpetrator is? Examining the "acting white" accusation from in-group and out-group members in black and Latina/o/x college students.

Ferguson, A. A. (2010). *Bad boys: Public schools in the making of black masculinity.* Ann Arbor: University of Michigan Press.

Ford, J. D., & Gómez, J. M. (2015). Self injury & suicidality: The impact of trauma and dissociation [Editorial]. *Journal of Trauma & Dissociation,* 6, 225–231. doi: 10.1080/15299732.2015.989648.

Freyd, J. J. (2009). Journal ethics and impact. *Journal of Trauma & Dissociation, 10*, 377–384.
García, N. M. (2018, May 22). Growing roses in white concrete. *Diverse Issues in Higher Education*. Retrieved from http://diverseeducation.com/article/116880/#.WwVoUiQ60ch.facebook.
Gilbert, K., & Ray, R. (2016). Why police kill black males with impunity: Applying critical race and public health theory to address determinants of policing behaviors and the justifiable homicides of black men. *Journal of Urban Health, 93*(1), 122–140.
Gómez, J. M. (2012). Cultural betrayal trauma theory: The impact of culture on the effects of trauma. In *Blind to Betrayal*. Retrieved from https://sites.google.com/site/betrayalbook/betrayal-research-news/cultural-betrayal.
Gómez, J. M. (2014). Ebony in the ivory tower: Dismantling the stronghold of racial inequality from the inside out. In K. J. Fasching-Varner, R. Reynolds, K. Albert, & L. Martin, (Eds.), *Trayvon Martin, race, and American justice: Writing wrong* (pp. 113–117). Rotterdam, Netherlands: Sense.
Gómez, J. M. (2015). Microaggressions and the enduring mental health disparity: Black Americans at risk for institutional betrayal. *Journal of Black Psychology, 41*, 121–143. doi: 10.1177/0095798413514608.
Gómez, J. M. (2016a, June 23). Black, raped, shamed, and supported: Our responses to rape can build or destroy our community. *The Black Commentator*, 659. Retrieved from http://www.blackcommentator.com/659/659_campus_rape_gomez_guest.html.
Gómez, J. M. (2016b, May 11). *Cultural betrayal trauma theory* [Dissertation]. Retrieved from http://dynamic.uoregon.edu/jjf/theses/gomez16.pdf.
Gómez, J. M. (2017a). Does ethno-cultural betrayal in trauma affect Asian American/Pacific Islander college students' mental health outcomes? An exploratory study. Advanced online publication. *Journal of American College Health, 65*, 432–436. doi: 10.1080/07448481.2017.1341896.
Gómez, J. M. (2017b). Does gender matter? An exploratory study of cultural betrayal trauma and hallucinations in Latino undergraduates at a predominantly white university. Advanced online publication. *Journal of Interpersonal Violence*. doi: 10.1177/0886260517746942.
Gómez, J. M. (2018a, April). Cultural betrayal trauma theory: New horizons in trauma research. Invited talk. Seventh Black Psychology Research Conference, Virginia State University, Petersburg.
Gómez, J. M. (2018b). Dr. Jennifer M. Gómez. Retrieved from http://jmgomez.org.
Gómez, J. M. (2018c, February 16). A time for arrogance: A minority scholar describes the challenges she experienced on the academic job market [Op-Ed]. *Inside Higher Ed*, Conditionally Accepted Blog. Retrieved from https://www.insidehighered.com/advice /2018/02/16/minority-scholar-describes-challenges-she-experienced-academic-job-market-opinion.
Gómez, J. M. (2019). Group dynamics as a predictor of dissociation for black victims of violence: An exploratory study of cultural betrayal trauma theory. *Transcultural Psychiatry*. *56* (5), 878–894.
Gómez, J. M., & Freyd, J. J. (2017). Psychological outcomes of within-group sexual violence: Evidence of cultural betrayal. Advanced online publication. *Journal of Immigrant & Minority Health*. doi: 10.1007/s10903-017-0687-0.

Gutiérrez y Muhs, G., Niemann, Y. F., González, C. G., & Harris, A. P. (Eds.). (2012). *Presumed incompetent: The intersections of race and class for women in academia*. Logan: Utah State University Press.

hooks, b. (1992). *Black Looks: Race and Representation*. Boston: South End Press.

Hurston, Z. N. (2017, July 8). Zora Neale Hurston quotes and life lessons. *Literary Ladies Guide: Inspiration for Readers and Writers from Classic Women Authors*. Retrieved from https://www.literaryladiesguide.com/author-quotes/zora-neale-hurston-life-quotes/.

Jackson, R. L. (2006). *Scripting the black masculine body: Identity, discourse, and racial politics in popular media*. Albany: State University of New York Press.

Jones, C. (2018, April 4). The whisper campaign of academic trauma. *Student Voices*. Retrieved from https://mystudentvoices.com/the-whisper-campaign-of-academic-trauma-fc917686fcc3.

Matthew, P. A. (Ed.). (2016). *Written/unwritten: Diversity and the hidden truths of tenure*. Chapel Hill: University of North Carolina Press.

McClelland, S. I., Rubin, J. D., & Bauermeister, J. A. (2016). Adapting to injustice: Young bisexual women's interpretations of microaggressions. *Psychology of Women Quarterly*, 40(4), 532–550.

Mercado-López, L. (2018, May 18). Want to retain faculty of color? Support them as faculty of color. National Center for Institutional Diversity. Retrieved from https://medium.com/national-center-for-institutional-diversity/want-to-retain-faculty-of-color-support-them-as-faculty-of-color-9e7154ed618f.

National Academy of Sciences (2018). Ford Foundation Fellowship Programs. Retrieved from http://sites.nationalacademies.org/pga/fordfellowships/.

Ray, R. (2017). "If only he hadn't worn the hoodie . . .": Race, selective perception, and stereotype maintenance. In S. McClure & C. Harris (Eds.), *Getting real about race: Hoodies, mascots, model minorities, and other conversations* (pp. 72–84). Los Angeles, CA: Sage.

Sensoy, Ö., & DiAngelo, R. (2017). "We are all for diversity, but . . .": How faculty hiring committees reproduce whiteness and practical suggestions for how they can change. *Harvard Educational Review*, 87(4), 557–580.

Sue, D. W. (2010). *Microaggressions and marginality: Manifestation, dynamics, and impact*. Hoboken, NJ: John Wiley & Sons.

United Nations Office on Drugs and Crime (2018). Empowering women and girls when tackling drugs and crime: UNODC, United Nations in Vienna launch new gender equality strategy. Retrieved from https://www.unodc.org/unodc/en/frontpage/2018/March/empowering-women-and-girls-when-tackling-drugs-and-crime_-unodc-united-nations-in-vienna-launch-new-gender-equality-strategy.html.

Van Cleve, N. G. (2016). *Crook County: Racism and injustice in America's largest criminal court*. Stanford: Stanford University Press.

TWENTY

Through a White Woman's Tears

Fragility, Guilt, and the Journey toward Allyship

Rachelle A. C. Joplin

My journey as a White woman toward allyship with Women of Color has been deeply personal, painful, and liberating. I have not yet arrived. But my hope is that by sharing the processes I have encountered along the way, I can provide a roadmap for other White women who desire to wrestle with their privilege and intersectional identities in the interest of becoming an ally to People of Color. This journey is a profoundly uncomfortable space to occupy. However, learning and growing toward a liberated and liberating existence is, necessarily, uncomfortable. I have split my journey into several distinct, yet interactive, processes. These stages cover ignorance, reckoning, fragility, tears, guilt, savior complex, and finally, allyship, all situated within my experience as a White, heterosexual, cisgender woman.

My intent is to be honest, accurate, and up-front. I provide concrete examples of situations and beliefs in my life that defined these stages, and how these examples made—and still make—me feel. I have deep sympathy for the inevitable reader of this chapter who will find the processes discussed too harsh, too real. I have been there. I am still there, at times. Ultimately, I argue that the discomfort of encountering these sticky processes is necessary and healthy, as long as we don't stay stuck.

THE BEGINNING AND THE RECKONING

As a burgeoning scholar, my feminism was flat. I assumed that all women were in a fight against the patriarchy. In addition, we all experienced oppression and desired liberation in ways that were similar enough to allow for one united strategy. I deeply resonated with what Stephanie Shields termed an "unthinkingness" in the first volume of *Presumed Incompetent* (2012): I was never faced with the stark differences between my experiences and the experiences of Women of

DOI: 10.7330/9781607329664.c020

Color—or any other identity, for that matter. This unthinkingness bred a blinded ignorance to the struggles of Women of Color. I felt that, surely, all women agreed on the definitions of gender equity. All women could agree that the climate of acceptance for women in power had shifted significantly toward the positive. Most important, we White women feminists were firmly part of the solution, and only the solution.

Little did I know that, in fact, White women were still very much part of the problem. During my first semester of graduate school, I took a Queer of Color critique course taught by a queer Woman of Color. One of the earliest works we read was *This Bridge Called My Back: Writings by Radical Women of Color* (Moraga & Anzaldúa, 2015). These brutally, refreshingly honest narratives were my first exposure to the vastly differing stories of Women of Color. To me, this book represented the breaking of my blindness to the experiences of Women of Color, and the convictions I was responsible for bearing as a White woman. I vividly remember reading Gloria Anzaldúa, Cherríe Moraga, and Audre Lorde. I recall reading their messages about exhaustion with White women "not getting it" and how White women were another "master's tool" that had harmed their movement toward liberation, and desperately thinking, "Wait . . . why are you attacking me? I thought we were all on the same page!"

As we discussed these readings in class, I frequently contributed to the conversation, voicing my frustrations: how was I, as a White woman, supposed to be part of the movement toward equity and liberation if I was constantly being blamed? Rather than allowing me to sit comfortably in my arrogance, my professor encouraged me to dig deeper, to allow these narratives to move me toward a new understanding of feminism and justice. Partially to placate her, and partially to assuage my rapidly building guilt, I planned and produced a seminar paper that aimed to define allyship through the works of *This Bridge Called My Back*, *Presumed Incompetent*, and Sara Ahmed's *On Being Included* (2012). When my professor and I had our one-on-one meeting about my paper, she admonished me for not writing the paper she knew I should have written—incidentally, something much like this chapter, about what allyship had to do with Women of Color feminism in the academy. We completed our meeting with her telling me that if this was the work I wanted to engage in, I would be permanently occupying a space of discomfort, shifting allegiance, and unlearning privilege.

WHITE FRAGILITY AND WHITE WOMAN TEARS

Now that I have established the sequence of events, I want to unpack the underpinnings of my reactions, behaviors, and emotions. As I explained, when I read the narratives contained in *This Bridge Called My Back*, I reacted with frustration, anger, and defensiveness to the idea that part of the oppressive hierarchy was "my fault." This defensiveness became external in class discussions and in my writings for the course, as I attempted to impose my blindness back onto myself and onto my professor and classmates. I did not want to be held responsible for something I felt I had no part of: the oppression of Women of Color, the silencing of their voices, the patriarchal norm that I thought I had been fighting against. I needed the narrative to indicate that there were, in fact, still good White women.

People of Color have been naming this phenomenon for years, but it is time for us, for me, to name, claim, and discuss it. These emotions I felt, and defensiveness I enacted, were key expressions of my White fragility. This fragility is marked by defensiveness and emotional manipulation when a privileged individual—in this case, a White person—is confronted about her ignorance about and complicity in oppression. My insistent questioning of my professor in class about what actions I had taken that made me responsible for the oppression I was reading about is a classic example. I would argue further that the behavior is gendered; although White fragility can and does occur across gender boundaries for White people, my particular enactment of it has been colloquially named "White woman tears." The sensation of White woman tears is marked with the age-old concept that White women's protection is paramount for the survival of society. Thus, as a White woman, if I feel my status as the protected identity is threatened, I can name that threat and ensure that my protection erases the narrative causing the threat. For example, if a Woman of Color were to note that a diversity committee within a department was made up entirely of White individuals, and a White woman on the committee were to respond, "But I'm a woman, so we do care about diversity, and if you care so much, why don't you just replace me?" that would be an enactment of White woman tears to silence a Woman of Color.

Two key themes of each space I describe in this chapter are the labor required of Women of Color while the White woman occupies it, and the relationship the space has with sympathy and growth. The phenomenon of White woman tears requires the most labor for Women of Color, by far. In this space, we are identified by our complete inability to hear and listen to narratives that challenge our status quo. If we identify as feminists, it's even more sinister: we believe that we must be revolutionary enough already, so any indication otherwise is treated with derision and as an attempt to "divide the soldiers." Between steep publishing requirements that prioritize White methodology, mentoring labor that is significantly higher than that of other academics, and the continual legal and epistemological violence enacted on their existence by the institution, Women of Color must fight to simply exist in the academy. Women of Color must somehow manage to communicate their narratives as organically as possible while also attending to the fragile emotions and defense mechanisms of White women, all while already existing in a system that wants nothing more than their silence.

My intent is not to villainize White women, but rather to hold us accountable and to name and explain these processes in an attempt to move through them. There is significant value in acknowledging and working through the depths of White women's complicity in the oppression narrative, and in order to do that, we must put aside our assumed innocence for the benefit of Women of Color. White woman tears is a particularly sticky space where, if left unchecked, I would have been happy to fiercely defend my comfort for the foreseeable future, relying on my unacknowledged privilege, my perceived feminism, and my deep fear of being held responsible for unspeakable violence and oppression. This space is a part of the process of allyship, but is too deeply associated with purposeful stagnation to exist in for a lengthy period of time. To move on, I had to put aside my White fragility and be willing to feel conviction.

WHITE WOMAN GUILT

After completing my Queer of Color critique course, I maintained a relationship with my professor, ultimately asking her to be on my MA exam committee, write a recommendation letter for my PhD applications, and review my application materials. She acquiesced, and encouraged me to add several readings from her course to my exam list. However, she also encouraged me to revamp the paper I had written for her course, to use it as the writing sample for my PhD applications. I balked at the idea: surely I could not occupy that space again. I was clearly not qualified to speak on issues of allyship and oppression, I was a White woman! I, once again, allowed fear to prevent me from processing through this space.

It was clear that my interest in what allyship meant to White women was becoming my desired trajectory. My stumbling block was the process I refer to as White woman guilt. Moving past White woman tears required active conviction on my part that I was, in fact, implicated in the oppressive narrative Women of Color had been espousing. This conviction incited guilt within me, marked by seeing structural inequality all around me. The academy assumes that Whiteness belongs within it, so while my space as a woman is sometimes questioned, my race is invisible. My worth to the academy is preconceived, and it is a bonus when I do the required elements of my job, such as mentor students or publish. Women of Color have their space in the academy questioned on multiple levels, and are constantly being required to prove themselves by mentoring more, publishing more, being more. However, Women of Color are also told to be sure they are not "too much," at the risk of threatening White men and White women.

My White woman guilt forced me to see these assumptions of my worth as what they really were: attempts to oppress marginalized voices, disguised as objective professionalization expectations. I was also confronted with the truth of the patriarchal bargain, a system of compromises through which women oppress alongside White men to alleviate pressure on themselves. As a White woman who claimed feminism as a priority, I assumed that I was exempt from this temptation; I was fighting the patriarchy alongside *all* women! However, the truth was I was more than willing to silence and "tone down" the voices of Women of Color to make feminism a more palatable concept for others. I was accepting the bargain all along.

The realization of these inequities was brought about by my White woman guilt. This space is notable for its shift of some labor onto White women: the mental and emotional effort of recognizing the gross amount of inequality surrounding us, and how we are inherently complicit in it, is our burden to bear.

The strange intersection of oppressed and oppressor is a complex space, one in which all White women exist. This space of conviction and guilt is one that garners the most sympathy from me, as we never truly leave it completely. Guilt and complicity will only end once the systems causing them end. The pain of guilt is a real pain that we feel, one that can encourage massive growth and organic partnership with Women of Color. But we must not stay here. For me, that meant processing what I heard from Women of Color, rather than only allowing the affect of conviction to wash over me. In short, I was motivated to seek forms of forgiveness and penance.

WHITE SAVIOR COMPLEX

As I began my PhD program, I was determined to align my behaviors with my newfound understanding of oppression. My desires for forgiveness and penance led to a manifestation of what I describe as "White savior complex," a firm belief that I should seek to save Women of Color from the oppressive regime around them. For example, I would tell my professors, especially my Women of Color professors, that I had a tendency to talk a lot in class, and that if I had talked "too much" to ignore my raised hand. In addition, if I felt I had talked too much during a discussion, I would ask my non-White colleagues what they thought about the discussion. I placed the burden of creating space for other voices on the professor, and I called out students who may have preferred to be silent due to precarity or hidden fears.

My White savior complex was a fervent attempt to shed the moniker of oppressor. However, my actions still continued the narrative of Women of Color as weak and needing help, especially from White women. I had recognized that the color-blind racism and narrow-mindedness of White woman feminism was not what I wanted to align myself with, but my manifestation of allyship was still centered around my experience and what I saw as a priority for Women of Color. I believed that I should stand up and speak for them rather than listen to them. The inherent danger in this behavior, even with the best intentions, is the continued elision of the narratives of Women of Color.

This is the space I find myself returning to again and again, to unlearn and relearn various ideas, assumptions, and experiences. As I drafted this very chapter, the first manifestation was a how-to for White women to enact allyship, which was actually an explanation of how to be a savior. If we can get beyond guilt, White savior complex can quickly become an equally sticky space to occupy if we allow it. For me, my religious understanding of penance held—and still holds—me here. As retribution for my complicity in the oppression of Women of Color, I must now turn into their voice, their champion. They want me to serve for them; they need me to serve for them.

By living out my White savior complex in this way, I guaranteed the continued silence of Women of Color while also assuaging my own guilt. What was actually happening was a processing of my guilt and conviction for my own comfort rather than for the destruction of hierarchical structures. This selfish epistemology inevitably leads to feeling sorry for Women of Color, which is fundamentally not helpful, and offensive to the autonomy and power Women of Color hold. However, seeing Women of Color as victims of an oppressive regime in which I am a key participant is a required, painful step in the process toward understanding allyship.

Throughout the two years over which this journey has taken place, I have returned to the first volume of *Presumed Incompetent* many times. For a long time, I read the narratives and recommendations contained within as fundamentally about me and my story. As I continue to mature and walk through the process of deconstructing my White privilege, I recognize that the necessary piece of allyship that I have been missing is a key component of the practical recommendations in *Presumed Incompetent*: decenteredness of the White narrative. Not elision or ignorance or erasure. But a dethroning of its space as the default and the assumption. The idea that Women of Color were victims whom I must save is, at its core, a reifying of the White-centric narrative. To move forward from White savior complex, I must feel and understand decenteredness as coming alongside Women of Color.

ALLYSHIP AS JOURNEY

I continue to struggle with being an ally of Women of Color. I am careful with my language, because if I simply stop the sentence at "I want to be an ally," the inevitable, natural completion of that sentence, as a White woman, is "for myself, so I can help Women of Color, so I can protect them." The necessity of decenteredness is clear here: to be an effective ally, I must become an ally of Women of Color, but not for my own benefit. Women of Color do not want a savior, a white knight who parades their feminism like a flag. Women of Color want an ally. As a White woman, it is my responsibility to deconstruct my privilege, my guilt, my tears, and to understand my role in the larger narrative of oppression, in order to deconstruct it as well.

There is a tension in the requirement of decenteredness. This chapter, and this journey, is my story. However, the work of allyship is about destroying the oppressive system. It is simultaneously very much about me, but it is also fundamentally beyond me. It is difficult and painful. But true allyship is about working with Women of Color to ensure that your allyship, someday, will no longer be needed. The ideal conclusion to the process of liberation is the removal of allyship, and this conclusion should be what I work toward. The key difference between being a savior and being an ally is processing the narratives I hear and the worlds I encounter as being about the system in which we are all implicated. I am not saving Women of Color from a world in which I am removed. I am aligning myself with Women of Color, bringing my own experiences and stories to the table, in the hopes that we can create an entirely new table.

Throughout this piece, I have given several real examples of the stickiness of my process toward allyship. And as I mentioned earlier, this piece began as a practical, how-to guide for White women to be successful allies. I hold by my advice, but with a very different frame. These methods are simply the spaces in which I processed through these stages most effectively. My intent in sharing them is to encourage White women to allow themselves to occupy these practical spaces, in the hopes that their epistemological spaces are impacted as well. For example, White women should mentor one another on matters of allyship and working through White guilt. The labor of creating and maintaining allies falls disproportionately on Women of Color, and White women must learn to share this burden.

As graduate students, we should take courses with feminist and anti-racist scholars, and seek professional certificates in interdisciplinary fields such as women and gender studies. Much of my growth was facilitated by these courses. Techniques like strategic silence and active listening—useful in these courses, but also in spaces like department meetings—have taught me that oftentimes a valuable contribution is lurking in a space I need to learn to leave open. Instead of placing the burden of not calling on me on a professor, or worse, calling on another student myself, I can simply take notes and leave my hand down! However, as Yolanda Niemann reminded me, the perspectives of Women of Color are oftentimes met with silence, and are therefore invalidated. Thus, I encourage White women, and myself, to be more willing to relinquish the safety of silence to validate Women of Color's voices and to lessen the burden of discussing difficult topics that is typically placed upon already-oppressed individuals.

My last piece of advice is deceptively simple: read—and if you can, teach—texts by Women of Color. A key part of my journey through these stages has been consistent engagement with the work Women of Color are already doing. I would never be writing this chapter if it weren't for *This Bridge Called My Back* and *Presumed Incompetent*. As I have explored, continual decenteredness and a willingness to remain uncomfortable are keys to impactful growth in understanding our positionality within allyship. This decenteredness and discomfort can be accomplished best by engaging continually with scholarship that challenges the structures under which some bodies are privileged and others are marginalized and destroyed. In short, we should never stop reading scholarship that challenges the subject positions that are in power, especially in the academy. The more recent scholarship has bibliographies that any willing student can mine for even more rich resources about feminism, intersectionality, and liberation. Reading is fundamental.

My journey of understanding my religion has been one of lifelong learning about guilt, forgiveness, and living out essential teachings. Allyship, I have realized, is no different. Both require continual sanctification. I am not through the guilt and the savior complex yet. I will probably never be entirely free from them. The important work is constantly dismantling the systems that cause the fragile tears, the guilt, and the assumption of victimhood. The journey toward allyship is essentially self-reflective, recognizing where we are and where we want to go. My Queer of Color critique professor taught me that the core value of allyship is in the discovery of self as a privileged individual first, as a lifelong student second, and as a worker for liberation third. To err is human; to learn from mistakes and continue forward is allyship. This work will not end with this chapter: for me, for White women, or for Women of Color. We will continue to wrestle with these spaces. I hope, however, that I have at least removed the blindfolds.

REFERENCES

Ahmed, S. (2012). *On being included: Racism and diversity in institutional life.* Durham, NC: Duke University Press.

Moraga, C., & Anzaldúa, G. (Eds.). (2015). *This bridge called my back: Writings by radical women of color* (4th ed.). Albany: State University of New York Press.

Shields, S. (2012). Waking up to privilege: Intersectionality and opportunity. In G. Gutiérrez y Muhs, Y. F. Niemann, C. G. González, & A. P. Harris (Eds.) *Presumed incompetent: The intersections of race and class for women in academia* (pp. 29–39). Logan: Utah State University Press.

TWENTY-ONE

And Still We Rise

Adrien K. Wing

Whenever I feel overwhelmed or depressed, I think of one of my favorite poems—Maya Angelou's "Still I Rise" (Angelou, 2010).[1] It is a wondrous anthem to the strength of Black women. Angelou first published it in 1978, the same year I graduated from Princeton. I loved the poem then, and I love it even more now that I am in the twilight of my career as a law professor and associate dean. I have had a wonderful life—beyond my wildest imaginings in 1978. I earned a master's of arts degree in African studies from UCLA as well as my doctorate of jurisprudence from Stanford Law School. Then I worked for five years as an international lawyer in New York City. And now I have spent over thirty fantastic years at the University of Iowa (UI) College of Law, a place I could not have imagined visiting, much less living in, back in 1978. I have written over 130 publications, primarily in areas involving race, gender, and international human rights. I have served on prestigious nonprofit boards, and won numerous awards. I have visited about 100 countries, and helped draft three constitutions. I have mentored countless junior colleagues across the country and hundreds of law students. Yes, I, the daughter of a widowed African American mother who raised three children on her own in suburban New Jersey, have indeed risen.

So what is there for me to say or do at this point other than take a bow and ride off into the sunset of retirement? Most conversations with my baby boomer peers usually discuss this issue at some point. Some have already retired or are de facto retired because they cannot get suitable work at our age. Others are counting down the months or years to leave jobs they dislike. Many have mentioned moving to warmer weather, spending more time with grown children and

1. Special thanks to my research assistants Golnoosh Mostoufi, Amanda Ndemo, Aileen Nguyen, Vy Nguyen, and Nicolle Rhim.

DOI: 10.7330/9781607329664.c021

grandchildren, dealing with health issues, getting involved in new or old hobbies, and winding down projects that may or may not ever be finished. Some have said that they will never retire because what else would they do? Others have said that they cannot afford to retire.

When I read selections from the comprehensive *Presumed Incompetent* volume and other sources, the emphasis in the literature continues to be on the challenges for Women of Color in being junior professors, getting tenure and promotion, as well as campus climate, faculty/student relationships, and allies (Gutiérrez y Muhs, Niemann, González, & Harris, 2012; Wing, 1990–1991). A few articles, including my own, specifically discuss mid-career challenges (Wing, 2010, 2012).

There are very few publications discussing the end of work life in the legal academy for women. I have often speculated why so little has been written. One reason could be that there are relatively few senior women, especially Women of Color. Another reason is that most writings occur in the earlier career stages, well before the issues of retirement are even imagined. Senior women may have become administrators, with no time for scholarship. Some may feel disconnected from the profession or burnt out, perhaps focusing on interests outside the ivory tower. Finally, some may not want to bare their spirit-injured souls. Spirit injury is a term that I have been using throughout my career to characterize emotional and psychological damages from various sources (Wing, 1990–9191, p. 186).

Professor Meera Deo has produced *Unequal Profession: Race and Gender in Legal Academia*, which is part of the Diversity in Legal Academia (DLA) project. She collected empirical data from ninety-seven law professors throughout the United States to yield a rigorous examination of intersectional race X gender challenges and opportunities. The quantitative and qualitative data reveal patterns involving privilege, bias, and discrimination associated with race, gender, and the combination of these devalued identity characteristics. Senior scholars and administrators were specifically included in the study, with associated challenges detailed in the book (Deo, 2019).

Deo's work reinforces that challenges remain in the senior years. As a senior scholar interviewed for the book said, "Competition for merit increases, or chair, or whatever gets a little more fierce" (2019, p. 41). Professors feel that even though they have seniority, they do not dare to say no to teaching more and to doing extra service requests, even at the expense of their own health (p. 49). Even with many years of experience on the faculty, scholars may feel their relationships are distant with their colleagues (pp. 52–53).

So, in this brief chapter, I will contribute to the literature by tackling a few issues regarding the end of a career phase of academic life for Women of Color under the headings "Love Is All There Is"; "Spirit Injuries Can Fester until the End"; "Privileging Multiplies—How to Handle It"; and "The Struggle Is My Life."

LOVE IS ALL THERE IS

Love is more important than footnotes, and love can manifest in many ways and with many people. I gave birth to two sons, and I knew that I must have done something right when these grown sons said that they had appreciated my untraditional mothering that emphasized global engagement and service rather than baking cookies from scratch and creating homemade Halloween costumes. Additionally, I became a surrogate mom to five other youngsters, including three biracial boys from Iowa and two young ladies who came from Ethiopia as refugees. So far, I have fifteen grandchildren, with the oldest two in college already. I could become a great-grandmother before my youngest child becomes a parent. These children and grandchildren are my prides and joys, and are my hope for the future of our country and the world.

All those great accomplishments mentioned in the opening paragraph of this chapter could not have happened without the love and support of my partner James Carl Sommerville, an independent commercial artist who works from home. I have known him for nearly forty years, and he has been with me in Iowa for over twenty years.

James is central to my universe, and spending my quality time with him may be far more important than a day job. He moved from San Bernardino to Iowa and helped parent all the various children and surrogate children, none of whom are his own biological children. He is not only the one who deals with so-called male chores of fixing the car, taking out the garbage, mowing the lawn, raking the leaves, and snowblowing; as a Stanford-trained engineer, he handles the technology for our family, an area where I am an illiterate. Moreover, he is a great cook, does the housecleaning and laundry, shops for the groceries, and even picks out jewelry to go with my outfits when I am traveling.

While I am grateful for all of the things that James has done to truly enable my career for the last twenty-plus years, I am most thankful for what he did for my mother. Both my grandmother and mother had Alzheimer's. We brought my mother from New Jersey for her final years. James is the one who generally managed her care in its various sad phases so that I could work. First, he parent-sat, watching and interacting with her while she still had lots of periods of quirky coherence. When that became too difficult and stressful, he took her to adult day care centers in both Iowa and California, where we spent one semester. When she no longer had appropriate behavior for day care, James supervised the very expensive home health aide company, which we could only afford to pay for forty hours a week at best. By this phase, Mom rarely knew us, and it was James who sometimes had to assist with her bathing and toileting. We had to clean her up in the shower, sometimes more than once a day. Finally, for the last seven months of her life, James made the daily trips with me to Mom's dementia unit at the Solon Care Center, and even visited her when I was out of the country running Iowa's France summer program.

It was James who zoomed to the airport to pick me up from a trip so that I could get to the dementia unit for what they said were Mom's last days. I made it in time and lay in the bed next to my mom as she breathed her last. And it was James who comforted me as I wept. The horror of that difficult time was somewhat alleviated because she died on October 8, the same day that my father died some forty-eight years earlier. Now they were together again. So you can see why James's well-being is beyond priceless to me.

I realize that I might have to make a sudden decision concerning my retirement not based upon my own health, but that of James. My former dean, Gail Agrawal, stepped down from her deanship early due to her husband's health. James was recently diagnosed with emphysema in addition to his preexisting high blood pressure and arthritis. His most severe struggle to date has been living with being bipolar, a horrific condition that many sufferers will not even reveal due to the severe stigma. James came out as mentally ill on Facebook a few birthdays ago, and it has been a big emotional and spiritual relief. While we are very proud that he has not been hospitalized for this condition during his decades in Iowa, that could always change. We are pretty sure that he is well past life expectancy for mentally ill African American men in the United States (NASMHPD, 2006). Our entire lifestyle could end if he can no longer handle the strain.

With respect to my own health, any small lapse in my behavior makes me dread that I will get Alzheimer's too. What will be my attitude toward working if I have a limited and declining amount of coherent time? I have three books on the back burner and I want to get them done before I can never finish them. What if both James and I are seriously impaired? Love will carry us through—love from each other, our children, our family, our colleagues.

SPIRIT INJURIES CAN FESTER UNTIL THE END

If you have been treated badly throughout your career, that is likely to continue until the end. Everything you struggled to achieve or represented can be wiped out within the institution without a trace. My mother was mistreated for decades as an English teacher, and the school system ultimately took three years before they even featured her at a retirement dinner. Many Women of Color have discussed the intersectional discrimination they have faced on account of their race, sex, class, and other identities (Crenshaw, 1989). This field of study is often called critical race feminism, and I am the editor of an anthology on this topic in domestic law (Wing, 2003) as well as a companion volume on the global level (Wing, 2000). Even though Women of Color may change jobs, get promotions, or even disconnect as much as possible from toxic environments, spirit injuries they have ignored or even addressed will continue to eat into their souls.

At the end of my career, one form of discrimination I now face that is a source of new spirit injuries is ageism. My children are now older than almost all my students. Do I need to get out of the way, make space for younger people who are up to speed with technology and the culture of the students? Will I know when it is time to go? Will I recognize when people roll their eyes or patronize me? Will I recognize the signs of Alzheimer's or will someone else so I do not embarrass myself? Why did I not cherish each year instead of always bemoaning the fact that the prior year/decade was gone? Now I try to be proud of my years and embrace them, but it is very hard as everything in society features youth.

Thus, another source of spirit injury involves what I call stature identity. Stature is how one looks within a society (Wing, 2001, pp. 841–842). If a woman fits the model of beauty—young, blond, and Barbie doll–like—then she will usually do better in school and in the labor force. Older women generally get "stereotyped as pathetic, powerless, querulous, complaining, sick, weak, conservative, rigid, helpless, unproductive, wrinkled, asexual, and ugly" (Healey, 1986, p. 59).

Additionally, most Black women do not fit the Barbie image, and may deal with a lifetime of negativity on account of their skin color, hair, nose, size, and so on. In my own case, *matronly* would be a kind term, more reminiscent of being a "mammy." My once-brown hair would be white if I did not have the vanity to keep coloring it, and it is certainly thinning. None of the clothing featured is designed for my size or age. I have adopted the style of wearing black every day, with varying scarves, jackets, and so on. I vacillate between rejoicing at being freed from the dictates of fashion and cringing that I still care about my image. Each woman must navigate these shoals, and it does not necessarily get easier, especially for Black women.

My worst spirit injuries involve the devastating blow to my psyche and my family due to the suicide of my brilliant physician father in 1965, when I was nine. For almost fifty years I suppressed it. Sometimes I can voice my pain. Whenever another brilliant African American person ends her life, as Northeastern law professor Denise Carty Bennia ("Denise Carty-Bennia," 1990) and New York judge Sheila Abus-Salaam did (Quinn, 2017), I feel it viscerally. I am sensitive to suicidal pain that may be radiating from students or friends. I embrace those with mental illness, including James, who is bipolar, and my late former mother-in-law, who was schizophrenic (Wing, 2005, pp. 663–664).

There is a large literature on the physiological and psychological effects of racism on Blacks (American Psychological Association, n.d.). Additionally, while gains have been made, Blacks under sixty-five have higher death rates than Whites, and Black life expectancy is three and a half years lower than that of Whites (Achenbach, 2017). The term *weathering* has been used to describe the premature aging and health decline that Blacks experience, which can accumulate across a lifetime or perhaps even across generations. It may be due to the consequence of psychosocial, economic, and environmental stressors (Achenbach, 2017).

It is clear that many Black law professors have died before their time. In my view, the cause of death has probably been influenced in part by the severe spirit injuries that even the most elite members of our community face. Patricia Roberts Harris, the first African American woman to be a law dean, US ambassador, and US cabinet member, died of cancer at sixty (Williams, 1985). Goler Butcher, a Howard law professor and former Carter administration official, died of a heart attack at sixty-seven (Pearson, 1993). Marilyn Yarbrough, the first Black female dean of a predominantly White law school, died at fifty-eight, and she had suffered from diabetes ("Marilyn Yarbrough," 2004). American University Law School professor Pamela Bridgewater died of cancer at forty-five ("Pamela D. Bridgewater Toure," 2015). Northeastern law professor Hope Lewis, who struggled for years against the effects of diabetes that made her blind, died at fifty-four (Amann, 2016). Duke law professor Jerome Culp suffered from kidney disease, and died after a kidney transplant at fifty-three ("Duke Law Professor," 2004). Harvard law professor and former diplomat Clyde Ferguson died of a heart attack at fifty-nine (Hinger, 2015). Professor Edwin "Rip" Smith, the first Black law professor to get tenure at USC, died at sixty-six of a heart attack while he also battled multiple sclerosis (Phillips, 2016).

The first Black New Orleans mayor, Ernest Dutch Morial, died at sixty after an asthma attack led to a cardiopulmonary collapse (Marcus, 1989). The first Black Chicago mayor, Harold Washington, died of a heart attack in his office at sixty-five (Johnson, 1987).

Beyond law, a number of prominent Black intellectuals also died too young. UC Berkeley professor Barbara Christian died of lung cancer at age fifty-six ("Barbara Christian," 2000). Prolific author June Jordan died of breast cancer at sixty-five (Smith, 2002). Brilliant lesbian feminist Audre Lorde died of liver cancer at age fifty-eight ("Audre Lorde," 2019). Iowa English professor Darwin Turner died at age fifty-nine of a heart attack ("Darwin Turner," 1991). We will never know the degree to which spirit injuries affected the longevity of any of these brilliant people.

It also seems strange to me that two outstanding Harvard law professors, Charles Ogletree (Helm, 2016) and Lani Guinier (Emmons, 2017), would both get Alzheimer's at relatively young ages. Alzheimer's affects Blacks at twice the rate of Whites (Helm, 2016). What role might spirit injury play in the emergence of this disease?

The recent Supreme Court confirmation hearings of Judge Brett Kavanaugh opened up deep spirit injuries that I try to keep buried. These same feelings had been released by the treatment of Professor Anita Hill in the Clarence Thomas confirmation hearings. The bottom line is that men have acted in sexually inappropriate ways with me and said inappropriate things to me from the time I was a child. I was sexually harassed at every institution I attended, most jobs I ever held, and most organizations to which I dedicated my energies. The men were loved ones and strangers. They were mentors and peers. They were Black and White. They were famous and unknown. They were US citizens and foreigners. They were younger than me and much older. I now realize that relationships that I had considered really cool when I was young were actually statutory rape. Even though I am a grandmother and apparently no longer subject to new incidents, I realize that I must tackle these harms or I will take them unresolved to my grave.

I took a first step recently when I attended an anniversary conference of an organization that I was heavily involved with early in my career. In a session on the Me Too movement, I brought up sexual harassment issues that dated back to the early 1980s in the organization. In our discussion, which included a significant number of men, I was heartened by the fact that men said they were sorry that things had happened to women in the group and they did not know or looked the other way. Men apologized if they might have inadvertently said or done something offensive, even if many decades ago. It was a good start.

PRIVILEGING MULTIPLIES: HOW TO HANDLE IT

While I am now wise enough to know that I will be dealing with various types of discrimination for the rest of my life, I must also deal with my simultaneous privileging. As a law professor, I am incredibly humbled by the fact that I have been able to live a life of the mind, in which I am paid to administrate, research, teach, and give service. While I still work way more than forty hours per week, my time is relatively flexible. I have been able to handle child care, illnesses, and emergencies without losing my job. In over three decades, I have never been bored and have always been able to innovate ever year. I have been blessed to work with wonderful colleagues around the world. I enjoy teaching and learning from students, including many who have been my research assistants and mentees. I smile as through Facebook I watch their careers blossom.

While I will never earn the millions of dollars that some of my White male lawyer colleagues do, I am content that I make more than most African Americans and most women in the world. Residing in a vibrant low-cost college town has enabled me to live very well. I have been able to use my resources to expand my biological family and to help people in other countries. I have created the Wing Fund to enable Iowa law students to work or study abroad. When I pass away, the fund will be endowed so the future students who will never have met me will benefit from my resources.

This relative privileging will be further augmented shortly, even before retirement. In addition to obtaining full Social Security at sixty-six and four months, I can still continue to work and receive my salary. When I retire, my substantial TIAA-CREF (Teachers Insurance and Annuity Association-College Retirement Equities Fund) assets will supplement Social Security so that I will have a very comfortable situation. When I pass away, I will be able to bequeath sizable wealth, although it may not equal that of most of my White professor colleagues. Meanwhile, I have relatives who will have to live only on Social Security. It will be a fraction of my payment because they earned far less and worked fewer years. More Black women marry later, never marry, or have a higher divorce rate, which definitely affects their retirement income (Raley, Sweeney & Wondra, 2015).

I have relatives who will not even collect Social Security because they did not work forty quarters on the books. What will be their plight, especially if they have no children or their children cannot assist them? As a group, African American women have only $100 in median wealth compared to $7,900 for African American men (Chang & Bowie-Singh, 2013). My children have done well so far in their careers and are self-supporting. There is no doubt that they would assist James and me if this should ever be necessary.

So what to do with this relative privilege even while Women of Color are still facing discrimination? I plan to expand the reach of my resources. I have established trusts for James and my extended family, and plan to expand my giving to more of the organizations I am affiliated with as well.

THE STRUGGLE IS MY LIFE

When Nelson Mandela was in a South African prison for what he thought would be forever, he made a statement that the struggle was his life (Mandela, 1990). He had no idea that he would be released and become the first Black president of his country and win a Nobel Peace Prize. None of us knows how long we have. I do know that we will not cure the many kinds of discrimination on this planet during my lifetime or the lifetime of even my youngest grandchild. The late professor Derrick Bell, a founder of critical race theory, thought that racism is cyclical (Bell, 1992, p. 98), and I have gone through several cycles in my life. Perhaps I will witness several more. Bell also thought that perhaps racism might be permanent (p. 13), like alcoholism, which can be managed but is never eliminated. Thus, I will not waste time and energy in becoming depressed about the vicious-isms and their perpetrators. Instead, I will want to be judged by the quality of my struggle for justice and for taking steps forward rather than just accepting sliding backward.

I stand by things I have previously emphasized. Professors must do more than the minimum required and they must keep learning themselves. They must always mentor or "othermother," whether male or female (Wing, 2012). In recent years, I have enjoyed mentoring more junior women who are participants in the Lutie Lytle conferences designed for African American women. At Iowa, we held the first and tenth conferences, the latter featuring 125 African American women at all stages of their careers (Onwuachi-Willig, 2017). They must take care of themselves and give credit where the credit is due. They must always engage in service, which in my case has been on the university, local, state, national, and international levels (Wing, 2012).

For over ten years, I have been associate deaning and directing. I am realizing my limitations. I might never be that law school dean or college president. I might not be an ambassador in an administration I would embrace, but I can still contribute greatly in the multiple hats I wear.

Despite the obstacles I have faced as a Woman of Color in academia, I would go through it all again. As I noted in my earlier work, "When the bombs are dropping—literally or figuratively—you need to keep calm and carry on" (Wing, 2012, p. 362). And still we will rise!

REFERENCES

Achenbach, J. (2017, May 2). Life expectancy improves for blacks, and the racial gap is closing, CDC reports. *Washington Post*. Retrieved from https://www.washingtonpost.com/news/to-your-health/wp/2017/05/02/cdc-life-expectancy-up-for-blacks-and-the-racial-gap-is-closing/?utm_term=.036b623ff9aa.

Amann, D. (2016, December 9). In passing: Our sister Hope Lewis. *Intlawgrrls*. Retrieved from https://ilg2.org/2016/12/09/in-passing-our-sister-hope-lewis/.

American Psychological Association. (n.d.). Physiological and psychological impact of racism and discrimination for African-Americans. Retrieved from https://www.apa.org/pi/index.aspx.

Angelou, M. (2010). Still I rise. *Sister Namibia, 22*(1), 36. Retrieved from http://proxy.lib.uiowa.edu/login?url=https://search-proquest-com.proxy.lib.uiowa.edu/docview/608854180?accountid=14663.

Audre Lorde. (2019, Apr. 16). *Biography.com.* Retrieved from https://www.biography.com/people/audre-lorde-214108.

Barbara Christian, professor and pioneer of contemporary American literary feminism, dies at age 56. (2000, July 12). *Berkeleyan.* Retrieved from https://www.berkeley.edu/news/berkeleyan/2000/07/12/christian.html.

Bell, D. (1992). *Faces at the bottom of the well: The permanence of racism.* New York: Basic Books.

Chang, M., & Bowie-Singh, L. (2013, August 26). *Black women face wealth gap 50 years after the march. Ebony.* Retrieved from https://www.ebony.com/news-views/black-women-face-wealth-disparities-500.

Crenshaw, K. (1989). Demarginalizing the intersection of race and sex: A black feminist critique of antidiscrimination doctrine, feminist theory and antiracist politics. *University of Chicago Legal Forum, 1989* (1), 139–167. Retrieved from http://chicagounbound.uchicago.edu/uclf/vol1989/iss1/8.

Darwin Turner, professor of English. (1991, February 21). *New York Times.* Retrieved from https://www.nytimes.com/1991/02/21/obituaries/darwin-turner-59-a-professor-of-english.html.

Denise Carty-Bennia, law professor, 43. (1990, September 29). *New York Times.* Retrieved from https//nyti.ms/29wzvxO.

Deo, M. (2019). *Unequal profession: Race and gender in legal academia.* Palo Alto, CA: Stanford University Press.

Duke law professor Jerome Culp dies at age 53. (2004, February 6). *Duke Today.* Retrieved from https://today.duke.edu/2004/02/culp_0204.html.

Emmons, E. (2017, June 26). The history makers return to Denver. *Denver Urban Spectrum.* Retrieved from http://denverurbanspectrum.com/articles/231442.

Gutiérrez y Muhs, G., Niemann, Y. F., González, C. G., & Harris, A. P. (Eds.). (2012). *Presumed incompetent: The intersections of race and class for women in academia.* Logan: Utah State University Press.

Healey, S. (1986). *Growing to be an old woman: Aging and ageism.* In J. Alexander et al. (Eds.), *Women and aging: An Anthology by women* (pp. 58–62). Corvallis, OR: CALYX.

Helm, A. (2016, July 10). Harvard law professor Charles Ogletree calls his Alzheimer's diagnosis a blessing. *The Root.* Retrieved from https://www.theroot.com/harvard-law-professor-charles-ogletree-calls-his-alzhei-1790855967.

Hinger, C. (2015, May 6). Clarence Clyde Ferguson, Jr. (1924–1983). *Blackpast.org.* Retrieved from https://blackpast.org/aah/ferguson-clarence-clyde-jr-1924-1983.

Johnson, D. (1987, November 26). Chicago mayor Harold Washington dies after a heart attack in his office. *New York Times.* Retrieved from https://www.nytimes.com/1987/11/26/obituaries/chicago-s-mayor-washington-dies-after-a-heart-attack-in-his-office.html.

Mandela, N. (1990). *The struggle is my life.* New York: Pathfinder.

Marcus, F. (1989, December 25). Ernest Morial, former mayor of New Orleans. *New York Times.* Retrieved from https://www.nytimes.com/1989/12/25/obituaries/ernest-morial-former-mayor-of-new-orleans.html.

Marilyn Yarbrough, law prof, ex-Tennessee dean, dies at 58. (2004, March 11). Retrieved from http://lawschool.com/yarbrough.htm.

NASMHPD (National Association of State Mental Health Program Directors Medical Directors Council). (2006, October). Mortality and morbidity in people with serious mental illness. Retrieved from https://www.nasmhpd.org/sites/default/files/Mortality%20and%20Morbidity%20Final%20Report%208.18.08.pdf.

Onwuachi-Willig, A. (2017). The promise of Lutie A. Lytle: An introduction to the Tenth Annual Commemorative Lutie A. Lytle Black Women Law Faculty Workshop *Iowa Law Review* Issue. *Iowa Law Review*, *102*(5), 1843–1846.

Pamela D. Bridgewater Toure. (2015, January 16). *Legacy.com*. Retrieved from https://www.legacy.com/obituaries/WashingtonPost/obituary.aspx?pid=173869009.

Pearson, R. (1993, June 13). Goler Butcher dies. *Washington Post*. Retrieved from https://www.washingtonpost.com/archive/local/1993/06/13/goler-butcher-dies/60c3dabf-2f4f-40ba-bcc7-c3dbd9f4e1b1/?utm_term=.9bfc6fcc5337.

Phillips, A. (2016, August 13). Edwin "Rip" Smith, first minority tenured professor at USC law, dies at 66. *Los Angeles Times*. Retrieved from http://www.latimes.com/local/education/la-me-edwin-smith-20160812-snap-story.html.

Quinn, R. (2017, July 27). Medical examiner: Judge drowned herself. *Newser*. Retrieved from http://www.newser.com/story/246330/medical-examiner-judge-drowned-herself.html.

Raley, R., Sweeney, M., & Wondra, D. (2015). The growing racial and ethnic divide in U.S. marriage patterns. *Future Child, 25*(2), 89–109. National Library of Medicine. Retrieved from https://www.ncbi.nlm.nih.gov/pmc/articles/PMC4850739/.

Smith, D. (2002, June 18). June Jordan, 65, Poet and Political Activist. *New York Times*. Retrieved from https://www.nytimes.com/2002/06/18/arts/june-jordan-65-poet-and-political-activist.html.

Williams, J. (1985, May 24). Patricia R. Harris dies at 60. *Washington Post*. Retrieved from https://www.washingtonpost.com/archive/politics/1985/03/24/patricia-r-harris-dies-at-60/fc328a6a-5758-4713-8747-95f75069fbc5/.

Wing, A. K. (1990–1991). Brief reflections towards a multiplicative theory and praxis of being. *Berkeley Women's Law Journal*, *6*(1), 181–201.

Wing, A. K. (2000). *Global critical race feminism: An international reader*. New York: New York University Press.

Wing, A. K. (2001). Polygamy from Southern Africa to black Britannia to black America: Global critical race feminism as legal reform for the twenty-first century. *Journal of Contemporary Legal Issues, 11,* 811–880.

Wing, A. K. (2003). *Critical race feminism: A reader* (2nd ed.). New York: New York University Press.

Wing, A. K. (2005). Examining the correlation between disability and poverty: A comment from a critical race feminist perspective—Helping the Joneses to keep up! *Journal of Gender, Race & Justice, 8*, 655–666.

Wing, A. K. (2010). One l redux. *University of Missouri Kansas City Law Review, 78*(4), 1119–1126.

Wing, A. K. (2012). Lessons from a portrait: Keep calm and carry on. In G. Gutiérrez y Muhs, Y. F. Niemann, C. G. González, & A. P. Harris (Eds.), *Presumed incompetent: The intersections of race and class for women in academia* (pp. 356–371). Logan: Utah State University Press.

TWENTY-TWO

Closet Chair and Committee Side Piece

Black Women STEM Faculty at HBCUs

Marcia Allen Owens

This essay gives voice to a faculty member who is the first African American woman to earn tenure in her science, technology, engineering, and mathematics (STEM) field at her historically Black college and university (HBCU). Comprising less than two percent of faculty nationwide, Black women are in the minority everywhere, even at HBCUs. Women faculty in STEM, at all institutions, face challenges in disciplines with few female colleagues and administrators. Most of the women at HBCUs—faculty, staff, and students—are Black. While we may not confront issues of race in the manner that may be encountered at majority institutions, Black women at HBCUs do face challenges when race, class, gender, academic discipline, and history intersect in a context where Black women students are the majority, but where Black women STEM faculty are the minority.

HBCUs were initially founded in the 1800s to offer the rudiments of educational instruction, reading, writing, and arithmetic to newly freed slaves (Kendi, 2017). Their articulated missions varied from institution to institution, reflecting the interests of their founders or benefactors. As of 2016, 105 HBCUs were in operation; yet their storied histories remain buttressed by the persistent beliefs of presumed racial superiority and inferiority which result in characterizations of HBCU students as low-achieving and faculty as less qualified (Gasman & Nguyen, 2015).

GENDER AND HBCUS

Black women are often lost amid the intersections of race and gender at HBCUs by the focus of studies on Black men. Similarly, in studies of gender, White women are cast as the "universal woman." Rendered invisible in scholarship, Black women, who are the majority in the student ranks at HBCUs, remain in the minority in faculty and administrative ranks, are less likely to be tenured, and

DOI: 10.7330/9781607329664.c022

are less likely to ascend to the rank of "full" professor (Bonner, 2001; Gasman, 2007; Gasman& Commodore, 2014).

SCIENCE, TECHNOLOGY, ENGINEERING, AND MATHEMATICS (STEM)

Although HBCUs comprise only three percent of colleges and universities, they produce 27 percent of African American students with bachelor's degrees in STEM fields (US Department of Education, 2016). Comprised of Africans, Indians and other Asians, and European Americans, HBCU faculties are much more diverse than their traditionally White institutional (TWI) counterparts (Bradley, Cook, McDonald, & North, 2009.) Described as "minorities among minorities," Black women STEM faculty at HBCUs are markedly outnumbered by both males and females from other ethnic/demographic groups (Bradley et al., 2009).

My institutional context is representative of this trend. My faculty is 70 percent Black, 19 percent White, seven percent Asian/Pacific Islander, and four percent Hispanic. In terms of gender, 54 percent are male and 46 percent are female. Noting that published faculty data do not report the intersections between gender and ethnicity, and in preparation for a National Science Foundation (NSF) grant proposal, a colleague and I sat and did just that.

Counting and naming the women STEM faculty and social and behavioral sciences (SBS) faculty, we found that the largest percentage of women is at the rank of instructor (50 percent) and conversely, the smallest percentage (17 percent) is at the rank of full professor, with associate and assistant professors at 40 percent and 38 percent, respectively. The School of the Environment has had as many as three women, all White, at one time. I was the second Black woman to ever be hired, and the first to stay long enough to apply for tenure and promotion to associate professor. As the sole remaining woman, I comprise ten percent of the current school faculty composition.

Microassaults, Microinsults, and Microinvalidations

As an untenured faculty member, I wrote about my practice of keeping a journal (Owens, 2012) in which I chronicled years of microassaults, microinsults, and microinvalidations (Sue et al., 2007) experienced through the actions of faculty, staff, and students. One might expect that post-tenure, there would be fewer such interactions, but this is not the case.

These racial and gendered attacks do not always originate with men. Much of the work of Black women involves invalidating racist stereotypes and perceived lower social stratification by non-Blacks and Black people who are covetous of Whiteness (Westfield, 2008b). Prior to becoming tenure-track faculty, I directed a center. New to the institution and still surveying the landscape, I noted the hostility of a Black woman member of the support staff. She finally erupted and told me that I was too young for the job, and that she should have had the position since she had done so much work on the grant that supported its founding.

She then sought to minimize my terminal degree, as well as my actual and perceived status, and told me that I should put my pantyhose on one leg at a time, just like she had. With her insider knowledge of the grant budget, she added that I was paid $10,000 less than the budget allowed, and that a White woman candidate had been preferred. In this microassault, which had White superiority at its foundation, this Black woman staff person venerated an unhired White woman and weaponized her existence in an effort to "bring me down a few pegs" and put me back "in my place."

PATRIARCHY

The environments of HBCUs perpetuate "heteronormativity and stringent gender roles," while also reinforcing White supremacy (Njoku, Butler, & Beatty, 2017). Explaining patriarchal norms in the Black community and institutions, Robert Staples (1979) described a Black community consensus that men would serve out front as leaders during the civil rights movement of the 1960s. I recall the stories of my own mother who, when she was interviewed about her life as an educator in Mississippi in the 1950s, was asked to take a less vocal supporting role in the movement once my father became involved (Owens, 2001).

Manipulative Paternalism

Like women in the modern civil rights movement, Black women at HBCUs are forced to choose race over gender, and men with status are sometimes manipulatively paternalistic in their attempts to control choices and outcomes. One year, I was elected to the University Tenure and Promotion Committee. A male full professor who missed the election approached me under the guise of concern and mentorship and suggested that I should decline to serve because of the time commitment. He had served the previous year and would be glad to continue if I stepped down. As an environmental policy professor, I am interested in processes. Although advisory, this committee reviews and makes recommendations for every promotion and tenure application across the university. I thanked him for his concern, and responded that if I needed to give up something, I would give up one of my many other service commitments. I further informed him that this would be a new experience and something else to put on my CV, and since I still have to go up for full professor, it is critical that I understand how the process works.

He persisted, taking a stab at emotional manipulation in his expectation that I would yield to his leadership without interference (Jackson & Wu, 2015; Williams, Dempsey, & Slaughter, 2014). My mother had recently passed; and he asked how I was doing. I happened to have her obituary on my desk. Reading and noting her accomplishments in higher education, including her retirement as executive vice president at Jackson State University, he said, "I see where you get it from. Your mother did too much too." I served two years on the university tenure and promotion committee.

POACHING AND GENTRIFICATION

Consistent with a growing body of knowledge (Benderly, 2017), my experience indicates that the potential of Black students is not always predicted by "subjective" measures such as Graduate Record Examination (GRE) score or grade point average (GPA) alone. Rather, I very closely read their personal statements, which share their stories, to fill in gaps. In one instance, I pushed for admission of a Black woman who had graduated from a TWI with a GPA below 3.0, but who had high GRE scores. Somehow, the numbers did not tell the full story. Internally, I asked, why the discrepancy? In reading her eloquent personal statement, in conjunction with looking at the timing of her academic struggles on her transcript, I discovered that her grades began to slip after her family lost everything in Hurricane Katrina. With that understanding, I said, "I'll take her."

The response from my White woman colleague was, "You have to justify your decision." I responded, "No one else has had to justify their decisions, so neither do I." The student was admitted, did well in her coursework, and finished a two-year master's program in two years and a summer. Reviewing her application to our doctoral program, White faculty members openly sought to advise her, although she clearly declared in her personal statement that she wanted to continue to work with me. When I objected to this blatantly disrespectful attempt at poaching and gentrification of a student whom they now valued, I was told that technically, she was a new student applying to a new program and that everyone should have the opportunity to work with her. I reminded them that this was the same student whom I was asked to justify admitting in the first place.

Without my knowledge, the White woman faculty member told staff members and the dean that she should be added as co-adviser; and without my knowledge, consultation, or agreement, the student was notified of the new co-advisement arrangement. Thankfully, a more senior student warned me that her colleague was about to leave the program because of this arrangement, which she thought I had agreed to. I sought out my distraught student, whose parents were already planning the trip to move her home. She and her mother did not understand the change. They told me that the student would not continue her work in our program under that particular co-advisement arrangement. I actually had to fight to continue to advise my own student, who remained at my institution and went on to complete her PhD, winning fellowships and awards and other national accolades.

VENERATION OF WHITE WOMEN IN A PREDOMINANTLY BLACK SPACE

Even in a historically Black space, White women enjoy protection and privilege. At HBCUs, White women's tears are potent, concentrated, and effective in their weaponization to villainize and silence Black women, and to influence Black men to prioritize their wishes (Accapadi, 2007; Hamad, 2018). During one incident in a Faculty Senate meeting, I was cast as the stereotypical mean, angry Black woman when I opposed an action that blatantly disrespected disciplinary boundaries and conventions. A White woman faculty member had convinced the Black male Senate leadership that any faculty members engaged in environmental work should have to report to her so that she could make monthly reports on environmental research and service activities. However, neither her faculty appointment nor credentialing were environmental. I questioned how her hobby and special interest could require those of us who had environmental careers to report to her, when we had a School of the Environment. Enter White fragility. The tears appeared, the conversation shifted toward her comfort and away from the substantive issue at hand; I became the villain because she did such "good work."

I simply refused, and still refuse to advance the faulty perception that meaningful environmental research could only be done by Whites.

A DIFFERENT KIND OF MAID

Harley (2008) referred to Black women at TWIs as the "maids of academe," in contrast to their White female counterparts, who "are the daughters of White men, and subsequently benefactors of White privilege" (p. 20). Black women are "deprivileged," as they are subjected to "gendered racism" through misconceptions, abuses, and stereotypes (p. 20).

Being referred to as a maid in Black spaces is racially and historically charged because of Black women's historical and current roles as domestic workers. At least three generations of the women in my family worked in domestic roles in Grenada, Mississippi. On the maternal side, my mother was the last, because at the age of fourteen, she dared to fight back against the sexual advances of a young man in the household in which my grandmother worked. At that point, my grandmother told her, "You have to go to school," because her fierceness and sharp tongue would get my grandmother fired and the entire family killed. My mother went on to be class valedictorian, graduate of Jackson College for Negro Teachers (now Jackson State University), and a high school teacher who earned an EdD from the University of Mississippi before retiring as an HBCU senior-level administrator.

Regardless of terminology, label, or faculty status, Black women faculty members are expected to uphold traditional household roles, at all types of institutions. When the committee lists came out, I was shocked to find my name on the Hospitality Committee, even though I was already on several academic committees. One of the things that the Hospitality Committee was responsible for was the annual homecoming cookout. I responded, "I'm neither domestic nor domesticated. I don't even do this kind of stuff at home!" When I was a new faculty member, there was also a White woman faculty member who was placed on the Hospitality Committee. However, as the only Black woman faculty member, I experienced myriad emotions upon being handed a spoon and gloves to serve food to and clean up after male faculty, students, and alumni—a strong reinforcement of the intersectionality of race, gender, and class. My name has been removed from the committee list, but the expectation is still there. So, every year, I help to underwrite the cookout. I don't attend regularly; I actually stopped going for two years. When I do attend, I arrive quite late and do not venture anywhere near the serving tables.

ACADEMIC MOTHER BECAUSE DOCTORS ARE MALE

Other gendered perceptions and expectations that impact my existence involve naming and titles. My institution, as is true of many HBCUs, tends to be very formal with respect to using titles, "a historical practice that may have been born to combat the microaggressions of majority culture" (Owens, 2012).

Imagine my dismay when, on a day I had chaired two successful doctoral dissertations, one newly minted PhD, after thanking the male scholars present and another Black female committee member offered his profuse thanks to me as his chair, calling me his "academic mother." My face flushed, and I literally ducked my head.

To be labeled an "academic mother" is not inherently bad. In fact, it is complimentary in Black culture and is indicative of warm demander pedagogy (Ware, 2006). However, being labeled "mother" is tricky for Black women in the academy. The mother is valued for nurturing and other characteristics that are inherently feminine, but not for her intellect. Mother is loved but is not respected as a scholar. So, by labeling me "mother," not "scholar," "researcher," "scientist," or "mentor," the student created the perception that I nurtured him into success with love, not knowledge or intellect.

At dinner after his defense, and in the presence of his own biological mother, I explained the awkward pain of his statement as the other woman faculty member and I perceived it. The newly minted doctor apologetically explained that in his (Caribbean) culture, the mother is loved, respected, and held in the highest regard. My rebuke might be perceived as an attempt to shame the new doctor, but that was not my intention. I offered this professional perspective as a teachable moment, like others commonplace at HBCUs; if I had not engaged with the issue, the PhD might have unknowingly made the same mistake, costing him career opportunities in the future.

Similarly, another male student invariably called me "Mrs." I asked him why was I being addressed according to my marital status rather than according to the academic credential that qualified me to be a professor. He paused and then explained that there was no slight intended when he called me "Mrs." rather than "Dr." because "Dr." was masculine.

In a similar situation, when I asked a student to name his professors for the semester, he called all his White and other non–African American women professors "Dr.," while I was "Mrs." When I asked about the difference, the explanation had to do with me being likable and approachable.

BUT WE'RE ALL WOMEN, RIGHT?

The opening for my current position occurred when an untenured White woman, one of three total, abruptly resigned two weeks into the semester. I was asked to become an adjunct professor, teaching two night classes in my field of environmental policy. The position was not advertised right away, so I taught as an adjunct for two years in addition to holding down my position as a center director.

Once the position was advertised, the search for my current position narrowed down to me, with a JD, a PhD, and nearly twenty years' experience practicing environmental law and teaching environmental policy, versus a White woman with only a law degree and practice in a different specialty who had taught one class as an adjunct. By the time we reached the interview phase, a second White woman had resigned, which meant that there would be only one White woman remaining who had successfully navigated the tenure requirements. After the job talks, the lone remaining tenured White woman faculty member sent a Black woman graduate student to tell me that I should withdraw from the search because I was not qualified. Black women sometimes willingly participate in anti-Blackness and in their own oppression if it suits their case (Kendi, 2017). Similarly, Black women also have the capacity to advance racist ideas and to internalize and project misogynoir when racism and misogyny combine to oppress Black women (Bailey, 2010; Solis, 2016). White women do not hesitate to use Black women's internalized oppression to advance their desires.

In the mind of the White woman faculty member, it was perfectly logical for an academic unit at an HBCU to have three White women faculty and no Black women faculty, even when the majority of the students are Black women. Such logic seeks to nullify intersectionality in an effort to lull Black women into the notion that "we are all women."

"THE FACULTY DIDN'T WANT YOU"

I spent four of my untenured years under a Black male administrator who used the contentious search process as a control mechanism. In evaluations and when I would resist an uncompensated overload of administrative assignments such as assessment, he told me, "The faculty didn't want you. The only reason that I picked you was because you could do assessment." When I was hired, I was told that assessment would rotate every two years, as it was time consuming and only counted as service, of which I had plenty. I functioned as a committee of one. When the two years elapsed and it was time to rotate to someone else, the rotation was denied because "you do a great job!" And, remember, "The only reason that I picked you was because you could do assessment." A two-year rotation turned into a permanent assignment with no reduction in course load or research requirements, because I did a "great job."

This structurally violent and manipulative statement that "faculty didn't want me" disallowed my sense of belonging, invoked feelings of doubt, and undermined my confidence in my own competence. His representation that the faculty did not want me remained relatively secret until a full faculty meeting more than five years and two deans later. Again, the topic was assessment. At this point, I was tenured and had returned from a leave of absence to an uncharacteristically high teaching load for men in our school. A committee of three men had failed to successfully develop an assessment plan and report while I was gone.

CLOSET CHAIR AND COMMITTEE SIDE PIECE

Students want the knowledge, warmth, and support of Black women faculty, but often seek it out secretly. Some dissertation chairs choose supervisory committee members rather than allowing the students to choose for themselves. I rarely serve on committees for chairs that engage in that practice. However, their students often seek me out, asking me to become the "closet chair" of doctoral committees, which are comprised of five members. Despite not choosing me, year after year, students ask me questions that could have been answered with minimal research. I am treated like a human search engine; the insights of my dictation are considered the Holy Grail. While I wish to help students, I need to do creditable work for tenure and promotion. If their visit is secret, and I am not on their committee, the interaction typically remains off the record, as a few have actually shared that their advisors have instructed them not to talk to me. I cannot even list this work as service.

Some of these interactions are more blatant: a student's thesis or dissertation chair actually sends the student to "pick my brain." Yet, there was no room for me on the five-member supervisory committee. I call this being a "committee side piece" because it is an interaction in which the principal partner in the formally recognized relationship knows about me, but I'm relegated to being the "chick on the side." As I have progressed up the tenure ladder, I have learned to exhibit a healthy self-interest by saying no more often.

MEN ARE ALWAYS IN CHARGE, EVEN WHEN THE WOMAN IS THE COMMITTEE CHAIR

Likewise, my contributions to the work of my own students are often expected to be hidden. In one dissertation defense, I served as chair—one of two Black women on the committee. The other woman faculty member attended virtually, so I was the only Black woman in the room. Patriarchy took over. My authority as a Black female chair to direct the meeting was deemed insignificant and insubordinate to maleness. The Black male dean, who is an ex officio member of all committees, decided to remain for the committee's discussion, something that he does not routinely do. As my student struggled to navigate a particular question, the dean actually told me to "be quiet" as I tried to guide my student. I sat in disbelief at the level of disrespect and disregard. This was not my first dissertation defense, and I actually have produced more doctoral students than he. The other men, who were substantively on the committee, just watched, further normalizing the disrespect. Encountering the forced choice of clearing the room to set and maintain authority, I just took the blow, pushed through, and kept the goal of the student's successful defense as priority.

"I WILL KICK YOUR ASS!"

In addition to disrespect and structural violence, I have also faced threats of physical violence, the most notable occurrence being during a dissertation defense. Proud parents and other family members often attend thesis and dissertation defenses. After one memorable incident, I have requested that students prepare their families for the tough questioning that might occur in the oral defense.

In that case, I served on a committee (and as closet chair) and the student forgot some information that was foundational to her research and the academic discipline. Exercising my best warm demander pedagogy (Ware, 2006), I pushed and prompted her into a successful clarification of an answer. As the audience was dismissing for the private session with the committee, a Black woman approached me and said, "I'm from Chicago! I will kick your ass!" Realizing that this was the student's mother, I backed up and responded, "Ma'am, I'm just doing my job." I said to the student's husband, who was familiar with the doctoral process, "You need to get her and explain what is going on." Although I was introduced as a member of the dissertation committee and participated as such, I was not worthy of respect, nor of apology.

The sharing of this sampling of experiences makes me understand the question "are Black girls are ever worth fighting for?" (Cooper, 2018, p. 83). Indeed we are, but when we fight for ourselves rather than others (as we are often enlisted to do), we are subjected to negative stereotypes and perceived as angry and aggressive. I ask this question regarding my treatment and that of other Black women faculty, and when I listen and redress concerns and grievances involving Black women students. Though patriarchy is clearly a structural problem, often there is a refusal to confront it, because to do so makes it seem like Black women are "picking on" Black men (Cooper, p. 84). Naming the terrible things Black men have done to Black women gets too frequently read as "man-bashing and hatred" (Cole & Guy-Sheftall, 2003, p. xii). Male colleagues have witnessed much of the behavior discussed in this narrative but have said nothing publicly. A few come to me after the meeting to render support that they were unwilling to provide during the meeting. The silence of my colleagues is memorable.

WHY I STAY

After reading my own experiences, I ask myself: Why am I still here? Why do I stay? In this instance, I have only described events that I have experienced as a Black woman STEM faculty member at an HBCU. In the overall scheme of things, what I have shared pales in comparison to my experiences of growing up in the segregated South, graduate education at TWIs, career stints where I was the only Black person, and daily experiences of navigating the nation and the world as a Black woman. Regardless of the complicated and often painful encounters at my HBCU, I am called to teach and to make a difference in the lives of students. As an HBCU STEM graduate, I know that my foundational grounding has provided me with the resilience to withstand daily intersectional assaults. My existence as the first and only means that I am a visible example of achievement and success for Black women students, but also for students and colleagues who represent myriad intersections of race, ethnicity, gender, and privilege.

PERSPECTIVES FOR CHANGE

All my life, Black men and patriarchy-supporting Black women have been telling me what I can and cannot do or be. In the fourth grade, when I encountered my first White woman teacher, the limiting and oppressive perspectives of White women were directly added to my educational and career aspirations. Yet since that time, I've managed to exceed their low expectations and continue to excel while encouraging others to do so as well. So, if you have no interest in supporting me, I have limited time or inclination to teach you how to help me. I will, however, gladly have a discussion if you show evidence of attempting to do your own work.

For those who seek to be helpful in addressing inequities, I would advise first: do no harm. Part of my incredible privilege to share a measure of success in the face of intersectional inequities is that I am often asked to provide solutions for the problematic behavior of would-be allies in the midst of being microassaulted by that very behavior. Just know that a Black woman with a terminal degree has likely dealt with a lifetime of microagressions at every educational and professional level, and she has persisted in the face of and in spite of them.

Her persistence has been accompanied by hidden pain because patriarchy and racism have developed controlling stereotypes that prevent us from expressing the full spectrum of human emotions. Whereas White women's tears are powerful weapons, if a Black woman cries, she defies conventional logic because she is no longer the "strong Black woman." If we use passionate or other expressive vocal inflections, then other negative stereotypes apply: "sassy," "loud," using a hostile "tone," being the "angry Black woman." The life of a Black woman faculty member is often lived in an attempt to navigate the perilous norms of Whiteness and maleness with no visible show of emotion.

Check your assumptions. If you assume that a Black woman got into her top-tier graduate program because of her race and gender, also assume that she caught hell trying to graduate, also due to her race and gender. Do not assume that Black women work at HBCUs because we cannot find jobs at "better" institutions. Further, if we changed careers to get the terminal degree, do not assume that we were a failure in our prior careers. In fact, our successful career experiences add the depth of real-life experience to our teaching. One Black woman at an HBCU can plant hundreds of seeds of success in the lives of Black students by supporting the mission to provide educational opportunities in an environment where we can also enjoy the culture and the relative decrease of racism.

Honestly, being at an HBCU is a virtual guarantee for Black women that we can go to work and every day see multiple other Black women in various roles. At many STEM professional conferences, we are the only Black woman in the breakout session or exhibit hall. When that is the case, more than a few people will make service requests based on their erroneous assumptions that we work at the conference venue since we do not look like we belong.

I would like for my default position to be to give everyone the benefit of the doubt, but with more than four decades of experience of flying with a lead cape over my wings—Black patriarchy (by men and women), White fragility and privilege, and White women's tears—I live with a hermeneutic suspicion. However, I do this work in hopes that younger Black women may have a default setting of freedom and authenticity, as well as personal, professional, bodily and emotional autonomy.

With every cathartic revision I wondered whether I should file or delete this essay. However, writing it means that I am owning everything that happens to me and telling my own story (Lamott, 1995). In service of normative Whiteness, patriarchy, and HBCU traditions, I, as the token Black woman STEM faculty member, am expected to maintain respectable and smiling silence that is neither enjoyable (Hurston, 1937) nor protective (Lorde, 1980). I remain committed to the mission and work of HBCUs, but I am also committed to making them better for everyone by speaking and modeling a life lived fully in the intersections.

REFERENCES

Accapadi, M. (2007). When white women cry: How white women's tears oppress women of color. *College Student Affairs Journal, 26*(2), 208–215.

Bailey, M. (2010). They aren't talking about me. *Crunk Feminist Collection.* Retrieved from http://www.crunkfeministcollective.com/2010/03/14/they-arent-talking-about-me/.

Benderly, B. L. (2017). GREs don't predict grad school success. What does? (column) *Science,* June 7, 2017. Retrieved from https://www.sciencemag.org/careers/2017/06/gres-dont-predict-grad-school-success-what-does.

Bonner, F. B. (2001). Addressing gender issues in the historically black college and university community: A challenge and call to action. *Journal of Negro Education, 70*(3), 176–191.

Bradley, J., Cook, D., McDonald, D., & North, S. (2009). "We, they, and us": Stories of women STEM faculty at historically black colleges and universities. In W. R. Brown-Glaude (Ed.), *Doing diversity in higher education* (pp. 103–118). New Brunswick, NJ: Rutgers University Press.

Cole, J. B., & Guy-Sheftall, B. (2003). *Gender talk: The struggle for women's equality in African American communities.* New York: One World/Ballentine.

Cooper, B. (2018). *Eloquent rage: A black feminist discovers her superpower.* New York: St. Martin's Press.

Gasman, M. (2007). Swept under the rug? A historiography of gender and black colleges. *American Educational Research Journal,* 44(4), 760–805.

Gasman, M., & Commodore, F. (2014). *Opportunities and challenges at historically black colleges and universities.* New York: Palgrave Macmillan.

Gasman, M., & Nguyen, T. (2015). Myths dispelled: A historical account of diversity and inclusion at HBCUs. *New Directions for Higher Education,* 2015 (170), 5–15.

Hamad, R. (2018, May 7). How white women use strategic tears to silence women of colour. *Guardian.*

Harley, D. A. (2008). Maids of academe: African American women faculty at predominately white institutions. *Journal of African American Studies, 12*(1), 19–36.
Hurston, Z. N. (1937). *Their eyes were watching God*. New York: Harper Perennial Modern Classics.
Jackson, F. J., & Wu, E. Y. (2015). Must we deploy drones in the twenty-first century to target under the radar discrimination against minority women at law schools at historically black colleges and universities? *Columbia Journal of Gender and Law, 31*(1), 164–195.
Kendi, I. X. (2017). *Stamped from the beginning: The definitive history of racist ideas in America*. New York: Nation Books.
Lamott, A. (1995). *Bird by bird: Some instructions on writing and life*. New York: Anchor.
Lorde, A. (1980). *The cancer journals*. San Francisco: Aunt Lute Books.
Njoku, N., Butler, M, & Beatty, C. (2017). Reimagining the historically black college and university (HBCU) environment: Exposing race secrets and the binding chains of respectability and othermothering. *International Journal of Qualitative Studies in Education, 30*(8), 783–799.
Owens, A. N. (2001). Dr. Mildred J. Allen. Unpublished interview. Emory University, Atlanta, GA.
Owens, M. A. (2012). Is that healthy? Experiences of microagressions by black women at historically black institutions. Retrieved from http://www.thefeministwire.com/2012/11/is-that-healthy-experiences-of-microagressions-by-black-women-at-historically-black-institutions/.
Solis, M. (2016, August 30). Meet Moya Bailey, the woman who created the term "misogynoir." *Mic*. Retrieved from https://mic.com/articles/152965/meet-moya-bailey-the-black-woman-who-created-the-term-misogynoir#.8sL5GKqB4.
Staples, R. (1979). The myth of black macho: A response to angry black feminists. *Black Scholar, 10*(6/7), 24–33.
Sue, D. W., Capodilupo, C. M., Torino, G. C., Bucceri, J. M., Holder, A.M.B., Nadal, K. L., and Esquilin, M. (2007). Racial microagressions in everyday life: Implications for clinical practice, *American Psychologist, 62*(4), 271–276.
US Department of Education. (2016). FACT SHEET: Spurring African-American STEM degree completion. Retrieved from https://www.ed.gov/news/press-releases/fact-sheet-spurring-african-american-stem-degree-completion.
Ware, F. (2006). Warm demander pedagogy: Culturally responsive teaching that supports a culture of achievement for African American students. *Urban Education, 41*(4), 427–456.
Westfield, N. L. (2008a). *Being black, teaching black: Politics and pedagogy in religious studies*. Nashville: Abindgon.
Westfield, N. L. (2008b). Called out my name, or had I known you were somebody . . . The pain of fending off stereotypes. In N. L. Westfield (Ed.), *Being black, teaching black: Politics and pedagogy in religious studies* (pp. 61–78). Nashville: Abingdon.
Williams, J. C., Dempsey, R., & Slaughter, A. (2014). *What works for women at work: Four patterns working women need to know*. New York: New York University Press.

TWENTY-THREE

In Name Only

A Principal Investigator's Struggle for Authority

Nellie Tran

Grants are often either an amplifier of or barrier to academic success, especially tenure and promotion. Not only is access to funding a challenge for Women of Color because of the topics that we care to study and the methods we choose to study them (Turner, González, & Wood, 2008), so too are the opportunities to engage in mentorship and advice around federal grant writing and work. In this chapter, I share the story of what happened when my vice provost brought me, an assistant professor, onto a two-institution collaborative grant team because of my scholarly expertise in microaggression intervention work. I led the smaller research component of the grant, and then I inadvertently ended up as the principal investigator (PI) of a $750,000 federally funded grant. Specifically, I describe my experiences working with more senior, White women and how, despite being the content expert, and leader, I came to be the PI—in name only. I also share my personal struggle with "not being enough" and the ways that I had to learn and insist that I am an expert, a leader, and worthy of compensation. In sharing my experiences pursuing and working on a large federal grant with other academic women, I highlight how tokenism, exploitation, and forced mentorship caused me heightened anxiety, emotional pain, and stifled my productivity. Through sharing my experiences, I hope other junior faculty Women of Color who desire to pursue collaborative team grant funding will go into the process better informed of possible barriers and traps, but also with more knowledge of the process and the relationships needed to be successful, productive, and to maintain one's psychological wellness.

PERSONAL HISTORY AND EARLY CAREER EXPERIENCES

Here, I share the early experiences that shaped the lens through which I interpret the grant experience. I am the US-born daughter of Vietnamese refugee boat

DOI: 10.7330/9781607329664.c023

people. Although I am bilingual and bicultural, I spent a great deal of my youth harboring a very anti-Asian viewpoint, steeped in a racially color-blind ideology. Like many other minoritized and racialized children in predominantly White school contexts, I tended to internalize my experiences of "otherness" as personal deficits instead of structural oppression (Tatum, 2017).

My personal "not good enough" story intersects with my academic journey in critical moments that provide an additional layer to understand my experiences. I was not accepted into a four-year university out of high school, resulting in two years of community college where, thankfully, I discovered psychology. In attempting to get into a doctoral program, my soon-to-be graduate school advisor informed me that my too-low GRE verbal score would not be a problem were I Latino or Black. Asians, on the other hand, were not considered minorities. I am Asian and therefore required to meet the same standards as White students. This presumption of my incompetence based on my inability to meet White standards of academic success set a form of internalized oppression in motion that made writing more difficult and even impossible at times. In my first tenure-track position, senior faculty regularly reminded me that I was their third choice and ought to feel grateful for my position. Upon reflection, these statements indicated that this workplace upheld norms of incivility, disrespect, and harassment of colleagues. What other purpose did these constant reminders serve but to "put me in my place"?

I am not the Asian American stereotype of a model minority. My hard work and dedication did not overcome my exposure to discrimination, leading to my successes (Suzuki, 2002; Tran & Birman, 2010). At each step, White folks told me I was not worthy, not smart enough for an Asian, and that they did not perceive me to be oppressed enough to deserve accommodations. They made it clear that if they, as judges of my oppression, perceived me to be more disadvantaged, things would be different. The dominant White institution perpetually judged my level of oppression and worthiness of receiving resources and opportunities, ones that Communities of Color, including Asian Americans, fought for during the civil rights movement (Chan, 1991). My experience of feeling the pressure to assimilate and be perceived as valuable and worthy within the academic institution permeates all layers of this story.

THE GRANT

In year two on my tenure clock, I received a phone call from my vice provost for research. She invited me to join a two-institution team working to obtain a federal grant to improve the recruitment, retention, and promotion of women in science, technology, engineering, and mathematics (STEM) disciplines because of my scholarship on microaggression interventions. I was ecstatic that for the first time in this position, someone saw me based on my professional scholarship rather than my ethnic identity and migration story. The year before this included tokenization in the form of misguided invitations to collaborate on immigration work and an offensive request to play tour guide and translator in Vietnam for the university. Hindsight makes me question whether the thrill of receiving an invitation based on my actual expertise after feeling invisible and misunderstood clouded my judgment. I wish I had proceeded more cautiously.

The team included administrators, staff, and faculty at two large state public institutions, including institutional centers invested in faculty advancement, research productivity, diversity and inclusion, social science faculty researchers, and several psychology researchers across a broad spectrum of topics. Most team members were personally committed to the work of recruiting, retaining, and promoting women in the STEM disciplines.

Research Team Leader

At my first meeting with the two-institution team, I encountered immediate challenges to my expertise. The team used the term *microinequities* to refer to subtle gender biases that occur within academia. Within the academic scholarship, micro*inequities* are the inequities that occur due to the expression of subtle biases (Rowe, 1990). Micro*aggressions*, on the other hand, are the subtle slights, invalidations, and insults that people experience on a daily basis that suggest negative messages about a person's marginalized group identities (Russel, 1998; Sue, Bucceri, Lin, Nadal, & Torino, 2007). It baffled me to see the definition of microaggressions associated with the concept microinvalidation. When I questioned the choice in terminology, the group responded that they chose to disregard the literature because microaggressions sounds "aggressive" and would cause defensiveness in White men. Despite my insistence, the group would not budge. Some of the most vocal oppositions came from team members with little to no experience conducting social science research or bias and discrimination work. After months of negotiations, we landed on "subtle gender bias" as the overarching concept. In my opinion—and this is one that is shared by leading scholars on the topic—calling microaggressions anything else protects the psychological health of perpetrators, failing to provide the peace of mind that the accurate term offers victims.

As an early-career, thirty-something, exceptionally young-looking Asian American, I had plenty of experiences where people questioned my authority and expertise. Although this experience infuriated me, it also felt typical and even normal. It played in well with my feelings of being an imposter and the messages my department colleagues relentlessly taunted me with about being unworthy of my job. It led to my internalization of being not expert enough, not good enough to be the leader. I questioned what I knew about the topic, reading about it endlessly to ensure my perfect and precise understanding of my work. While I certainly held an internalized need to be perfect, the women on my team also demanded the perfect, extensive, and precise articulation of the literature for me to be expert. This same requirement, however, was not expected of team members advocating for terminology that protected White men. I began to see why Women of Color have to be exceptional in order to be included, hired, or promoted.

As the research team leader, I wrote a five-page research proposal that complemented the larger million-dollar grant. The real test of my power and leadership would come when I began to ask for basic resources: participant incentives, a research assistant, and summer salary. The senior leaders denied each request. I came to realize that my White female colleagues created space for me and my work only when I provided checkmarks to their tasks and lent my expertise in areas where they did not have any. These were the additional signs that they would only grant opportunities and access to serve their own careers and goals. I held very little actual power. It also felt like they were setting up a trap: should I complete the project on such meager resources, I would surely be invited to participate in future projects to repeat this incredible feat. My failure, on the other hand, would provide evidence of my incompetence.

On Becoming the Inadvertent PI

Ironically, the funding agency rejected the grant but decided to fund my smaller addendum research project. The program officer called me to offer $750,000 to specifically fund my smaller project under a different name, and I became the new PI.

To further complicate matters, I was pregnant with my first child when I received word of my award funding and new leadership role. The grant funding arrived as I began my maternity leave. Federal grants and large multi-institutional projects often do not have options for parental or medical leaves. The option to delay funding was also not considered because many people from both institutions counted on the funding to pay their salaries. In hindsight, that my team would move on with me on leave tells me they lacked depth in their commitment to create more socially just and equitable workplace environments. A couple weeks after giving birth, I sat at home with my newborn feeling exhausted, still recovering, and leading my team in conference calls. I sat on the floor of my living room, laptop on the coffee table, and rocked a baby bouncer with one foot. Half my brain was on leading the team, the other half praying the baby stayed asleep. I cried silently nearly every day after each meeting. And yet, as I now know is typical for this workplace, the people on my team and at my institution most committed to the well-being and success of Women of Color academics did not care enough to hold off on starting.

The White women who felt most entitled to my work presumed power over me and provided me with constant unsolicited feedback in the name of "mentorship." This began as suggestions on how to communicate with senior colleagues when women on the team believed me to be slacking and unable to attend to the details of the position. It led to suggestions about how to run meetings, who to employ, and how to manage my research staff. One woman even line-edited my budgets and would give a second approval of my decisions after I gave a first approval. She would likely tell you that I wasn't getting it done, that I needed her help. In reality, she kept me on a leash and micromanaged my leadership. Both White women from each institution bombarded me with emails demanding updates and descriptions of my whereabouts.

At one point, one woman's emails criticized me in humiliating and racially charged ways, attacking the extent to which I lacked graciousness and humility. She asked me to be more grateful for her and our colleague's work and suggested I begin each meeting with more gratitude for their contributions and support. At one point she noted that to restore my graciousness, she recommended that I not feel so "entitled" to the summer salary that I budgeted for the PI. She aggressively demanded that I think more about the staff that could work on writing blog posts and tweeting about the project, rather than paying myself. Note that these would be additions to the project that were unnecessary and not in the original budget. I was then and am now the "cheapest" faculty member on the team. I should not have had to say it then or now, but I did feel entitled to that money. I deserved it. Most important, it was in the original budget approved by the funding agency. No other reason should have mattered. It was my idea, my grant, my budget, and my money.

Halfway through the project, I decided to leave this position for the one I now hold as assistant professor at San Diego State University. If you ask the people on this project or from my previous academic department, they will tell you that I returned to San Diego because my family is here. They will deliberately leave out the information I reported during my exit interview regarding the ways that I felt bullied and harassed within my department and this team. This very team devoted to understanding Women of Color's experiences of hostile academic settings will also continue to fail at discussing these specific cultural climate issues. I left the grant in place, with PI status going to a trusted Woman of Color (who left the team after funding ended). Everyone agreed that I would remain the lead of the project in all aspects, with the exception of the formal listing with the funding agency. Two years after leaving, I learned that the team had moved on and scrubbed their website of any mention that I led their first project. Again, I needed to request that my name be listed with proper acknowledgment of my work. I also had to make it abundantly clear that any mention of this project must always list my name.

REFLECTION AND LESSONS LEARNED

Reflecting back on this work and the path I took, I wish I had known my personal issues with my self-worth and the impact my academic and racial socialization would have on me. I wish I had realized how smart I am and how much I had to offer this project. I wish I had not believed the messages that I should feel lucky and grateful for the opportunity. I don't regret having done the project. Honestly, this grant made it possible for me to leave this aggressively hostile workplace and has propelled me to focus on work that truly aligns with my racial justice agenda.

It is important to note that fault in this situation and others like it rests not just with my White woman colleagues, but also with the oppressive academic institution more generally. For systemic oppression to exist, all players at each level within the hierarchy must play their part. Therefore, I must have played a role as well. Why did I allow myself to be involved in a project that refused to use correct terminology? Why did this experience not signal their lack of commitment to working on microaggressive climates? Had I trusted my expertise in microaggressions and acknowledged the lack of influence I had on the team's work, when would I have left? Even these questions are too simple. Higher self-esteem and confidence would likely not have been enough. I also needed to understand how deeply I had internalized over three decades of academic and racial socialization that led me to seek out White approval. I had been socialized to long for White colleagues to mentor me, love me, validate me—save me. I would have had to acknowledge that nothing I did for myself would be enough without their approval.

Why wouldn't this be the case? The majority of the work I read and perspectives I had been trained within represented that of White scholars educating White students to engage with Communities of Color (Guthrie, 2004). To be successful within these predominantly White institutions, People of Color have often had to assimilate to Whiteness (Fordham & Ogbu, 1986; Marinari, 2005) and seek approval from the White people who dominate those spaces. Educational institutions upholding color-blind racial ideology are more likely to employ White educators and enroll White students who hold beliefs that People of Color are inferior to them (Apfelbaum, Norton, & Sommers, 2012). Therefore, People of Color surviving in predominantly White school environments that uphold racial color-blindness are also likely to require Students of Color to assimilate to Whiteness as well as beliefs in their own second-class citizenship. When Women of Color faculty have this early socialization within predominantly White institutions, their mistreatment becomes almost normal and expected. Why then would my vice provost, a Woman of Color, invite an expert onto a team of White woman and then allow them to talk down to me? I trusted her, but I also knew her limits. She cared about me, but perhaps she was more invested in maintaining the "peace" and funding, rather than standing up for justice.

Beyond my academic training and socialization, I also needed to have awareness regarding the role of my Asian American socialization. Asian Americans have long been triangulated between White and Black communities to uphold White supremacy (Kim, 1999). The use of Asian Americans as honorary Whites (Tuan, 1998) allows the illusion of an American Dream to exist. In other words, Asian Americans are often allowed to either assimilate to Whiteness to obtain validation and worth from people and institutions upholding Whiteness, or they can align with other Communities of Color to fight for liberation (Tran, Nakamura, Kim, Khera, & AnhAllen, 2018). To do this, however, Asian Americans need to acknowledge the "false charity" granted to them by their oppressive White superiors (Freire, 2000, p. 45). My White colleagues needed me on their team to benefit them in their quest for funding and to support views of themselves as White allies. I would not be heard as an equal at that point or any point.

We have long known that including more Folks of Color would not be enough to bring diverse and inclusive perspectives to the academy, that it would require a more profound and intentional approach to diversifying the pillars that form the foundation of the academy (Sheurich & Young, 1997). In practice, it appears that many White academics are continuing to strive for this first step of bringing diverse people onto their team and giving them these charitable opportunities to lead (on benevolent racism, see Glick & Fiske, 1997; Swim, Aikin, Hall, & Hunter, 1995). The question is whether your White colleagues are looking to advance their goals or yours. In my case, this opportunity gave me a chance to work with senior scholars and high-ranking administrators on a topic that I cared about deeply. However, I should have accepted the message that I heard when I saw the lack of congruency between their words and actions.

The potential danger of this "add-on" method of diversification and inclusivity is that it does not address the racial dynamics inherent in interracial interactions. For example, stereotype activation for well-intentioned White colleagues is well documented in the social psychological literature (Fiske, 2000; Macrae & Bodenhausen, 2000). Consequently, the well-intentioned, liberal White women who worked with me are likely to have missed the implicit activation of Asian American stereotypes whereby I must be a model minority and expected to meet White standards of success. When I lacked obedience to elders, was too vocal and aggressive for an Asian, and did not assimilate to White work culture and leadership norms, they reprimanded me. Research on expectations suggests that when people of lower status perform/behave differently than superiors expect, they are often met with negative and sometimes hostile reactions (Rosenthal & Jacobson, 1966). Moreover, when individuals perceive themselves to be higher, better, or otherwise more superior to fellow team members, they set up self-fulfilling prophecies that perpetuate these dynamics. More specifically, when individuals believe in the incompetence of their colleagues, they treat them in demeaning ways that create reactions that provide evidence for their incompetence.

In my case, my White female colleague decided to "mentor" me into being a leader, one that would serve her and her needs. It is possible that she did not believe in my leadership skills. However, self-fulfilling prophecy and Pygmalion effect studies suggest that it is not necessary to have clarity, certainty, or even confirmation of my colleague's "real" beliefs so long as her behaviors suggested to *me* that she believed in my incompetence. Within the teacher-student relationship, this pattern has been shown to lead to learned helplessness (Maier & Seligman, 1976). For example, when people feel as though they do not have control over the outcome of a situation, they internalize it as their fault, thus leading them to learn to be helpless within that context. These same dynamics occurred within my relationship with my colleague. The difference is that she presumed her role as my mentor without my consent. She would never come to see me as an equal, nor as the leader of what she felt and treated as her project.

The sad reality is that fighting to preserve the sanity and health of women Faculty of Color in this situation did not work. It only highlighted how deeply the women on this team had internalized the need to protect and support White men, even on a project set up to recruit, retain, and promote faculty in minoritized and racialized situations. This event taught me to play the game differently.

I could not appeal to their sense of justice and equity. I had to highlight their absurdity and punctuate it with my threat to depart from the project.

It is this last point that is worth noting—my threat to leave the project. Despite the opportunity and the investment of time and work I had put into the project, I had to know when enough was enough. These moments require personal self-awareness. While we may not be able to avoid working in situations where we are tokenized, racialized, and minoritized, our self-awareness of these social locations and circumstances allows us to set our boundaries and plan for the inevitable oppression. In my case, it was my strength and determination to do good science that protected me and allowed me to maintain a curriculum vitae that showcased my research skills and talents. This is what allowed me to be lead this grant and also subsequently to walk away from this hostile project and work environment.

MY ADVICE TO YOU

Lessons on Grant Writing

Throughout the experience that I had at this job and on this grant team, I stayed vigilant of the research process and maintained the integrity of the science. This has been my saving grace. By ensuring that my work reflected my personal and professional values, I allowed myself to have options outside of this institution and project. If you are embarking on such a project, here are some questions to consider. Why did you want to be in this profession? What goals will this grant enable you to achieve? What part is for you? How much will it cost you?

Nothing is free, including your time, effort, and psychological health. Compensation can come in many different forms, including summer salary, course buyouts, research assistants, stipends, space, equipment, publications, and even titles. Make sure you have a clear understanding and get as much as possible in writing as you lay the foundations of the grant and project guidelines. Make sure to note who will have access to and "own" research data, who will get first and last author (depending on your discipline norms), and how you will be explicitly paid. Know your worth and behave accordingly. If you don't ask to be paid, chances are that you will not be.

Lessons for Working with Others

It sounds like a cliché, but is still worth repeating: when people show you who they are, believe them the first time! Look for signs that you and your collaborators are working toward goals that align—or not. In my case, I cared about the science because it was personal. They did not care about the science, nor the impact on individual stories. They cared about the funding and prestige that would come to their center and institutions. I could have seen that had I believed the signs I saw. My team cared more about perpetrators than victims. They treated me as disposable. They cared about STEM Women of Color in the abstract but not the one actually on their team.

Perhaps this is a more difficult suggestion if you are new to an institution or have limited time to show productivity. However, it may be worth the time to work on smaller projects with potential collaborators first before jumping into significant, long-term projects. This process could allow you to consider the effectiveness and productivity of the partnership. Large projects, especially those funded by grants, are much more challenging to stop, should the collaboration go sour. Collaborative groups are successful if the team is able to work together effectively. You are not required to continue working on teams that do not function well or that mistreat you. Over time, it is okay to pivot your work and move into collaborations with new partners.

Lessons for the Self

The story begins and ends with you, the individual. Believe in your worth. You deserve to be in your position. You deserve resources. You don't owe anyone for treating you with the dignity and worth that you have always deserved. Anyone who mentors you to achieve goals they set for you to benefit them and not you is not your mentor. Worse still is a mentor who makes you feel as though you owe them for treating you as a colleague and doing their job. The oppressive systems that I have survived set me up to believe that I did not deserve resources. My cultural upbringing taught me not to over-rely on others and to pull myself up by my bootstraps. These messages have been oppressive and ineffective. It was therapy that helped me to heal from early graduate school and early career traumas. I hope that you will do the revolutionary thing and make yourself a priority by allowing yourself access to any and all resources that are available to you.

As I finish writing this chapter, I am preparing to submit my materials for tenure. I have been at my current position for four years and have come to understand the parts of my current and past institutions that are consistently and inherently oppressive. My first semester here, a senior colleague invited me for coffee. He shared his reflections of my interview and thoughts he had about my future work. I had never had a department colleague speak so clearly about my worth and potential. I walked back to my office and cried. It had not dawned on me how much I had internalized the messages that I was incompetent and an academic imposter. I have come to understand what it looks and feels like to be valued and have freedom to work and live my values. Sometimes, it's impossible to see clearly when you are sitting in the eye of the storm. Thankfully, my work has improved the academic work conditions of at least one academic STEM Woman of Color—my own.

REFERENCES

Apfelbaum, E. P., Norton, M. I., & Sommers, S. R. (2012). Racial color blindness: Emergence, practice, and implications. *Current Directions in Psychological Science, 21*, 205–209. https://doi.org/10.1177/0963721411434980.

Chan, S. (1991). *Asian Americans: An interpretive history.* Boston: Twayne.

Fiske, S. T. (2000). Stereotyping, prejudice, and discrimination at the seam between the centuries: Evolution, culture, mind, and brain. *European Journal of Social Psychology, 30*(3), 299–322.

Fordham, S., & Ogbu, J. U. (1986). Black students' school success: Coping with the "burden of 'acting white.'" *Urban Review, 18,* 176–206. https://doi.org/10.1007/BF01112192.

Freire, P. (2000). *Pedagogy of the oppressed.* New York: Bloomsbury Academic. (Original work published in 1968.)

Glick, P., & Fiske, S. T. (1997). Hostile and benevolent sexism: Measuring ambivalent sexist attitudes toward women. *Psychology of Women Quarterly, 21,* 119–135. doi:10.1111/j.1471-6402.1997.tb00104.x.

Guthrie, R. V. (2004). *Even the rat was white: A historical view of psychology.* Upper Saddle River, NJ: Pearson Education.

Kim, C. J. (1999). The racial triangulation of Asian Americans. *Politics & Society,* 27(1), 105–138.

Macrae, C. N., & Bodenhausen, G. V. (2000). Social cognition: Thinking categorically about others. *Annual Review of Psychology, 51*(1), 93–120. doi: 0.1146/annurev.psych.51.1.93.

Maier, S. F., & Seligman, M. E. (1976). Learned helplessness: Theory and evidence. *Journal of Experimental Psychology: General, 105*(1), 3–46.

Marinari, M. (2005). Racial formation and success among Korean high school students. *Urban Review, 37,* 375–398. doi:10.1007/s11256-005-0019-x.

Rosenthal, R., & Jacobson, L. (1966). Teachers' expectancies: Determinants of pupils' IQ gains. *Psychological Reports, 16,* 115–118. doi:10.2466/pr0.1966.19.1.115.

Rowe, M. (1990). Barriers to equality: The power of subtle discrimination to maintain unequal opportunity. *Employee Responsibilities and Rights Journal, 3,* 153–163. https://doi.org/10.1007/BF01388340.

Russel, (1998). *The Color of Crime.* New York: New York University Press.

Sheurich, J. J., & Young, M.D. (1997). Coloring epistemologies: Are our research epistemologies racially biased? *Educational researcher,* 26(4), 4–16. https://doi.org/10.3102/0013189X026004004.

Sue, D. W., Bucceri, J., Lin, A. I., Nadal, K. L., & Torino, G. C. (2007). Racial microaggressions and the Asian American experience. *Cultural Diversity & Ethnic Minority Psychology, 13,* 72–81. doi: 10.1037/1948-1985.S.188.

Suzuki, B. H. (2002). Revisiting the model minority stereotype: Implications for student affairs practice and higher education. *New Directions for Student Services, 97,* 21–32. https://doi.org/10.1002/ss.36.

Swim, J. K., Aikin, K. J., Hall, W. S., & Hunter, B. A. (1995). Sexism and racism: Old-fashioned and modern prejudices. *Journal of Personality and Social Psychology, 68*(2), 199–214.

Tatum, B. D. (2017). *Why are all the black kids sitting together in the cafeteria? And other conversations about race.* New York: Basic Books.

Tran, N., & Birman, D. (2010). Questioning the model minority: Studies of Asian American academic performance. *Asian American Journal of Psychology, 1,* 106–118. doi: 10.1037/a0019965.

Tran, N., Nakamura, N., Kim, G. S., Khera, G. S., & AnhAllen, J. M. (2018). #APIsforBlackLives: Unpacking the interracial discourse on the Asian American Pacific

Islander and black communities. *Community Psychology in Global Perspective, 4*(2), 73–84. doi: 10.1285/i24212113v4i2p73.
Tuan, M. (1998). *Forever foreigners or honorary whites? The Asian ethnic experience today.* New Brunswick, NJ: Rutgers University Press.
Turner, C.S.V., González, J. C., & Wood, J. L. (2008). Faculty of color in academe: What 20 years of literature tells us. *Journal of Diversity in Higher Education, 1*(3), 139. doi: 10.1037/a0012837.

SECTION FIVE

ACTIVISM, RESISTANCE, AND PUBLIC ENGAGEMENT

TWENTY-FOUR

Spectacular Bodies

Racism, Pregnancy, and the Code of Silence in Academe

Julia H. Chang

El lenguaje silencioso engendra fuego.
El silencio se propaga, el silencio es fuego.
Era preciso decir acerca del agua o simplemente apenas nombrarla, de modo de atraerse la palabra agua para que apague las llamas del silencio.

Silent language engenders fire.
Silence self-propagates, silence is fire.
It was urgent to say something close to water or even to simply name her, in order to attract the word water so that she would extinguish the flames of silence.

(PIZARNIK, 2016, KINDLE, LOCATION 1224)

Silence is endemic in academe, its embers ravenous and consumptive. But the courageous act of speaking is enough to quell its fire. This essay explores the ways in which universities silence People of Color by rendering us spectacles. I deliberately play with the semantic polyvalence of spectacle as something unsightly whose ontological status relies on a visible regime of surveillance, as well as something extraordinary—as in spectacular—and thus, meant to be shown off, to glisten, to improve the image of the university. Here, I draw on Sara Ahmed's conceptualization of diversity as a "form of institutional polishing: when the labor [of diversity] is successful, the image is shiny" (2017, p. 102).

In interrogating the thorniness of visibility, I want to draw attention to the persistence of a colonial logic within universities that aligns diversity with conspicuousness, exhibition, and display. As universities launch campaigns for racial diversity and so-called inclusiveness, People of Color must negotiate the uneasy relationship between representational politics and spectacle. We are increasingly burdened with the labor of being hypervisible within universities and at the same time are expected to conform to norms defined by elite exclusivity and

DOI: 10.7330/9781607329664.c024

Whiteness. Often this means adhering to a code of silence. But what happens when our bodies get loud, so to speak?

In what follows, I recount how I came to file a hostile work environment and discrimination complaint as a faculty fellow in a prestigious research seminar. This arduous process was, tragically, bookended by two miscarriages. As is true of so many women and Women of Color, my struggle within the academy cannot be neatly disentangled from the challenges that I faced in my personal life. In fact, these concurrent events were jointly restrained by a culture of silence.

Before I continue, I feel it is important to acknowledge that I was in a unique a position to break this code of silence, since by the time I filed my complaint I had accepted a job offer elsewhere. Still, I felt reluctant to challenge the institution that had so graciously invited me to be a guest in its house. I worried that doing so would paint me as a "difficult person"—a label that clings too easily to Women of Color—and I feared this reputation would follow me to my next job. (Indeed, I believe that it has.) I still have lingering trepidation over putting this story in writing, and yet I feel it is necessary to resist the asphyxiating silence of academia. I hope that my story opens a window, ushering in a gush of fresh air.

THE IMPOSTER SYNDROME

I landed a tenure-track position at an Ivy League university right out of graduate school. When the euphoria faded, I was overwhelmed by a sense of survivor's guilt from a brutal job market. But mostly important, I felt like an imposter. For me, the imposter syndrome stems from my family's immigrant roots in this country. Painful memories of clumsily navigating Anglo-American culture are interwoven into my sense of not belonging. A professor once told me that the Argentine Jewish poet Alejandra Pizarnik never felt at home in any of the languages she spoke. This story pierced me to the core. I was born in the United States, and yet English still sometimes fails me. Actually, it often feels like *I* fail *it*. "What is a 'watershed moment'?" I recently asked my partner. "How do you pronounce 'penury'?" On rare occasions I stutter, as though my mouth were no longer my own but instead my mother's. I chew through my Rs like they are a piece of crusty bread unexpectedly jammed between my teeth. How ironic that I became a professor of Spanish language and literature. In the fourth grade, I found myself in a remedial class, taught bilingually in Spanish and English. Later in life, when I achieved fluency in Spanish, I found it provided me with a surrogate home. It gave me reprieve from English, and with it friendships with other children of immigrants. It did not, crucially, come with the same cultural baggage as Korean, my parents' native tongue. In Spanish I felt free; in Korean I was, much more so than in English, woefully inadequate.

Writer and translator Carina del Valle Schorske (2017) expounds on her relationship to "hand-me-down" Spanish, her grandmother's native tongue. *Ensimismada*, del Valle Schorske explains, is really just the feminine adjectival form of "en si mismo," meaning "in itself."

> Walter Benjamin once wrote that "content and language form a certain unity in the original, like a fruit in its skin." And shouldn't we all feel "a certain unity" at home in our own skin? For some, this feeling comes easily: If you and the world agree about who you are, if your social context has been designed to support your sense of individual coherence, if English is your first language and the language of the state, then you might not worry much about how you would be read in a foreign context. You might not worry about how you would translate. (del Valle Schorske 2017, n.p.)

The imposter syndrome causes me to feel precisely this: that I am not one with my skin, as though I had the encasing of one fruit and the flesh of another.[1] The long accumulation of racist acts, ranging from racially motivated violence to racist sexual harassment, and the more difficult to call out microaggressions, persistently confirm this. These acts of oppression have caused me to doubt myself, to fumble for words, and ultimately to buckle in the face of White-Anglo institutional power.

This sense of fraudulence reignited when I started graduate school and further intensified when I began my first academic job. Spanish no longer represented freedom and cross-cultural solidarity but became yet another arena in which I had to prove, but doubted, my competence. Moreover, I thought I would never be at home at an Ivy League institution, having completed my PhD at a public university. The committee that hired me was comprised entirely of Ivy grads. Most of my colleagues welcomed me with open arms, for which I was grateful, but in spite of, or perhaps because of, their enthusiasm, I felt stilted by a sense of indebtedness, which stemmed from this feeling of being an outsider.

These circumstances subtended an already institutionalized culture of silence that began to govern my way of being. There was a seemingly unshakable disciplinary force to this culture that appeared to have a well-understood code: *Keep your head down. Lie low, and just focus on your work.* An early workplace conflict drove home this point. A colleague questioned my intention to have a family and surmised that the department would not be supportive of me doing so. While the colleague later apologized and made clear that they were projecting their own anxieties around parenting while on the tenure track, at the time I was distraught by what felt to me like an invasive conversation.

I sought the advice of my official university mentor. Of course, the challenge here was raising this issue without revealing that I was planning to have children. Untenured faculty and graduate students go to great lengths to conceal this information for fear it might impact the perception of our tenurability or hireabilty. The mentor recommended that I let it go, suggesting that chairs do not want to know that faculty are not "getting along." I was stunned. I cleared up the matter on my own with my colleague and was glad I did so. But what this experience taught me early on was the imperative to stay silent in the face

1. I am reminded here of the nectarine, a hybrid of the peach and plum invented by Korean Americans in Hawaii.

of power. This culture of lying low, however, presents particular challenges to junior Faculty of Color who are made hypervisible, as the value of our "diversity" remains tethered to our visibility. This is a tough balance to strike when we are in precarious positions within the institution.[2] What a fine line to walk—to be visible but unheard, to be marked different, but conform.

SPECTACULAR BODIES

In *Talking Back*, bell hooks (1989) reflects on her reluctance to speak about the personal: "In all this talking I was concerned that I not lose myself, my soul, that I not become an object, a *spectacle*" (p. 3; my emphasis). The fear of becoming a spectacle, a feeling intimately tethered to my being a Woman of Color, is one that I felt deeply. Universities recruit People of Color to uphold an image of diversity, rendering our bodies conspicuous. But should we challenge institutional power with unruly speech, we risk making an unsightly spectacle of ourselves. We are expected to be visible but compliant—in a word: disciplined. For hooks, defiant speech becomes a matter of survival and self-preservation. Maintaining the code of silence is, in part, what allows for systematic forms of discrimination to persist in the university. As hooks describes it: "In the act of overcoming our fear of speech, of being seen as threatening, in the process of learning to speak as subjects, we participate in the global struggle to end our domination" (p. 18). Of course it would have been easier in some respects for me to stay silent, but I felt it necessary to risk making a spectacle of myself. Even as I write this story, I continue to challenge the pervasive code of silence that dominates academe. Audre Lorde (1984) reminds us that silence is not a form of protection. I respectfully disagree. Silence within universities *can* protect us from certain things, being labeled "difficult" for one, but it comes at a great cost: our self-worth, freedom, and dignity.

THE MASTER'S HOUSE

My second year on the job, I was a faculty fellow in a prestigious research seminar that was at best hostile to intellectual diversity, and at worst promoted racist beliefs and anti-Black pedagogy. In a seminar of a couple dozen participants, we were three People of Color: two of us faculty, none of us tenured, and all of us women. At our first meeting, a world-renowned, White male faculty member publicly intimidated me and would later continually dominate the room. After this first meeting, rarely did I have the courage to participate in discussion. Not long after, our meetings became entirely unbearable. The first particularly egregious incident occurred when the same faculty member asserted that "racial othering can be liberating rather than oppressive." In yet another instance he argued that race played no role in the transatlantic slave trade, noting that Romans had

2. Here I am thinking of David Palumbo-Liu's essay "Un-diversifying the Professoriate" (2017), in which he deals with the alarmingly low tenure rates for Faculty of Color.

enslaved other Romans, at which point the seminar leader confirmed that this latter comment was true. I naively assumed that such remarks would not be tolerated in a seminar housed by a center devoted to the teaching and research of women. I would certainly never allow this in my own classroom. But I was dead wrong. I reached out to a participant who explained that they "just ignored" the racist comments. The Women of Color clearly did not have the privilege to *just* ignore such remarks. Our bodies were obviously conspicuous in that space, and the racism affected us directly. Ultimately, whether participants actively pandered to the racist professor or silently remained complicit, the seminar cultivated a hostile environment that impacted the Women of Color in the room and what few allies we had. Lesson learned: You cannot trust those with institutional power to defend the vulnerable, no matter the gravity of the injustice.

In response to the inaction on the part of the seminar leaders, I met with the two other Women of Color and a few other participants, comprised mostly of graduate students, who were outraged. As a way to combat the racist, we sought to revise the group's reading list. Together we attempted but ultimately failed to have our research interests—race and gender—adequately represented in weekly discussions. As the participants with the most precarious status, our actions were risky, and our defiance did not rectify the injustice. Race and gender, we were repeatedly told, were not relevant to our focal themes—aesthetics and beauty. At that point, I began to feel I could no longer continue. Thankfully, my chair fully supported my decision to leave. Before withdrawing, I sought the advice of a colleague in the seminar. She advised me not to disclose my reasons for leaving, asserting that it would do more harm than good. Again, I stayed silent in the face of power and politely withdrew. In response to my decision, I was met with further hostility. The director threatened to hold my department financially responsible if I did not immediately return. In that instant, I was reminded of whose house I occupied. My body needed to be visible to polish the image of the seminar but emphatically compliant to earn my keep. (Tellingly, even after my name was removed from the seminar's website, my image continued to circulate in the center's promotional material.) Even after our initial act of defiance—challenging the content of the seminar—the power of the code of silence still loomed large, while the need for diversity remained.

Soon after, I met with the university's diversity officer, who was extremely compassionate in our first meeting. She emboldened me to explain, in writing, my decision to leave and informed me of my right to file a hostile work environment complaint. I began the former immediately. The complaint, however, seemed at once empowering and intimidating, as it entailed involving the dean of faculty and the provost. The fear of becoming a spectacle crept in again, as I knew my action would make this a public fight. I thought carefully about my options. There was the "easy" route: I could quietly return to the seminar and simply disengage. This option would protect me, so to speak, and save me time and labor, thereby allowing me to focus on my research and teaching. At the same time, doing so would be injurious to my sense of self. To return to the aforementioned bell hooks passage, I realized the importance of overcoming the fear of appearing threatening—this defiant act of speech was necessary for me to reclaim my personhood. Ultimately, I felt it important to have these acts of racism formally documented. (I later discovered that the research seminar had a long history of excluding the voices of women and People of Color.)

In the midst of this laborious tumult, I learned I was going to have a miscarriage, which made my ability to perform professionally suddenly all the more daunting. Silence and the fear of spectacle shaped this experience as well—I was afraid to publicly mourn, as I did not want to reveal that I was trying to conceive. Moreover, multiple medical practitioners informed me that my early miscarriage would be akin to a "heavy period," ignoring the devastating emotional and physical pain along with the taxing hormonal fluctuations that I would later learn accompany this kind of loss. Their dismissiveness led me to ignore self-care, and I continued with work as usual, filing my complaint and teaching my classes as I quietly miscarried. What agony . . .

In the United States, we do not have established rituals for mourning miscarriages, which our society treats as a mother's failure to reproduce, wrongly equating it with infertility, rather than the loss of a pregnancy. Moreover, the silence around miscarriages (and pregnancy) within the academy, combined with the failure to recognize the toll it takes on the mother's body, forecloses the possibilities of asking for medical leave and other forms of institutional support (Winegar 2016). As a result, many women feel ashamed and suffer in silence, and our careers pay a price.

As is true for so many Women of Color, my professional life could not be bracketed from the personal challenges that I faced due to my race and gender. Furthermore, all of this was amplified by the difficulty I experienced with my physical, emotional, and hormonal well-being. I could not adhere, for example, to the euphemistic phrase "work/life balance," which by definition implies that work and life are discrete entities. Quite frankly, it became difficult for me to show up to work and maintain a sense of steadiness at home. As one scholar describes her experience, "My body didn't cooperate with the need to do well in my job, stay sane, and get pregnant" (Winegar 2016, n.p.). I broke down into tears, for instance, when my office manager greeted me one morning. I also avoided many social interactions, feeling that I could neither mask my miscarriage nor safely disclose it. My world quickly shrank.

In academia, the boundaries between work and life are infamously blurred. But for some, maintaining a separation between the personal, the political, and the professional is not just a matter of individual choice. I, for one, could not simply leave my hormonal fluctuations at home, though I tried my best to hide them. The body is not this neutral vessel that can easily be controlled, sanitized, and tamed. Thus, while my miscarriages and the hostile work environment may appear to be disparate events, in fact, these concurrent challenges were joined by the pressures of visibility experienced by People of Color, and an all-pervasive culture of silence within the academy. Silence enables the persistence of workplace conflicts around race and gender, especially while on the tenure clock. Junior faculty, as I have mentioned, are told to lie low, while racial and gender hierarchies make it all the more risky to speak up. Similarly, silence also masks issues around pregnancy. As I noted earlier, untenured faculty and graduate students rarely speak openly about their plans to have children, fearing they will not be seen as serious scholars, and disclosing a miscarriage falls into the same camp. The mother to be, the mother in mourning—both are spectacular bodies.

THE MASTER'S TOOLS

Despite all of this, I labored forth with my complaint. Much to my surprise, the university failed to adhere to its own procedural guidelines for conducting an investigation. As the process dragged on for months, the diversity officer became less and less transparent in our exchanges. I requested to see the statements from the seminar leader and the director of the center that housed the seminar. I was told that while I had a to provide a written statement, they did not. I then asked the diversity officer for a copy of the investigation report and was denied. In my final days of employment and after much persistence, I received a letter from the provost, who determined that there was no proof of "systematic discrimination" or a "hostile work environment" in this research seminar. I later learned that not a single one of my witnesses had been contacted. In sum, there was no way of knowing whether an investigation had been conducted at all. This is what happens when you attempt to dismantle the master's house with the master's tools! One by one, all of the Participants of Color left the seminar. Even so, the administration denied any evidence of discrimination. This disavowal of racism perfectly illustrates what Sara Ahmed (2017) describes as an intersectional feminist experience: "When you become a feminist, you find out very quickly; what you aim to bring to an end some do not recognize as existing . . . So much feminist and antiracist work is the work of trying convince others that sexism and racism have not ended . . . Even to describe something as sexist and racist here and now can get you into trouble" (pp. 5–6). Unwilling to go quietly, once again, I contemplated different strategies to contest the botched investigation.

If my first act of bravery had been breaking the silence around the longstanding discrimination in this seminar, my second act of bravery was making the decision to end the institutional fight and take care of myself. The provost's decision arrived shortly before I went to the emergency room and learned that I would have a second miscarriage. This time I chose to make healing a priority. I wrote a frank letter to the provost, denouncing the acts of discrimination and the administration's active complicity and then made peace with this situation. Fortunately, during this time, I was supported by an amazing Woman of Color therapist who specialized in issues around race and racial discrimination and had a wealth of knowledge on grief. Eventually, under her care, I came to terms with the fact that I was mourning the loss of life and unable to thrive without help. At the same time, she affirmed my experience with racial oppression in the seminar. With her guidance, the support of my partner, and a few trusted friends, I began to reclaim my voice and my power. I did this by allowing myself to take up emotional space in public, something frowned upon in academia. I also broke the silence around my miscarriage and my hostile work environment by opening up with friends and other Faculty of Color from whom I had kept these things a secret. Speaking frankly with people about my loss *and* my complaint led me to discover an unexpected world of solidarity.

The code of silence in academe is unrelenting. I came up against it not once but several times: in my department, in the research seminar, with administrators, with well-meaning colleagues, and finally with the editors of a seemingly important and well-intentioned volume. An earlier version of this essay was initially selected for a collection of personal narratives that centered the voices of Women of Color in academia. I was shocked that I experienced the disciplinary force of silence from this volume's editors. To cite a few examples, they questioned whether enduring two miscarriages could be considered "brave." They asked me to separate my personal narrative (my miscarriage) from the professional one (the hostile work environment), noting that it was confusing to include both in the same essay. Finally, I was asked to share my emotions at various junctures, while pressured to eliminate "superfluous" details regarding the racist incidents I and others experienced. Coming up against another wall of silence, I ultimately stood my ground, pointing to the ways in which I felt my story was being censored and manipulated. The editors responded by stating my essay was no longer a good fit for the collection because the "trauma and fear" outweighed the "joy and strength." While I believe the editors had good intentions, the amalgamation of these comments eerily mirrors academia's sanitizing of diversity. It promotes a vacant celebration of differences that actively glosses over the painful ways in which universities make Faculty of Color peripheral to institutional life. I can't help but wonder if the editors were influenced by this fear of being made into a spectacle. This experience was a sobering reminder that the silencing effect of White institutional power can pop up where we least expect it.

RECLAIMING MY POWER

My story begins and ends with speech—making public that which ought to remain hidden—but it also begins and ends with my body. Academe rewards us for our minds, while diversity profits from our bodies. Our bodies, moreover, allow us to carry out the work that we do, and our bodies are often the first to give out. My miscarriages were devastating, but with each pregnancy and subsequent loss, I was able to connect with a reserve of physical resilience I had never known before. Eventually, I had a full-term pregnancy and delivered a healthy baby. This long trajectory of loss, resilience, and life left me in awe of my physical strengths. Speaking out against the injustices at work while dealing with emotional devastation and physical loss were spectacularly brave acts. But on a day-to-day basis, simply "showing up" and surviving this chaos were also incredible feats. If the experience of becoming a woman under patriarchy is to feel a deep sense of inadequacy in one's body (skin and flesh), these experiences radically challenged these ideas. They helped me confront my fear of becoming a spectacle by tapping into my body as a source of spectacular power.

While my defiant speech rendered me a spectacle in the university, speaking up in other spaces proved crucial to reclaiming my sense of strength and dignity. After I filed my university complaint, I began reaching out to faculty and Students of Color across campus, eventually establishing an important network of solidarity and support. Not surprisingly, I was not the only one who experienced this kind of injustice on campus. While the miscarriages were seemingly unrelated, I was equally afraid of sharing my story in this regard. Sometimes I had to ask my partner to speak on my behalf. But as we began to share our tragic news, we discovered a similar network of support and learned of a staggering number of women in our lives who had silently experienced pregnancy loss. In both instances, silence led to isolation, and finding these communities played a vital role in my path to healing.

By sharing this story, I hope I have offered some insight into the inner workings of silence and power and an affirmative account of resistance in and beyond the academy. Writing about these intertwined experiences of exclusion, silence, and spectacle challenges the ways in which universities uphold a division between private and public, personal and political. For many women and People of Color, maintaining neat boundaries between these two spheres is simply not a choice. As intersectional feminists have shown, the personal is always political. While my experiences by no means make me an expert on these issues, I close with some tips I wish I had known before I embarked on this journey. I hope they prove useful as you continue yours.

Things to be mindful of when filing a complaint (formal or otherwise) within the university:

Reach out to people you trust for advice—official mentors may not necessarily be trustworthy. Be wary if your confidants appear to minimize your experience. Trusted senior faculty members with institutional knowledge can offer strategies for navigating the administration. Do this with the understanding that confidentially can never be guaranteed.

The only person who is required to maintain confidentiality is the university ombudsperson. He or she cannot advocate or intervene on your behalf, but may provide you with useful information for navigating university channels.

Diversity officers cannot be blindly trusted to represent your best interests since they are members of the administration. I have a great deal of respect for their work and the challenges they face, but even the most well-meaning practitioners have limits to how they can protect faculty interests.

It is your right to use whatever formal channels the university offers to file complaints, but understand that these systems are at best flawed and at worst designed to protect the university. Filing complaints may not yield anything meaningful, but the university must keep a record of them. One immediate benefit for untenured faculty may be having documentation of the incident in question in your file.

Seek support elsewhere. Filing the complaint alone may not bring about any justice, and may add further insult to injury. It is important that you find solidarity, healing, and personal nourishment elsewhere. In my case, this meant sharing my story with a trusted community of Faculty and Students of Color on campus.

Know that you have other options available to you outside the university channels, such as legal recourse, an open letter, a petition, or collective action. These options are, of course, risky for junior faculty but are likely to put more pressure on the university.

There are therapists who specialize in issues pertaining to race. Having a therapist with this background proved crucial for legitimizing my experience and finding my voice.

For anyone going through a miscarriage:

Know that you are not alone. Approximately 15–20 percent of pregnancies in the United States end in miscarriage. If you are ready to open up to family, friends, and colleagues, you will begin to discover a network of people who have experienced some form of pregnancy loss—many of whom have suffered in silence.

For some, minimizing an early miscarriage allows them to move on, but this is not a universal experience. Knowing how common it is should not downplay the emotional and physical pain that can accompany this kind of loss. For me, it was important to allow myself adequate time to grieve and recover. Honor your experience.

Prioritize your health. Once I was able to recognize how taxing a miscarriage and pregnancy can be on one's body, I felt more emboldened to say no to others and yes to myself.

There are therapists who specialize in pregnancy loss and fertility issues. I found this kind of support crucial for helping me make sense of the grieving process, for which medical doctors did not prepare me.

REFERENCES

Ahmed, S. (2017). *Living a feminist life.* Durham: Duke University Press.

del Valle Schorske, C. (2017. October 26). Translation. *New York Times.* Retrieved from https://www.nytimes.com/2017/10/26/magazine/letter-of-recommendation-translation.html/.

hooks, b. (1989). *Talking back: Thinking feminist, thinking black.* Boston: South End.

Lorde, A. (1984). *Sister outsider: Essays and speeches by Audre Lorde.* Berkeley: Thinking Press.

Palumbo-Liu, D. (2017, May 18). Un-diversifying the professoriate. *Huffington Post.* Retrieved from https://www.huffingtonpost.com/david-palumboliu/un-diversifying-the-professoriate_b_10012544.html.

Pizarnik, A. (2016). *Extracting the stone of madness: poems 1962–1972.* (Y. Siegert, Trans.) New York: New Directions.

Winegar, J. (2016, November 29). The miscarriage penalty: Why we need to talk more openly about pregnancy loss in academe. *Chronicle of Higher Education.* Retrieved from http://www.chronicle.com/article/The-Miscarriage-Penalty/238526.

TWENTY-FIVE

Hashtag

Social Media as a Source for Developing Community

Meredith D. Clark

Communities of Black women can form a healing space, as bell hooks wrote in her 1993 book, *Sisters of the Yam: Black Women and Self Recovery*. The book was published the same year that Netscape introduced widespread internet access to those who could afford it, and its themes are still applicable to the networks of Black women in academia who have found comfort and collegiality among one another on social media, particularly Twitter.

I am one of them. Diagnosed with major depression in the second term of my first year as a PhD student, I turned to Twitter—specifically, Black Twitter—to connect with clusters of Black women intellectuals (both in and outside of academia) whose online company provided a public-in-private space for simultaneously processing my illness and the demands of my program outside the gaze of my classmates, instructors, and advisor, most of whom were not on the platform at the time. The collective experiences of Black women in media, education, and social justice, tweeted out in regular updates of 140 characters or fewer, created a footpath for me to learn more about the Black feminist epistemology that shapes my work and centers my personal ethos, and offered a bridge between the promise of a more successful life via higher education and the reality of pursuing that version of the American Dream in a fat Black body. In my case, the Twitter-based online communities of Black women and Women of Color I connected with during the four years of my PhD program were essential in providing the intellectual and emotional support I needed to finish the program with a well-researched and soundly structured dissertation, and with my dignity and sanity firmly intact.

Despite the inherent technocultural influences that allow Twitter's functions to be weaponized as a tool of misogynoir directed toward Black women online (Bailey & Trudy, 2018), the platform can also connect us to a digital system of wraparound support. It has the potential to create a digital commons for

DOI: 10.7330/9781607329664.c025

public acknowledgment of the Black woman's unique experiences in academia, structure channels for networked transmission of cultural knowledge about navigating academic professional and social cultures, and serve as a potential site for digital self-archiving work where valuable individual and community reflections can be drawn upon as sources of knowledge for our legacies in the post-digital age.

In this chapter, I offer a reflection of my own experiences as a Black woman academic who found an online community of practice and support on Twitter. Through online conversations that combine collective wisdom and resource sharing in a fairly open digital space, Women of Color in academia may find social media, particularly Twitter, to be a useful tool for constructing networks of emotional, social, and scholarly support.

FINDING COMMUNITY CONNECTION

At my core, I am and will always be a journalist, though that part of my occupation identity is somewhat shunned in academia in favor of my scholarly pursuits as a media studies researcher. Both of these professional identities drove my Twitter use. As an opinion writer, I joined the platform in 2008 to open the editorial board's closed-door conversations about political endorsements in local elections. Derided by my colleagues as a place where people went to post about their lunch, Twitter existed as a microblogging platform where individuals could broadcast messages to audiences of hundreds of thousands, if not millions, of people in real time. Within two years, it would figure largely as part of the internet communication toolkit activists in the Arab Spring, Occupy Wall Street, and later the Black Lives Matter movement would use to draw attention to political and social oppression in their communities. I attribute part of the strength of the Black Lives Matter movement as it existed online to Black Twitter, the same core network of Black users among whom I found a fascinating population for ethnographic research, and a digital support system of Black women as agents of knowledge (Collins, 2000).

Black Twitter, the focus of my dissertation, is a multifaceted online phenomenon of Black social media users discussing issues of concern to their respective communities. But for members of the emerging professoriate, this Twitter subculture—and others like it, bound within an intersectional matrix of structural power defined by race, class, gender identity, and more—offers a digital surrogate cohort and an interdisciplinary mentoring system that address critical information and socialization needs.

FINDING COMMUNITY CONNECTION

Two-thirds of the people who use social-networking platforms said they do so to stay in touch with friends and family members and, to a lesser extent, to build new connections (Smith, 2011, p. 2) And since the Pew Research Center for the Internet and American Life first started measuring the number of social media users by racial group in 2005, Black Americans have continued to outpace nearly every other racial group's representation on the platform (Pew Research Center, 2018). As of 2018, nearly a quarter of Black Americans who use the internet also use Twitter, and overlapping figures on race, gender, education, and income suggest that Black and Hispanic women on Twitter are well represented among folks with college degrees making more than $60,000. So it makes sense that one of the highest and best uses of social-networking platforms like Twitter for Women of Color in academia is to connect with one another to provide solidarity, guidance, and support. To complicate Sherry Turkle's argument that "we look to the network to defend us against loneliness even as we use it to control the intensity of our connections," (2011, p. 13), we can and have demonstrated how to use social media to abate our alienation in graduate programs, and control the extent to which our tokenization robs us of the intensity of grounded, connecting, loving community.

Like me, Jameelah Jones is an HBCU (historically Black college or university) graduate who found a support network on Twitter to be a microcosm of the environment she experienced at Paine College. "I was tweeting my way through all of it," she said of her time in a master's degree program at a large midwestern university.

> When you're vocal about needing something, someone sees you. It's the literal illustration of putting something out into the atmosphere . . . When I was trying to figure out a research topic, I would tweet my way through that. I was talking to my followers, really frustrated. I told Twitter I was going to drop out of school and get a job at the bank [*she laughs*]. *Everyone* was like, "No, please don't do this, absolutely not. You will not do this. One last push. You will do this if we have to push you across the finish line."

Social media gives us the ability to be vulnerable, to drop the mask in public in ways that we dare not attempt among members of our cohort or in front of faculty. Online, though, we can tell an imagined but very real community that we are struggling, and find encouragement. "A lot of people [online] are going to tell you that you're not alone. I think the institution tries to teach you that you're alone in your experiences, and therefore if you push back against things, no one will be behind you," Jones said. "I still have people on Twitter saying, 'Write the paper, write the abstract, why would you not?' Twitter helps you find people that study what you study. So you know that you're not alone academically and politically" (personal communication, 2018).

BLACKADEMIC TWITTER: THEORY AND PRACTICE

Early cyberculture studies identified an imagined audience in the tradition of imagined communities—networks of individuals fostering weak social ties online via communication practices that helped them to feel like influential individuals within a larger collective (Marwick & boyd, 2011). On Twitter, where Black users outpaced other groups by nearly a third for the better part of a decade (Pew Research Center, 2018), these practices were particularly noteworthy. There, in 140 characters or fewer (pre-2018), Black technologists abandoned the code-switching practices that often govern our conversations in mixed company offline. Through the sheer strength of our numbers, we influenced digital discourse through our everyday interactions, punctuating them with hashtags, pictures, pithy phrases, memes, and gifs as we created Black digital culture that provided real-time counternarratives of our own lived experiences in the United States and beyond.

Black women in academia gathered around the #SayHerName hashtag as we collectively grieved #SandraBland, another college-educated woman whose death haunts us, in part because, as so many women I've spoken to have said, "That could have been me." We discussed our experiences as first-generation working-class women for whom being #BlackAtWork meant navigating both corporate and academic culture. In proclaiming #ILookLikeAProfessor, a hashtag created by three Women of Color in 2015, we engaged in "networked vanity" (Pham, 2015, p. 244), offering curated images of ourselves to demonstrate diversity in the professoriate.

By posting a selfie along with two of my friends and colleagues, I saw my participation in the hashtag as a strategy for providing multiple images of what a professor might look like today: women in varying shades of brown, different sizes, rocking our natural hair and enjoying life. Online, these selfies demonstrated that we were part of a larger community of Women of Color in academia, strengthening our ties across time and space. We saw each other, recognized each other, and invited others to do the same. Through the hashtag, I found amazing Women of Color, queer folks, and "Others" to connect with as part of my Blackademic online neighborhood. These connections were the mid-level point of the social ties that supported me online. Through my personal community, academic community, and the meta-network of Black Twitter itself, I found sustenance for naming every obstacle I encountered in graduate school: depression, isolation, alienation, and the like.

HOW BLACK TWITTER CREATES AND CONNECTS COMMUNITIES

Black Twitter's first and most intimate level of connection is personal communities. These are reciprocal (I follow you, you follow me) online relationships between users on the platform who are usually preacquainted via offline spaces. The second level of community connection are "thematic nodes," clusters of people who find one another through online conversations about topics and issues of interest the users return to again and again. One research participant, @Karnythia, referred to them as "neighborhoods." Another participant, Allison, described exactly how her core neighborhood was designed: "Anyone on Twitter who is Black and in a PhD is getting followed by me." Everyone who uses Twitter regularly (read: daily) has one or more neighborhoods they belong to.

The third level of connection, the meta-network, is what most media outlets and regular folks are referring to when they talk about "Black Twitter," used this way as a digitized heuristic similar to "the Black community." Both indicate a collapse of Black existence and culture that allows Black people to be more easily defined and read in the dominant worldview. The connections at this level are the most ephemeral, linking together Black-identifying individuals and the online neighborhoods they belong to, like Voltron, when an incendiary event sends us to the internet to tweet our frustrations. As hashtags and algorithmically recognized phrases are repeated among our numbers, our sentiments trend and ignite mass media's agenda-setting function, to kick off a new round of media coverage.

In a uses-and-gratifications framework, Blackademics' use of Twitter is governed by a series of needs-fulfillment activities: *information seeking*, such as advice on how to write personal statements for our grad-school applications, searching out scholarship by People of Color, and collective resource management in bartering access to paywalled journal articles; *collective identity maintenance*, including sharing perspectives on our mental health struggles and the microaggressions we manage on a daily basis in order to remain productive and in our right minds as we balance self-care and self-preservation with our studies; *entertainment* through participation in second-screening and social viewing of television and web-based media with others; *social interaction* in everyday conversations about our lives as graduate students, professors, and academic-adjacent folks; and *escape* in the simple act of using Twitter instead of attending to other tasks, like grading papers or working on an R&R. At the end of each term, my own Twitter account, populated with neighborhoods split among Faculty Members of Color, former students, and news professionals, helps pull back the veil about what professors *really* do in our professional work.

HELP IN A HASHTAG

On Twitter, hashtags have been useful in indexing our conversations, carrying them beyond the healing places of meeting groups like the Sisters of the Yam, while serving as a beacon to connect users who have the same mindset and concern about particular issues. In the process of Black digital resistance, they are critical tools for signaling information and belonging to other users, and for highlighting conversations of note to social media users outside our communities who need to learn more about our experiences.

During the rise of the Black Lives Matter movement, college students across the country adapted hashtag protest techniques to create online conversations about the higher-ed experiences of People of Color to foster collective visibility unseen since the affirmative action debates of the late 1990s.

VISIBILITY

By searching out hashtags such as #BlackGradLife, #SisterPhD, or #FirstGenDocs, users can locate communities developing shared meaning through talking about the issues and themes the hashtag represents, add their personal perspectives, and in some cases, offer others suggestions and strategies as a form of support. Hashtags such as #ConcernedStudent1950, which accompanied tweets about racial harassment and abuse experienced by students at the University of Missouri, were instrumental in drawing attention to student activism on the campus, including a hunger strike and sit-in. #BeingBlackatMichigan and #BlackatYale called out hostile conditions at predominately White institutions (PWIs), aligning the intimate experiences of a generation of Black students with racial justice work to demand change on campus. Professors, too, took note of hashtag activism as a means of disrupting normative beliefs about who belonged where on campus.

For me, #NoShame, the hashtag created by activist Bassey Ipki and eventually used as part of the Siwe Project's #NoShameDay, was one of the first digital tools I used to begin talking about my struggle with depression and anxiety in my graduate program. Engaging in the process of Black digital resistance, those of us who tweeted with the hashtag when Bassey first spoke about her own battle with bipolar disorder on Twitter were able to identify with her experience, affirm one another, and eventually find vindication (via the production of resources and alternative coping mechanisms) as the hashtag was affixed to links and recommendations for professional mental health workers, books, and other tools to help us campaign for eliminating the stigma of mental illness within Black communities. Being able to talk with other Black women about the dilemma of being caught between imposter syndrome, which pushes us to perform academic feats of mastery, and depression, which makes it difficult for me to perform the basic series of tasks (sleep, shower, eat, dress, drive, speak) culminating in attending class, meetings, and social events on time and with some semblance of presence, was the bridge I needed as I searched for a culturally competent counselor in my area.

While my institution provided a generous six hours of mental health counseling for graduate students as part of our benefits package, I found online contact with other Women of Color who had experienced similar hardship to be exponentially more useful than spending my campus health therapy sessions trying to manage the details of my family history so as not to alarm the campus therapist (fresh out of grad school herself) assigned to my treatment. The hashtag signaled that others were there: listening, sympathetic, and even experiencing similar struggles.

FINDING COMMUNITY AND HEALING SPACES ONLINE

To paraphrase Roxane Gay's (2014) take on a "typical first-year professor" in our collective experience:

> We go to school for a very long time and get some degrees and finally move to a very small town in the middle of a cornfield. We leave someone behind. We tell ourselves we have worked so hard we can't choose a partner over a career. We want to choose the partner over the career . . . Many of our students have never

had a black teacher before. We are the only black professor in our department. This will probably never change for the whole of our career . . . We are used to it. We wish we weren't.

Our "neighborhoods" on Twitter are places where we can discuss the politics of academia without (too much) interference. They can serve as an interactive healing place for many Women of Color who find themselves isolated from communities of care as a consequence of choosing the academic's life. Within these self-selected networks we find space to compare notes on our respective experiences, to ask questions without shame, and to learn about the dynamics of what I call the #TenureTrackHustle: strategies and practices for making the recipe of research, teaching, and service plain rather than continuing to perpetuate the myth of scholarly alchemy that leads so few Scholars of Color to tenure.

POLITICS OF CITATION

Conversations and resource sharing around the politics of citation are one way Black women are using Twitter to bring Black girl magic into academia. #CiteASista, a hashtag created by Brittany Williams and Joan Collier in 2016, subverts the invisible college by equipping academics on Twitter to share their own work and that of Black women scholars using the hashtag. Similarly, #ScholarSunday, an academic spin on #FollowFriday, through which users post who they're following and why, creates greater visibility among Researchers of Color. Created by @raulpacheco, an environmental politics scholar who has written prolifically on academic productivity, the #ScholarSunday hashtag is another tool that Women of Color on Twitter are using to amplify the voices of their mentors, colleagues, and students. I learned of the hashtag via @jentrification, a user who studies and practices public relations. And through the hashtag, I found womanist biblical scholar @drnyashajunior, among others.

Twitter also allows us to collectively manage resources, and reallocate our good fortune among colleagues who lack access to certain knowledge banks. In light of restricted access to certain databases, and consequently journal articles, some academics have taken to employing a call-and-response crowdsourcing approach to finding the materials they need to do their work. The opposite of self-promotion of new and relevant publications, when we log onto Twitter and ask if "anyone has access to . . ." we engage in a useful form of cooperative economics.

The she-ain't-heavy, she's-my-sister attitude among Black women academics who share their stories of navigating academia's toxic relationships and structural obstacles is a worldview in diametric opposition to the individualism espoused in our programs through coded language that discourages asking too many questions as "hand-holding." Structured conversations through hashtags created by Academics of Color, like Bennie Niles's #TrynaGrad, are often held on a weekly basis, and cover everything from the details of conducting a systematic literature review to learning how to read faculty interactions in order to avoid conflicts among committee members to developing a strategic approach to conference attendance and involvement that will ultimately produce relationships with potential intellectual sponsors whose contributions (in the forms of job-market and later tenure-review recommendations), a mix of technical and practical skills that are essential to our long-term success. Digital knowledge curation also includes self- and cross-promotion of the scholarship of other Academics of Color. #BlackTwitterstorians, for instance, chronicles the work of Black historians, and is a mechanism for holding important conversations about historical context around contemporary crises, and for introducing wider audiences to Black scholars and their work.

RISK MANAGEMENT

While Twitter may provide space to create and curate an online "healing place" for Women of Color in academia as well as a repository for our collective knowledge, I am steadfast in my belief that there is no *safe* space online for women color. High-profile scholars, including Anthea Butler, Dayna Chatman, Saida Grundy, Tressie McMillan Cottom, have found themselves subjected to racial hatred and abuse online related to their work and simple existence as Black women in White spaces. Butler and Grundy became targets of online hate after their tweets critiquing White men's hubris were picked up in conservative blogs, prompting an onslaught of harassment. Butler, a tenured religious studies professor at the University of Pennsylvania, was on sabbatical when her criticism of a film mocking Muslims was amplified by a right-wing blogger (Butler, 2012). In Grundy's case, online statements about White, college-age men being identified as a "problem population" were recirculated after she was hired by Boston University (Grundy, 2017). The institution was silent for days as the online maelstrom raged around the pre-tenure professor, and colleagues rallied behind the #ISupportSaida hashtag on Twitter. Chatman was forced offline for a few weeks when her dissertation research on Black Twitter and the ABC television show *Scandal* was improperly framed in a press release by her graduate institution, which erased her from the project altogether (Chatman, 2014). Cottom takes down trolls, critics, and antagonistic liberal White folks on a daily basis via her Twitter feed.

The propensity for unchecked abuse, ranging from persistent online vexation to outright threats of violence on Twitter, can be overwhelming, and institutions remain poorly equipped to handle it and provide support for their faculty members, particularly those of us whose work centers race, gender, and social justice.

Jameelah, who engaged in online activism while finishing her master's degree, said she was warned by others on campus to "watch what you tweet," as she reacted to hashtag memorials and crises raised during the Black Lives Matter movement in 2014. "I had to really commit to the idea that any academic space that did not like what I tweeted, I wouldn't want to be here. I had to let go of that carrot of elite institutions," she said (personal communication, 2018).

We are also right to be concerned about governmental, social, and corporate surveillance, like Meghan, a PhD student who planned a much-desired pregnancy during her PhD program. "On my first Mother's Day, and I almost posted on Twitter about how I'd waited for this miracle baby. I thought about how future employers might be biased against me because I'm a mother," she said (personal communication, 2018).

Still, as a critical cyberculture and journalism studies scholar, I encourage us to take up space everywhere we go—including online. Personal blogging creates Black digital enclaves where we can largely control the narrative about our lived experiences (Steele, 2018), and may ultimately lead to opportunities for engagement in public scholarship on more wide-reaching platforms. Engagement on social media allows us to connect with others and bring them into our more private spaces online, and, if we choose, into our personal lives away from the internet.

LEAVING A DIGITAL LEGACY

No one can know how long Twitter, as a platform, will last, and the chilling reality of social media exploitation by corporate entities, foreign agents, and individuals surveilling the online activities of their students and peers all pose clear and distinct threats to the creation of online communities that support Women of Color in the academy. I offer two sets of suggestions—one technical, one practical—for digital citizens who wish to pursue graduate education and those already working in academia.

First, we must recognize that creation of intellectual property hosted on third-party sites and servers is essentially digital sharecropping. In a single paragraph, Twitter asserts that users "retain [their] rights to any content [they] produce" while operating under a license that allows the company to "make your Content available to the rest of the world and allow others to do the same." In short, nothing we create on the platform is truly ours. It can be coopted by other scholars, companies, and the public at large. It can be removed at any time. Digital data is ephemeral, and can be corrupted, confiscated, or erased altogether. One participant in my early research, Genie Lauren, learned this firsthand when her Twitter account—which she successfully used in 2014 to block publication of a book about the acquittal of George Zimmerman, the White Hispanic man who killed Trayvon Martin, an unarmed Black teenager, in Sanford, Florida, in 2012—was deleted by the company without warning or explanation in early 2018. A following of more than 31,000 people, an archive of more than 530,000 tweets spanning ten years—gone without any recourse (Lauren, 2018).

I also encourage those of us who use social media for any purpose to consider the implications of such investment in terms of creating our own digital archives. Though not all online conversation rises to the level of discourse, and not all discourse is worthwhile to our academic and professional lives, the data we create via social media engagement demands that we think critically about who gets to preserve our online legacies, how that preservation will be carried out, and what legacy of cultural knowledge about Black women's experiences in academia have been captured on these platforms. Digital Archivists of Color take note of the importance of the letters, jottings, and personal papers of scholars including Zora Neale Hurston, Anna Julia Cooper, and Audre Lorde. Their authors might have considered these just reflective writing, but they have survived and been preserved as contributions to a Black feminist epistemology. That the written reflections of Black intellectual women of earlier generations, especially those with less recognizable names, may have been lost due to disregard for Black intellectual capability and our own ignorance of their importance, should urge us to consider how we will store our data in this present age. How should we engage in the practice of self-archiving our online lives and the texts that capture our sense-making on digital social media?

As I stress to every student I teach, "ownership" of one's name online is a fundamental concern in digital self-preservation of data. Buy your name as a web domain. Buy every permutation of it you can think of, and keep these records up to date. Consider purchasing space on a server to store your digital data, including the seemingly banal online conversations you've participated in via Twitter. Make a point to regularly download archives of your online data.

Second, as queer Black archivists have recommended, I encourage us to think about all of our online activities in terms of "digital legacy making," which Neal and Broadnax (2018) describe as "intentional centering of the individual and the memories, experiences and histories created in the digital space, influenced by four lenses of the digital self: personal, communal, social, and professional." The knowledge we're creating on Twitter and other digital and social media platforms may seem ephemeral, but in the same way that the personal writings of scholars before us offer some of our most treasured insights, our contributions today represent thousands of perspectives as data points that may one day prove invaluable to the scholars who will follow us. Taken together, the digital media tapestry of our networked social experiences as Black women scholars will serve as witness to how we collectively navigated a hostile system, leaving a legacy of . . . for our students, our children, and even for ourselves. As one of hooks's students mused, "Healing occurs through testimony, through gathering together everything available to you and reconciling" (hooks, 1993, p. 17).

REFERENCES

Bailey, M., & Trudy aka @thetrudz. (2018). On misogynoir: Citation, erasure, and plagiarism. *Feminist Media Studies, 18*(4), 762–768. doi: 10.1080/14680777.2018.1447395.

Butler, A. (2012, September 13). Opposing view: Why "Sam Bacile" deserves arrest. *USA Today.* Retrieved from https://www.usatoday.com.

Chatman, D. (2014). In reply: My reflections on comments about our research on Black Twitter. Retrieved from https://dchatman3.wordpress.com/blog/.

Collins, P. H. (2000). Black feminist thought: Knowledge, consciousness, and the politics of empowerment (2nd ed.). New York: Routledge Press.

Gay, R. (2014). *Bad feminist*. New York: HarperCollins.

Grundy, S. (2017). A history of white violence tells us attacks on black academics are not ending (I know because it happened to me). *Ethnic and Racial Studies*, 40(11), 1864–1871.

hooks, b. (1993). *Sisters of the yam: Black women and self-recovery*. New York: Routledge.

Lauren, G. (2018). *Theroot.com*. Retrieved from https://www.theroot.com/twitter-stole-from-me-and-they-can-steal-from-you-too-1823548501.

Marwick, A. and boyd, d. (2011). I tweet honestly, I tweet passionately: Twitter users, context collapse, and the imagined audience. *New Media & Society*, 13(1), 114–133. Retrieved from https://doi.org/10.1177/1461444810365313.

Neal, J., and Broadnax, M. (2018). Preserving our digital selves. Paper presented at the National Forum on Ethics & Archiving the Web, New York.

Pew Research Center. (2018). Social Media Fact Sheet. Washington, DC. Retrieved from https://www.pewresearch.org/internet/fact-sheet/social-media/. 5 February 2018.

Pham, M.T. (2015) "I click and post and breathe, waiting for others to see what I see": On #FeministSelfies, outfit photos, and networked vanity. *Fashion Theory, (19)*2, 221–241.

Smith, A. (2011). Why Americans use social media. Pew Research Center. Retrieved from http://www.pewinternet.org/2011/11/15/why-americans-use-social-media/.

Steele, C. K. (2018). Black bloggers and their varied publics: The everyday politics of black discourse online. *Television & New Media*, 19(2) 112–127.

Turkle, S. (2011). *Alone together: Why we expect more from technology and less from each other*. New York: Basic Books.

TWENTY-SIX

My Tenure Denial

Grace Park

A tenure denial is made to seem as if it is the sole responsibility of the person denied tenure, but it is also evidence of a department's and institution's collective failure to adequately mentor, integrate, and help their junior colleague navigate the hidden rules, culture, and politics of their specific institution. It is ultimately a shared responsibility, but because the process is not transparent, systemic patterns of bias may never be addressed, thereby perpetuating the myth of meritocracy in academia and rendering the challenges Women of Color face in the tenure process invisible.

Yet some senior colleagues pride themselves on the fact that there was no formal system of mentoring when they came up for tenure. They do not acknowledge that as White men they were already part of an old boys' network, and that White women can also create their own parallel structures. They believe they did it on their own. They find requests for mentoring unnecessary. They believe that if mentoring is offered, it is done equitably across junior faculty, and that it is not dependent on race, gender, or sexual orientation. What they fail to understand is that mentoring is also informal and based on socialization, which can be quite subjective, arbitrary, and influenced by unconscious bias. Just as there is implicit bias with respect to hiring and which students we take on as mentees or encourage to apply to graduate school or fellowships, there are inequalities in this informal mentoring and socializing "system." These inequities contribute to deepening gaps in advancement and sense of belonging between White and non-White junior.

Color blindness perpetuates the myth of meritocracy and the idea that persons who get tenure do so because they worked hard and deserved it. Color blindness allows White straight men to fail to recognize that there are certain affinities and relationships built over drinking, sports, having children in the same school district, and shared notions of what they think is valuable research.

DOI: 10.7330/9781607329664.c026

I was not given the same kind of attention and informal mentoring that my White junior colleagues received. Later, as I spoke up about inequities in workload and mentoring that I believed were a result of bias, and when I asked for discussions for more inclusive pedagogy and practices, my department became more hostile toward me.

The myth of meritocracy can produce and perpetuate a system of exclusion and even violence against Women of Color who dare to speak up about the inequalities in workload or when they advocate for themselves and their students in matters of race or bias. Those in power were not willing to admit that I might experience academia differently as a minority woman. They truly seemed committed to this idea that academia is color-blind and based on merit. Accommodations or requests from me were seen as requests for exceptions and accommodations for the minority woman. There was no compassion or understanding that I would experience being on the tenure track differently. They saw academia only through their own experiences as White Americans.

In this chapter, I reflect on my experience as an Asian American woman in a predominantly White institution (PWI) in a rural location. I the hope that my experience will motivate well-intentioned White senior colleagues and administrators to consider the ways in which mentoring can also be subject to racial bias and favoritism. I also hope that this reflection alerts Women of Color in larger multicultural universities and cities to the realities of living in a mostly White rural area and working in a PWI, such that they may go from being part of a majority to a highly visible minority. Some of us are drawn to these locations by the job security and benefits, especially after years of surviving as poor graduate students in cities where we could barely afford the cost of living and housing, so we leap to take these tenure-track offers with great salary and benefits. We look forward to being able to purchase a home and actually provide for our families and help our parents on one salary—*but think twice*. Think very hard about the importance of community, inclusion, and the daily toll of dealing with your difference. Think about having to justify and explain your existence and credentials on and off campus, especially to the people you have to see almost every day.

Tenure denial is a shared and collective responsibility. Institutions must bear some of the responsibility for the damage and the violence that can be done to Women of Color who dare to claim a stake in the culture and practices of their institution and who try to make positive changes that will benefit others. The systems and practices that conceal and protect the ways in which senior colleagues can shirk their responsibilities must be investigated and accounted for as well. All parties must reflect on what can happen.

HOW COLLEAGUES SET ME UP FOR FAILURE

I did not know that there was bias and favoritism in mentoring by race and cultural fit until three junior colleagues were hired after me: two White men (one who left only after a year), a White woman, and a biracial (half White and half Asian) woman who identified as and passed for White. It became evident that my experiences were not comparable to the way my senior colleagues welcomed and socialized with my junior colleagues. There was a significant deficit in how I was mentored in comparison to my junior colleagues. I learned that who is mentored is subjective, and influenced by culture, race, class, gender, sexual orientation, and even geographical affinities.

White senior colleagues and chairs often search for junior colleagues who are reproductions of themselves and what they deem to be a good fit for the profession, their department, and institution. In my former department, that meant that a certain type of research is favored (quantitative American politics and international security), and a certain kind of person is deemed fit for leadership (masculine and domineering). In a department with several Americanists who are male and two women who are openly lesbian, I was in a culture that seemed accepting of sexual minorities, if they were White women who were more masculine presenting and performing, but not of racial minorities. Women who succeeded in my department were women who behaved much like the older White men.

The social life of the department revolved around those who had more in common than not. I have heard and witnessed comments and jokes by both senior and junior colleagues about minority students and job candidates that revealed how cultural fit and professionalism are defined in ways familiar and comfortable to my colleagues' Whiteness, their Americanness, and their privileges.

I was hurt to see a newly hired biracial Woman of Color leverage her Whiteness for professional advancement. She saw me as liability. She did not want to have anything to do with me and my advocacy for Students of Color, despite my sincere efforts to try to mentor her, be her ally, and welcome her to my community of minority students and staff. I learned that just because someone shares half your heritage it does not mean she is your ally, shares your views on race, or is willing to take the risks you are to speak up for them. Her seemingly internalized racism would come out in hurtful jokes and comments about people from our culture. She likened us to animals. Because she did not make race an issue, as I did with White colleagues, she was favored and supported by my White senior colleagues and students (especially by those in athletics and the fraternities), while I was fighting to advocate for marginalized students on campus.

She was the good half Asian. I was the full-on Asian, ethnic Asian, and Asian American troublemaker complaining about the lack of this or that in the department and more aligned with students than faculty. She actually said during a department meeting that intellectual diversity was more important than racial diversity. Her statements fit with the older White men in the department who resented being told to revise their job ads and try harder to diversify their applicant pool. She chose their side and belittled me for proposing something else. This half–Asian American woman ended up being one of the most conservative voices in the department. She was rude, abrasive, and condescending to me. There is a saying that not all skin folk are your kinfolk, and that was certainly true. It did not help that she was very masculine in her demeanor and looked out only for herself. I went to all of her research talks, but she never showed up to mine. I tried to promote sisterhood, but she treated me as if I was some kind of competition, which was totally unnecessary since we are in different subfields and work on very different issues, but she made her choice. I felt completely isolated in the department.

My White senior colleagues collaborated with and even published with my junior colleagues. They left me on my own and dismissed me when I asked about impact factors and alternative venues for my work, which is more interdisciplinary. This is informal mentoring—regular meetings to discuss research, drafting, submitting, and revising work and initiating junior colleague into the publication process. I was taught how to write a good dissertation, but I was not aware of the hidden rules about publishing and gaming it, not only to find the right venue, but to find one that can publish your work quickly. My White senior colleagues co-published with my White male junior colleague. Other junior colleagues got to understand how the institution works, especially with respect to fitting in and navigating the culture, politics, and administration. They received greater hands-on advice about the journal publication process and were given regular feedback and encouragement. They had their choice of mentor while I was actively fighting for any mentorship.

I learned that mentoring is based on friendship, and that is how you fit in my former department. I was not comfortable being friends with my colleagues because I never felt White, masculine, or American enough for them. I now understand that it was on me to have tried harder and to have looked more closely at the culture of the institution and department before moving across country. I also thought that you did not need to be friends with your colleagues as long as you were each doing your work and doing it well. However, they were looking to hire and retain people they liked and wanted to hang out with and be friends with for a long time. That is why sharing geographical and cultural origins and being part of a familiar culture informs who fits, and who is supported, mentored, sponsored, and promoted. For that department, it meant being quiet about comments that were racist and insensitive to people like me.

I also understand that it was up to me to be more aggressive and proactive about how I integrated and presented myself to these senior colleagues. But frankly, it became harder as I experienced more and more microaggressions. I heard racist comments in department meetings about Students of Color and Job Candidates of Color. I think our differences of opinion on matters of race made it harder for me to fake politeness. It got to a point where we just worked and shared space in a department; we were becoming factionalized. I became isolated. My classes were all scheduled on Monday and Wednesday mornings, while almost everyone else taught on Tuesdays and Thursdays. Even if that was unintentional at first, a good leader would have stepped in, but my chair, who is also lesbian, did nothing to foster community and belonging, but instead further isolated me while favoring her protégé.

I take responsibility for my part in the lack of socialization and the increasing isolation within the department. I understand that I was punished for choosing not to participate in the department culture of drinking, playing poker, and being part of conversations about football in the hallway. Even White male visiting faculty were also treated much more warmly. After a while, I became resentful that no one was asking about the region I was studying, my family, or my world. Because they could not relate to me, perhaps it was easier to just avoid engaging with me and revealing how ignorant they could be about race, immigrants, or people like me who speak English as a second language.

I could have tried harder, but I resented that it was I who had to do the work to try to fit a culture that didn't necessarily share my values about inclusion and equity. I was not the docile model minority Asian woman, by any means, which I think also made them uncomfortable. I did not match the stereotypes. Instead I was vocal, created initiatives, and took leadership in promoting inclusion during my several years at the institution, something that to my knowledge they had not done before my arrival because it was not really a part of their consciousness or a priority to them.

TENURE DENIAL

So my tenure denial should not have been a surprise. I had directly confronted and challenged colleagues on their microaggressions. I had advocated and mediated on behalf of students who came to me with their frustrations and concerns over how my White colleagues treated them. And I was active and took on leadership roles to change hiring practices and to push for greater inclusion. This "activism," in my colleagues' eyes, was a distraction from research. I was told, "We are scholars, not activists," but we can be both. My scholarship was demeaned and devalued, with colleagues openly disparaging the entire region of my work and ignoring the fundamental tenets of my research methodology when reviewing my work. I was told that North Korea was a fad and that I would not be able to fill two sections of a class on East Asian politics, which revealed some serious ignorance about Asia's role in the twenty-first century.

These colleagues literally closed their doors on me when I walked down the hallway. Over the preceding year they had effectively stopped talking to me and inviting me to departmental and social gatherings. I think that was because I dared to ask questions and challenge certain practices and mindsets (e.g., bringing race into discussions, trying to find a more diverse pool of applicants, asking that we look more carefully at the distribution of labor, especially in mentoring).

The half–Asian American woman emailed me job announcements the week of my annual review. I emailed her and asked if she knew something I did not know, because I was working to get tenure. I had become so used to the way the others dismissed me and my research interests, and the lack of mentoring and communication, that I understood that tenure was not guaranteed. I thought it might be a close vote. For months leading into the fall of my tenure submission my department did not even have a chair, and all my attempts to secure senior guidance were rebuffed.

While I believed in my work, I knew that I had not been as productive as I had wanted to be because of the work I was doing for Students of Color. I understood that a case could and would be made against me. However, I had seen people win tenure in previous years with fewer publications in similarly established venues, so I thought I had a chance. It is hard for me to look at the White colleagues who received tenure who did not publish as much as I did, and who did nothing for Students of Color. The chair wrote in my tenure letter that she regularly mentored me and met with me "one to two times a year." Some interest in my work and treating me courteously might have helped.

FILING A GRIEVANCE

After my tenure denial, I filed an appeal and then a grievance, partly to force the department to reevaluate its practices. I wanted to ensure that misrepresentations and errors were corrected with documentation, and that evidence that had been deliberately excluded would now be on the record. I appealed and filed a grievance to set the record straight and to expose my department to the provost and other committees. I no longer wished to have tenure and work with such people after I saw what they wrote and how they tried to push me out, but I had to make sure others would see what they had tried to do to me.

THE PAIN OF THE TENURE DECISION

Two things surprised me. The first was the indifference of the Professional Standards Committee to my external reviewers. All of my external reviewers recommended tenure for me, and five of them were very supportive of my work. It was validating and gratifying to find support from the field, but I was surprised to find that it had made no impression on the committee's decision. The second surprise was that my department members, with one exception, had submitted letters that not only demonstrated a coordinated effort against my candidacy, but were also filled with inaccuracies, easily identifiable misrepresentations of fact and, in three cases, doctored evidence. The lengths to which my colleagues were willing to go in order to rid themselves of me stunned and paralyzed me, and still does. I was immobilized by the way in which they denied me tenure—with letters full of inaccuracies that could have easily been verified had anyone actually worked with me in putting my file together. The lack of socialization, communication, and inclusion was showing its effects in my dossier. There were things I did not know to include or explain. For instance, it was so obvious to me that my publications were peer-reviewed. I did not understand how it could even be questioned or that they would claim so confidently that my work had not been peer-reviewed. There were misunderstandings and misrepresentations that were small in themselves but were blown up as evidence of my incompetence. That hurt me the most—-to realize that my colleagues did not know me at all, and that they would not give me the benefit of the doubt as they would to a White junior colleague. Instead, I was just deemed incompetent.

Despite how things ended there for me, I had started out strong and had a great first year and a good second year. I had an excellent first annual review and teaching observations. Then I had a very good interim review, in which the only warnings I was given were to work harder on returning graded assignments sooner (an issue I fixed the next semester by giving shorter assignments and using grading rubrics), and to publish articles instead of book chapters. However, I was told that I was on the right track in terms of publishing productivity and that I was making good progress. In my interim review, the Professional Standards Committee even said I was more productive in scholarship than most.

However, I knew immediately on reading my next annual review that something was off. For starters, the previous year, at the urging of a previous department chair, I led two honors theses. I was told that if I didn't help out, the students wouldn't be able to do their honors projects because other senior colleagues had already said no. I had previously led a successful honors thesis in my first year of teaching, so I believed that I had the current chair's support to lead these two projects. Of the two, one failed and one passed, but the chair at the time only wrote about the thesis that failed. Even more disturbing, the review criticized me at length for taking on too much work, even though it had all been approved by a previous chair. I had the registrar send me copies of the forms that were signed approving the thesis projects, but this made no impact on the Professional Standards Committee. Faced with this distortion of the record, I talked to the dean and provost and filed a letter challenging that part of the review by the chair at the time. This was the first incident in which I would not just take it or have someone who did not really know me or the situation misrepresent what happened. I stood up for myself. It made both chairs look negligent.

I think this may have been the beginning of the souring of my relationship with them, and whatever minimal formal mentoring I received (discussion after my annual review), became even more limited. I really felt I was on my own in the tenure process. When I asked the dean and provost for mentoring, they said to rely on my existing networks, and that I should know how to do this by now. They put the onus on me to figure it out because "figuring it out" is part of getting tenure. But that is easier for a White person who is actually liked and mentored informally by other White colleagues, not so for the uppity Asian woman who keeps asking questions and works for changes that would help minorities feel more included in the major and college.

So these were the first concrete warning signs. If people want to keep you around, they focus on overall patterns, either explaining the outliers or disregarding them completely. If they want to get rid of you, they use your one mistake, or outlier comments in one class you taught for the first time, as representative of your character, professionalism, and competence. They will also keep records to build their attack. In my case, my colleagues flat-out lied or made things up about my work. This is why you must document every little thing. Keep every peer review and every email about every honors thesis. These are the things that will help you if someone tries to build a case against you or misrepresent you. Save everything because minority women are not given the benefit of the doubt nor believed. I had no idea that being an assistant professor meant having a paper trail and saving emails over the years. I did none of these things because

I never anticipated that I would be in a position where I would have to prove myself in so many ways.

Institutional knowledge and field advice that passes between mentor and mentee was not available to me. The result was that I appeared naive, uninformed and, as my former chair wrote in her tenure letter, "unsophisticated." When I found the courage to raise this point with another senior colleague, a White male, he assured me that "we" all got the same treatment and that no one had helped *him* in any particular way. But "we" don't all get the same treatment from mentors, and it can be hard for some White colleagues to understand this. For example, when I requested a meeting to discuss my interim review with my dean (Latina) and my chair (White; both women are lesbian), I was demeaned and dismissed, attacked for asking questions and told that I was "passive."

This last comment stung me. Asian and Asian American women are often stereotyped as passive. I went to UCLA on Pell Grants and went to graduate school on fellowships as a low-income first-generation student. I wrote a dissertation while mothering my small child, and landed a tenure-track job in the worst academic job market for political science. Passive? My whole time in this rural town and school was about fighting the limitations and prejudices people put on me because I am an Asian female, but I never expected these would come from other women, especially other Women of Color. They had survived academia at a time when there were so few women, fewer who were openly gay, and even fewer yet who were openly gay and non-White. Yet my approach of seeking advice, community building, and advocating for Students of Color were signs of weakness to them. I began to wonder if the way I presented myself made it impossible for them to see me as competent, which was a huge blow to my sense of self. I had a child and a challenging custody situation. I was divorced, I didn't drink, I didn't follow sports. Were these issues? I couldn't say. But I can say that I was not able to bond with anyone in my department because of or in spite of these critical identifying issues. I realized that even women who are part of minority groups or lesbian can have internalized prejudices about Asian women and minorities, as well as deeply sexist and masculine ideas of leadership.

I can see now that it was soon after I spoke out about racism on campus that I was marked as a problem. Yet, in a PWI with marginalized minority students, I was not willing to stay silent or look the other way to get tenure. In a meeting one colleague said, "I can't be racist. I am lesbian! I am persecuted more than Black people. I can lose my job at anytime." This woman also erased all of my work with minority students in her tenure letter, saying, "We all do the same service." This is a woman who prides herself on her work on LGBTQ issues, but she has a serious blind spot about race.

Regarding formal service, the tenure committee counted all official advisees but failed to count the unofficial ones who regularly visited me each week to talk about their struggles at the institution, and these are struggles that you do not just ignore. As a human being and educator, if you are a White tenured faculty member, do not tell the minority junior colleague to just say no and keep her door closed. As a human being and Person of Color, you cannot do this to students who may not have the same support as White students. I would really like people in our field to think about what they are saying about themselves and our profession when they do not help our students who are struggling and isolated. My students were hurting and needed compassion, support, understanding and, frankly, representation of their lives and communities in the curriculum, but they were not getting any of these things. I would not be passive or accepting of any of this. I think that's why I was pushed out.

The way my department isolated me in the last two years was cruel and caused me to develop anxiety and depression. I dreaded just going to work. The tenure denial has also made me wonder how and why we perpetuate a system that makes it acceptable to ignore minority students who struggle, just so that we may be rewarded with tenure.

THE DAMAGE OF THE PAIN

It is still too painful to relive this. I walked away from filing with the EEOC and filing a lawsuit, even though my lawyer offered to help because he saw that I could not function. It was summer and both my kids were at home. I just wanted to be present for them at that time. The grievance process exhausted and damaged me. For the first few days I could not get out of bed. I do not even know how I was able to file and appeal in that state. I always thought that in times of injustice, you must fight. I learned that you can be incapacitated by shock, grief, rage. I learned that you may not be able to take the action you need as your body is trying to process your pain.

I am used to racism, but nothing so coordinated and intentional. I am still recovering from the way in which my department isolated me once I reported the bullying and favoritism. Some people call this mobbing—it is a way of making the person who disrupts the organization and its culture pay for that disruption through exclusion, isolation, and silencing. This kind of hyper-masculine aggression and the importance of hierarchy were more pronounced among the women in the department. I now absolutely regret assuming that other Women of Color and sexual minorities were my allies. These women were as blind as anyone on campus to their own privilege.

It has also become clear that at every stage, there was no Person of Color involved in my tenure case, appeal, and the grievance. Such as person might have known about the effects of inequitable treatment, but who knows?

MOVING ON

I had the great good fortune to find a contingent position the summer after my tenure denial. I left my institution immediately after the denial. The physical distance from my former department was so important because it was only with that literal and figurative distance and being in a new environment that I could really see how toxic and abusive the former institution was for me. I now work in a school that is not highly ranked, but has the diversity I need. I went from teaching the White children of the 1 percent to teaching in a majority-minority campus with mostly first-generation students receiving Pell Grants—my community. I work with colleagues who know and care about Asia. They invite me to lunch every week. For the first time, I have a Black woman colleague who has become a dear friend at work. I have an Asian woman chair who has been giving me stellar reviews and sponsoring me by encouraging me to apply to conferences and giving me opportunities to address the campus community on international issues—things my colleagues at the former institution never did for me. I also have White male sponsors who look out for me and explain the culture, norms, and unwritten rules of the institution without me having to ask. They are aware of what happened to me at my former institution, so they go out of their way to meet with me to explain how things actually work. We also have an Asian American dean whose mere presence makes me feel that I can belong. There are People of Color across the administration, staff, and faculty who make me feel like it is possible to grow and develop here.

Since the move, I have published more than ever before because I have mentoring and interest in my work. Also, there are other Faculty of Color so I am not responsible for caring for as many minority students and they do not have the same kind of racialized issues that my students faced at my former institution. There are just more People of Color at all levels and no one has a problem talking about Black Lives Matter or police brutality on campus.

I have research and professional momentum like never before, but no tenure or permanent job. I just keep trying to move forward and apply for jobs, no matter how discouraged I sometimes feel. I am not ready to give up. I want to proceed on my own terms, not because of several people who could not deal with me questioning them wanted me to fail.

It has been so healing for me to be in this environment. I have no idea what the future holds, but being a visitor here has been a gift.

PARTING THOUGHTS

What price are you willing to pay for tenure? Accept that if you have to speak out, you will make enemies, and that in all-White institutions, White faculty—no matter how progressive—don't want to be made uncomfortable about their privilege and aren't prepared to deal with race. White fragility can make the Person of Color who raises these issues the problem. As Sara Ahmed says, those who identify the problem become the problem. Just by asking questions we become problematic. How uncomfortable *we* are willing to be may still be the measure of our chances for successfully challenging and changing a system that does not want us, but that needs us more and more.

TWENTY-SEVEN

In Lak'ech

The Interconnectedness between Faculty and Students of Color

Yessenia Manzo

I grew up in a migrant community on a Native reservation in Washington State. The community consisted of a majority Mexican population working in the fields. My father and I were the only ones in our immediate family living here undocumented. Daily life was filled with the awareness and fear of possible deportation. Despite the hard work of both my parents, we grew up constantly having to move, at one point becoming homeless. Through poverty and instability, I found strength and constancy in education. School was always easy for me. It was a space of familiarity, no matter how unfamiliar it was to my family and community. But school was also a place of oppression, and that has remained true at all levels of my education.

My higher education has encompassed an undergraduate degree from a private institution, a graduate degree, and now law school. Each phase of education, although unique, was characterized by the same underlying thread of having to push against a racist system. In primary school, I was placed in special education because the teachers assumed I could not speak English. In high school, I was told the only life skills I needed were to look busy and be on time. As an undergraduate, I was treated as the affirmative action charity case. In graduate school, I was the tokenized and silenced minority. In law school, I am the Student of Color constantly advocating for professors to utilize a racial justice lens in their curriculum. Through this process, I have found that advocacy for racial equity cannot be done without the support of Faculty of Color, and without supporting them in return.

Over the past two years of law school I have been reflecting on the concept of *In Lak'ech* as it applies to my academic experience. "In Lak'ech" is a Mexican indigenous saying that means "You are my other self" (Lopez, 2008). This is a teaching I learned through our *danza* community and elders. It is a philosophy of empathy and understanding that human beings are interconnected. So

DOI: 10.7330/9781607329664.c027

intricately connected are our experiences that anything we do to another, we simultaneously do to ourselves. Intentions aside, the moment I give you love and respect, I give the same to myself. The moment I harm you, I am harming myself. This is not merely a philosophy, but a reflection we should be engaging in on a daily basis.

Our indigenous philosophies of deep interconnectedness offer much insight to the world of academia. There is a fundamental interconnectedness between the experiences of Faculty of Color and Students of Color. My experience as a Mexican indigenous woman is deeply tied to the experience of my Faculty of Color. When Faculty of Color are presumed incompetent, the detrimental effects on Students of Color are multilayered, complex, and long term.

EXPERIENCES WITH WHITE FACULTY

Without systems in place to promote and maintain racial equity in the classroom, my experience becomes dependent on the individual racial identity of each faculty member, on the extent to which they use a critical race lens, and on their personal level of cultural competency, resiliency, and ability to lead discussions on race.

Starting with White faculty, I have noticed several patterns. The first pattern is the White professor who has not even considered how themes of race and social equity affect curriculum or classroom dynamics. These professors are not ill intentioned; they simply have never had to consciously think about race because they possess racial privilege. My approach with these professors is to broach the topic in a direct yet nonconfrontational manner. A simple question, in an individual conversation—"How will you incorporate themes of racial and social equity into your curriculum?"—can lead to conversations that deepen awareness and even produce changes in the curriculum. This is not to say that all professors will respond with humility or that this tactic will always be successful, but I have preferred it over ignoring the topic altogether.

One of my most positive experiences with a White faculty member was in my ethics course in law school. Explaining his curriculum on the first day of class, the professor made no mention of race or social equity. I wanted to ask him how he was planning to incorporate those themes into his curriculum. But instead of asking in front of my classmates, putting him on the spot and possibly coming across as aggressive or critical, I waited until after class. When I asked him, his response was "Honestly, I had not thought about that before." He let me know he was open to dialogue and ideas. He followed up with an email reiterating his openness.

I decided to engage with my professor yet avoid taking on the responsibility of providing solutions. Instead of supplying him with a list of answers, I gave him with a list of questions that I as a Student of Color have in his classroom. The intention was to spark dialogue and critical thinking, and to ensure that themes of race and equity would not be excluded completely from our learning experience. This particular professor responded with humility, transparency, and a commitment to action. He humbly accepted that he was not an expert and demonstrated his willingness to actively listen. He openly and readily acknowledged the ways in which he understands the experience of marginalization and the ways he does not. Most important, he committed himself to action. In addition to adjusting some of the content he would teach, he also invited guest speakers from diverse backgrounds who were skilled in addressing the nuances of race and social justice in legal practice.

The second pattern is the White professor who is clearly conscious about race, but too afraid to address it directly. My constitutional law professor, whose course began just as the Trump administration transitioned into the White House, is a good example. The professor was a White female whose reading assignments reflected concern for marginalized populations. As the class went on, it was clear that although she did think about issues of race and gender, she was not adept at initiating or facilitating difficult classroom conversations on these topics. This placed an immense burden on Students of Color, who wound up raising issues of race in class and offering their views and insights. However, as students, there is a limited amount of insight we can provide since we are studying this material for the first time and are not experts.

The third pattern is the White professor who thinks about race, but treats it as a side topic. These professors are well intentioned but unprepared. They are unprepared because the very act of relegating race to the periphery of the course demonstrates a lack of understanding of the complexity, subtlety, and pervasiveness of racial dynamics. This opens the door for racial microaggressions from White students who regard any discussion of race as a distraction from the curriculum. My approach with these professors is to validate the importance of addressing the topic of race, while also providing alternative methods.

In one of my classes, a White professor allocated two days for "race and equity." Taking a direct but nonconfrontational approach, I wrote him an email expressing my concern about treating race as a side topic. I provided material from cultural competency trainings that I have utilized to educate a wide variety of professionals. Although my suggestions in this case were noted but placed aside, initiating the dialogue opened the door for further discussion when racial tensions became evident in his classroom.

Treating race as a side topic divorced from the rest of the course subjects Students of Color to racial backlash from White students who do not see race as a problem and resent having to devote two days of class time to the topic. This approach is also a disservice to the learning process for White students who are deprived of the opportunity to understand how race is interwoven into all areas of law and policy. Studies have shown that a majority of White individuals in the United States think that *Whites* are the victims of racism (National Public Radio, 2017). This attitude is reflected in our classrooms and needs to be navigated cautiously.

The professor in this course introduced race as a stand-alone topic through Guest Speakers of Color without assessing the classroom climate or providing students with the requisite background materials to appreciate these presentations. One speaker was a Latina attorney lecturing on the relationship between the law and race. The lecture triggered some of the strongest racial microaggressions I have experienced in the classroom. White students made dehumanizing statements about indigenous peoples, mocked the concept of implicit bias, and used personal anecdotes to claim that the legal field is now diverse. The White professor did not address the racist tone of the student comments and the contempt and disrespect with which the Latina guest speaker was treated. Students of Color remained silent throughout the entire class.

While this White professor was not equipped with the tools to address the racist comments and the disrespectful tone toward our guest presenter, I could not leave the class without drawing attention to the problematic dynamics. This time my intervention was in the form of confrontation. As the lecture was coming to an end, I raised my hand to speak up. I was angry that I had to speak up. I was angry that this Woman of Color was experiencing disrespect and racist backlash. I was angry with my White classmates who had no background in critical race theory and spoke as if their opinions based on anecdotes were more insightful than the information presented by the guest speaker. I was angry with my White classmates who did have a background in critical race theory yet remained absolutely silent. I was angry that my White male professor, in a clear position of authority, did not intervene. I was angry that I had to intervene. But I had to. I raised my hand and found a way to directly address the dehumanizing comments that were made in class while framing it as an appreciation of the difficult work that this guest presenter was carrying forward.

In addition to speaking up in class and debriefing with some classmates, I also spoke to the White male professor directly. This time, my message was not simply placed to the side. The professor responded with humility and a desire to engage in the conversation, while acknowledging it was not my responsibility to educate. Although he is correct that it is not my responsibility to educate White individuals, much less my White professors, it is my responsibility to continue to advocate for our Communities of Color. I met with him in person, discussed ideas on how to apply a more systemic and intentional approach to addressing themes of race in the classroom, and provided him with clinical tools utilized to facilitate conversations about race. The next time we had a class discussion on race, those tools were applied. These are the experiences that demonstrate the benefit of humility on both sides. There are White professors who are willing to learn, and mistakes are part of that process. As a White male, my professor has the responsibility to educate himself in order to educate his students. As a Student of Color, I have the opportunity to provide insight and advocate for our voices by engaging in challenging conversations with people in authority.

The final pattern is the White professor who is aware of issues of race and social equity and consistently, systematically, and unapologetically incorporates these issues into the curriculum. These professors are powerful. They are powerful not because they are perfect in their delivery, but because they use their privilege to bring validity to our struggles as People of Color. When Faculty of Color discuss race in the classroom, they are met with student resistance, questioning of their authority, and devaluation (Perry, Moore, Edwards, Acosta, & Frey, 2009). White professors do not face the same obstacles and do not have to fight for their credibility in the same manner.

For me, the White individual who utilized her advantage and credibility was my criminal law professor. My first day of law school I entered my criminal law classroom with absolute dread. I was not ready. I was not ready to reenter White academia. I sat in the back, scanned the room, and observed that I was the only Mexican student. I already knew Mexicans did not make up a large percentage of the legal profession, but I did not realize that we were not even counted. According to the American Bar Association, five percent of attorneys (American Bar Association, 2017) and four percent of judges (American Bar Association, 2010) are "Hispanic." Since the term *Hispanic* covers such a broad range of cultures and identities, all this tells me is that we as Mexicans make up less than five percent of attorneys (even though we constitute 17.8 percent of the US population), and that Mexican women are even further underrepresented (US Census Bureau, 2018).

Sitting in the back, feeling the weight of isolation, I looked at my White professor. I sat with a feeling of dread, awaiting her introductory remarks. I was not ready. And then, she introduced herself and the course in a manner that far exceeded my expectations. "One, this is criminal law, and we will be talking about race a lot. And when I say a lot, I mean *a lot*. You cannot talk about criminal law without talking about race. And two, as I scan the room, this city has a problem." The professor was a visiting professor who lived and taught at a university in a predominantly Black community. She was not part of the passive-aggressive, overwhelmingly White culture of the Pacific Northwest. She was direct, unafraid, and unapologetic. And best of all, she started the class by setting the expectation that White students would be required to step out of their comfort zones and grapple with race and racism.

During the class break, I went up to her to ask for the assignment. Somehow, I had not been added to the email list for the course. She responded with absolute kindness, told me not to worry about it, assured me I would be added, and ended by acknowledging my Latina identity. "This field is struggling in general, Students of Color are few, Latina students are fewer. I'm happy you're here. And while I do not expect you to take up the burden of topics of race, you will see me scanning for you every once in a while, for solidarity." In one class, this White woman upended my entire graduate school experience. This professor utilized her identity and privilege to address racism, recognized my Latinidad instead of lumping me into the "general minority" category, and committed to carry the burden of discussing race as opposed to placing it on my shoulders. She is an example of White professors who not only create an inclusive environment for Students of Color, but also model that the responsibility to address racism does not fall only on the backs of Faculty of Color.

EXPERIENCES WITH FACULTY OF COLOR

Though my experiences with Professors of Color have been few, I have noticed three main patterns. First, there are the Professors of Color who never mention race or equity. I feel empathy for these professors because they are either ignoring race due to intense pressure to assimilate, or they have internalized the notion that race must be eliminated from their narrative in order to have any credibility. At times, it is a complex combination of both.

A few semesters into law school I had my first ever Mexican male professor. I was ecstatic. While I cognitively understand the deprivation of not having professors that mirror your background, when you finally have one, the emotional realization of that deprivation sets in. With a White professor, my tactic is usually to address themes of race and social justice right away and head on. With Professors of Color, I am much more patient and hesitant. With this professor, I waited several weeks before asking him to incorporate themes of equity into his curriculum. His response was defensive, saying race simply had nothing to do with this topic. And while I understand that race is not central to every topic, there are always layers of racism within any topic in the law. Race does not have to be a central theme, but it is a necessary lens.

Second, there are the Professors of Color who are identified as social justice experts, but who do not incorporate this knowledge into their teaching. Their classrooms are devoid of a social justice lens and filled with racial microaggressions. These are the most difficult professors to approach, because their identity is centered around social justice but their practice contradicts this identity.

These professors can also be the most harmful to Students of Color. With these professors, my strategy consists of maintaining a safe distance, with minimal and careful confrontation if needed. During my second year in law school, I had a male Professor of Color well known for his work on racial justice issues, in both the school and the community. The class I took from him was a required course and not one heavy with racial justice issues. I was not surprised or bothered by the absence of these discussions since most of the content was very technical. What troubled me the most was the classroom dynamics he perpetuated. It was clear he was not thinking about race as it applied to his classroom setting or his own ways of interacting with students.

In the first few weeks of class, I raised my hand to pose a question. He answered and throughout his response I nodded and quietly, but out loud, said, "Oh, right." It was just an expression as I was gaining understanding through his answer. He abruptly stopped and said, "You say, 'Oh, right,' but do you *really* know what I mean?" His expression carried a tone of disbelief in my ability to grasp what he was telling me. This man had no prior experience or interaction with me. We did not have a relationship. He had no knowledge of my academic background or capacity. With a condescending tone, even if unintentional, he conveyed to the class that I was not smart enough to comprehend. I had no response for him. I immediately understood that my participation in his class would henceforth be minimal and that he did not intend to create a welcoming and inclusive environment in his interactions with Students of Color. Perhaps he treated all students this way, but if he behaved this way with a White student (who does not bear the presumption of incompetence), the consequences would be different. By treating me in a condescending manner in front of my classmates, he reinforced the cultural stereotype that Mexican women lack the intellectual capacity to undertake rigorous academic work.

Aside from not creating an inclusive environment for Students of Color, this professor demonstrated the same behavior toward his Colleague of Color. The class scheduled just prior to his was taught by an indigenous man who is not only a professor but also a tribal judge. This judge was quite passionate about the course material and would often stay during our break to have individual conversations with students. If the judge was still in the classroom when the professor came in to set up for his class, he would demonstrate contempt toward his colleague. These manifestations of contempt included rolling his eyes at him, demonstrating clear annoyance, and even walking up to students who were talking with the judge (on our break time) to instruct them to step outside if they wanted to continue having a conversation. He would not address his colleague; he would address the student as if the student was being disrespectful. By treating his indigenous colleague in this manner, this professor normalized student hostility toward their indigenous professor. At one point, I overheard one White student complaining about our indigenous professor, saying, "I just don't do stupid well."

Nationwide, there are so few Native individuals in judicial careers that the percentage is literally at zero. (American Bar Association, 2010). And yet this White student felt entitled to blurt out for others to hear that this Native professor is "stupid," without any consideration of the immense barriers he has had to overcome to hold his judicial position. This hostility is reinforced when Faculty of Color model disrespectful behavior toward him in front of White students. Not only does disrespect between colleagues in academia fuel student hostility, it also carries with it a strong message of devaluation to Students of Color. No matter what we accomplish as indigenous peoples, we cannot attain the respect of our Colleagues of Color, even those identified as social justice experts.

Finally, there are the Professors of Color who are aware of issues related to race, incorporate them successfully into their curriculum, and possess the skill to facilitate highly charged discussions in their classrooms. These professors are powerful and scarce. These are the professors who truly create a sense of inclusivity for Students of Color as well as holistic education and growth for White students. These are the professors whose accomplishments deserve to be recognized, valued, and emulated by academic institutions. Sadly, these are also the professors who do heavy lifting in the classroom that is often not rewarded by universities and who carry a heavy burden as they navigate systems of oppression within their own institution.

During my second semester in law school, I had a Latina professor who was knowledgeable and fierce. Her brilliance was evident to students, no matter their background. She carried clear expertise on the course topic and was also a talented educator. But there was more. There was something impacting about her. I could not explain it, but I could feel it. Then one day, I realized what it was: I had never met anyone like her. I had gone my entire education either without Faculty of Color, or with Faculty of Color who were treated as incompetent by both faculty and students. Furthermore, I had never had an educator who reflected my identity as a Latina woman, and one who did so while commanding respect in what seemed to be an effortless manner.

I knew it was not effortless. There is no way that she navigated oppressive academic institutions effortlessly. This was intentional, calculated, meticulous, and most likely incredibly exhausting. And I admired all of it. In silence. I did not have a relationship with her. I did not know the details of her experience. She taught the required content while never divorcing it from its social context. She had an ability to challenge students to widen their lens while not being threatening. And she was incredibly intentional about preventing and mitigating microaggressions in class.

One example was the day we discussed transgender discrimination within the law. As with most classes in law school, students need to be prepared to answer questions about assigned cases. Professors call on students without advance warning. However, in preparation for discussion of a case that included violence toward a transgender male, she contacted me to let me know I would be called on. Through my class participation, she knew that I had a background in racial and social equity trainings. The fact that she let me know beforehand as a way of allowing me to prepare was one example of her intentionality. On top of that, the day of this particular discussion, she started class by providing clear, definite boundaries. She instructed students on how they would be expected to refer to this individual's gender. She set specific parameters with the expectation that they would not be broken. The way in which she set up the class, from beginning to end, was such a powerful example of ways in which educators can create an inclusive environment by intentionally mitigating microaggressions. She did not coddle students or make them feel comfortable. She made it clear that she was here to instruct us, to guide us, to challenge us, and to help us grow. She was not here to entertain; she was here to educate. She approached students with high expectations, setting us up to meet those expectations. Whatever burdens she carried as a Latina woman navigating an oppressive institution, she made sure to lift some of those burdens off the shoulders of the marginalized students in her classroom.

CONCLUSION

Improving the learning experience for students of all backgrounds means ensuring we have access to racially diverse professors. Without inclusive spaces for Faculty of Color, inclusive spaces for Students of Color will be impossible to create. As a Student of Color who has had limited access to Educators of Color in academia, and who has observed harmful and disruptive White student backlash toward Faculty of Color throughout my education, including students scolding our professors and even walking out on them, I have several messages to convey.

First, for Students of Color who struggle in the alienating White spaces of academia, you are not alone and you are not powerless. There are constructive interventions you can make to engage with faculty and improve the learning environment for all. These constructive interventions are not about taking on the burden of educating White professors or peers, but about establishing a collective space to support one another as we navigate the barriers in academia and in our future professions. We may not have an obligation to deconstruct racism for those in power, but we do have an obligation to establish our own empowerment.

For White professors who have not considered how racial and social equity apply to their curriculum, please make an effort to utilize that lens. Utilizing the lens starts by asking the question, seeking education or consultation, and implementing changes into your curriculum, even if those changes are small. For White professors who are incorporating themes of racial and social equity into their curriculum as a side topic, please keep pushing forward to identify ways in which that education can be incorporated in a more seamless manner. Mistakes will be made along the way, but those mistakes are an unavoidable part of the learning process. For White professors who address the topic unapologetically and challenge their students, we need the credibility you bring in light of the conscious and unconscious bias Faculty of Color face when addressing the same topic.

For Professors of Color who are too afraid to address the topic of race in their curriculum, I realize the issue is complex, and that you may be operating out of self-preservation, but your students and Colleagues of Color are suffering and need the benefit of your insights. For Professors of Color who self-identify as social justice experts, please be conscious of the ways that your words and actions can harm students and colleagues in similar and unique spaces of marginalization. You have an even higher responsibility to remain vigilant, self-aware, and self-critical in order to avoid reinforcing the presumption of incompetence.

For Professors of Color who are unapologetically and skillfully navigating issues of race in your classrooms and in your work environment, your work does not go unnoticed. Some students do perceive the ways in which you manage racial backlash and move the conversation forward. Some of us do see how you work to enhance our learning experience and the learning experience of our White peers. The space of inclusivity you create for your Students of Color is deeply appreciated as it is rare and in stark contrast to the rest of our academic experience. Without you, we cannot succeed. In Lak'ech.

REFERENCES

American Bar Association (ABA). (2010.) *National database on judicial diversity in state courts*. Retrieved from https://apps.americanbar.org/abanet/jd/display/national.cfm.

American Bar Association (ABA). (2017.) *National lawyer population survey.* Retrieved from https://www.americanbar.org/content/dam/aba/administrative/market

_research/national-lawyer-population-10-year-demographics-revised.authcheckdam.pdf.
Lopez, M. (2008.) The language of resistance: Alurista's global poetics. *MELUS, 30*(1), 93–115.
National Public Radio (NPR). (2017.) *Poll: Most Americans think their own group faces discrimination.* Retrieved from https://www.npr.org/sections/health-shots/2017/10/24/559116373/poll-most-americans-think-their-own-group-faces-discrimination.
Perry, G., Moore, H., Edwards, C., Acosta, K., & Frey, C. (2009.) Maintaining credibility and authority as an instructor of color in diversity-education classrooms: A qualitative inquiry. *Journal of Higher Education, 80*(1), 80–105.
US Census Bureau. (2018.) *Facts for features: Hispanic heritage month 2017.* Retrieved from https://www.census.gov/newsroom/facts-for-features/2017/hispanic-heritage.html.

TWENTY-EIGHT

Securing Support in an Unequal Profession

Meera E. Deo

Destiny is a tenured African American law professor who is renowned as both a scholar and a teacher. Yet she has found some first-year students shocked to see her behind the podium on their first day of law school, their palpable disappointment seemingly based on her race X gender. When they exhibit what Destiny sees as a "tone and attitude that they just don't have with some of my male colleagues," she attributes it to "a disbelief [that a Black woman is their professor, which results in their] saying things that they would not normally say." After fifteen years in legal academia, her "students still get kind of [confrontational, with an attitude like] how dare you try to teach them." These ongoing confrontations "can be challenging" for Destiny to manage, and also disruptive for the class as a whole.

This presumption of incompetence based on intersectional (race X gender) characteristics does not stop with students, but extends to faculty colleagues. When an Asian American named Cindy was hired as an assistant professor at the same time as a White male, she experienced "a major difference in how he was treated and how I was treated." Cindy "was treated like the 'dumb one,' sort of an affirmative action hire in the worst sense of the word [meaning that I was unqualified, but hired because of my race and gender,] and he was the 'real one.'" After ongoing "favoritism towards him from particular faculty members," Cindy initially internalized her colleagues' intersectional discrimination until she too "felt like he was the real deal, and I'm not." Tellingly, "as it turned out, it was kind of opposite," with Cindy outperforming her colleagues' expectations to achieve both academic and administrative success while the White male hire fizzled out.

How do underrepresented and marginalized faculty overcome the presumption of incompetence to nevertheless succeed in legal academia? Cindy, Destiny, and fellow Women of Color law professors rely on various sources of support to reach their full potential. Destiny considers herself "a big family person," which

DOI: 10.7330/9781607329664.c028

includes close connections to "my parents, my sister, my brother, my sister-cousin, the people who raised me, grew up with me, and helped propel me to this point. Those are the people I rely on, and very close friends." She makes clear, "My support group comes from outside of my particular faculty," including "a cadre of faculty at other academic institutions" and identity-plus-academic "organizations that I'm associated with." Cindy's law school faces many of the same challenges "that plague any institution that is male dominated and dominated by White people," including a tendency to hire and promote more White men. Yet, "the [White male] dean has been very supportive," as have the few White women and Faculty of Color at her school, plus external mentors. She also notes, "My husband is fantastic. He's really a great co-parent," which is essential to her ability to maintain some semblance of work/life balance.

This chapter draws upon original empirical data from the book *Unequal Profession: Race and Gender in Legal Academia* to explore how, in the face of considerable institutional challenges, Women of Color draw from various support systems to succeed in the legal academy (Deo, 2019). The first section introduces statistics on current law faculty as well as the Diversity in Legal Academia project, the first formal multi-method study on law faculty in the United States—which generated the empirical data presented in this chapter. Building on *Presumed Incompetent: The Intersections of Race and Class for Women in Academia* (Gutiérrez y Muhs, Niemann, González, & Harris, 2012), the first part also provides a theoretical foundation for this work, including the concepts of intersectionality, privilege, and implicit bias. With this framework in place, the chapter's second part examines empirical findings on the sources of support that help female Faculty of Color overcome barriers to success in legal academia. The chapter concludes with a third section, which proposes first-step strategies derived from the data that allies in administration and institutional leaders should utilize to create a more equitable and inclusive workplace for all faculty.

BUILDING ON *PRESUMED INCOMPETENT*

Women of Color have always been underrepresented in legal academia and remain so today. There are only 771 Women of Color law professors, representing just 7 percent of the 10,965 law teachers (American Bar Association, 2013; Deo, 2015c).[1] As compared to the 5,090 White male law professors (46 percent of the total), and even the 2,741 White women (25 percent of the total), Women of Color are significantly underrepresented in the legal academy (American Bar Association, 2013; Deo, 2015c). Few studies have explored the challenges facing

1. AALS no longer publishes this data online, though tables and analysis relying on AALS tables can be found in Deo, 2015c. Because AALS data include many non-tenure-track positions, they are overinclusive when considering the tenured or tenure-track, nonclinical/legal writing/library participants in the study presented in this chapter. Data from AALS are similar to those published by the American Bar Association (ABA), available online at https://www.americanbar.org/groups/legal_education/resources/statistics.html.

Women of Color legal academics, let alone reliable mechanisms and structures for supporting them through professional trials.

Presumed Incompetent, volume 1, revealed the ongoing sexism, racism, and classism of academia, as "higher education is not immune from the inequities that plague the rest of American society" (Harris & González, 2012, p. 2). Theoretical frameworks involving intersectionality, privilege, and implicit bias also help explain the creation and maintenance of these inequities. *Intersectionality*, a cornerstone of critical race theory, recognizes the interplay between identity characteristics in shaping the experience of individuals, especially those from multiple devalued groups (Crenshaw, 1991; Delgado & Stefancic, 2017; Harris, 1990). Intersectionality teaches us that while women from all backgrounds may share some similarities, White heterosexual nonimmigrant wealthy women cannot be the norm for all women any more than the "reasonable man" standard can apply to all people (Cahn, 1992).

Privilege, the "systemic conferral of benefit and advantage [based on] affiliation, conscious or not and chosen or not, to the dominant side of a power system," is also instructive (Wildman, 1996, p. 29). The privileged set the norms and expectations; the less privileged are expected to follow, and are punished or excluded for deviance (Wildman, 1996). Those in power may purposefully utilize their capital to maintain the status quo through overt discrimination (Bonilla-Silva, 2001; Bourdieu, 1996). Additionally, people acting under *implicit bias* "operate without conscious awareness" that their actions lead to discriminatory results (Kang & Lane, 2010, p. 467). Even actors who believe themselves to be nondiscriminatory "make subconscious determinations that draw from race and gender stereotypes, negatively affecting those with less privilege, especially those with intersectionally devalued identity characteristics (i.e., Women of Color)" (Quintanilla, 2013, p. 187).

Research has shown that the "precarious and tentative" foothold (Arriola, 2012, p. 378) of underrepresented faculty is characterized by the *silencing* of Women of Color (Onwuachi-Willig, 2012), *identity performance* (Kupenda, 2012; Lazos, 2012), and *academic caretaking* (Guarino & Borden, 2017), with little reward (Wing, 2012) and additional "chronic stress" (Brooks, 1986, p. 419; Harris & González, 2012, p. 7). Perhaps the greatest contribution of *Presumed Incompetent*, volume 1 is to reveal how these challenges are not simply individual, but also structural—so embedded in the fabric of legal education as to be commonplace, expected, and often tolerated. When a Woman of Color professor enters building after building with walls covered in pictures of "dead White males and some living ones," she knows she has not belonged historically and may not be welcome now (Wing, 2012, p. 359).

Law students report high levels of satisfaction with law faculty as a whole, including 76 percent finding faculty "available, helpful, and sympathetic," and 93 percent believing that their instructors "care about my learning and success in law school" (Petzold, 2018). Yet only a handful of studies have conducted empirical research with law faculty to better understand their experiences on a structural level. Law faculty pioneers Derrick Bell and Richard Delgado piloted an informal racial analysis of legal academia thirty years ago, revealing "discrimination in hiring and promotion, alienation among faculty colleagues, hostility from students, and a lack of financial support for research and professional development" (Delgado & Bell, 1989, p. 349). They predicted little improvement in coming years without dedicated attention to ameliorating the problems they had documented. More recent findings from an empirical study of tenured law professors conclude that "despite significant progress toward more diversity, Women and Scholars of Color face continued difficulties" (Barnes & Mertz, 2012, p. 512). A full 35 percent of Women of Color law professors "believed that the tenure process was not fair," compared to only 12 percent of White males (pp. 516–517). Other "common negative themes" reveal "the effects of implicit bias in the tenure process," which create "differential impacts on women and on scholars of color" (pp. 521–522).

Building on these earlier studies, the Diversity in Legal Academia (DLA) project is the first formal, comprehensive, multi-method study of the law faculty experience. It utilizes an intersectional lens to investigate the experiences of Women of Color legal academics at all stages of their careers, across the United States, at both private and public institutions, and from elite to more accessible schools. Ninety-three law professors contributed to the survey and interview data collected in the DLA study. Sixty-three Women of Color—including African American, Asian American, Latina, Middle Eastern, multiracial, and Native American women—comprise the core sample of the study, while the control sample consists of thirty Men of Color, White women, and White men. Research subjects completed online surveys before participating in interviews, with data coded and analyzed using ATLAS.ti, Excel, and Stata.[2] The quantitative data tabulate survey responses of DLA participants. The quotes that are highlighted throughout the chapter represent the qualitative data—allowing the actual voices of participants in the DLA study to share their experiences, with names anonymized to protect confidentiality (Deo, 2019).

A collection of published articles and a book drawing from DLA data have explored the full range of challenges facing Women of Color faculty (Deo, 2019). These traditional outsiders face overt discrimination as well as implicit bias in hiring, tenure/promotion, and leadership (Deo, 2015b; Deo, 2018). Jane, a multiracial law professor, was overlooked for an associate dean position, though she and another female colleague "already do a lot of this work [without] any of the recognition." Problematic interactions with fellow faculty range from invisibility and silencing during faculty meetings, where colleagues *hepeat* (Dodgson, 2017), *mansplain* (Solnit, 2012), and *Whitesplain* their remarks, to a mask of collegiality covering hostility, and even denigration of the identity-based or nontraditional research that many Faculty of Color pursue (Deo, 2015c; Deo, 2018). Elaine, an Asian American professor, would frequently say something in a faculty meeting "and no one paid attention to it"—until a male colleague repeated

2. Detailed methods are provided in the appendix to Deo, 2019.

and claimed her idea for his own, "and then everyone would pay attention to it." Some students openly defy Women of Color faculty, being sullenly unresponsive or brazenly disrespectful in class (Deo, 2015c). Keisha, a Black professor, recalls a student openly telling her he "had other things to do than to do my written assignments." Other students leave biased comments on teaching evaluations that focus more on their Women of Color professor's personal appearance than on her curriculum, pedagogical approach, or mastery of the material (Deo, 2015a). Carla, a Latina professor, notes, "As a woman, there is a constant kind of student concern with my looks," with "attractiveness" essentially counting as "another element on which I get graded" on student evaluations. These challenges result in Women of Color leaving academia at higher rates than their peers (Deo, 2018). Mia, a Native American whose colleagues pushed her out of law teaching, "was terrified" to share her appalling experience even with a mentor, worrying, "I felt like I had failed her."

Of those who remain, some are thwarted at the tenure or promotion stage while others fight for success, drawing support wherever they can. *Presumed Incompetent*, volume 1 assures us that through persistence and perseverance many Women of Color faculty "have developed resources for naming their wounds and healing them, including friendship, alliances, and poetry" (Harris & González, 2012, p. 7). The remainder of this chapter discusses mechanisms for securing support for Women of Color law faculty and structural solutions to overcome these challenges.

INDIVIDUAL SOURCES OF SUPPORT

Women of Color in legal academia rely on various sources of support to help them survive and even thrive in the face of ongoing professional confrontations and challenges. Table 28.1 displays the most common bases for faculty support. Academics from all backgrounds rely heavily on family, friends, and faculty—including external mentors—to sustain them through their careers. Professional organizations play a key role for many faculty, while some also rely on religion.

The qualitative data—presented as actual quotes from study participants—expound on the survey responses, adding detail and nuance to the raw numbers displayed in table 20.1. A Latina professor named Valeria has a representative experience; she gets "a lot of emotional support from a lot of different people in my life," including "a great family," "parents," and "a significant other that I talk to very often; and two really great friends from law school [and] a mentor/best friend."

Family—including partners, parents, and children—are a primary source of support for most faculty, and especially for Women of Color. Elaine had the "good fortune" to find "a very supportive partner who not only views things like family life as something he should partner in, but actually probably enjoys it more than I do." Her partner's investment in their home life gives Elaine the flexibility to be both "real active with my kids [and] real active with my work life," instead of carrying the load as the *default parent* (Blazoned, 2014). Similarly, a

TABLE 28.1. Support from various sources, by race and gender, DLA 2013 ($n = 92$; multiple responses permitted)

		Family	*Friends*	*Internal faculty*	*Mentors*	*Professional organizations*	*Religion*
African American women	Number	21	20	21	20	17	12
	%	100	95	100	95	81	57
Asian American women	Number	15	14	15	14	11	6
	%	100	93	100	100	73	43
Latinas	Number	11	12	12	12	10	4
	%	92	100	100	100	83	33
Native American women	Number	5	5	4	5	4	1
	%	100	100	80	100	100	50
Middle Eastern women	Number	2	2	2	2	1	2
	%	100	100	100	100	50	100
Multiracial women	Number	7	7	7	6	5	2
	%	100	100	100	86	71	29
Men of Color	Number	9	10	10	9	8	4
	%	90	100	100	100	80	40
White women	Number	11	11	10	9	9	4
	%	100	100	100	90	82	36
White men	Number	8	8	8	7	6	0
	%	100	100	100	88	75	0
TOTAL	Number	89	89	89	84	71	35

Black faculty member named Patrice says that she and her husband are "essentially fifty-fifty" at home, rather than her shouldering the bulk of the *invisible work*, with him doing "a lot of child care, a lot of housework, grocery shopping [and] at least 80% of the cooking" (Wade, 2016). His support at home is critical to Patrice's professional success.

Extended family also provides much-needed encouragement and assistance. Laila, a Middle Eastern law professor, sees her life as "exponentially easier" living near extended family because they "help a lot" with her children and provide emotional support. Years ago, a Latina law professor named Camila juggled being a single parent with her first faculty position; today, she says, "Probably my biggest source of emotional support are my children," who are now adults living nearby.

Friends are also critical.[3] Vivian, an Asian American professor, has "a wonderful network of [local] friends" who help her move past daunting institutional

3. Friendships sustain many faculty through difficult times. Others lament their lack of friendships. Elaine sees friendship as a casualty of her professional success, noting, "I regret not having more of a friendship group," though she believes that in academia "you felt like you had to be so strong you couldn't share . . . so that means you couldn't have friends."

challenges. Lola, a Latina junior scholar, appreciates that "a small group" of her "closest friends" for decades "are really my support system." While she and her work colleagues "get along and [occasionally] go out and have a good time, I really, at the end of the day, don't say or share confidential information or personal experiences because I just don't trust them at all." This distrust stems from firsthand experience with colleagues removing the mask of superficial civility to reveal underlying intersectional hostility (Deo, 2015c). For instance, when Lola's race X gender contributed to a recent promotion denial, "no one at school knew the pain and the betrayal I was feeling and that [it] was incredibly exhausting to come to work every day and pretend like nothing was wrong." Instead of opening up to her colleagues, Lola "really had to rely on my family and close friends for [some] relief of the stress and disappointment."

Many Women of Color faculty credit mentors with providing critical support that enables their success. Frequently these mentors are at different institutions; sometimes they themselves are Women of Color who have experienced similar intersectional bias, so can suggest strategies to overcome them. Melissa, a Native American professor, wishes she had a mentor who had "been through the entire process who is a Woman of Color and [could share] what the landscape is like." Jane admits, "I don't know that I've ever really had mentors here at my own institution." Her colleagues, like Lola's, have not earned Jane's trust—instead showing time and again their preference in hiring and otherwise maintaining the predominantly White male status quo. Yet just before she entered law teaching, Jane met a Woman of Color law professor who had taught the same subject for years and "immediately offered me all of her stuff—meaning her lecture notes, syllabus, old exams—and made herself available to me to talk about any [substantive] questions that I may have when I was prepping that class." Jane was comfortable reaching out to her for help, sometimes "more than once a week," and sees that relationship as "absolutely invaluable" to her success. When Marjorie first entered academia, she found "tough love" from a fellow Black female scholar who over many years had learned how to navigate her professional environment. When a colleague was dismissive of Marjorie's reliance on critical race theory as a scholarly framework, her mentor "was like, 'This will not be the first time or the last time that some White man annoys you, or somebody dismisses your work because of the work you do. Suck it up and get back out there! [Don't] let them make you stop!'"

Allies come in all shapes and sizes. Sofia, a multiracial professor, credits "a White man who took me under his wing" with being the person who "made my career." Michelle, a Black professor, names her White male dean as "the biggest factor" in her decision to pursue a university-wide administrative position, primarily because he promised her, "'I will do everything in my power to help you succeed.'" He thereby *sponsored* Michelle's professional success, rather than seeing her as an academic caretaker (Deo, 2015c; Guarino & Borden, 2017). Peer mentors can also be critical (Deo & Griffin, 2011). A Black professor named Brianna applied for a senior administrative position only after many colleagues who were "Faculty of Color and outsider faculty, [told me], 'Yeah, you should do this!'" Though she had few "people who were already advanced in their careers who were reaching back" to pull her forward, numerous same-stage colleagues "were supportive of me pursuing [leadership] opportunities." Without them, she would not be the successful professor and administrator she is today.

Professional organizations and academic conferences provide another avenue of necessary support. Having a space to identify with others both personally and professionally is a key resource for those who are marginalized (Deo, 2013). Grace, a multiracial professor, says her "closest friends are within the academy, not within the same school necessarily, but in other schools." They regularly reunite at conferences around the country. Jane met her first mentor at an academic conference geared toward Faculty of Color. Now, she regularly attends meetings organized by the Coalition of Asian Pacific American Law Faculty (CAPALF), noting, "When we are at CAPALF, I feel comfortable"—as compared to the unease she feels on her predominantly White campus. Annie, an Asian American professor, credits "coming to these conferences" as sustaining her through decades of intersectional race X gender challenges, stressing, "I think I couldn't have done it without [faculty I met through professional organizations who] have just been strongly supportive over the years." Meetings of the Northeast Corridor (a group of "Women of Color, mostly African American but not all, from New York down to Washington") provide a Black professor named Josephine "a way for me to have a larger network of Women of Color" than the very few at her own school, and include "people who modeled for me what it meant to be a Woman of Color in academia" when she was new to academia.

Navigating the landscape and potential landmines of privilege and implicit bias requires skilled guidance from senior scholars. Alexandra sees "groups like SALT and LatCrit and [others] aimed at supporting people of color [as] absolutely critical" for retaining marginalized faculty.[4] She participates in the Lutie Lytle "Black women's writing group" annually, "not just [to] socialize," but to gather "critical sources of information" unavailable elsewhere. Imani regularly attends Lutie because "I need that boost. I need that recharging of people who have experienced similar things that you have, just reaffirming you, and helping to get you through it." Especially with few other female Faculty of Color at their own institutions, gathering together creates a *critical mass* of underrepresented scholars who inspire one another and reaffirm their collective commitment to

4. The Society of American Law Teachers (SALT) is a "Community of Progressive Law Teachers Working For Justice, Diversity and Academic Excellence." More at https://www.saltlaw.org. LatCrit grew out of a meeting of like-minded scholars focused on "Latina/o Communities and Critical Race Theory," who "aim to center Latinas/os' multiple internal diversities and to situate Latinas/os in larger inter-group frameworks, both domestically and globally, to promote social justice awareness and activism." For more about LatCrit, see http://www.latcrit.org/content/about/.

succeed.[5] In addition to professional benefits, participants build trust and then social capital by bonding at these retreats—all of which contribute to future success (Deo, 2013).

Some faculty also draw sustenance from religion, spirituality, or faith. Imani puts faith "first and foremost," specifying, "I'm very religious, so I definitely rely on God and my spirituality for support." An Asian American professor named Annalisa credits her husband and children as being "the ones that make me happy and make me whole and put a smile on my face." Their family ties are strengthened because they regularly "go to church" together: "We're becoming more engrained in our church and that's important to us." Kayla, a Black professor, sees yoga and meditation as a "spiritual practice [which] has definitely been a source of support." Other forms of grounding help too; a Latina named Melanie appreciates that "being outdoors," whether "running, hiking [or otherwise] being physically active and getting out of the city," helps her "detach and gain some perspective" to "return my soul."

THE STRUCTURAL NEED FOR INSTITUTIONAL SUPPORT

To combat the presumption of incompetence and related race X gender difficulties, female Faculty of Color draw from diverse support networks, including family, friends, mentors, organizations, and religion. Yet individual strategies initiated by Women of Color faculty are not sufficient; overcoming structural challenges requires structural support. Marginalized faculty must not only find their own way forward, but also have faith that their own administrations and institutions will support them. DLA data propose numerous opportunities for law schools to initiate and participate in structural solutions.

Parental leave is a perfect example. Decades ago, as the first member of her faculty to be pregnant, Elaine recalls she "had my baby one day and I was back to work the next week." Carolina, a Latina professor, recalls, "When I had my first child, my last class was Friday and I gave birth Monday." There was no institutional support for new mothers to adjust emotionally or heal physically. Today, while more law schools offer parental leave, faculty are nevertheless pressured to not take full advantage of vague or imperfect policies. Emma, a multiracial professor and new mother, is grateful to have "a parental leave semester which will relieve some teaching and some service," though she is nervous that her tenure clock ticks on. The default should be that all parents-to-be (regardless of gender, and whether a child arrives through birth, adoption, or otherwise) as well as

5. The Supreme Court has defined critical mass as referring to "'meaningful numbers' or 'meaningful representation' . . . that encourages underrepresented minority students to participate in the classroom and not feel isolated"; in other words, "numbers such that underrepresented minority students do not feel isolated or like spokespersons for their race" (Grutter v. Bollinger, 2003). That definition is adapted here to Faculty of Color in the employment context.

others with urgent family circumstances are offered leave—including a complete break from teaching, service, and scholarship.

Administrators should also set the tone for service—by openly and enthusiastically applauding it, but also by providing direct rewards for the extra meetings, student mentorship, and additional burdens Women of Color carry while they are "taking care of the academic family" (Guarino & Borden, 2017). Cindy suggests that schools provide a financial bonus for service work equal to what some give for well-placed scholarship, asking, "When we're doing this kind of work, why don't we get compensated for it in the way that writing an article that lands at *Yale* [*Law Journal*] gets compensated?" Deans, vice deans, associate deans, and law school board members must create "institutional accountability for fixing gender service imbalances" (Flaherty, 2017). As Melissa says, "I think there definitely has to be recognition for all the many roles often Women of Color play in the law school; the advising and the retaining students role is completely undervalued." Michelle proposes that leaders truly invested in retaining diverse faculty "protect them from themselves. Many Women of Color, People of Color, have a very [deep obligation to] service that can hurt them" when it comes time for tenure or promotion review. Service should be equally valued and distributed equitably.

Administrators should also take responsibility for educating their full faculty on the challenges facing female faculty—from the presumption of incompetence in the classroom to the value of nontraditional scholarship. Sofia led a successful "session on gender in the classroom" during a faculty retreat to educate colleagues who otherwise "were not really thinking about [how] gender affected [teaching]." Rather than placing this additional burden on individual Women of Color, administrators should arrange for outside facilitators and expect full faculty attendance at anti-discrimination trainings, workshops on race X gender in the classroom, and other events showcasing support for diversity and inclusion.

Faculty hiring provides law school leaders a unique opportunity to make meaningful change. Joe, a White male professor, believes that his colleagues blindly perpetuate a White male status quo: "As institutions tend to do, they've hired people who look like themselves." Rather than waiting for recalcitrant faculty to acquiesce to increased diversity, a Black professor named April suggests that administrators who "want to increase the number of women in academia [simply] hire them, obviously. I mean, there's not a dearth of applicants out there. But you have to have a commitment to do it. It's not rocket science." Aisha, an Asian American professor, wants administrators to "stop finding reasons to *not* hire" Candidates of Color. She has witnessed colleagues who "will find reasons *not* to hire People of Color and find reasons *to* hire White people [because] they give alibis to the deficiencies of White people but . . . look for the holes in [a Person of Color's] record to keep [them] down." Similarly, Imani urges committees to consider the discrepancy between a White male "Candidate A," whose stellar CV was the result in part of "a stay-at-home wife that can take care of the kids while [he does] a [visiting assistant professorship] and clerkship," facilitating publication of "two or three articles," and a Woman of Color "Candidate B, who's been working full-time, still has the passion and drive, and will be a great professor, but yet did not have those structures to help them produce and turn out these articles." Biases can be both implicit and explicit. April states, "I think there's so few women in legal academia because White people won't hire them. [They] feel for some reason that we can't take a 'risk' on someone who doesn't fit [the standard] profile," even when these candidates have qualifications signaling their likely success. Instead, law schools should follow the lead of the corporate world—where various industry giants from MetLife to Facebook have issued "diversity ultimatums" requiring prescribed diversity in the membership and leadership of their legal teams (Rosen, 2017; Sullivan, 2017). Faculty appointments committees should treat candidates fairly and equitably, with full awareness of the potential for implicit bias along with the avoidance of direct discrimination and a purposeful determination to maintain meaningful diversity at every stage of the hiring process.

The suggestions outlined here are but a few of the necessary steps institutions must take to prove their investment in Women of Color faculty and to improve diversity and inclusion in legal academia at initial hiring and through retention. While support from friends, family, and others can further the professional goals of individual Women of Color faculty, institutional support is necessary to move beyond current race X gender challenges and toward a more equal profession.

REFERENCES

American Bar Association (ABA). (2013). Online statistics. Retrieved from https://www.americanbar.org/groups/legal_education/resources/statistics.html.

Arriola, E. R. (2012). No hay mal que por bien no venga: A journey to healing as a Latina, lesbian law professor. In G. Gutiérrez y Muhs, Y. F. Niemann, C. G. González, & A. Harris (Eds.), *Presumed incompetent: The intersections of race and class for women in academia* (pp. 372–392). Logan: Utah State University Press.

Barnes, K., & Mertz, E. (2012). Is it fair? Law professors' perceptions of tenure. *Journal of Legal Education, 61*, 511–539.

Blazoned, M. (2014, October 28). The default parent. *Huffington Post*. Retrieved from http://www.huffingtonpost.com/m-blazoned/the-default-parent_b6031128.html.

Bonilla-Silva, E. (2001). *White supremacy & racism in the post-civil rights era*. Boulder, CO: Lynne Rienner.

Bourdieu, P. (1996). *The state nobility: Elite schools in the field of power*. Stanford, CA: Stanford University Press.

Brooks, R. L. (1986). Life after tenure: Can minority law professors avoid the Clyde Ferguson syndrome? *University of San Francisco Law Review, 20*, 419–427.

Cahn, N. R. (1992). Looseness of legal language: The reasonable woman standard in theory and in practice. *Cornell Law Review, 77*, 1398–1446.

Crenshaw, K. (1991). Mapping the margins: Intersectionality, identity politics, and violence against women of color. *Stanford Law Review, 43*, 1241–1299.

Delgado, R., & Bell, D. (1989). Minority law professors' lives: The Bell-Delgado survey. *Harvard Civil Rights-Civil Liberties Law Review, 24*, 349–375.

Delgado, R., & Stefancic, J. (2017). *Critical race theory: An introduction* (3rd ed.). New York: New York University Press.

Deo, M. E. (2013). Two sides of a coin: Safe space & segregation in race/ethnic-specific law student organizations. *Washington University Journal of Law and Policy, 42,* 83–129.

Deo, M. E. (2015a). A better tenure battle: Fighting bias in teaching evaluations, *Columbia Journal of Gender and Law, 31,* 7–43.

Deo, M. E. (2015b). Trajectory of a law professor. *Michigan Journal Race and Law, 20,* 441–484.

Deo, M. E. (2015c). The ugly truth about legal academia. *Brooklyn Law Review, 80,* 943–1014.

Deo, M. E., & Griffin, K. (2011). The social capital benefits of peer mentoring relationships in law school. *Ohio Northern University Law Review, 38,* 305–332.

Deo, M. E. (2018). Intersectional barriers to tenure. *U.C. Davis Law Review, 51,* 997–1037.

Deo, M. E., & Griffin, K. (2011). The social capital benefits of peer mentoring relationships in law school. *Ohio N.U. L. Review, 38,* 305–332.

Dodgson, L. (2017, September 26). Men are getting the credit for women's work through something called "hepeating." *Business Insider*. Retrieved from http://www.businessinsider.com/what-is-hepeating-2017-9.

Flaherty, C. (2017, April 12). Relying on women, not rewarding them: Study finds female professors outperform men in service—to their possible professional detriment. *Inside Higher Ed*. Retrieved from https://www.insidehighered.com/news/2017/04/12/study-finds-female-professors-outperform-men-service-their-possible-professional.

Grutter v. Bollinger. (2003). 539 US 306.

Guarino, C. M., & Borden, V. H. (2017). Faculty service loads and gender: Are women taking care of the academic family? *Research in Higher Education, 58*(6), 672–694.

Gutiérrez y Muhs, G., Niemann, Y. F., González, C. G., & Harris, A. (Eds.). (2012). *Presumed incompetent: The intersections of race and class for women in academia*. Logan: Utah State University Press.

Harris, A. (1990). Race and essentialism in feminist legal theory. *Stanford Law Review, 42,* 581–616.

Harris, A. P., & González, C. G. (2012). Introduction. In G. Gutiérrez y Muhs, Y. F. Niemann, C. G. González, & A. Harris (Eds.), *Presumed incompetent: The intersections of race and class for women in academia* (pp. 1–14). Logan: Utah State University Press.

Kang, J., & Lane, K. (2010). Seeing through colorblindness: Implicit bias and the law. *UCLA Law Review, 58,* 467–520.

Kupenda, A. M. (2012). Facing down the spooks. In G. Gutiérrez y Muhs, Y. F. Niemann, C. G. González, & A. Harris (Eds.), *Presumed incompetent: The intersections of race and class for women in academia* (pp. 20–28). Logan: Utah State University Press.

Lazos, S. R. (2012). Are student teaching evaluations holding back women and minorities? The perils of "doing" gender and race in the classroom. In G. Gutiérrez y Muhs, Y. F. Niemann, C. G. González, & A. Harris (Eds.), *Presumed incompetent: The intersections of race and class for women in academia* (pp. 164–185). Logan: Utah State University Press.

Onwuachi-Willig, A. (2012). Silence of the lambs. In G. Gutiérrez y Muhs, Y. F. Niemann, C. G. González, & A. Harris (Eds.), *Presumed incompetent: The intersections of race and class for women in academia* (pp. 142–151). Logan: Utah State University Press.

Petzold, J. (2018, September 6). Law student perceptions of faculty [blog post]. Retrieved from http://lssse.indiana.edu/uncategorized/law-student-perceptions-of-faculty.

Quintanilla, V. (2013). Critical race empiricism: A new means to measure civil procedure. *UC Irvine Law Review, 3*, 101–130.

Rosen, W. (2017, April 2). Facebook pushes outside law firms to become more diverse. *New York Times*. Retrieved from https://www.nytimes.com/2017/04/02/business/dealbook/facebook-pushes-outside-law-firms-to-become-more-diverse.html?mcubz=0.

Solnit, R. (2012, August 12). Why mansplaining is still a problem. *AlterNet*. Retrieved from http://www.alternet.org/why-mansplaining-still-problem.

Sullivan, C. (2017, April 3). Deadline for diversity issued by top MetLife lawyer. *Big Law Business*. Retrieved from https://biglawbusiness.com/deadline-for-diversity-issued-by-top-metlife-lawyer.

Wade, L. (2016, December 28). The invisible workload that drags women down. *Money.com*. Retrieved from http://time.com/money/4561314/women-work-home-gender-gap.

Wildman, S. M. (1996). *Privilege revealed: How invisible preference undermines America*. New York: New York University Press.

Wing, A. K. (2012). Lessons from a portrait: Keep calm and carry on. In G. Gutiérrez y Muhs, Y. F. Niemann, C. G. González, & A. Harris (Eds.), *Presumed incompetent: The intersections of race and class for women in academia* (pp. 356–371). Logan: Utah State University Press.

TWENTY-NINE

Healing Is Speaking

Stories Evolving Perceptions of Microaggressions, Abuse, and Racial Battle Fatigue—The Good Mind in Action

Melissa Michal Slocum

One chilly afternoon waiting for the university's bus, I encountered a former professor who only ever looked at the first page of my paper until it was perfect. This resulted in three entirely different rewrites *after* she then looked at a few more pages. She asked what I was working on. After explaining that I was theorizing through a term connected to American Indian trauma, a term not yet critically analyzed, she said, "Oh, you mean your methodology." I replied, "No, I'm theorizing through how this term differently highlights trauma specific to American Indian experiences." She replied again, "Yes, methodology." I shook my head and looked away. I knew theoretical arguments were classed higher, that I was in fact theorizing, and that she meant for me to think I was doing less.

Half of the authority figures I worked with as a graduate student—including trusted American Indian mentors—consistently abused power in fear-inducing ways, like that moment with my professor, creating unsafe spaces. Those moments might seem small, perhaps easy to brush aside from an outsider's perspective, but because they occurred daily, the result was a slow and painful degradation of self. For seven years as a graduate student and continuing into a visiting position, as a Haudenosaunee woman and first-generation college student, and now as a scholar, I have experienced mental and emotional abuse from mentors, faculty, and fellow graduate students both Native and non-Native. So, too, have most other American Indian scholars and scholars from underrepresented groups. Because I am a junior colleague in an untenured position, I cannot write about my experiences in as much detail as is important to share. I am semi-silenced in this regard, as were some of the women I interviewed to discuss the still-present abuse of colonized thinking. It was the undergraduates and tenured women I spoke to who were able to be more forthright. This need to protect our ability to obtain a job is one of the many ways others in the system have power over us.

DOI: 10.7330/9781607329664.c029

Normed expectations are engrained, and those who are outside of those norms make those in power afraid we will take their power.

Recently, I had a phone conversation with a gentleman from my community, keeper of some of our Haudenosaunee stories, and distanced from home like I. He is now retired from sociology. I relayed to him recent issues asserting our kinds of arguments. What he said next struck me. Academia is based on fear: either instilling it or reacting out of it. Sometimes the same person can both cause fear and react to it. Fear-based thinking is what we call the Clouded Mind, a mind filled with reactions and relationships far from the Haudenosaunee Good Mind.

The Good Mind is an intricate lifeway and a spiritual ideology in which individuals and ancestors build a consciousness for a community. As Oren Lyons, an Onondaga faithkeeper, outlines, the Good Mind theorizes through three principles: "peace in mind and community," equity resulting in community justice, and "the power of the Good Minds, which embodies good health and reason" (Dragone, 2002, p. 47). These principles institute peace and connection to a world where no one wars or presumes they are worth more than another and where no knowledge or way of being takes over another.

My argument means to lift the Clouded Mind caused by our silenced fears, the first step in healing. The Good Mind sees us working through this process first before we can move into peace and connection with others. Without this first step, we cannot help others through the healing process and we cannot keep ourselves from remaining in fear and passing it on in hurtful ways. To start healing, we have to first label what's happening and recognize that we have survived such fears. Then, we must talk more openly in safe spaces because this is what clears the air. Importantly, no one can leap through healing. In my community, we have what's called the Condolence Ceremony. See *Peace, Power, Righteousness* by Taiaike Alfred (1999) and *The Edge of the Woods* by Jon Parmenter (2010) for more discussion of the ceremony. The Condolence Ceremony is meant to move someone through grieving for a loved one who has passed on. Eventually, the ceremony connects a person with someone who will fulfill—not replace—the role of the deceased, filling in the gaps the loss creates. We see healing as a process that involves the *entire* community. Before this final connection, in order to move through the grief, there are many people working with you even before the ceremony. Within academia there exists a death of our personhoods. When we must constantly navigate a system where we are outside of "the norm," we must each day decide how much of our personhood we can actually incorporate in this project or interject in this department dialogue or into our curriculum. Over time, that etches away selves. And the Clouded Mind grows cloudier and more impactful in how we react out of fear.

These experiences are more than microaggressions, the casual daily degradation of underrepresented peoples or issues, or even hazing, challenging initiations into social systems. The microaggressions and hazing rituals imposed on students and scholars of difference compound and *are* mental and emotional abuses because they are specific to breaking a person away from their identity.

I use "person of difference" (POD) instead of Person of Color because indigenous peoples do not ascribe to social categorizations and because those with disabilities and those within the LGBTQ communities also experience hazing and microaggressions. First, I will discuss microaggressions and academic hazing to connect how daily encounters add up to abuse and how they are specific to the university. Then I will discuss emotional abuse, connecting the elements of abuse with microaggressions and hazing. Following this, the women's stories will act as experiential evidence of abuse that when spoken out loud releases the toxicity into the air—a start to healing, but not a finality. This argument shows that there is a cycle to abuse. The recognition of that cycle lifts the Clouded Mind so that we no longer hold onto those fears and so that we release the trauma each time we tell our stories. In my Haudenosaunee community, healing comes from naming, and then feeling and releasing the emotions *first*.

My methodology for this chapter was to collect stories in order to analyze through multiple voices, not simply my own experiences, thus revealing a more rounded story. I interviewed female undergraduate students, junior colleagues, and tenured colleagues. I use a polyvocal narrative tone and writing style I term "narrative critical framing" so as to invoke oral tradition into the criticism that includes more casual language and sentences, contractions, repetition, and intense description. I am grateful to those who bravely voiced their stories for this essay in order to evoke orality. But I must also mention those graduate students who were afraid of, even triggered traumatically by, the very idea of telling their stories. They assumed it would harm them on the job market. That reaction is the result of being so aggressively hazed and abused from kindergarten through to their graduate careers that the impulse is to remain quiet.

ABUSE COMPILED AND GROOMED: RACIAL MICROAGGRESSIONS AND RACIAL ACADEMIC HAZING

Hazing for graduate students is not an unknown consequence of going through the master's and PhD systems. When the layperson thinks of hazing, is it often physical abuse tied to sororities, fraternities, and other campus undergraduate groups, but it also takes place within the classrooms and the offices of mentors. Clifford Madsen, Robert O. Lawton Distinguished Professor of Music at Florida State University, argues for ridding what he terms academic hazing from the master's and PhD process. He states that "academic hazing still exists today concerning any number of 'rites of passage' . . . or any other impediment to real scholarship and developing a passion for learning and research. It is a curious club that psychologically bludgeons its prospective members over a long period then smilingly welcomes them into the fraternity" (2003, p. 77). Sadly, *bludgeon* is the right term here. There is shocking violence against the mind when, for example, there are consistent verbal admonitions against your work with no offers of help to refine arguments. Take the example I mentioned in the opening, of my professor who would discuss only the first page of my paper. When she asked what my argument was, I pointed to the second page, but was severely criticized for not focusing on the first page. Cameron Whitworth Jenkins, considering Madsen, investigates academic hazing in music education and finds that these "rites of passage" are prevalent and preventing development of *sound* research (2014, p. 3). At another university in a course outside of my field with a female professor of difference, my three emailed requests to meet were ignored. Feedback was never given on any projects after the first month, including paper topic ideas. I then emailed a draft of my final paper to request at least written feedback, only to be yelled at in several paragraphs for not understanding earlier (unclear) feedback on a different project and applying it to this one. When mentors, from whom both Madsen and Jenkins argue this most often occurs, induce such pressures to be immediately perfect without formal field training, no person can write clearly or develop newer scholarly critique.

When the hazing that is already in place piles on top of racial microaggressions, the result is a traumatic forcing out of identity. As William Smith, ethnic studies professor at the University of Utah, argues, consistent microaggressions mean that the targets go to battle every day. As defined by Smith et al., (2005) racial battle fatigue is the result of a process of daily interactions that constantly seek to deny a Person of Color's humanity and are "subtle, stunning, cumulative, verbal and non-verbal insults layered with racism, sexism, elitism, and other subordination," which "cause unnecessary stress to People of Color while privileging Whites . . . likened to the stress soldiers experience during battle" (2005, p. 300). One interviewee, a queer Latina senior scholar, Ronnie, works on social justice education. She believes we must add to our critique of and the definition of racial battle fatigue, which she calls multidimensional battle fatigue because of the many spaces and people's intersections that play a role in the aggression:

> I like *battle fatigue* because it equates it with a much more serious physical, psychological, and spiritual toll that it takes on our bodies and our communities. People will say, "Oh, this is just rude behavior" . . . but literally you are attacking our spirit . . . Our spirits, our minds are being murdered and/or destroyed and/or warped by all of these symptoms . . . It's not just what racism does to us. It's about what *combating* racism does to us.

There is a severeness that is violent and disruptive to our ways of thinking and being that must be acknowledged. But more important, the ways microaggressions act are *subtle*.

My term *academic difference hazing* extends Smith's and Madsen's work to argue that in the education system, racial battle fatigue is a result of abuse because those kinds of microaggressions are so severe, *and* tied to our identities, that they fit the patterns of abusive relationships. It's incredibly important to note that this is specific to the university system so that we have a foundation for understanding how uniquely the education system affects minds and bodies. It's also important that we voice this as abuse because, as Ronnie argues, it is causing a spiritual death. Neither rudeness nor unkindness does that. The microaggressions specific to the academic system groom us to become extremely different people, much further from our origins than we might be if we hadn't been abused. Knowing that specific set of patterned experiences then allows us to better heal ourselves from both within and without the American educational structures. Hazing in these situations is always about the differences of the POD and how those differences go "against" dominant Western academic standards in the work, in discussions, in curriculum expectations, in the writing styles or source types, and in teaching and research expectations. This is something that often stops for White scholars upon graduation because they are then perceived as equal. That perception of equality rarely occurs for those of difference.

ABUSE DENIES SOVEREIGN EDUCATION

Victims of abuse so often have been mind-controlled in ways that keep them from informing on their abuser. As Dr. Stephanie Sarkis, clinical specialist in child and adult counseling, outlines, the abuser makes a person question their reality and sets in place situations where the abuser's lies and manipulation become the reality for that person and those around them. In university systems, the racial microaggressions used to instill fear in students become part of the hoops students leap through to weed out the "weak." But we of difference are seen as weak not simply because of lack of institutional knowledge, but because of our worldviews. Our Good Minds are harmed and severely clouded here.

Defining our microaggressions and hazings as abuse is necessary to help in two ways: (1) it allows those of us of difference experiencing these situations to heal from such trauma through naming and recognizing; and (2) it shows both those causing these abuses and those witnessing these situations that this is not simply "how academia is," but how the system, and those abusing power within it, significantly harms others. Naming reverses the lies and manipulation through our recognition, returning our power back to us to heal. Quite frankly, these experiences deny our rights to a just education and existence within academia. As Mvskoke/Creek scholar K. Tsianina Lomawaima and Teresa L. McCarty (2002) argue, diversity and democracy are, and should be, intimately tied together. Because democratic ideals are connected to institutionalized education systems without proper critique of such ties to differences, we are displaced in the systems that should actually raise us up (p. 281). As an indigenous woman, I have a sovereign right to an education that values my background and perceives me *not* as a threat but as someone adding important critiques to the dialogue.

Abuse is the mistreatment and misuse of one thing by another where there is a relationship between the two. Presumed is that a standard exists about how objects, people, and places should be treated. When one human abuses another, because physical or emotional pain is involved, the result is a broken "social contract," "based on a common understanding, drawn from various religious, ethical and enlightened government principles and traditions, that hold out the idea that human beings are not things to be owned, but rather beings having innate rights and worth as independent creatures who are all roughly equal" (Patricelli, 2005). When one in power repeatedly breaks this social contract, abuse then becomes the pattern of that relationship. Abusive actions cause severe damage to those in this relationship. As people of difference, our worth has been categorized by those who don't allow our backgrounds to be an accepted, understood, and balanced part of the system. We are never roughly equal. Academic difference hazing, when confronted through the relationships a person of difference must regularly encounter, where they are presumed unworthy of consideration and kept thinking less of themselves because of their background, is abuse. Encountering situations where identity and knowledge base are presumed incompetent is emotional abuse.

When I began researching racial microaggressions, the resulting battle fatigue sounded akin to survivors of trauma and abuse. Below, from Vancouver Coastal Health (2017), are signs of emotional abuse:

1. Threats of violence or abandonment
2. Intentionally frightening
3. Making an individual fear that they will not receive food or care they need
4. Lying
5. Making derogative or slanderous statements about individuals to others
6. Socially isolating an individual, failing to let them have visitors
7. Withholding important information
8. Demeaning an individual because of the language that they speak
9. Intentionally misinterpreting traditional practices
10. Telling an individual they are too much trouble
11. Ignoring or excessively criticizing
12. Unreasonably ordering an individual around; treating an individual like a servant or child

At first glance, the list above may not seem to fit within an academic setting. But let's break this down within the contexts of the professional development of students and colleagues from undergraduate up through to assistant professor positions, where interactions are based on how those POD assert their backgrounds or are "read" by outsiders. The list that follows outlines a combination of examples that many of the interviewees said happened to them:

1. Threatening to abandon a student because they won't complete a project in a perceived academic way
2. Giving no positive comments and threatening to not allow them to move on to the next step
3. Making them fearful they will not graduate or taking away certain research privileges
4. Lying about abilities, either to them or to others
5. Interfering illegally with a job process and lying about interactions or abilities

6. Not allowing the student to show work to others or not allowing outside peer reviews of articles
7. Keeping from the student important career information, including how to "jump" through the hoops, feedback geared toward publishing, and how to respond to difficult interview questions or dialogues with colleagues
8. Demeaning an individual because of their writing style or tendencies, even if used in the field
9. Intentionally misinterpreting or avoiding getting to know a group's traditional ideas and practices and making assumptions about these ideas
10. Using abusive language on commentary
11. Unreasonably ordering a student to take research out of the work or to change the argument to look more academic/White

If these experiences occur daily and are the direct result of a person's differences, then racial battle fatigue will result. The stories of my interviewees and their emotional reactions to my questions about their experiences with microaggressions and racial battle fatigue arose out of traumatized states. As we dialogued about their experiences, each person commented that this was healing.

THE NECESSARY STORYTELLING: RELEASING ABUSE'S TOXINS

What the students and colleagues I spoke to recognized is that microaggressions begin early on and continue, from elementary school on through college-level work and then into university careers, where the compounding there makes racial battle fatigue take over. The system has set up students of difference to consistently feel less valuable than others with passive-aggressive mistreatment that places students of difference at a disadvantage and behind in the system's expectations. It's a pattern of dominoes slowly put into place that causes students of difference to either remain silent so as not to fight, to assimilate to the dominant ways, or to fight and receive constant pushbacks that exhaust the body and the mind. Throughout this degrading process, we lose our trust in people and in the system that broke us down. I interviewed five female students of difference ranging in age from twenty-three to twenty-eight, two junior scholars, and two senior scholars. Some students had heard about racial battle fatigue. Some hadn't, but recognized it from their own experiences. The advanced scholars already knew of racial battle fatigue, but they too had a hard time defining it within their own experiences prior to discussing it in the interviews.

Earlier experiences show an increasing pattern of grooming students of difference to be fearful of their identities. These moments scaffold a mindset that we don't matter and that we can't be successful within the systems. Once we see those earlier moments as just as valuable to our understanding of the process of academic difference hazing, it becomes more possible to intervene in the system. In response to the definitions of emotional abuse and racial battle fatigue, Ray, an African American and Puerto Rican undergraduate student, said the definitions make the distinction clear between our experiences and those of other students and colleagues: "It's letting everyone know, 'You don't all fall into this. So don't think that you do.' . . . Women of Color don't get the acknowledgement. We don't get the care . . . We are very much in this gray area where nobody wants to talk about us and nobody wants to care. It's like such a fight."

Ray recalls being shocked at how little she learned about herself and injustices before college: "You don't learn that you are being taught wrong until you can afford to go to college . . . You're just kind of pushed through the system . . . You feel like you just have to do what you're told because you don't want to push back." Ray echoes what all the students feel. If they do not move ahead and fit into the system, they will be knocked down time and again. We are taught not to fight, but to keep things moving along smoothly.

Another student, Cass, shares a college experience readying a presentation, a comparison between Donald Trump and Iago from *Othello*. As soon as she gave the title students asked her not to present. Cass was raised by those who remain afraid of being deported. She is Latinx and has belonged to several activist groups. She has been deconstructing the system for many years. In most classes, she speaks up and corrects histories, word choice, and definitions given by mostly White male professors. This was a student who, by the very problematic curricula taught across coursework, felt she could never relax as she *must* become the teacher. The students were probably prepared for what they considered her "teaching" moments and so reacted negatively. In response to students telling her to stop talking, her White male professor said, "Yeah, I think they're right" and didn't allow her to even explain her argument, which in the end was not what they would have presumed. Later, Cass was granted permission to present—but only after already being traumatized by the assumptions made. Students of difference later told her they should have "stuck up for you." She is being groomed to not question the system and to not become the angry female of difference, and others of difference are groomed to either remain quiet or to quiet her as well. We become something false and negative in others' perspectives.

College becomes this space of awakening for students of difference during those early stages. We learn we cannot trust fellow students, let alone professors, because there are no safe spaces. We have a way of getting used to this so that it becomes part of our way of being—an acceptance that these things will continue happening even though they are completely inappropriate and unethical. What we have found, and what these interviews revealed, is that most of the time, we *are* being judged incompetent, but in such subtle ways that outsiders will redefine this for us: "That's nothing" or "You're imagining it." These earlier moments teach us we must hold back how we assert these identities.

Junior and senior colleagues echoed similar early experiences. However, throughout graduate school, the grooming intensified. One indigenous scholar, Lisa, recounts a graduate school experience that eventually placed her behind in her studies. She had been specifically sought out to attend a university through email exchanges with the one American Indian scholar in that department. When she accepted the university's offer, she was assigned that scholar as her mentor for the first year, with the underlying assumption that he would be her dissertation chair thereafter.

> I didn't have a choice in the matter . . . Then come to find out, this mentor had no real background knowledge in American Indian studies. He had been hired because of his name made in other ways. So when I pursued other professors as potential dissertation chairs, they wouldn't touch me. I was *his* student. And my dissertation ideas made them uncomfortable because I was incorporating my community and our ways. They assumed they wouldn't know how to help me with that. I just needed help with making my argument stronger, which he never gave feedback on. His comments were just word choice changes.

Years into the PhD program, she began to uncover even more things about her mentor that made her uncomfortable, but that also revealed she was still just a check box to the university.

> There were other departments that explicitly kept their Native female students away from him. The underlying feeling was that he was "too friendly" with the pretty, younger female students . . . I noticed that if I wore a dress, he would kiss me on the cheek. When I mentioned all of this to both the department chair and another American studies professor, they said that they knew. But they couldn't tell me. I had to find out for myself . . . They also told me I should stay with him as there weren't other options. Where was my protection? I spent two years with someone who not only would not help me become more academically sound, but who abused power with female students. And to be another Native, too. It all hurt. We truly do not matter, so long as we give them more diversity to advertise.

The department was aware of the issue, but seemed unaware of the harm this caused to Lisa's career, and of the harm the professor could have caused physically. This creates an unspoken rhetoric that not only are we not safe, we aren't allowed to be safe. Too, we come to understand that no one, not even those in our own intersections, values our bodies or our minds.

Another junior indigenous colleague, Christina, encountered issues with two male indigenous scholars. As she notes, it's much more painful to know your own group so negatively affects you. She had published her book only two years after graduating. She then worked on a project with another indigenous colleague, a man, who did none of the work. At a luncheon with other indigenous scholars celebrating said project, he was praised by another male Indigenous scholar. She was not. It was common knowledge that her book is out and that she co-ran the project and her name was on the program. He never apologized. He didn't correct the wrong or speak with her at all during the rest of the event. What we experience in abuse does not come just from those outside our groups. Some of those in our groups have taken on the fear and stalled their own healing.

Ronnie contends that if we don't recognize what happened, we can easily become like our abusers—adding to miles of already instilled fatigue. This is particularly true if "we forget the anger . . . forget how it felt to go through the system." What she is referring to here is when those of difference are complacent and shake our heads when students of difference discuss any hardships, as if "I had to go through it, then so do you." If we remain unhealed, that complacency, derived from exhaustion, will affect others like us. That makes it ever more difficult for us to then help others through their racial academic hazing or to stop the aggressions.

As chair of her department, Ronnie encountered several situations managing money in the department, including paying students for events they helped to host or correcting a miscommunication on agreed-upon jobs for students. The department did not see it as necessary to replace a lost check right away or for an overload to be agreed upon. She fought to pay back students of difference who could not afford to live without this money. Those fights took quite a bit of time and her own money to sort through. Shortly after these two situations occurred, Ronnie needed to present to the incoming class and find a teaching replacement for a course, the same week that DACA was repealed, while also enduring media coverage of Trump's rhetoric attacking multiple people of difference.

> We took care of the mistake with teaching. But the next time that I met with the dean, he came down on me punitively for that mistake and all of the other mistakes. And what was really the icing on the cake was when he said, "I know today is a hard day because DACA got rescinded, but I have other bad news . . . I feel like you have your priorities mixed up." . . . That was the intention of the conversation, that maybe I should consider a different role for myself . . . A chair is about dotting the Is and crossing the Ts . . . Of course that is my priority as well . . . I said to him, "As an ally one of the biggest mistakes that you can do is come to me and acknowledge that the world is falling apart that people's lives are at stake and yet come to me about bureaucracy . . . and say that that is more important than people's lives . . . Even though I support your diversity work, I still feel like you aren't doing your job as well as you should."

If diversity work was truly supported, then an understanding of what those differences bring with them has to follow, which, in this case, the dean could not see. Had Ronnie not fought for students receiving their money and instead prioritized the lecture and teaching duties, her actions would have been more acceptable. But that also meant that those students possibly would have had to leave school, not pay rent, and/or not moved forward in the manner that they had intended. The dean was used to a chair who followed rules to the letter and waited for the red tape to clear. But those rules don't consider students of difference who cannot take on these financial hardships on top of all of the other racial microaggressions. Ronnie went on to discuss three other students who lost their teaching jobs due to a paperwork. Those students can no longer afford school, through no fault of their own. Ronnie is presumed incompetent because of how she views what could work in the institution to support and retain students, which inherently rises up out of her differences. Too, framing Ronnie as incapable in her job because she made such small mistakes blows out of proportion what occurred and misses the extra work we put in to create safer atmospheres for other students of difference. "I still believe and have hope that we are shifting practices," she says. Battle fatigue can rip that away from us. So she emphasizes both having hope that our colleagues will develop into allies and that they are trying. She believes her dean, even with these kinds of moments, has grown and changed his perception.

We need to be prepared to continue to fight even after the healing and, therefore, to continually seek to heal. I heard healing happening through sharing, cleansing crying, and anger that dissipated with time. We must say what has occurred; otherwise we hold this inside of ourselves to simmer and eat away at our souls in the same way the original treatment does. Some of my healing has come from currently working at a university that values and validates my experiences, with colleagues who agree this was abusive and toxic, and who care about the triggers I experience because of my past. However, it is a rare institutional mindset of social justice and inclusive practices that are expected at every level. As someone in a visiting position, I know I may not find this sense of peace and wholeness at another institution, and those of us here know how lucky we truly are to experience education in this way. But it shores me up for the next round of challenges, and it gives me hope that this kind of education is indeed possible. It's not a rose-colored dream that we all have. My students have given so much to this dialogue, whether interviewed or simply sitting in seats in front of me. They are the next generations we must take care of.

This book you hold does not signal the end of academic difference hazing or battle fatigue. Believing will. Hearing will. Speaking will. We of difference in academia have been torn apart, not just hurt. Those pieces are very difficult to put back inside our souls. There was one documentary that affected me so greatly and brought me into my journey to speak openly about education: *Our Spirits Don't Speak English* (Rich-Heape Films, 2008). This film describes how debilitating and tortuous American Indian boarding schools were, to the point where we couldn't speak to our ancestors any longer because those spirits don't speak English. We were broken again and again by American institutionalized forced education. The more those stories are heard and understood, the more we can all have our ships and our canoes that do not disturb one another, but move along the same river.

I survived these moments and so much more. I cannot allow these experiences to go unheard. That's also my healing. I write good into the system, and I teach my students to think differently, to care, and to be kind. I think about my students and how they crave these conversations. How they crave to have their experiences discussed and understood rather than be the lone Latinx or African American females who just heard a slur or racist remark in the hallway or who cannot simply read any more White writers and scholars or who are treated differently because of how they look or what they speak up about. Something they believe they cannot talk about, which becomes the cycle where abuse rises up and becomes an ugly, silencing, harmful, living being. Healing and transparency lead to a Good-Minded pathway meant not simply to help us as individuals but to create an atmosphere where this no longer happens to students or to faculty.

Our healing is making change. Now the stories call each of you to tell your story and to believe the stories of others.

REFERENCES

Alfred, T. (1999). *Peace, power, righteousness: An indigenous manifesto.* Vol. 171. Toronto: Oxford University Press.

Dragone, N. (2002). *Haudenosaunee literature: A view from outside the culture.* Unpublished master's thesis, University of Oklahoma, Norman.

Jenkins, C. W. (2014). Academic hazing in music education. University of Mississippi, Oxford. *Proquest Dissertations.* Retrieved from https://search-proquest-com.ezproxy.library.unlv.edu/docview/1559962353/fulltextPDF/769660DB3A614806PQ/1?accountid=3611.

Lomawaima, K. T., and T. McCarty. (2002, Summer). When tribal sovereignty challenges democracy: American Indian education and the democratic Ideal. *American Education Research Journal,* 39(2), 279–305. Retrieved from http://journals.sagepub.com.ezproxy.library.unlv.edu/doi/abs/10.3102/00028312039002279.

Madsen, C. K. (2003). Instruction and supervision of graduate students in music education. *Research Studies in Music Education,* 21, 72–79. Retrieved from http://journals.sagepub.com.ezproxy.library.unlv.edu/doi/abs/10.1177/1321103X030210010601.

Parmenter, J. (2010). *The edge of the woods: Iroquoia, 1534–1701.* Lansing: Michigan State University Press.

Patricelli, K. (2005). Abuse defined. *Mentalhelp.net.* Retrieved from https://www.mentalhelp.net/articles/abuse-defined/.

Rich-Heape Films. (2008). *Our spirits don't speak English: Indian boarding school.*

Smith, W., et al. (2005). Challenging racial battle fatigue on historically white campuses: A critical race examination of race-related stories. In C. A. Stanley (Ed.), *Faculty of color teaching in primarily white colleges and universities* (pp. 299–327). San Francisco: Jossey-Bass.

Vancouver Coastal Health. (2017). About adult abuse and neglect. Retrieved from http://www.vchreact.ca/read_psychological.htm.

THIRTY

The Social Ecology of Tokenism in Higher Education Institutions

Yolanda Flores Niemann

> We must remember that the university was developed with white males in mind as students, and people of color have only recently in our history been admitted to some universities. Tokenism has sufficed to appease the masses and prevent national revolt from people of color. If we are to have a truly integrated society, it will never develop through tokenism.
>
> (KING, 1966)

As evident from the pervasive university student activism of the last two years, the likes of which have not occurred in half a century, and with demands for more Faculty of Color, tokenism is no longer appeasing the masses.[1] The cost of this tokenism and race-related activism can be measured in dollars required to address demands, in damaged careers, in student time and energy, and in the compromised reputation of higher education. The greatest damage of tokenism, however, may well be to the careers of Faculty of Color who work in predominantly White institutions.

More than six decades after the implementation of the federal affirmative action policy, Faculty of Color remain significantly underrepresented on college campuses. According to the National Center for Education Statistics, in 2013, of the total numbers of all instructional faculty—692,302—White males and females made up 75 percent, or 520,703. In contrast, the combined, collective total of African Americans, Latinas/os, Asian Americans, American Indians, and Native Hawaiians made up roughly 19 percent, or 131,228 (the remaining percentage were of international and/or unknown ethnicity). The numbers were worse with respect to tenure-track Faculty of Color. Out of 275,217 tenure-track

1. Reprinted with permission from *Peace Review: A Journal of Social Justice, 28* (4), 451–458.

DOI: 10.7330/9781607329664.c030

faculty (professors, associate professors, and assistant professors) in the United States in 2013, 79 percent were White men or women. The combined, collective group of African Americans, Latinas/os, Asian Americans, American Indians, and Native Hawaiians made up only 17.8 percent of the total number of faculty on highly coveted and prestigious tenure tracks. These heavily skewed numbers create a social ecology fertile for the tokenization of Faculty of Color. In this essay, I build on the extant literature on tokenism and related constructs to present an applied theory of the social ecology of tokenism in higher education institutions. The theory posits that the structural social ecology of higher education is the foundation for the creation and maintenance of tokenism for Faculty of Color who work in predominantly White institutions.

The tokenized status of persons in educational contexts is not a new concern. At the height of the civil rights movement, for instance, Martin Luther King Jr. addressed tokenism in multiple speeches. In 1966 he said,

> Massive resistance has given way in the South to a kind of sophisticated kind of resistance embodied in tokenism. If we are to have a truly integrated society, it will never develop through tokenism. We get a few Negroes in formerly all-white schools and say we have integrated schools. The fact is that this kind of tokenism is much more subtle and can be much more depressing to the victims of the tokenism than all-out resistance. And so we have a long, long way to go in dealing with this problem, but it is not only a Southern problem that we face, it is a national problem.

Malcom X (1963) also addressed tokenism in educational systems:

> What gains? . . . It has been nine years since the Supreme Court decision outlawing segregated schools, yet less than ten per cent of the Negro students in the South are in integrated schools. That isn't integration, that's tokenism! We must have a permanent solution. A temporary solution won't do. Tokenism will no longer suffice.

Experientially, tokens are rare persons of their demographic groups within the context, especially in contrast with majority numerical dominants. In her classic work on power dynamics in the workplace, *Men and Women of the Corporation,* Kanter (1977) concluded that the perceptual processes associated with tokenism generally occur when the numerical minority constitutes 15 percent or fewer of the total persons in comparison to the dominant majority group the workplace context. The skewed group structure is the foundation that affects interactions and perceptual phenomena associated with the nondominants, or tokens. These perceptions relate broadly to three overarching phenomena. The first is visibility and awareness—tokens capture a larger share of awareness due to numerical proportions; the smaller their proportions, the greater the awareness. The second is polarization—dominants are more aware of commonalities with and differences from the tokens, and differences between tokens and dominants are exaggerated. The third is assimilation—tokens' attributes are distorted to fit preexisting generalizations about their social types.

The low numbers of Faculty of Color in the midst of high numbers of dominant, White persons afford exaggeration of differences between Whites and

People of Color in the university context. This exaggeration of differences leads to a high level of distinctiveness in the environment, providing the environmental supports that evoke tokenism and its consequences. *Environmental supports* are the generative sources of perception found not in the individual, but in the physical and social world. As Gibson (1966) argued, the properties of the physical environment afford the direct perception of physical objects in a certain manner. Gibson referred to the information attributes of the visual array as *affordances*. That is, the basis of perception lies in what is afforded in the environment. In the case of tokenism, the overarching affordance is the very low numbers of Faculty of Color relative to the numbers of White faculty. These disproportionately low numbers become evidence that supports attributions of belongingness and of perceptions about which particular roles are more appropriately served by Faculty of Color rather than by Whites.

The affordances derived from the chronic distinctiveness of Faculty of Color are also social identity contingencies, which Purdie-Vaughns and her colleagues (2008) define as possible judgments, stereotypes, opportunities, restrictions, and treatments tied to one's social identity in a given setting. That is, features or cues in a setting may create the expectation that a person's treatment will be contingent on one of their social identities. Among the most overt cues is the number of individuals in the setting who share a given racial identity. Because there are so few Faculty of Color in typical research universities, their racial identity becomes their most distinctive feature. Their chronic distinctiveness is the mechanism that moves the nondominant, or token, Faculty of Color beyond being a data point within the low numbers to high visibility and exaggeration of differences between themselves and the dominant group members.

The skewed proportions shape the power dynamics, perception of, and interaction with Faculty of Color to such an extent that their identities are disrupted. Faculty of Color enter their positions as colleagues, scholars, and experts in their field, but their overarching identity quickly shifts to being the Black, brown, Asian, or Indian faculty member. Their racial identity becomes the lens through which they are perceived, especially for the diversity-related needs of the university and communities within and around it. In other words, for the perceivers, including White dominants and People of Color, the environment affords seeing Faculty of Color mainly through the salience of their racial group membership. Such identity disruption is reflected in Kanter's finding that

> tokens not merely deviants or people who are different from other group members along any one dimension. They are people identified by ascribed characteristics (master status such as sex, race . . .) or other characteristics that carry with them a set of assumptions about culture, status, and behavior highly salient for majority category members. They differ from dominants, not in ability to do a task or in acceptance of work norms, but in terms of secondary and informal assumptions. Tokens can never be just another organizational member while their category is so rare . . . In these contexts the word token reflects one's distinctiveness in the context and status as a symbol of one's kind. (1977, p. 968)

Due to conscious and unconscious biases, including racial stereotypes, it may seem quite obvious and natural for White faculty peers, students, staff members, members of the community at large, and university administrators to believe that matters involving race and/or diversity are best handled by the non-White persons in the context. Faculty, staff, and administrators may impose upon Faculty of Color roles they perceive to be best suited to non-White faculty, irrespective of their expertise in the task or activities associated with those roles. For instance, White administrators may place Faculty of Color in the spotlight when it is in the interest of their unit, their grant, or the university brand, for example, touting diversity as a priority. Faculty of Color may be asked to teach race-related curricula, irrespective of their expertise in that scholarly domain. White colleagues may believe they have a right to place the names of Faculty of Color colleagues on grant proposals when the granting agency values diversity, with or without their permission. Countless possibilities of this tokenization arise, as reflected in the narratives written by Faculty of Color. Tokens experience constant challenges of being viewed as "other," including lack of professional support systems; excessive scrutiny by peers, superiors, and students; an unstated requirement to work harder to gain recognition and respect; assumptions that positions are acquired through affirmative action and that, therefore, these Black women lacked the necessary qualifications; and denial of access to power structures normally associated with their positions.

As the forces at play call upon their racial identity to meet the needs of the university, the predominant perception of tokens as racial persons, rather than as faculty peers and professors with disciplinary expertise and valued scholarship, is exacerbated and compounded. Tokens' distinctiveness leads dominants to assimilate Faculty of Color to their preconceived notions about their group and to question their goodness of fit for a given environment, role, and/or occupation. As a result, Faculty of Color may be evaluated under different, and more stringent, criteria than their dominant colleagues. They also attract disproportional attention and causality. Due also to their racial salience, Faculty of Color are perceived as homogeneous, with associated actions, decisions, values, and mannerisms interpreted in a stereotype-consistent manner. These stereotypic expectations may lead to the encapsulation and entrapment of tokens in particular roles, such as specialists in ethnic or gender matters and symbols of workplace diversity. Suddenly, instead of—or in addition to—teaching the courses within their research areas of expertise, tokens may find themselves teaching the "diversity" courses within the department. They may be called upon to represent the university administration's response to the last student protest, or to local or national racial concerns. Students and local community members may also call upon tokens to be engaged in race-related matters, whether or not they have expertise in the particular issue or concern at hand. They may become the university's symbol in Martin Luther King Jr. events.

As the needs of the context override their intent and motivation, the identity of Faculty of Color is further disrupted. Their agency is obscured, perhaps even rendered irrelevant at worse and secondary at best, relative to the university's needs for them to fulfill diversity-related rhetoric and action. The situation becomes cyclical and compounding—the more tokens engage as racial entities, the less they are perceived as scholars, and the more they are called upon to function through their racial identities. Yet, these Faculty of Color in token positions often have no real choice. They typically enter the university in less powerful roles, especially relative to Whites in dominant positions, whose large numbers and historical status in the academy ensure representation in the most powerful positions. Faculty of Color who turn down administrative or colleagues' requests risk being accused of not being team players, with potentially career-ending consequences. Those who turn down community organizations and/or Students of Color risk being perceived as selfish at best, or as traitors at worst.

The social ecology imposes identity and behaviors, *irrespective* of the identity beliefs of Faculty of Color. In his classic tome, *Black Skin, White Masks,* Franz Fanon, a famed psychiatrist and one of the twentieth century's most renowned theorists of colonialism and racial difference, wrote of his token experience,

> It was always the Negro teacher, the Negro doctor . . . I shivered at the slightest pretext. I knew, for instance, that if the physician made a mistake it would be the end of him and of all those who came after him. What could one expect, after all, from a Negro physician? As long as everything went well, he was praised to the skies, but look out, no nonsense, under any conditions! The black physician can never be sure how close he is to disgrace. I tell you, I was walled in: No exception was made for my refined manners, or my knowledge of literature, or my understanding of quantum theory. (1967, p. 117)

The weight of the needs of the university structure relative to any matters related to race is placed on the few visible Faculty of Color, leading to their assignment to tasks and roles that the dominant group perceives requires engagement by Faculty of Color. Tokenism is thus a function of the needs of the organization and dominants' expectations and perceptions of the appropriateness of Faculty of Color to fulfill these needs and related roles, coupled with dominants' power to impose their will along these expectations. As a result, because the university structure consistently includes only a few Faculty of Color, the social structure creates and maintains tokenism.

Tokenism is a disrupted identity, a psychological state imposed upon Faculty of Color. It is a function of a social-ecological context that Faculty of Color are typically left on their own to navigate. Irrespective of individual, their personal racial identity (and lack of), political ideologies, expertise, credentials, character, and so on, Faculty of Color become caught up in the needs and perceptions of others. The complexity and consequences of marginality increase when race, ethnicity, and gender intersect, as for Women of Color. In some cases, these faculty members, especially those new to the academy, may not have the experience, mentoring, or understanding to be conscious of the effects of token status or to understand how to minimize the negative aspects of the situation. The same can be said for their White colleagues, who may want Faculty of Color to succeed, but also lack the knowledge to help their colleagues diffuse the damaging ramifications of tokenism.

The weight of the social ecological structure and resulting needs impose psychosocial consequences on Faculty of Color, including high visibility, cultural isolation, tensions with colleagues, loneliness and isolation, cognitive busyness, focus on impression management, representativeness, attributional ambiguity, role encapsulation, stereotyping, and racism. For further elaboration on these concerns, please see Gutiérrez y Muhs, Niemann, Gonzáles, & Harris, 2012; Hewstone et al., 2006; Niemann, 2003; Niemann & Dovidio, 1998; and Sekaquaptewa & Thompson, 2002.

The foregoing discussion affords and supports a theory of the social ecology of tokenism with the following ten interconnected tenets. The first is that tokenism is imposed on Faculty of Color and maintained by the institutional context and structure. Second, the primary foundation, or environmental support, of the tokenized context is the low numbers of tokenized group members, which make Faculty of Color highly distinctive, relative to the skewed numbers of dominant group members. Third, the tokenized context creates and maintains the phenomenological realities of the perceived and perceiver. Fourth, tokens do not differ from dominants in ability to do a task or in acceptance of work norms, but rather, in terms of secondary and information assumptions associated with the perception of their belongings in the context. Fifth, tokenism results in identity disruptions that impact tokens' institutional role, job description, career success, and career path, as well as their psychosocial realities. Sixth, tokenism has no regard to the competence or character of the tokenized persons, nor for their qualifications, accomplishments, character, motivations, or intentions. Seventh, tokenism does not necessarily arise from intentional prejudices of White persons or Persons of Color in the workplace, whose conscious and unconscious biases and perceptions are affected by the context. Eighth, dominants in the context have the power to intercede in the identity disruption through interventions that facilitate belonging, inclusiveness, identity integrity, valuing of research of concern to communities of nondominant groups, and applied community relevance. Ninth, through the power of their hiring practices and rules of success, members of the dominant group create and maintain the tokenized context. The tenth tenet is that dominants have the power to change the context such that it does not support or maintain tokenism.

University leaders can diffuse the negative impacts of tokenism by facilitating a context that places meaningful value on Faculty of Color: rewarding them for race- and diversity-related service with merit increases, tenure, and promotion, and celebrating their presence. In such environments, the distinctiveness of Faculty of Color will be positive, rather than stigmatizing and demoralizing. To reduce the strain on Faculty of Color, White faculty can be rewarded for having knowledge of Communities of Color that they apply to areas of teaching, research, and community service.

Numbers matter. Ultimately, hiring decisions create tokenized contexts. For decades, phrases such as "Women and minorities are encouraged to apply" or "University X is an affirmative action employer" were common. However, as noted earlier in this chapter, the percentages of Faculty of Color have hardly changed since affirmative action became the law of the land in 1964. Administrative leaders have been content to espouse rhetoric about the importance of diversity without facilitating any real change through their leadership and/or examination of biases in the hiring process. As the demographics of the United States continue to change toward an increasingly non-White majority, students and community members are increasingly likely to demand change such that faculty and students reflect the demographic makeup of the community. We are at the point that Martin Luther King Jr. (1963) warned us about when he said,

> But tokenism can now be seen not only as a useless goal, but as a genuine menace. It is a palliative which relieves emotional distress, but leaves the disease and its ravages unaffected. It tends to demobilize and relax the militant spirit which alone drives us forward to reach change . . . The day for assessing that experience is at hand. Token gains may well halt our progress, rather than further it . . . There segregation, the evil heritage of slavery, remains.

REFERENCES

Fanon, Franz. (1967). *Black skin, white masks.* New York: Grove Press.

Gibson, J. J. (1966). *The senses considered as perceptual systems.* Boston: Houghton Mifflin.

Gutiérrez y Muhs, G., Niemann, Y. F., Gonzales, C., & Harris, A. (2012). *Presumed incompetent: The intersections of race and class for women in academia.* Logan: Utah State University Press.

Hewstone, M., Crisp, R. J., Contarello, A., Voci, A., Conway, L., Marletta, G., & Willis, H. (2006). Tokens in the tower: Perceptual processes and interaction dynamics in academic settings with "skewed," "tilted," and "balanced" sex ratios. *Group Processes & Intergroup Relations, 9*(4), 509–532.

Kanter, R. M. (1977). *Men and women of the corporation.* New York: Basic Books.

King, Martin Luther, Jr. (1963, March 30). *Nation.*

King, Martin Luther, Jr. (1966, March 17). SMU. retrieved from https://www.smu.edu/AboutSMU/MLK.

Malcolm X. (1963, October 11). *Racial separation.* University of California, Berkeley.

National Center for Education Statistics. (2017). Digest of education statistics. Retrieved from https://nces.ed.gov/programs/digest/d17/tables/dt17_315.20.asp.

Niemann, Y. F. (2003). The psychology of tokenism: Psychosocial realities of faculty of color. In G. Bernal, J. E. Trimble, A. K. Burlew, & F. T. Leong (Eds.), *The handbook of racial and ethnic minority psychology* (pp. 110–118). Thousand Oaks, CA: Sage.

Niemann, Y. F., & Dovidio, J. F. (1998). Relationship of solo status, academic rank, and perceived distinctiveness to job satisfaction of racial/ethnic minorities. *Journal of Applied Psychology, 83*(1), 55–71.

Purdie-Vaughns, V., Steele, C. M., Davies, P. G., & Diltman, R. (2008). Social identity contingencies: How diversity cues signal threat or safety for African Americans in mainstream institutions. *Journal of Personality and Social Psychology, 94* (4), 615–630.

Sekaquaptewa, D., & Thompson, M. (2002). The differential effects of solo status on members of high- and low-status groups. *Personality and Social Psychology Bulletin, 28,* 694–707.

THIRTY-ONE

Why I Clap Back against Racist Trolls Who Attack Black Women Academics

Stacey Patton

> **SPADE500** @DrStaceyPatton "If it wasn't for Europe you wouldn't have modern mathematics, modern science, modern technology, modern medicine, etc."
>
> **Stacey Patton** @Spadedust "Without Africa, which birthed ALL of humanity, your ancestors would have never mutated into the whiteness u think is so superior."
>
> **Larry Darrell** @DrStaceyPatton "How could you possibly know what it feels like to be white and called a racist? Short answer . . . you don't and never will."
>
> **Stacey Patton** @LarryDarrell "But why would I ever want to know what that feels like? How blessedly melaninated am I to have been spared such a burden!"

I reside at the intersection of scholar, journalist, and online clapback artist. If some racist internet troll insults me, I very publicly burn them back and then I showcase the clapback by reposting it on my social networking pages to the delight of myself and more than 60,000 followers. While many professors and reporters would rather avoid confrontation, I believe that clapping back is an act of self-care and a way to build a buffer between myself and the hate from racist and sexist trolls who want to silence Women of Color and keep us living in fear or chronically on the defensive. When I clap back, it allows me to recast myself from victim to an empowered woman who is not to be fucked with.

Some people say, "Don't feed the trolls," especially if you are a college professor or a journalist. As Academics and Professional Writers of Color, we are expected to take the so-called high road and to keep some critical, dispassionate distance from the issues we study even when echoes of our research and the stories we write keep sounding off in our own personal lives. We are supposed to

DOI: 10.7330/9781607329664.c031

put our perspectives, our lived experiences, our anger and fears into a box so as not to disrupt mainstream narratives and the fallacy of objectivity. Meanwhile, all that toxicity too often becomes biologically embedded into our bodies, saps our emotional energy, and makes us physically ill. This is exactly what online harassment aims to achieve.

For Women of Color in academe, the knowledge that there is nothing to protect your personal or professional safety can be devastating. It changes everything. And if you are judged, criticized, or attacked for doing what you believe is right—in the classroom, in mainstream media, and in the internet streets—with curses, slurs, nasty insults, and even threats, it's more common for your department chair, dean, or college president (the people who profit from your hard work and diversity optics) to stand over your shoulder ready to chastise you, demanding your apology or silence. As my fellow historian Deirdre Cooper-Owens eloquently put it, "Disrespecting black women is historical practice" (2016).

For writing and speaking publicly about race as a journalist and college professor, I've been called nigger, cunt, bitch, monkey, whore, and other derogatory names. My favorite slight is when the trolls put quotes around "Dr." Racists have just as much disdain for Black female PhDs as they do for Reagan's so-called welfare queen. Sometimes the messages are even more personal—"I know where you live." I've been told to kill myself and have received death threats as well as creepy phone calls and anonymous letters to my campus office. My current department chair, university president, and even the Board of Regents have been flooded with phone calls demanding that I be fired from my tenure-track position at Morgan State University. Fortunately, my university has responded in a manner that protects my academic freedom and due process rights. But for many Scholars of Color, merely responding to the dehumanization of those slurs and attacks is deemed unprofessional and worthy of suspension or termination. It seems that colleges and universities are more insulted by Scholars of Color standing in defense of our own and collective humanity than by the racist vitriol ejaculated onto us by the dredges of our society.

In recent years, Black women academics have increasingly come under fire by right-wing internet-based journalistic organizations because of politically charged comments they posted on social media platforms such as Twitter and Facebook and the content of their academic publications that deal with issues of race and inequality. One notorious case involved former University of Memphis professor Zandria Robinson, who in the summer of 2015 came under fire for declaring that "whiteness is most certainly and inevitably terror," that the Charleston shooting at Mother Emanuel AME church was just another example of "white people acting how they're conditioned to act," and that "death and rape threats . . . are the ultimate expressions of love from conservative whites these days" (Chasmar, 2015).

Earlier that spring, Boston University professor Saida Grundy received backlash when she posted on Twitter that "white men are a population problem" and that "white masculinity is THE problem for America's colleges." She also tweeted, "Deal with your white s**t, white people. Slavery is a *YALL* thing" (Wells, 2015).

Flash forward to May 2017. Princeton University Black studies professor Keeanga Yamahtta-Taylor, who endured right-wing racist attacks as a graduate student at Northwestern University, gave a commencement speech at Hampshire College in which she referred to Donald Trump as a "racist, sexist, megalomaniac" (Jones, 2017). After Fox News aired a clip from the speech, she was deluged with intimidating emails, including death threats. Taylor eventually canceled scheduled talks in Seattle and San Diego as a result (Flaherty, 2017b).

These Black women scholars and countless others, who represent a range of academic ranks and teach on campuses that are distinct from each other, have experienced the dizzying effects of being targeted by trolls, conservative blogs, and news sites like The Last Tradition, The College Fix, Campus Reform, Daily Caller, YoungCons, Breitbart News Network, and Fox News. In April 2018, NPR reported that at least 250 university professors had been targeted via right-wing online campaigns because of their research, their teaching, or their social media posts (Kamenetz, 2018). Some scholars have been placed on The Professor Watch List, a list of over 250 left-wing professors who have been accused of liberal bias against conservative students and for criticizing Donald Trump's policies. In some instances, professors have lost their job, and others have had to take security precautions to protect their family's safety.

From 2011 until 2015, I was a reporter for the *Chronicle of Higher Education*. As one of two Black journalists in that predominantly White newsroom, I covered graduate education, faculty life, adjunct working conditions, and race and diversity issues. My reporting experiences and conversations with hundreds of academics over the years have yielded some useful observations about these attacks. Let me first say that because universities have increasingly turned curriculum and policy over to corporate interests and demands, the very presence of Scholars of Color and the research we produce is threatening to the status quo. Our bodies and our work challenge some fundamental truths . . . that America is not a post-racial society, that race and gender matter, and that issues of race and justice remain at center stage culturally and politically.

Women of Color in academe challenge narratives of American exceptionalism and the "American Dream." Our work, which is often dismissed as lacking intellectual rigor, lays bare the uncomfortable truth that White successes are about privilege, and not that White people are innately blessed with merit. Not only do our presence and scholarship make Whiteness and all its insecurities visible, there's unspoken resentment about the inability to effectively use Scholars of Color as demonstration projects to nurture the lies about our alleged inferiority.

It's a narrative we have witnessed play out in the controversial *Fisher v. the University of Texas* case in 2016. Rather than pull herself up by her proverbial boot straps, Abigail Fisher blamed her shortcomings on phantom less qualified "minority" students who supposedly took her spot and not the forty-two White students with lower grades and test scores who were accepted instead of her (Ng, 2016). Fisher and her supporters knew that playing into the popular stereotype of Black people as innately intellectually inferior and incapable would shift the spotlight away from her mediocrity and paint her as the victim of "reverse racism."

I saw the conceit firsthand in my own classrooms when I taught at predominantly White universities. I can tell you that as a Black woman professor whose teaching career has mostly been set in White classrooms, I observed that White students were in no way more advanced than Students of Color. I enjoyed teaching my students, but I found a good number of them to be lazy, entitled, shallow thinkers whose writing and analytical skills were severely underdeveloped. They plagiarized papers, cheated on tests, made excuses for why they could not get assignments done on time, and treated professors like customer service representatives. And then they had the audacity to comment on their course evaluations about how "articulate" I was, how I "knew my stuff," that I was "unpatriotic," and how I made them "feel bad about being White" in an African American history course.

I should note that attacks against Scholars of Color are not a new phenomenon. They have a long heritage stretching back to the civil rights movement, with notable examples such as the professors at Alabama State who faced repercussions for assisting with the Montgomery bus boycott of 1955. In the late 1960s and early 1970s, ethnic and Black studies professors faced threats for writing publicly on racism (Davis, 2017). The post–civil rights era has witnessed another rise of a bigoted, paranoid, and shrill brand of White conservatism on American college campuses. This time around, social media have helped fuel the incessant attacks on Scholars of Color, especially Black women, who speak and write publicly on issues related to anti-Black racism.

In this historical moment, as evidenced by the election of Donald Trump, the serial police killings of unarmed Black people, the White supremacist march and attacks at Charlottesville, White people calling the police on innocent Black people going about their daily business, tensions on campuses across this country, the NFL's backlash against players taking a knee to protest police brutality, and the brutal separations of undocumented immigrant parents and children at our borders, conversations and scholarship on race are needed more than ever. Not surprisingly, in response to those conversations there has been amped-up hostility toward scholars who participate in them.

Irrespective of the commonplace claims that colleges and universities are liberal and progressive havens, they are actually a staging ground for protecting the racist status quo. Our institutions still remain bastions of Whiteness despite the rapid diversification of the student body and the persistent decline in White student enrollment at both the undergraduate and graduate levels. American colleges are failing to live up to their purported mission as spaces to facilitate social change. They do not serve as models for justice and equality, or as spaces that genuinely value diversity beyond a tired marketing ploy. Predominantly White institutions appear more interested in cosmetic diversity and counting the numbers of Bodies of Color to show incremental progress, rather than in genuinely creating a culture of inclusivity and equity.

While many colleges produce marketing materials that look like old-school Benetton ads, and talk a good game like Starbucks, their campuses have become increasingly hostile to students and Faculty of Color. The latest available data from the US Department of Education show that in 2014 there were 804 reported hate crimes on campuses in the United States—45 percent of them motivated by race. The most common type of hate crime reported by institutions was intimidation (343 incidents) (Bauman, 2018). The Southern Poverty Law Center reported a rise in hate crimes after Trump's election, which worsened a political climate already inhospitable to academic freedom. The center documented 900 such incidents in just the ten days following Trump's election (Miller & Werner-Winslow, 2016).

Adding to this ecosystem of hate, conservatives have continued to portray colleges as beset by "leftist tyranny" and "liberal excess" (Schmidt, 2015). As such, Professors and Public Intellectuals of Color are suspect and have become visible targets for neoconservative racial projects whose purported mission is to reform higher education's alleged tendency toward hating America. The corporate takeover and colonization of academe by right-leaning forces has brought amped-up attacks on tenure, academic freedom, ethnic studies, and student and faculty diversity efforts.

A major force in academe's ideological battles and attacks against Scholars of Color are the more than 100 biased and sensationalist right-leaning publications (Schmidt, 2017). Each is devoted to the same cause—protecting the rights of students from "politically correct multiculturalism" and faculty "indoctrination." The editors, student writers, and their financial backers are protecting their vision of the world and preserving the narrative that White people are victims of "minority rights" and "political correctness."

Their tactics are not a mystery. These publications routinely publish stories exposing the "liberal biases" of faculty. They cite one another, and their stories often get picked up by *Fox & Friends* and then spread virally through social media, placing individual faculty members and colleges under intense pressure. The harassing phone calls, hateful emails, tweets, and cowardly threats to do harm spreads. The emails are also sent to department chairs and deans, putting the faculty member at risk of being labeled a troublemaker. University administrators, who succumb to pressure from alumni, donors, and legislators, throw the faculty under the bus, hate grows, and the rest of the faculty shuts down (Thomason, 2015).

Fox & Friends has shaped a narrative that progressive universities are hostile to conservative professors and students and that university culture discriminates against Whites, males, Christians, patriotic Americans, and the overall greatness of Western civilization. They are pushing a narrative that is popular among much of White America: that the tables have been turned against White people, who are now the biggest victims of discrimination (Gonyea, 2017).

Despite the embrace of rhetoric about "free speech" and universities as places of open conversation, these academic terrorists work to silence all too many Faculty of Color, who risk jobs, tenure, their mental health, and future prospects with each tweet, article, and lecture that challenges White supremacy. Over and over again, the belief in free speech and the principles of democracy or the defense of humor and satire are used as covers to allow anything they want to say.

Racial slurs in class equals free speech. A noose on a door equals free speech. Calling someone a "tranny" equals free speech. Hanging a symbol of hate equals free speech. A song about lynching equals free speech. A sexist comment in a faculty meeting equals free speech. A feces swastika smeared on a bathroom wall equals free speech. Telling a Black female professor that her PhD in Black studies is worthless, or calling her a monkey or a whore on Twitter, or demanding that she kill herself equals free speech (Davis, 2015).

Protecting the freedom to demonize and dehumanize, to silence, and to practice hateful speech creates a hostile learning and work environment. Ironically, it is these trolls and their friends, who are aided and abetted by campus administrators and the donor class, who contain conversations. They terrorize to silence our voices, using the cover of "free speech" when it is clear they are only targeting certain professors and certain departments.

And yet, there is a certain irony that White students will invoke victimhood and demand protection from conversations about White privilege and rape culture. Their helicopter parents at *Fox News* are ready and waiting, making sure that White students don't have their feelings hurt by the truth. Of course, the reality is that there are students and Scholars of Color and our allies who are truly being victimized on a daily basis, and no one is putting up trigger alerts or offering protections from racist comments in class, misogynistic evaluations, homophobic jokes polluting dining halls, Eurocentric curricula, and the violent and threatening backlash directed at those who protest the status quo.

Another key element to consider in this conversation is that state legislatures have divested from public education (Donachie, 2017). As such, universities are increasingly anxious about preserving what little funding is left. This gives legislatures, which because of gerrymandering are more right leaning, greater power. Because universities, both public and private, are so dependent on tuition and donations, the dollar is powerful. So when Faculty of Color are attacked, the facts are irrelevant because the university's mission is to protect the bottom line. This gives more power to the White racist oligarchy and all its constituents operating an ecosystem of hate—from the right-wing publications to the student-themed blackface and ghetto parties.

In this climate of hate, university administrators basically sanction threats by not standing in solidarity with the faculty or condemning their attackers for a number of reasons. Some departments don't have power and are trying to survive cuts, while others have bought into narratives of American exceptionalism or respectability politics. More broadly, donors and legislators take precedent over the work conditions for faculty and the learning environment for students, especially those of color. In addition, there tends to be a lot of blame placed on faculty who are said to be bringing the hate on themselves because of their tone, their selection of topics, and because they're being too political and not good academics.

Meanwhile, there's been a resounding clarion call from within the humanities that academics make their work more accessible to the broader public. This is troubling because Faculty of Color who have been doing this are often dismissed as "activists" and there are no efforts to protect scholars who are engaging with the public. To "go public" has a different set of consequences for our lives, and this is not hyperbole.

Universities want to create the illusion of diversity and to profit from that illusion, but they are showing little interest in making campus classrooms and curricula more inclusive, more welcoming, more honest, more intellectually rigorous. Once Faculty of Color are inside the building, once Students of Color pay their tuition and have their picture taken for the university website, all bets are off. The message we receive is clear: We got you for what we need, now sit down, shut up, and be counted for our diversity report while we pat ourselves on the back and call it "progress."

Some professors are standing up for themselves and other professors by simply continuing to do their work and speaking out, by posting foul voicemail messages and screenshots of racist and sexist comments on social media pages, and by organizing letter-writing campaigns in support of targeted professors. At the start of the 2017 academic year, eighty professors across the country began their classes by reading a statement against hate speech and threats against faculty who make controversial remarks. This act was part of the "Stand Up and Speak Out" campaign, a weeklong effort to defend Faculty of Color. The campaign's organizers said they were also trying to "persuade college presidents to stand by their instructors, not scold them or take sides, when they face possibly life-threatening criticism on social media for their controversial remarks" (Zamudio-Suaréz, 2017).

Two groups, the American Association of University Professors (AAUP) and the Campus Anti-fascist Network, continue to assist harassed faculty while pressuring university officials to stand behind scholars. After Trump's election, the AAUP began tracking incidents of targeted harassment by creating a website where faculty can submit their stories. The AAUP specifically "urges administrations, governing boards and faculties, individually and collectively, to speak out clearly and forcefully to defend academic freedom and to condemn targeted harassment and intimidation of faculty members" (Flaherty, 2017a). It also recommends that "administrations and elected faculty bodies work jointly to establish institutional regulations that prohibit the surreptitious recording of classroom discourse or of private meetings between students and faculty members" (Flaherty, 2017a). Like the AAUP, the Campus Anti-fascist Network (CAN) is a grassroots, multiracial collective of faculty and students that organizes letter campaigns and puts targeted faculty members in touch with others who have endured smear campaigns. CAN makes its presence known on campus through teach-ins and workshops on fascism and how to fight it. The group also prepares documents to help scholars defend themselves when attacked by fascists and also how to protest their appearance on campuses.

Sadly, as racial tensions continue to rise in the United States, these attacks on scholars will only worsen and have a chilling effect on academic freedom if there is no sustained resistance. We must all clap back. Silent, fearful, and obsequious faculty will become complicit in turning the university into a place that ceases being critical, innovative, and somewhat humane. Unless there is resistance, the university will merely reproduce the reigning hegemony.

REFERENCES

Bauman, D. (2018, February 16). After 2016 election, campus hate crimes seemed to jump. Here's what the data tell us. *Chronicle of Higher Education*. Retrieved from https://www.chronicle.com/article/After-2016-Election-Campus/242577.

Chasmar, J. (2015, June 30). University of Memphis professor: "Whiteness is most certainly and inevitably terror." *Washington Times*. Retrieved from https://www.washingtontimes.com/news/2015/jun/30/zandria-robinson-univ-of-memphis-professor-whitene/.

Cooper-Owens, D. (2016). How black women scholars navigate right-wing media attacks in the age of social media. Paper presented at the 101st Conference of the Association for the Study of African American Life and History, Richmond, VA, October 6, 2016.

Davis, K. (2017, February 17). The quiet history of how ASU shaped the civil rights movement. *Montgomery Advertiser*. Retrieved from https://www.montgomeryadvertiser.com/story/news/2017/02/17/quiet-history-how-alabama-state-university-shaped-civil-rights-movement/97969402/.

Davis, S. (2015, November 12). Mizzou releases photos of poop swastika, discloses details of previously unreported racial slurs. *Federalist*. Retrieved from http://thefederalist.com/2015/11/12/mizzou-releases-photos-of-poop-swastika-discloses-details-of-previously-unreported-racial-slurs/.

Donachie, P. (2017, August 24). Report details pattern of higher ed divestment by state governments. *Education Dive*. Retrieved from https://www.educationdive.com/news/report-details-pattern-of-higher-ed-divestment-by-state-governments/503347/.

Flaherty, C. (2017a, February 2). Standing up to trolls. *Inside Higher Ed*. Retrieved from https://www.insidehighered.com/news/2017/02/02/aaup-says-colleges-should-defend-professors-targeted-online-harassment-due-political.

Flaherty, C. (2017b, June 1). Concession to violent intimidation. *Inside Higher Ed*. Retrieved from https://www.insidehighered.com/news/2017/06/01/princeton-professor-who-criticized-trump-cancels-events-saying-shes-received-death.

Gonyea, D. (2017, October 24) Majority of white Americans believe whites face discrimination. NPR. Retrieved from https://www.npr.org/2017/10/24/559604836/majority-of-white-americans-think-theyre-discriminated-against.

Jones, S. (2017, May 29). Where is the outrage for Keeanga-Yamahtta Taylor? *New Republic*. Retrieved from https://newrepublic.com/minutes/143064/outrage-keeanga-yamahtta-taylor.

Kamenetz, A. (2018, April 4). Professors are targets in online culture wars; Some fight back. NPR. Retrieved from https://www.npr.org/sections/ed/2018/04/04/590928008/professor-harassment.

Miller, C., & Werner-Winslow, A. (2016, November). Ten days after: Harassment and intimidation in the aftermath of the election. Southern Poverty Law Center. Retrieved from https://www.splcenter.org/sites/default/files/com_hate_incidents_report_2017_update.pdf.

Ng, A. (2016, June 23). Abigail Fisher, loser in Supreme Court case against affirmative action, earns herself a new nickname: Becky with the bad grades. *Daily News*. Retrieved from http://www.nydailynews.com/news/national/abigail-fisher-becky-bad-grades-article-1.2685865.

Schmidt, P. (2015, September 8). Higher education's internet outrage machine. *Chronicle of Higher Education*. Retrieved from https://www.chronicle.com/article/Higher-Educations-Internet/232879.

Schmidt, P. (2017, June 22). Professors' growing risk: Harassment for things they never really said. *Chronicle of Higher Education*. Retrieved from https://www.chronicle.com/article/Professors-Growing-Risk-/240424.

Thomason, A. (2015, July 1). How one professor's tweets got her fired—Or so it seemed at first. *Chronicle of Higher Education*. Retrieved from https://www.chronicle.com/blogs/ticker/how-one-professors-tweets-got-her-fired-or-so-it-seemed-at-first/101375.

Wells, V. (2015, May 13). Too much or too real? Incoming black professor says white males are the problem for America's colleges. *Madame Noire*. Retrieved from https://madamenoire.com/533036/too-much-or-too-real-incoming-black-professor-says-white-males-are-the-problem-for-americas-colleges/.

Zamudio-Suaréz, F. (2017, September 13). How a group of instructors is standing up to the right-wing outrage machine. *Chronicle of Higher Education*. Retrieved from https://www.chronicle.com/article/How-a-Group-of-Instructors-Is/241192.

THIRTY-TWO

Unconquered and Unconquerable

A Chickasaw Woman's Quest for Tenure

Rachel Tudor

> Today I couldn't handle the pain of being an American Indian.
>
> —MELANIE FEY (DINE)

> As Indigenous women writers and artists we are continually trying to exist, live, and love in a world that doesn't always show its love for us.
>
> —TANAYA WINDER (DUCKWATER SHOSHONE)

> Even during a time of reconciliation, Indigenous people are faced with having to defend their identities from being mocked, used as a trend or form of entertainment every single day.
>
> —JESSICA DEER (MOHAWK)

The motto of the Chickasaw Nation is "Unconquered and Unconquerable." That is not to say that we are not the victims of America's ethnic cleansing and cultural genocide. Our motto is simply a testament to our resolve to never surrender. I have been battling for justice since Southeastern Oklahoma State University illegally denied me tenure and retaliated against me for complaining about its egregious violations of my civil rights. I never surrendered and on November 20, 2017, a federal court jury declared that Southeastern and the Regional University System of Oklahoma (RUSO) had committed sex discrimination and retaliated against me for reporting it. Most people would think the jury's verdict would be the end of litigation. After all, it is really very simple. I did nothing wrong. I was wronged. A jury has spoken. But that was not the end. Southeastern did not welcome me back. Litigation continues. After nearly a decade of wrestling with Southeastern for a position I earned, I face months, perhaps years, of continuing litigation, poverty, and anxiety.

Discrimination in education is not new to me. The first week of elementary school, a predominately White school in an impoverished neighborhood, a

DOI: 10.7330/9781607329664.c032

classmate asked me, "Are you Mexican?" When I said, "I'm Indian," the kids started making war whoops and running circles around me. You may be thinking, "Well, they're just kids." Yes, of course, but I was just a kid too. I felt humiliation and shame. I identify as Chickasaw or Native American, but the word *Indian* will always be a term of derision for me. As I moved from school to school, kids assumed that I was Hispanic and would mock me on the playground by adding an "o" to my name and chanting, "Go back to Mexico!" Of course, the joke was on them because I'm indigenous and they are immigrants to my country! Admittedly, that is not much comfort to a child who grew up eating alone in the cafeteria or being jumped after school and beaten up.

My favorite part of going to school was visiting the library. I thought books were my friends. One day I was looking at the content of a book of poetry when I came across the title "The Indian Student." I remember being excited to find a poem about me. I couldn't turn the pages of Philip Freneau's book fast enough. Here are the words I found: "No divine spark fired his mind / only sense enough the squirrel to find!" I was only a child, but I had a strong instinct to protect my mother from the hate in those bitter words so I swallowed them.

A few years later, in middle school, I was in a Texas history class taught by an Australian. The textbook's motif was the inevitable triumph of civilization over savagery—with Native Americans cast in the role of savages. One day a student asked the teacher, "What happened to all the Indians?" The Australian replied: "Your Indians are like our aborigines—they just can't survive in the modern world."

I entered a PhD program at the University of Oklahoma to study Native American literature without having heard a single lecture about Native American literature or history. As a PhD candidate I had to assemble a dissertation committee. I enjoyed my Victorian literature course and considered asking the professor to be a member. We shared an admiration for Dickens's novel *Little Dorrit*. He told me that I was the first student to ever make a reference to it in his class. However, a White graduate student advised me against choosing this professor because when he had told him that he was going to focus on Native American literature in his PhD program, this professor discouraged him by saying: "You're smart; you should study real literature."

My first university appointment was as a visiting assistant professor of Native American literature at the University of Idaho. I did not know it when I accepted the position, but the reason for the vacancy was that UI had denied a Native American woman tenure. Over the years I have met several other Native American women who were denied tenure or have never been hired on a tenure track. Shortly after the semester began, the LGBT student office was vandalized and a Pride flag was burned. The university's perfunctory investigation failed to uncover those responsible, but the perpetrators were proud of what they had done and felt free to boast. It turns out they included not merely students but the student body president and a student senator. No criminal charges were brought; they were not expelled. They were merely asked to resign from their leadership positions. What message did that send to these budding terrorists? The message to me was clear—UI was not a safe or welcoming place.

My next university appointment was at Southeastern. Southeastern is officially a "Native American–serving institution" located in the historic boundaries of the Chickasaw and Choctaw Nations. However, during my campus visit I became wary because Southeastern named its athletic teams "Savages" and "Lady Savages." The moniker *savage* was particularly disturbing given my experience with the term *Indian*. Also, there were no Native Americans on the hiring committee or among the administrators I met during my interview. Nevertheless, I accepted a position at Southeastern because of my desire work with Chickasaw and Choctaw students and teach in my area of expertise. I even declined an offer from another university with a higher salary, more comprehensive benefits, and a strong faculty union to accept the position.

I worked hard to earn the respect of my colleagues and students. For example, I was the chair of my department's Assessment, Planning, and Development Committee, served as Southeastern's professor of record for the state's prestigious Oklahoma Scholar Leadership Enrichment Program, served on the Five-Year Program Review Committee as well as various hiring committees, assisted with the Honor's Program and the English Honor Society, served on the Native American Symposium Committee and coedited the corresponding journals of the proceedings of the symposium, was elected to the Faculty Senate, served on the Faculty Senate Planning Committee and its Personnel Policies Committee, and published a record number of peer-reviewed journal articles. The university's aggregate assessment of student surveys ranked me as one of their highest-performing faculty members, and my department chair always complimented me in my annual performance assessment on the favorable comments students made about me. After years of service, I earned the right to think about my eudaemonia.

A flourishing life for a woman is one that allows a woman to live as a woman. Chloe Schwenke describes being unable to do so as a "tinnitus of the soul." This is well documented in memoirs by transgender womenare. Jennifer Finney Boylan's *She's Not There: A Life in Two Genders* (2003), is specifically about transitioning while working in an English department. However, one incident in her memoir troubled me: she recounts that her colleagues asked her why she transitioned *after* she was granted tenure—did she not trust them to do the right thing? I did not want my colleagues to resent me for not trusting them. Therefore, I made the decision to transition before I was tenured.

Tragically, the administration did not evaluate my tenure application on its merits. They violated policy, usurped norms, ignored faculty grievance outcomes, snubbed the Faculty Senate, failed to respond to inquiries from the American Association of University Professors, disregarded an online petition signed by thousands, and even violated the law to deny me tenure. My advice to any faculty member who is trans is to wait until you have tenure because you can do everything right and still lose.

Here's what happened: the Tenure and Promotion Committee, seconded by the department chair, recommended me for tenure and promotion in the fall of 2009. I received notification shortly before Christmas break. As you can imagine, that was a cause for celebration. I had worked toward this goal my entire life and felt I had finally found a home. But I also had a sense of foreboding. Maybe it is the historical experience of Native Americans or simply my own lived experience—I did not share the news with my two sisters. I knew how devastating it would be to me if the administration found some way to deny me tenure, and I did not want people I loved to feel that pain. I kept the biggest news in my life to myself. No celebration. No congratulations.

My fears were confirmed when shortly after the beginning of the spring semester 2010, I received a letter from the Dean of the School of Arts and Sciences indicating that she was recommending against granting me tenure. It was followed by a letter from the vice president for academic affairs (VPAA) informing me that he was also opposing granting me tenure. My department chair and my colleagues were appalled and dismayed at this turn of events. In the 100-year history of Southeastern, the administration had never before failed to follow the recommendation of the faculty in matters of tenure. Additionally, the Dean and VPAA both informed me that they would not respond to my request for an explanation in writing. They said I must schedule an appointment with their respective administrative assistants. I did as instructed. I scheduled appointments and waited. It was agonizing, waiting weeks for this urgent information. However, the only information I received when I went to my appointment with the Dean was that she was not going to discuss her rationale with me. I was astonished. Why did I have to make an appointment simply to be told that I was not going to be given an explanation? When I informed my department chair, the chair of the Faculty Senate, and colleagues in my department of what happened, they all encouraged me to file a grievance because, they asserted, we deserved an explanation.

I grieved the Dean's refusal to provide an explanation as required by policy to the Faculty Appellate Committee (FAC) on February 26, 2010. The VPAA also refused to provide an explanation and canceled our scheduled meeting as soon as he learned that I had exercised my right to grieve the Dean's action. Because they both failed to give me any explanation for their opposition, I added the VPAA to my grievance with the FAC. In my grievance, I specifically included letters attached to emails to the Dean and the VPAA wherein I respectfully asked: "In accord with Southeastern's goal of promoting faculty development and retention and in agreement with SE's principles of shared governance, please explain your rationale for not supporting the recommendations of the . . . Tenure and Promotion Committee and Department Chair. This information is important in order for faculty to understand your criteria and in what way your criteria differ from our own. I would like to call your attention to the following sections of the Academic Policies and Procedures Manual." Then I cited section 3.7.4, which clearly explains that faculty status is primarily faculty responsibility, why the primary responsibility lies with the faculty, and when administrators disagree with faculty judgment—which should only be in "rare instances and for compelling reasons"—those reasons should be stated in detail.

My grievance included the reasons I cited in my letters to the Dean and the VPAA as well as calling the FAC's attention to the necessity of "practices that promote confidence among faculty in administration and provide vital and timely feedback to promotion and tenure committees, department chairs, and candidates in order that all parties may actively participate and be partners in a process vital to the health and well-being of the university." The FAC agreed with my arguments and recommended that my "request for a detailed written explanation that clearly delineates the factors that led to [the Dean and VPAA's] decision to deny tenure and promotion be provided."

Well, that sounded reasonable and in accord with policy and best practices. I hoped my tenure application would get back on track. However, I received a letter from the assistant vice president for academic affairs informing me that the explanations would not be forthcoming because "there is no policy that stipulates that the Vice President and/or the Dean is compelled to provide reasons as to why tenure and promotion were denied." This was followed by a citation of section 3.7.3 referencing the "President's authority." The letter also informed me that "legal counsel" (via RUSO) had been consulted and he agreed that the President, VPAA, and/or Dean were not required to provide any explanation.

Although this outcome was an egregious undermining of the function of the FAC, the FAC decision was also thwarted in another way that was in direct violation of policy. For FACs to work, it is necessary for faculty to be informed of the outcome in a timely manner. The decision of the FAC was withheld from me until the end of April—until after the President had made his decision to deny me tenure. Withholding the information was a direct violation of policy that had well-defined guidelines concerning timely notifications of FAC decisions. Only after I and my department chair were informed of the President's decision to deny me tenure was I was notified of the FAC's decision. The VPAA then had the temerity to assert in his letter notifying me of the FAC's decision: "[The President's] decision, in my view, moots your appeal and has brought this process to an end."

I filed a formal appeal to the President to exercise a "spirit of shared governance that exceeds the minimum required by a diminutive reading of the Policy and Procedures Manual and honor the FAC's decision." I explained why it is important for faculty to understand why the Dean and the VPAA rejected the faculty recommendation, and why it was important for me to have those explanations as well in preparation for my reapplication.

I did not receive an explanation from the President.

Because of the many improprieties that occurred during my tenure and promotion application in 2009–2010, I filed another grievance with the FAC on August 30, 2010. Succinctly stated, it was a due process claim. The way the administration handled this grievance is very important to note. In order for FACs to preserve equity, the proceedings of the FAC must be equitable. It is only fair that when the administration meets with the FAC members, the faculty member discussed should have an opportunity to be present and heard. In this instance the administration brought RUSO legal counsel to their meeting with the FAC. In the spirit of fairness and equity, if the administration decided to bring legal counsel to meet with the FAC, shouldn't the faculty member be notified and have the same opportunity to be represented? I was not notified. I was not given the opportunity to be present or represented.[1] At the meeting, the RUSO attorney told the FAC that it "was not empowered to address the issue of due process as related to tenure and promotion" and was "unable to act on the grievance." The RUSO attorney's interpretation of policy was in stark contrast to what written policy actually affirmed to be the responsibility of the FAC. The FAC yielded to the RUSO attorney's ex parte intervention.

Southeastern's policy explicitly states and the norms provide that anyone who was denied tenure may apply again—as long as it is before the seven-year limit for receiving tenure. One of the norms at Southeastern is that the tenure application is viewed as an opportunity for the faculty to closely examine a colleague's work and provide critical feedback to candidates if needed so they may succeed in a subsequent application. This norm is different from that obtaining in many research universities, where it is "one and done." Thus, at the beginning of the 2010–2011 academic cycle, my department assembled a new Tenure and Promotion Committee, I submitted a new tenure application, discussed my application with my department chair, and received his approval to proceed. However, on October 5, 2010, I was notified that the VPAA was not going to allow me apply for tenure. Since 2010–2011 was my seventh and final year to earn tenure, he was effectively terminating me. His memo admitted that policy does not prohibit a subsequent application for tenure, but he was not going to allow it. He claimed that allowing me to apply would be "disruptive to the School of Arts and Sciences, create unnecessary work for both your department and the administration, and will inflame the relationship between faculty and administration."

The VPAA's memorandum prompted my third grievance to the FAC, on October 11, 2010. My complaint specifically addressed the issues of shared governance, academic freedom, professional values and standards, promoting the economic security of those who teach and research, and ensuring higher education's contribution to the higher good. I supported my arguments by citing policy and referencing long-standing norms.

My grievance asserted, in part, that the VPAA's action was "so far removed from the normalcy of practice and policy that it represents an alarming expansion

1. On hiring an attorney to represent you during your tenure application: if you are teaching at a regional university, the absence of qualified attorneys is acute. The first difficulty is finding an attorney with expertise in tenure—there are few. Next, those with expertise in education issues in general will be conflicted out because they will likely already have connections to the university. Also, universities are often cornerstones of local communities and attorneys do not want to be seen representing someone against the community's interest. Any honest attorney will tell you up-front that tenure cases are notoriously hard to win, very expensive, and will require years to litigate. And, finally, there is the practical matter of being able to afford to hire an attorney even if you are able to find one who is willing to take your case. Access to legal representation is a privilege that few can afford.

of the power of the office of the Interim Vice President of Academic Affairs and an unparalleled diminishing of the rights and responsibilities of the tenure-track and tenured faculty at Southeastern." His action was also in violation of RUSO policy 5.6 and 5.7, which prohibit acts of retaliation. I specifically addressed the VPAA's claim that if my tenure application were allowed to proceed it would "inflame the relationship between faculty and administration." I noted that the tension between "authoritarianism and share governance will be exacerbated, 'inflamed,' by the unprecedented act of arbitrarily and unilaterally suspending the right of tenure-track faculty to address any alleged deficiencies in an application in a subsequent application for tenure and promotion within the time limits provided by RUSO. In addition, [the] newfound assertion of the power of the office of Interim Vice President of Academic Affairs to allow candidates to address alleged deficiencies effectively removed the purpose of the explanatory letter from the President . . . it not only renders the explanatory letter meaningless, but arguably makes it an act of cruelty if it contains easily remedied technical deficiencies such as letters from the Tenure and Promotion Committee and Department Chair justifying their decisions to recommend a candidate for tenure and promotion (it did), or readily available documentation of accomplishments (it did) . . . Furthermore, it is unjustifiably punitive to begin forbidding ensuing applications because the process has recently become adversarial instead of cooperative." I also pointed out that since this is retaliatory on the face of it, it "has a chilling effect on other faculty exercising their rights under policy and law." Finally, I appealed to the FAC to act to ensure higher education's contribution to the common good. I wrote: "Civil society is dependent on a shared set of common expectations and values. One of the most important shared values in a democratic society is that everyone is treated equally and given the same opportunities as other members of the community . . . As an institution of higher education, whose mission and responsibility is to promote a more equitable and just society, Southeastern has a duty to exemplify not only the letter of the law, but the spirit as well."

Outcome: the FAC "unanimously agreed that I should be allowed to apply for tenure and promotion during the 2010–2011 academic year."

Well, once again, that sounds reasonable and in accord with policy and best practices. If the administration had followed the FAC recommendation, I would have spent the better part of the last decade working with my colleagues, educating students, conducting groundbreaking research, attending conferences, and serving my community. However, that did not happen. Instead, I received a letter from another assistant vice president for academic affairs informing me that the President's designee "concurs with the action taken by [the VPAA]." Thus, they effectively usurped the FAC's decision. This was unprecedented. It violated the norms. New rules were written, new policy implemented, without consulting the Faculty Senate or the Faculty Senate's Personnel Policies Committee (I was elected by my peers to serve on the Faculty Senate and selected by the Faculty Senate to serve on the Personnel Policies Committee, so I know they were not consulted) in order to deny me the opportunity to apply for tenure.

I followed the new rules and appealed to the President the decision of his designee not to allow me to apply for tenure. Keep in mind the decision I was appealing was the one directed by the President via VPAA. To be clear, the new policy meant I was forced to appeal the President's decision to the President! Could there be a more futile exercise? I cited facts: (1) The current policy (previous to being rewritten) invites the administration to share its perspective via the president's designee once the FAC has made its decision—but deliberately makes no provision for the president's designee to usurp the decision of the FAC because policy states that in matters related to faculty the administration should concur with faculty judgment; (2) Amending the faculty grievance policy without the advice or consultation of the Faculty Senate violates the principles of shared governance; (3); Amending the faculty grievance policy without the advice or consultation of the Faculty Personnel Policies Committee usurps the specific commission of the committee as well as violates principles of shared governance and due process; (4) Any amendments to policy should reflect established policy of privileging faculty in affairs related to faculty—as amended, the policy assigns equal weight to the singular opinion of the president's designee as it does to the considered judgment of three members of the FAC; (5) In accord with 3.7.4, any amendment to policy should clearly place the burden on the president's designee when the designee disagrees with the recommendation of the FAC; (6) The changes to policy were enacted in violation of the "outstanding memorandum" in effect since a shared governance forum in 2007; (7) The Faculty Senate passed a resolution on February 16, 2011, specifically requesting that the president honor the unanimous decision of the FAC; and (8) In the interest of equity and common sense, the rules may not be changed once a process commences—particularly odious and inequitable are rules that favor one party at the expense of the other.

On March 25, 2011, the President ruled in favor of his designee and did not allow my tenure application to proceed. This exhausted all my in-house remedies. But in addition to in-house remedies, I contacted the American Association of University Professors (AAUP) to inform them that Southeastern was in violation of their Statement of Principles as well as their Procedural Standards. On May 6, 2011, AAUP wrote to the President informing him that "we are concerned that favorable recommendations of the faculty, both in regard to Professor's Tudor's tenure case and her request for reconsideration, were overturned, that the faculty senate resolution went unheeded, and that faculty grievance policy appears to have been revised by the administration absent appropriate consultation with the faculty." The President failed to respond to this letter or a follow-up letter AAUP sent to him on May 20 stating: "We have yet to receive a response to our letter of May 6th." To my knowledge, the President never responded to the AAUP. I was hopeful that the AAUP would continue to pursue its inquiry and help me in my quest to be reinstated. However, once I was terminated the AAUP informed me that they would not be following up with Southeastern. I was heartbroken.

One of my colleagues started a Care2 petition online for my reinstatement that rapidly received 4,077 signatures from faculty, staff, students, and local community members as well as supporters across America. Unfortunately, the cry of so many supporters went unheeded.

I was terminated in May 2011.

Once I received the President's letter informing me that I was terminated, I immediately filed a complaint with the Equal Employment Opportunity Commission. On September 5, 2012, they informed me that they had determined that my civil rights had been violated on multiple counts. Keep in mind that the EEOC did not represent me. Their mission is to uphold the law in an unbiased and equitable manner. I accepted their settlement terms (confidentiality laws prevent me from disclosing the exact terms), but Southeastern rejected the EEOC's best efforts at an equitable and just solution. On March 29, 2013, the EEOC determined that any further attempts at conciliation would be "futile" in the face of Southeastern's and RUSO's unreasonableness and forwarded the case to the Department of Justice. The DOJ also found that Southeastern had violated my civil rights. However, Southeastern rejected equitable solutions for years. I had to wait until November 2017 for my day in court. On the eve of trial, US presidential administrations and leadership at the DOJ changed, and the DOJ entered a settlement agreement with Southeastern that did not include me. The DOJ settlement focused exclusively on policy changes and promises to stop discriminating. I continued to prosecute my own case with the support of private attorneys. Finally, after a weeklong trial in November 2017, a jury of Oklahomans examined the evidence and found that Southeastern and RUSO had violated my civil rights—two counts of sex discrimination and one count of retaliation. Nevertheless, Southeastern and RUSO continue to refuse to reinstate me.

My case against Southeastern and RUSO established new precedents in a range of issues, is cited in federal anti-discrimination regulations, and has been reported on by major newspapers and respected websites around the world. Professors in law schools and business schools lecture on my case, undergraduate and graduate students are discussing it in class, businesses are altering their personnel policies, and journal articles are being published referencing it. My case was the first of its kind to go to trial.

The trial was challenging on many fronts. Tenure discrimination and retaliation cases are notoriously difficult to win, and also I was subjected to uncivil personal attacks. Attorneys for Southeastern and RUSO, for instance, went so low as to repeatedly describe me to the jury as "the boy who cried wolf." But the jury found there are indeed wolves and that I was discriminated against because I am a woman. There were those who believed a woman who is Chickasaw and trans could not receive a fair and impartial jury trial—especially in Oklahoma—but the good people of Oklahoma proved them wrong! I have never been more proud of my fellow Oklahomans! If the courts reviewing my case will have as much respect for the jury as I do, the future will be one that rewards merit instead of bigotry.

Eight years (and counting) is a long time to live with the shame and humiliation of being denied tenure. Everything changed when I was denied tenure. I was not a prideful person, but my accomplishments provided me a certain amount of self-respect. I was not always right, but I believed my opinion mattered. I never felt I was indispensable, but I didn't feel I was disposable. I wasn't the life of the party, but I enjoyed quiet conversations and celebrating my colleagues and students when they were honored.

Of all the descriptors of who I am, the one that is the core of my identity is professor. Being a professor was never simply a job—it is who I am. I went to sleep at night thinking about the classes I taught that day and the classes I would be teaching tomorrow. If asked today who I am or what do I do—I simply have no response. Sometimes, the loneliness and isolation are unbearable. The years of struggle are heavy. I am still unemployed—or, more accurately, unemployable. It hurts that no university will hire me. After all the battles I have fought, it strikes me that all it would take to restore my sense of self is one department to welcome me.

However, being denied tenure anywhere—even illegally—is an impassable barrier to tenure everywhere. I have applied to universities for tenure-track jobs since 2011 and have not been invited to a single on-campus interview. Not one! Even if I eventually receive tenure somewhere, I will never be able to share that news with my sisters. They died in 2014. "Unconquered and unconquerable" does not mean the absence of deep hurt, recurring suffering, and profound loss—it means being unwavering in the quest for justice.

REFERENCES

Boylan, J. F. (2003). *She's not there: A life in two genders*. New York: Random House.

Charleyboy, L., and Leatherdale, M. B. (Eds). (2017). *#NotYourPrincess: Voices of Native American women*. Toronto: Annick.

Schwenke, C. (2018). *SELF-ish: A transgender awakening*. Pasadena, CA: Red Hen Press.

Afterword

Deena J. González

During my thirty-six years in the professoriate and in senior leadership positions, I have experienced many of the same humiliations and degrading treatment documented in these narratives. My generation built on the one before ours, which was repeatedly denied tenure and promotion. The four or five Faculty of Color at places as prestigious as UCLA, UC San Diego, UC Berkeley, and UC Davis were each denied tenure, followed by feeble attempts to placate them with lectureships or transfers. The handful that achieved tenure was so small that the UC system could not report single-digit percentages of tenured Faculty of Color until the end of the last century. It seems safe to conclude that some dynamics in institutions of higher learning have changed very little.

Yet in more than three decades as a member of the professoriate and over a decade as an administrator or university leader, I have indeed witnessed an increase in White women and People of Color as professional staff, faculty, and students. Most of us enter the academy with few resources, histories not affirmed in the names of buildings or statues on campus, and expectations different from those of our predominantly White male predecessors. In this context our service is expected to remedy racist, sexist, homophobic realities of institutions of higher learning, which proclaim a commitment to "openness," "diversity," and "welcome for all." We quickly realize that we are the change agents, while simultaneously faced with toxic environments that no amount of merit or salary increases, course release, extra summer salary, grant, or elevated status and authority can ameliorate.

The demographic shifts, including the racial fault lines that are upon us in almost every area of the country, are changing discourses—some for the better, some for the worse. The national political climate conveys messages about what is appropriate in classrooms and about how higher education is viewed by large segments of the electorate, who may never set foot on a university campus.

DOI: 10.7330/9781607329664.c033

It conveys information about how education will be reformed by policy makers, elected officials, and professors, many of whom need time to collect, digest, and analyze the discrimination in their workplaces but have little time to do so. Policy makers and academic leaders can learn from the experiences documented in volumes such *Presumed Incompetent* and *Presumed Incompetent II*.

Rachel Tudor's essay in the collection highlights the importance of first-person accounts. Her essay describes the hardship and disrespect that many Women of Color—and, in her case, transgender—endure, and yes, survive. We know that not all denials of advancement are erroneous, but those against Women of Color often include egregious substantive and procedural irregularities. Procedures are violated; stated policies are ignored; faculty and administrative allies seem few and far between; and resources for grieving or collecting evidence to document track records of denials are few. Even when the EEOC and the AAUP become involved, equitable review and resolution by those vested with protecting the institution and advancing its agendas seem impossible. When explicit policies, procedures, and manuals are ignored, negative outcomes are far more difficult to digest and to accept. The injustice fuels emotions that run high, especially when racial capital seems to be on trial. Tudor's essay, situated at the end of the volume, brings readers back to the fundamental question about what it will take to make universities more humane. Tudor reminds us that there is a civic responsibility embedded in these testaments that go beyond "speaking truth to power."

The testimonies rendered in these chapters are documentary evidence of the far larger social justice project with the message, "We are now here; we will be responsible, dignified humanitarians in describing our working, professional, academic, and community lives." The clarion calls in these essays involve not just taking notice but also interceding in bullying and other professional development barriers faced by highly competent students, faculty, and administrators. They demand that we not ignore the classed, raced, sexed, and gendered barriers to economic, political, and social advancement. They remind us that persons must be accountable and responsible for denials of human and civil rights.

Where, then, can we locate optimism and muster the hopefulness that being a member of the academy requires? We are not afforded the luxuries of cynicism, "taking a break," or "I will do this in retirement." Some strategies appear in these essays, such as locating a work/life balance, fostering alliances, remembering that student success—not prestige or awards bestowed—are the goal.

Navigating the academy has been difficult for previous generations, to be sure. Women across race/ethnicity, academics from working-class backgrounds, and Jewish scholars, to name just three groups, have provided documented testimonials about the barriers they have encountered. These historical experiences remind us that the challenges are persistent, even if their impact varies. To give in or give up, to leave or to take a leave, is not a crime, but without us present as our best selves, the university changes hardly at all.

Some women have found that their well-being demands that they close the door on academia. Examples include Nell Painter, a leading US historian who spent decades at Princeton, left the academy, and devoted herself to art. Others, like Tey Diana Rebolledo, have retired, sold or donated their libraries, and moved into creative spaces that feed their spirit and souls. The essays in this volume are written by those who are not quite there yet. We hope that the strategies in this volume will help them persevere and thrive. Yet they are faculty in the center of a festering set of circumstances worsened by the current political climate that promotes and demonstrates misogyny, racism, and gleeful misconceptions of the world, including the growing gap between rich and poor, the destruction to our planet, and power and (in)difference. Other eras in US history, marred by anti-Mexican or anti-Asian sentiment, Native decimation and removal, slavery, indentured servitude, and lynching have endured political discourses that threaten and intimidate. This era is no different.

Presumed Incompetent II reminds us not to yield to the pressures to oust us, to erase our experiences, to be silent in fear of the repercussions. For centuries, higher education has provided careers and empowering pathways to generations of Americans. This fundamental priority of a liberal education must not now be allowed to halt as People of Color are filing through college and university doorways. For institutions of higher education to move forward in the agenda of righting past wrongs, of acknowledging the contributions different perspectives and histories bring to the academy, of searching for truths, change, or justice, the goal is clear: they must, at minimum, reflect the demographics of the society across rank and status. The evidence provided in these narratives is key to surviving, and then thriving, once we make it through the door. Higher education provides first-generation, working-class, immigrant, and undocumented students, faculty, and staff the gateway to improved economic status, access to health care, and lives filled with purpose and promise.

About the Authors

SAHAR F. AZIZ is professor of law, Chancellor's Social Justice Scholar, and Middle East and legal studies scholar at Rutgers University Law School. Her scholarship adopts an interdisciplinary approach to examine intersections of national security, race, and civil rights, with a focus on the adverse impact of national security laws and policies on racial, ethnic, and religious minorities in the United States. Professor Aziz has received multiple awards, including the Research Making an Impact Award by the Institute for Social Policy and Understanding.

JACQUELYN BRIDGEMAN is the Kepler Professor of Law at the University of Wyoming College of Law and currently serves as the interim and inaugural director of the School of Culture, Gender and Social Justice in the University of Wyoming's College of Arts and Sciences. She has served as associate dean of academic affairs, associate dean of program development, and interim dean of the University of Wyoming College of Law. Bridgeman received her bachelor of arts degree with honors from Stanford University. She earned her JD degree from the University of Chicago.

JAMIELLA BROOKS is a Black mother-scholar of two, the first person in her immediate family to learn a new language and pursue a doctoral degree, and occupies multiple spaces of wife, daughter, believer, and descendant. She earned her PhD in French literature from the University of California, Davis, in 2018 and a BA in English from Oberlin College. She was a Mellon-Mays Fellow, McNair Scholar, and Fulbright Teaching Assistant in France. Currently she is associate director of the Center for Teaching and Learning at Berea College, focusing on anti-colonial pedagogical practices. In her spare time, she reads Afrofuturism and invents languages.

LOLITA BUCKNER INNISS is the Senior Associate Dean for Academic Affairs and a professor of law at Southern Methodist University Dedman School of Law. She earned an AB degree from Princeton University and a JD from the University of California, Los Angeles. She also holds an LLM with distinction and a PhD in law from Osgoode Hall,

York University in Canada. Her research addresses historic and geographic norms of law, especially in the context of gender and race. She is the author of *The Princeton Fugitive Slave: The Trials of James Collins Johnson* (Fordham University Press, 2019).

KIM A. CASE, PhD, is professor of psychology at the University of Houston, Clear Lake, and applied social issues director. Her mixed-methods research examines ally behavior, interventions to increase understanding of intersectionality and privilege, prejudice reduction, and creation of inclusive workplace and education settings. She is the author of *Deconstructing Privilege: Allies in the Classroom* (2013) and *Intersectional Pedagogy: Complicating Identity and Social Justice* (2017). As founder and president of the Lightning Bug Center, she provides faculty development, promoting intersectional allies, diversity, equity, and inclusion in K-12 and higher education settings. Her scholarship, blog, and teaching resources are available at www.drkimcase.com.

DONNA CASTAÑEDA is associate dean and professor in social psychology at San Diego State University, Imperial Valley. Her research focuses on interconnections between gender, ethnicity, close relationships, women's sexuality, and mental and physical health. She has investigated the role of close relationship factors, such as intimacy and commitment, in HIV sexual risk behavior among Latinx adults; the HIV prevention needs of women, in both the United States and Mexico; the close relationship context and how it affects intimate partner violence among young adults and adolescents; the relationship between mental health and marital satisfaction; and health and mental health among Latinx LGBTQ+ adults.

JULIA H. CHANG is assistant professor of Hispanic studies and a member of the core faculty in feminist, gender, and sexuality studies at Cornell University. Her areas of specialization include modern Spanish literature and culture, feminist and queer theory, critical disability studies, and the history of medicine. She holds a PhD in Hispanic language and literatures with a designated emphasis in women, gender, and sexuality from the University of California, Berkeley.

MEREDITH D. CLARK, PhD, is an assistant professor in the Department of Media Studies at the University of Virginia. Her work focuses on the intersections of race, media, and power, with specific concentrations on news media processes and social media audiences. She was named to TheRoot.com's list of the 100 most influential African Americans in the United States for her work on Black Twitter in 2015. Clark is a two-time graduate of Florida A&M University and holds a doctorate in mass communication from the University of North Carolina at Chapel Hill. She can be found on Twitter @meredithdclark.

SARAH AMIRA DE LA GARZA is a sixth-generation Tejana and Southwest Borderlands Scholar in the Hugh Downs School of Human Communication at Arizona State University, where she is also an affiliate faculty member of the School for Transborder Studies. A two-time Fulbright Scholar to México, she writes about de-colonial/indigenous methodologies, intercultural communication, and identity and performance. She is a founding member of ASU's Faculty Women of Color Caucus and is the author of *María Speaks: Journeys through the Mysteries of the Mother in My Life as a Chicana* (2004) and *Painting the White Face Red* (forthcoming 2020).

MEERA E. DEO, JD, PhD, is director of the Law School Survey of Student Engagement (LSSSE) and professor of law at Thomas Jefferson School of Law. Her research merges jurisprudence with empirical methods to interrogate institutional diversity, affirmative action, and racial representation. Her book *Unequal Profession: Race and Gender in Legal Academia* (2019) examines how race X gender affect workplace interactions, tenure, work/life balance, and more. Professor Deo has been a member of the California Commission on Access to Justice, consultant to the ACLU of Southern California, and chair of the AALS Section on Law and the Social Sciences.

PENELOPE ESPINOZA, PhD, is a cisgender female Mexican American. She is an associate professor of educational leadership at the University of Texas at El Paso. Dr. Espinoza holds a doctoral degree in social psychology from the University of Michigan and an undergraduate degree with honors in psychology from Stanford University. She has held Ford Foundation Fellowships, internships with the National Academy of Sciences and ETS, and grants from the National Science Foundation. Her research on social psychology in education includes stereotypes about women in STEM and persistence in higher education. She has the pleasure of raising her family in her hometown of El Paso.

YVETTE G. FLORES holds a doctoral degree in clinical psychology (UC Berkeley, 1982), and has been professor of psychology in Chicana/o studies at UC Davis for the past twenty-nine years. Her research focus has been substance abuse treatment outcomes, women's and men's mental health, and intimate partner violence. At present, she is co-investigator of a National Science Foundation Institutional Transformation grant to increase the numbers of Latinas in science, technology, engineering, mathematics, and medicine (STEMM) careers. Dr. Flores is a national and international consultant on cultural humility, prevention and treatment of trauma, and gender, migration, and mental health.

LYNN FUJIWARA is an associate professor of ethnic studies and is the author of Mothers without Citizenship: Asian Immigrant Families and the Consequences of Welfare Reform (2008), which received the Best Book Award in the Social Sciences from the Association for Asian American Studies. She is the coeditor of Asian American Feminisms and Women of Color Politics (2018). She co-created and coordinated the Women of Color Junior Faculty Project, "Women of Color, Borders, and Power: Mentoring and Leadership Development" through the Center for the Study of Women in Society from 2008 to 2010.

JENNIFER M. GÓMEZ, PhD, Ford Fellow, received her doctorate in clinical psychology in 2017 from the University of Oregon. She is currently a postdoctoral fellow in the Wayne State University Postdoctoral to Faculty Transition Fellowship Program, researching trauma in Black youth and young adults at Merrill Palmer Skillman Institute. Additionally, she is a coeditor of the upcoming special issue of *Journal of Trauma & Dissociation—Discrimination, Violence, & Healing in Marginalized Communities* (2018–2021). In proposing cultural betrayal trauma theory, Dr. Gómez incorporates interpersonal trauma in conjunction with discrimination to examine mental health outcomes in Black and other minority populations. http://jmgomez.org.

CARMEN G. GONZÁLEZ (BA Yale University, JD Harvard Law School) is a professor of law at Seattle University School of Law. She has published widely in the areas of international environmental law and environmental justice. Professor González was a Fulbright Scholar in Argentina, a US Supreme Court Fellow, and a visiting fellow at the University of Cambridge in the United Kingdom. In 2017, she served as the George Soros Visiting Chair at the Central European University School of Public Policy in Budapest, Hungary, and as the Norton Rose Fulbright Distinguished Visiting Professor at the University of Houston Law Center. Her most recent co-edited book is *Energy Justice: US and International Perspectives* (2018).

GABRIELLA GUTIÉRREZ Y MUHS, PhD, is a professor of modern languages and women and gender studies as well as the Theiline Pigott McCone Chair in Humanities. She is a poet, literary critic, cultural worker, and mother. She is the author/editor of eight books of poetry, criticism, and culture, and of multiple articles, encyclopedia entries, and opinion pieces. She has presented her work all over the world, multilingually, and specializes in expanding subjectivity. She was a commissioner for the arts for the state of Washington (2014–2017) and is the daughter of migrant farmworkers, as well as a past field and cannery worker herself.

ANGELA P. HARRIS is professor emerita and Boochever and Bird Chair for the Study and Teaching of Freedom and Equality at the University of California, Davis School of Law. She is a founding editor in chief of the *Journal of Law and Political Economy*, and a founder of the Aoki Center for the Critical Study of Race and Nation at UC Davis School of Law. Along with Carmen González, Gabriella Gutiérrez y Muhs, and Yolanda Flores Niemann, she was an editor of volume I of *Presumed Incompetent: The Intersections of Race and Class for Women in Academia* (2012).

DOROTHY E. HINES, PhD, is an award-winning writer and an assistant professor in the Department of African and African American Studies, and in the School of Education at the University of Kansas. Her research examines the societal and educational experiences of Black women and Black girls using justice-oriented and race-conscious frameworks. She received her PhD in education policy from Michigan State University.

PAMELA TWYMAN HOFF, PhD, is a mother, daughter, sista, and friend to many. She is currently an associate professor at Illinois State University in the College of Educational Administration and Foundations. She teaches courses in the social foundations of education and African American education. Dr. Hoff's career in education has spanned more than thirty years in numerous contexts. Dr. Hoff identifies as an activist scholar who believes that education should be transformative for the individual and the community.

RACHELLE A. C. JOPLIN is a White, female, cisgender graduate student earning her PhD in rhetoric, composition, and pedagogy at the University of Houston. Her scholarly projects center around the rhetorical implications of allyship, especially in the academy. She is interested in the application of affect theory and intersectional feminism to the teaching of rhetoric and composition and the study of pop culture. She is also the editorial assistant for *Peitho, the Journal of the Coalition of Feminist Scholars in the History of Rhetoric and Composition.*

JESSICA LAVARIEGA MONFORTI is the dean of the College of Arts & Sciences at California Lutheran University. She received her PhD from Ohio State University in 2001.

Her research primarily focuses on the differential impact of public policy according to race, gender, and ethnicity. She is specifically interested in the political incorporation and representation of Latino/as, immigrants, and women. She has coauthored two books and published over fifty articles and chapters. She has contributed to several newspapers and broadcasts, including the *New York Times*, *La Opinión*, and NPR's *All Things Considered*.

CYNTHIA LEE is the Charles Kennedy Poe Research Professor of Law at the George Washington University Law School, where she teaches and writes in the areas of criminal law and criminal procedure. She is the author or editor of four books: *Criminal Procedure: Cases and Materials* (2018; with l. Song Richardson and Tamara Lawson); *Criminal Law: Cases and Materials* (2014; with Angela Harris); *Searches and Seizures: The Fourth Amendment, Its Constitutional History and the Contemporary Debate* (2011); and *Murder and the Reasonable Man: Passion and Fear in the Criminal Courtroom* (2003).

YESSENIA MANZO is a recent graduate of Seattle University School of Law. Yessenia was born in Guadalajara, Jalisco, and grew up in a migrant community in Washington State. She was a first-generation student and obtained her BA in psychology from Whitman College and her MS in mental health counseling from Central Washington University. Yessenia has dedicated more than ten years to developing and implementing racial equity trainings. She has tailored curricula in a variety of settings, including nonprofit behavioral health organizations, high schools, Latinx community organizations, and the Department of Public Defense.

MELISSA R. MICHELSON earned her PhD in political science from Yale University and is currently professor of political science at Menlo College. Her work focuses on persuasive communication to shift attitudes toward LGBTQ rights, the political attitudes and behavior of Latinx immigrants, and randomized experiments aimed at increasing Latinx voter turnout. She is the award-winning author of four academic books and has published dozens of articles in top-rated peer-reviewed academic journals, including pieces in *American Political Science Review*, *Journal of Politics*, *Political Behavior*, and *International Migration Review*. In her spare time, she knits and runs marathons.

SUSIE E. NAM is the pseudonym of a faculty member in the United States. She wishes to remain anonymous to protect her career and her family.

YOLANDA FLORES NIEMANN is professor of psychology at the University of North Texas. She has sixteen years of administrative experience in multiple universities. An invited panelist for the White House Initiative on Educational Excellence for Hispanics, she has been principal investigator of over $42 million in federal outreach grants. Research interests include the psychological effects and social ecological contexts of tokenism. She has recently developed a training video on microaggressions (https://www.youtube.com/watch?v=ZahtlxW2CIQ). Her most recent book is *Surviving and Thriving in Academia: A Guide for Members of Marginalized Groups*, 3rd ed. (2017).

JODI O'BRIEN is professor of sociology at Seattle University and director of SU ADVANCE, an NSF-funded program for the advancement of women faculty. Her work focuses on everyday discrimination and transgressive identities and communities. Her books include *The Production of Reality* (forthcoming 2020); *Social Prisms: Reflections on Everyday Myths and Paradoxes* (1999); and *Everyday Inequalities* (1998). Her recent articles include "Stained-Glass Ceilings: Religion, Leadership, and the Cultural Politics of Belonging" and "Seeing Agnes: Notes on a Transgender Biocultural Ethnomethodology." She is also the editor of the *SAGE Encyclopedia of Gender and Society* and the recent former editor of the public sociology journal *Contexts*.

AMELIA ORTEGA currently works as a feminist psychotherapist through her practice Amanecer Psychotherapy and as an adjunct lecturer. Amelia believes her role in social work education and as a community-based clinician is an opportunity to build collective consciousness about identity, power, and liberation labor. Amelia's practice is trauma focused and she utilizes somatic experiencing techniques with clients to connect healing, post-traumatic growth, and philosophies of struggle. Amelia is inspired daily by the love of her parents for their work, by the writing of fellow queer, Chicanx, and working-class writers, and by the life partnerships created with her chosen family.

MARCIA ALLEN OWENS is associate professor of environmental science and policy at Florida A&M University (FAMU). An interdisciplinary scholar, she earned her PhD, JD, and MDiv degrees from Emory University and her BS degree from Jackson State University. As the principal investigator of the National Science Foundation ADVANCE Institutional Transformation grant at FAMU, her lived experiences as first tenured Black woman in her academic unit has informed interests in intersectional gender issues in science, technology, engineering, and mathematics (STEM), specifically at historically Black colleges and universities (HBCUs). Other research interests include environmental policy, ecojustice, environmental literacy, and religion and environment.

LAURA M. PADILLA joined California Western School of Law in 1992, after receiving her BS from Stanford University and her JD from Stanford Law School, where she was co-president of Stanford's Latino Law Students' Association. Her research focuses on gender, race, and property, and climate change/land use. Padilla was on the AALS Committees on Recruitment/Retention of Minority Law Professors and Bar Passage/Lawyer Performance, and is an ALI member. She was a Kellogg Fellow, received the San Diego County Bar Association's Service to Legal Education Award (2008) and the Stanford's Governor's Award (2009), and was a San Diego Daily Transcript's Top Attorney, academic category (2012).

GRACE PARK is a pseudonym for a faculty member in the United States. She wishes to remain anonymous to protect her career and her family.

STACEY PATTON, PhD, is an award-winning journalist and an assistant professor of multimedia journalism at Morgan State University. Her writings on race, higher education, and child welfare issues have appeared in the *Chronicle of Higher Education*, the *New York Times*, and the *Washington Post*, and she has appeared on MSNBC, Al Jazeera, CNN, ABC News, and other outlets. She is the author of *That Mean Old Yesterday* (2008), *Spare the Kids: Why Whupping Children Won't Save Black America* (2017), and the forthcoming *Strung Up: The Lynching of Black Children and Teenagers during Jim Crow*.

DESDAMONA RIOS, PhD, is an associate professor of psychology and director of the Latinx and Latino American Studies Program at the University of Houston, Clear Lake.

Her current projects involve mixed research methods and examine the relationship between culturally relevant cues in academic contexts for at-risk Latinx American high school students, and community-based comprehensive prevention and intervention programs for families in crisis. She has published on narrative identity among diverse groups of LGBTQ college students as well as her pedagogical practices. She is the recipient of several national teaching awards.

MELISSA MICHAL SLOCUM is of Seneca decent. Her creative work explores historical trauma and resilience within her own community. Her criticism focuses on trauma and representation of indigenous histories and literatures in educational curricula. She is a fiction writer, essayist, scholar, and professor. Her short story collection, *Living on the Borderlines*, was published by the Feminist Press in February 2019. She is working on a nonfiction essay collection and critical monograph, *Haudenosaunee Good Mind: Combating Literary Erasure and Genocide of American Indian Presence with Literature Curriculum and Literary Criticism.*

NELLIE TRAN, PhD, a first-generation daughter of Vietnamese "boat people," is a community psychologist working at a Hispanic-serving institution. Coming from a refugee family and being born in the United States, she has struggled to find her identity and place as an American and as Vietnamese, especially in academia. She is not your model minority. Each step of the way, White folks in the system told her she wasn't worthy or smart enough for an Asian person, but also that she was not enough of a minority in their eyes, and that things would be different if they perceived her to be more disadvantaged.

RACHEL TUDOR is a citizen of the Chickasaw Nation. She holds a PhD in English from the University of Oklahoma with a primary concentration in Native American and American literature and a secondary concentration in modernity and theory. Her scholarly research is on the subject of gender and genre in literature by and about indigenous American and global diasporic peoples. She is a recipient of the Bishop-Baldwin, Barton & Phillips Civil Rights Advocacy Award from Oklahomans for Equality. She continues to pursue her precedent-setting case through the courts while welcoming opportunities to advocate for justice.

ADRIEN K. WING is the associate dean for International and Comparative Law Programs and the Bessie Dutton Murray Professor at the University of Iowa College of Law, where she has taught since 1987. Additionally, she serves as the director of the University of Iowa Center for Human Rights, as well as director of the France summer abroad program. Author of over 130 publications, her courses include Critical Race Theory, and Sex Discrimination. She is editor of *Critical Race Feminism* (2nd ed. 2003) and *Global Critical Race Feminism* (2000). She holds degrees from Princeton, UCLA, and Stanford Law School.

JEMIMAH LI YOUNG, PhD, is an assistant professor at the University of Iowa. Her areas of expertise are multicultural education, urban education, and the sociology of education. Her specific research interests include the academic achievement of Students of Color; intersectional research of Black girls; educational outcomes for marginalized populations; and culturally responsive pedagogy. She can be reached at jemimah-young@uiowa.edu.

Index